UFO CASE FILES

OF

RUSSIA

UFO CASE FILES

OF

RUSSIA

Philip Mantle & Paul Stonehill

HEALINGS OF ATLANTIS

London U.K

www.HealingsOfAtlantis.com

Healings Of Atlantis Ltd

Hayes

Middlesex

England

www.HealingsOfAtlantis.com

First Published in Great Britain in 2010

By Healings of Atlantis

ISBN: 978-1-907126-03-1

A catalogue record for this book is available from the British Library.

Cover design by Mark Roberts and Lewis Webb

CONTENTS:

INTRODUCTION

Throughout the centuries, UFOs hovered over Russia, and USOs lurked in its waters. Our book will introduce you to the most important cases, observations, and sightings. We will describe efforts of those dedicated researchers who have stubbornly pursued UFO research in the Russian Empire, the USSR, and modern Russia.

Russia is a huge country. Many of its areas, especially in Siberia, Far Eastern provinces and the Arctic regions, have not been completely explored even today, in the beginning of 21st century. During the last one hundred years Russia has gone through bloody revolutions, wars, transformations of its economy, purges, famine, invasions, and other life-shattering events. Millions of Russians perished in concentration camps created by Soviet Marxist Leninists and German National Socialists. Hundreds of thousands, if not millions, died from famine and starvation. Others were exiled, banished, maimed, their lives torn apart by terrible events of the twentieth century, by totalitarian onslaught on humanity.

Of course, Ukraine, the Baltic nations, Central Asia, and countries of the Caucasus suffered greatly, too.

And yet, even in the darkest of times, there were those in the USSR who had observed strange and perplexing unidentified flying or submersible objects and found ways to preserve their observations. Such anomalous phenomena had been of great interest to Soviet Union's rivals throughout the nation's existence, as readers find out in our book. Such anomalous phenomena had never escaped attention of the Soviet rulers and the nation's Armed Forces.

Debunkers, skeptics and critics of UFO extraterrestrial hypotheses will be mentioned, as well as their views. We will not elaborate mutual accusations among some Russian Ufologists, for this is not the purpose of this book. Those few who openly express intolerance and brand their opponents in an uncivilized manner and those who label Western researchers and debunkers as "CIA agents" are in reality Pseudo-Ufologists. Such Russian, Ukrainian, and other "researchers" will not find a place in this book.

We thank those who have helped us in our endeavor: Mikhail Gershtein, Nikolay Subbotin, Vadim Chernobrov, Anatoly Kutovoy, Genrikh Silanov, Yuri Orlov and many other former Soviet and contemporary UFO researchers, kind, decent, intelligent and open-hearted people dedicated to the pursuit of knowledge.

Philip Mantle and Paul Stonehill

CHAPTER 1

ZNAMENIYA - UFOs OVER ANCIENT RUSSIA

The history of UFO sightings and contacts over the lands that later became known as Russia date back thousands of years. We have collected the most interesting episodes of this fascinating history; most of which have never been presented to Western readers before. They are now available for the very first time in the West. Whatever the UFO phenomena is, it is certainly not a modern invention as this unique history will clearly demonstrate.

UFOs AND ANTIQUITY

Around the 7th century B.C, nomadic Scythian tribes migrated north into the fertile Russian territories. Some tribes began to cultivate the land. Others traded furs and honey with Constantinople; eventually these merchants acted as middlemen between other settlements in the far north (inhabited by Finnish tribes) and the Roman Empire. The ancient Slavs who settled here built villages and towns, and protected them by kremlins (wooden citadels), cut from the rich forest timber. The inhabitants gradually occupied an area from the site of what is now modern St. Petersburg to Kiev. The Slavic tribes were united in the 8th and 9th centuries, when the Vikings (Varangians or Varyagi, in Russian), began their migrations south, and established their trade outposts with the Slavs. Later their strongholds were founded along the Neva River, and the Ladoga Lake. As we shall see, UFO sightings have been reported in these areas throughout the centuries.

In 880 A.D. Oleg (successor to the mighty Ryurik the Norseman, conqueror of Russian North) vanquished the Slavs in the South, and made Kiev his capital. As Varyagi united the conquered land, the State of Russia became a very powerful kingdom in the world of that age.

And yet, the UFO sightings occurred long before Oleg's times. There are ancient stone monuments in the Russian North that had been built at the same time as Stonehenge in England and the Egyptian pyramids. Smaller in size, the spiral "labyrinths" of the White Sea are no less enigmatic. They can be found on the Solovetski Islands, and throughout the area known as the Tersk Shores (southern portion of the Kola Peninsula). As we will show later in the book, this was also a destination point for an early expedition of A. Barchenko, a protégé of the Soviet secret police in the 1920's. One of the labyrinths lies near the ancient Umba, near the Lesnoi settlement. The locals have called it "Babylon" for many centuries. Nobody knows today how this name came about. Perhaps there is a connection to the ancient Sumer civilization? No one really knows.

The Saam hunters (descendants of ancient nomadic tribes, reindeer breeders) sighted UFOs over the area on numerous occasions. A number of Russian archaeologists who have studied the local legends consider the labyrinths as a gateway to an underground kingdom. Similar double spiral labyrinths have been found throughout the ancient world, in Egypt, China, and Scandinavia. They symbolise the Sun in the ancient cultures. What is more amazing, the same double spiral labyrinths were depicted on ancient Minoan coins, minted on the island of Crete, one of the most mysterious civilizations of the Neolithic age.

Andrei Nikitin, Russian archaeologist, researcher, and writer mentions a very curious incident. As a field archaeologist he had studied the labyrinths of various sizes throughout the Russian North. Once, Nikitin showed his drawings of the labyrinths to a physicist. The man asked him in amazement: why would an archaeologist draw direct transmission aerial (antenna) of broad frequency range? The physicist could not believe that he was looking at an ancient stone structure built on the shores of Northern seas thousands of years ago.

Russia is just like that labyrinth: full of secrets, enigmas, and mysteries. UFOs have hovered over it since the dawn of time.

ZNAMENIYA: UFOs OVER ANCIENT RUSSIA

In 904 CE (Common Era), Russian prince Oleg began his campaign against the Greeks. His huge army was comprised of Varangians, Slavs, Chud, Krivichians, and many other tribes when he marched it out of Kiev. The Greeks knew all these tribes as the Great Scythia. With this entire force, Oleg pushed on, by horse, ship, and apparently, flying apparatuses. Oleg had two thousand vessels with him, a powerful naval presence for those times. He arrived before Tsargrad (Russian name for Constantinople), but the Greeks fortified the strait and closed their city. Oleg disembarked upon the shore, and ordered his troops to beach the vessels. The war waged on, and many Greeks were put to death. Palaces and churches were burned and destroyed. The prisoners Oleg's troops captured were tortured, beheaded, or thrown into the sea. This was a cruel war, and too prolonged for Prince Oleg's taste. He decided to use other means to conquer the city. Oleg commanded his troops to make wheels, which they attached to the vessels. When the wind was favourable, they spread the sails and bore down upon the city from the open country. At the same time the Russians launched into the air "horses" that were well equipped and "of golden colour". From these horses the warriors hurled fiery arrows at Constantinople. But to ascend through the air for the purpose of bombing a city, the Russians would have to have advanced technology they definitely did not possess in 907. Where did the Russians borrow such "horses"? Who was interested in aiding them to conquer Constantinople? The emperors Leo and Alexander made peace with Oleg, and after agreeing to pay the tribute and mutually binding themselves by oath to him.

They invited Prince Oleg and his men to swear an oath likewise. According to the religion of the Russians, the victors swore by their weapons and by their deity Perun, as well by Volos, the god of cattle, and thus confirmed the treaty. His people called Oleg "the Wise". He was still a pagan, a ruler who apparently had powerful friends.

Russian chronicles tell of numerous znameniya (signs, including "signs in the sky"). Ukrainian researcher Valentin Krapiva and others studied them at length before compiling their research. Here are a few examples of these signs:

1028 CE: There was a serpent-like sign in the sky, so big that it could be seen from everywhere.

1111 CE: A fiery pillar, from the ground up to the sky, had appeared; lightning lit all around, there was a thunderous noise, and all could see the pillar.

1204 CE: There was a great sign in the sky: three suns had appeared in the East, and four suns in the West. In the middle of the sky, a giant moon-like sign was seen. This sign remained in the sky from morning until midday.

1317 CE: There was a circle over the city of Tver, and it moved toward the North. The circle had three rays: two pointed eastward, and one westward.

1319 CE: At night, over Russia, people observed "fiery pillars"; they extended from the ground toward the sky. Some also sighted a "heavenly arc". Yet others saw horse-like flying entities, equipped with "lanterns"

1403 CE: Three objects appeared in the sky, "sun-like", and they emitted blue, green, and crimson rays. Later something "like an arc" arrived. The last object was cross-like, great in size, it was right in the middle of the Moon, and hovered for almost half an hour.

UFOs OVER THE LAND OF VOLGA BULGARS

Ahmed Ibn Fadlan was an Arab chronicler. In 921 CE, the Caliph of Baghdad, Al-Muktadir, dispatched Ibn Fadlan with an embassy to the King of the Bulgars of the Middle Volga. Ibn Fadlan wrote an account of his journeys with the embassy; the account is properly termed Risala. The Bulgars (a nomadic tribe) settled in the northern Volga-Kama river region, which became known as "Magna Bulgaria", after the death of their great leader Kubrat. The Arab chronicler visited the ruler of the "volzhskih bulgar", Khan Blatavar, in 922 CE. The very first night spent in the palace of the King, Ibn Fadlan witnessed a very strange celestial phenomenon. Just before the sunset, the horizon became bright red, and from somewhere above came a low rumble. Ibn Fadlan raised his eyes to the sky and saw a fiery-reddish cloud moving above him. At the same time another cloud appeared, similar to the first one. The Arabs were frightened and kneeled in prayer. The locals, however, were amused by their guests' behaviour, and laughed out loud. As they later explained to Ibn Fadlan, the battles in the sky take place every night.

Ibn Fadlan and his companions gazed up into the sky and observed how one cloud joined itself with another, and how some time later the clouds came apart again. The clouds disappeared when the night fell. The chronicler described constantly moving shapes inside the clouds, human and animal looking. Ibn Fadlan saw weapons in the arms of the beings within the clouds. The shapes were quite clear one moment, and then would disappear the next. The "battle" he observed consisted of another formation ("black") attacking the other formation. The battle lasted for a long time. At one point the formations merged together, and then separated once more. Ibn Fadlan mentions that he could observe the "phenomenon" quite clearly. Finally, the "phenomenon" disappeared. He emphasised the loud noises, sounds, and visibility of the occurrence. The Bulgars explained the "riders in the sky" as Jinni (in Moslem legends, a supernatural being who can take human or animal form and influence human affairs), the "faithful" ones fighting against the "unfaithful".

Were the "horses" observed by Ibn Fadlan and his companions the same ones who aided Prince Oleg in his battle to conquer Constantinople some fifteen years before that?

Almost a thousand years later, on April 14, 1990 a Russian woman, V.N. Kuzminikh, observed a UFO, over the Tien-Shen Mountains (Soviet Central Asia). The object was iridescent, it broke into several parts, and then the parts would come together again into a single entity.

ZAPOROZHSKAYA SICH

The Zaporozhyan Sich was founded in the early 16th century. It soon became the military administrative and political organisation of the Ukrainian Kozaki (Cossacks).

The Zaporozhye Cossacks became masters of the lands beyond the rapids of the Dnieper River. The impregnable Khortitsa Island became one of the centres of Cossack civilization. The abolition of the Zaporozhskaya Sich took place in 1775.

The chronicle of Samoil Velichka deals with the history of the Zaporozhye Sich at the end of the 17th century. The ataman (Cossack chieftain) at the time was Ivan Sirko. The chronicle mentions December 15, 1680. Just before the sunset an unusual-looking star or a comet appeared in the sky. The people who observed this UFO became agitated, confused, and fearful. This "comet" hung in the sky over the Sich for almost a month. Another Cossack chronicler, Semovidets, indicated the very same date, December 15, 1680. He, however, described it as a small star that emitted a very bright great pillar, reaching "half of the sky". When the "comet" descended, the Cossacks fired on it from their "pischali" (harquebus) portable guns. The object hovered for a while before moving off.

UKRAINE

Dmitry Lavrov collected interesting reports about a possibility that Ukraine was visited by extraterrestrials long ago. We found his article online on the Internet, along with other reports and articles about Ukrainian UFO phenomena (www.geocities.com/d_dibenko/ukraine/ufo).

Lavrov describes silver figurines, discovered in the Martinovsky hidden treasure, buried near the Ros' River mouth (the Kiev region). The figurines bear a striking resemblance to the dogu figurines of Japan, and drawings of the "Great Martian god" of the African people from the plateau of Tassili (Lybia). We will describe other strange discoveries in Ukraine in another chapter of this book.

The Ukrainian figurines also have spacesuit-resembling attire, including their headgear.

Manuscripts from the days of the ancient Russia' contain stories that could be interpreted as UFO sightings; of course, people in those days used a different language, and perceived the world differently than modern Earthlings. One famous manuscript ("Povest' vremennikh let") has this curious account. In the year 1065 CE there was a znameniye in the western portion of the sky: a great star, and its rays blood-coloured. For seven days, each evening the star appeared after the sunset. At the same time, a baby was thrown into the Setoml' (a river that once existed in the Kiev area). Now, some fishermen caught this baby in their nets, brought him out of the river, and looked at the baby until the darkness fell. Then they threw him back into the river. They were frightened by the child's appearance and tossed it back into the river.

Here is how the baby looked: his face had "shameful" features, and more features that cannot be described because of "shame" they would cause. At that time the sun changed, too, and ceased being bright; actually it resembled the moon.

Who was that strange creature, asks Lunev, under the rays of the "bloody star"? Perhaps, it was a dwarf-like ET?

Another Ukrainian researcher and writer, Valery Kratokhvil, in his book, published in Kiev in 1993 (NLO-mashina vremeni), mentioned a medieval Russian miniature painting from the 16th century. A "flying saucer" and "angels" departing from it apparently observed the Kulikov Battle, a crucial event in the history of Russia. Still another manuscript, describing the Chudskoye lake battle (also, a crucial battle for the future of Russia, between the Slavs and foreign invaders), contains a curious miniature painting. A painter, whose name history has lost forever, depicted a UFO. A face of someone who observes the battle can be seen through one of its "portholes".

OTHER MANUSCRIPTS

A digest, published in Gomel', Byelorus, in 1990, contains more interesting accounts from the manuscripts of ancient Russia (FENID, NLO: za i protiv).

One, from the 16th century, is contained in the famous Uvarovsky Chronicle (1518). The place of the sighting was Vologda, according to the author of the Vologodsko-Permskaya Annals. That summer there was a znameniye in the sky: three suns rose from the east, and one rose in the West, and in the middle of the sky, big as a moon, an arc-like znameniye hung from the morning till the midday.

Something happened in 1111 CE that could relate to the experiences of Oleg's armies described above. It occurred on March 24 and 27, according to ancient chronicles. During a battle on the Degeya River between the Russians and nomadic Polovets tribe, the latter claimed to have been defeated by some "assistance" from the sky. This "assistance" allegedly helped the Russians by cutting off the heads of the Polovets warriors on the ground. There were substantially greater numbers of the nomads than of their enemies at the battle. When asked about their numerical advantage, the nomads replied to the Russians "how could we defeat you, when the others rode in the sky, with their bright and terrible weapons, helping you?"

To add another interesting touch to the Kratokhvil's mention of the manuscript describing the Chudsky lake battle of 1242, the digest reveals that many eyewitnesses among the Russian troops of Aleksandr Nevsky saw a "divine regiment". This "regiment" helped the Russians defeat German invaders.

Here is another interesting confirmation of the Kulikov Battle sighting (we mentioned the "flying saucer" above; see UKRAINE). The night before the battle, commanding officer of the Russian guards, Foma Katsibey, observed something very curious over the Chyurya River. Two heavenly "bright young men" uttered the words "Who willed you to destroy our Fatherland?" and with a lightning-like weapon they destroyed a regiment of the invaders.

That very same night, some warriors in the Dmitry Donskoy army witnessed battles in the sky. They revealed their observations to the prince Dmitry, who ordered them to keep everything in secret.

The battle itself was very unusual. Firstly, until three o'clock in the afternoon, everything was dark, and the battle could only start at six o'clock. It lasted three hours. Around nine o'clock the Russians weakened, and could lose, but then they received aid from the "heavenly armies". Two Russian warlords observed how "fiery arrows" of the heavenly warriors destroyed the Tatars. Finally, the Tartar leader Mamay and his entourage escaped to the Orda camp. Curiously, corpses of the "infidel Tatars" were found in the area where no Russian troops were present. The Tatars were chased to the river Mech, but the ensuing complete darkness ended the fighting.

Russian troops were as fortunate in yet other battles against their nomadic foes. A famous Russian explorer and conqueror of Siberia, Yermak, as well as his adversary Khan Kuchum, also observed znameniye. The latter gentleman observed a znameniye on October 25, 1582. He actually saw the sky open up in "the four corners of the Universe", and exiting it were "bright, armed, winged warriors". As they approached Kuchum's camp, the "warriors" surrounded it, and ordered the Khan to flee. He was shaken, and ordered his camp to leave. They left in fear, and hid in the forest, and it seemed to the Khan he was chased by some "heavenly armies".

THE ROBOZERO PHENOMENON

The most famous UFO sighting in the ancient Russian history occurred during the reign of Czar Alexei. Yuri Roszius and other Russian researchers of the paranormal phenomena have studied it extensively. The event occurred "in the year 171" (that is, the year 7171 from "the creation of the world"). It corresponds to the year 1663 C.E. The details of this amazing and enigmatic event have been preserved because of the efforts of the Archaeographic Commission. It published a collection of its Historical Acts in 1842. Among these acts was an authentic 17th century document. It was signed by Ivan (Ivashko) Rzhevsky, a "labourer"; a report to his "masters" about something that had happened 10 versts from their Loza monastery estate. Versta is approximately 3500 feet. Here is an account of the event, translated to contemporary terms.

On August 15, 1663, between 10 a.m. and noon, local time, a "great noise" resounded over Robozero Lake, located in the Vologda Region; about 50 kilometres southwest of Belozersk (see more about the Vologda area in OTHER MANUSCRIPTS, above). From the north, out of the clear sky appeared a huge flaming sphere no less than 40 metres in diameter.

From its fore part emitted two "flame" beams, about "20 sazhens ahead of it" (i.e. 40 metres or so; a sazhen is 2.13 metres). From its sides poured bluish smoke. This huge ball of fire, its height like that of a modern 15-story building, hovered over the lake.

The phenomenon was observed by a multitude of people. It was the day of the Assumption, and villagers from all of nearby villages gathered for mass at the parish church situated on the lake shore. The "great noise" occurred just as the thanksgiving singing had begun. Terrified by this noise, the people emerged from the church to the vestibule, but upon seeing the "frightful sight" they went back into the church and "prayed to the Lord and the Virgin Mary with tears and weeping", whereupon "the great flame and the two smaller ones vanished". However, soon after "the fiery flame" again appeared over the lake, somewhat to the west, "about half a versta (approximately 1750 feet) from the spot where it had vanished".

Its appearance was just as unexpected as the first time and it had "dimmed". A little later the same body, seemingly becoming even brighter and more terrifying, reappeared another half kilometre to the west, and then, moving westward, it dimmed and disappeared from view.

The "flame" hovered over Robozero for about an hour and a half". The lake is quite small, "two versts long and about one wide. Peasants were sailing in a boat in the lake at the time, but the scorching heat did not let them come closer. They saw the light from the unknown object penetrate the water, and reach the bottom of the lake that was "about four sazhens down". They saw "fish fleeing from the flame towards the shore". Where the flame touched the water, there appeared a brownish film of oxide on the surface, resembling rust ("just like rust"); it was later dispersed by wind.

Ivan Rzhevsky was an educated and intelligent man, as his observations reveal quite clearly. He went as far as to check out the testimony of an eyewitness, a peasant by the name of Levko Fedorov. He also received written confirmation from the local priests that "such a sign was observed on that date"; only then did Rzhevsky report the occurrence to his superiors. The Russian author provides a detailed description of the phenomenon, but does not offer any subjective interpretation of it.

Others tried to interpret the Robozero Phenomenon. Russian astronomer D. Svyatski, in his book "Astronomical phenomena in Russian chronicles" (Petrograd, 1915), claims that the eyewitnesses saw pieces of a meteorite that flew apart after an explosion. How could the people in the boat approach a hovering body? Some have tried to explain it as ball lightning. But there was no storm and no rain that day. A lightning's life span is short. Its diameter is not larger than a metre, certainly never 40 metres. Then, there were two rays that emitted from the body. Ball lightning does not emit rays.

Yuri Roszius analysed Rzhevsky's report. His detailed analysis included the study of one interesting episode related by eyewitnesses. The document notes a change in the outer appearance of the object: an increase in its brightness when it came into view for the third time. For some reason this change preceded the start of the object's progressive movement westward. In modern times, such increase in brightness could be attributed to the firing a cruise engines (increase in its trust). Is it by chance that the object's brightness increased before its departure?

A CURIOUS MANUSCRIPT

This ancient manuscript that mentions UFOs was discovered in the Kazan University, and researched by a historian in Moscow, M.D. Strunina. The manuscript tells the story of a boy named Yasha. He collected berries in the forest. Suddenly the boy saw a stranger, clad in white clothes, next to him. The stranger introduced himself as Timofei. Timofei placed Yasha in a giant "copper cauldron", and some unknown force ascended them both to Heaven. Yasha spent three years there. Timofei taught him different sciences, as well as "magic". Then the boy was brought back, in the same "cauldron", at the same spot in the forest. Timofei gave him two coins, as a present, one golden, the other made of silver.

WHO WAS BABA - YAGA?

Some Russian researchers who have studied ancient myths, manuscripts, legends, and tales have compared ancient Russian folk tales to the contemporary knowledge. Baba Yaga, a strange and powerful character in Slavic and Russian folk tales, is the archetypal Hag. She is an old, ugly crone who has a terrifying appearance, emaciated like a skeleton. She is the guardian of the frontier between the land of mortals and the spirit world. Of all the strange characters of the Russian folk tales, Baba Yaga is perhaps the one who occurs most frequently, and is the best known. She is usually depicted riding in a stupa (mortar; sometimes "fiery mortar"), rowing herself along with a pestle. She also uses a broom. She dwells in a strange house (izbushka na kuriykh nozhkah) in a forest. The house is described as a temporary abode; it has no windows, no doors, uncomfortable (for humans) and cramped. It also stands on "chicken legs".

Russian scientist Yuri Roszius, a noted researcher of UFO phenomenon, studied available accounts of the Baba Yaga. Her face, he concluded, was actually a description of a human-like, unusual appearance. "She" (her sex is not determined) actually uses a "fiery" broom to guide the "mortar". The "mortar" has some sort of "fire" underneath, and as it moves, trees fall down: the "mortar" is propelled by devils. The" mortar" has an aero dynamical shape. Those who see Baba Yaga become mute. And if we were to compare her "izbushka" to the Apollo lunar module design, we would find striking similarities. Unlike American astronauts, when Baba Yaga would leave her "module" she would behave in a strange manner. She destroyed mountains, and caused pestilence in animals and kidnapped human children. Baba Yaga also "charmed" young men. They stayed with her, were questioned extensively, and in the end, she gave them "knowledge of all things". Yuri Roszius interprets her actions in this fashion: some aliens acted according to their program, incomprehensive to humans; they collected samples of flora and fauna; they brought with them unknown viruses (animals had no immunity against them);

they contacted humans, looking for the young and the intelligent, to teach them skills and give them knowledge; such humans were "tested" before initiation to contact.

These are but a number of the ancient tales of mysterious phenomena that have haunted Russia down the centuries. Surely some can be explained but many others still leave us as puzzled today as the original observers. They do however give us an insight into the way our ancestors described what today we might term as UFOs.

CHAPTER 2

THE TUNGUSKA PHENOMENON, THEN AND NOW

JUNE 30, 1908, 7:17 AM

This arguably was the most famous Russian UFO case of the early 20th century. When something exploded over Siberia on June 30, 1908, it flattened more than 2,100 square kilometres of forest, left no craters, and no obvious fragments. What was it? This question has been on the minds of Russian scientists, researchers, and ufologists since at least the 1920s. Some of those who dared study the phenomenon died in concentration camps; some perished during their search; some were ostracised, forgotten, crushed by bloody history of 20th century Russia. The Tunguska, a vast area, remains a wilderness, full of mosquito-infested swamps and marshes. The surrounding taiga is, however, a most beautiful sight, but the journey to the area is a living hell.

There are conflicting reports about the occurrence, even regarding the direction of the object's flight. There are conflicting opinions, whether it was an "object" or something else; or even if there was an object at all. Yes, we have reports from various eyewitnesses, we have learnt about subsequent mutations and the ecological impact of the explosion, read a number of hypotheses and still the most important event of Russia's UFO history is still not that much closer to being solved. This chapter will attempt to present all points of view, and piece together scattered fragments of the ongoing quest to solve the mystery of the Tunguska Explosion.

1908

According to Pesach Amnuel, an Israeli astrophysicist and writer of Soviet Jewish origin, the year 1908 experienced an increase in solar activity. Y. Koptev, in his article published in NLO Magazine (Issue 2, 1997) presents detailed description of the strange phenomena in the sky above that had occurred that year, and might be related to the Tunguska Explosion.

On a clear February 22nd morning, local residents of the town of Brest (Russia) observed a bright spot (in the north-eastern direction). It was

V-shaped, and moved to the north. The object initially was quite bright, but later dimmed. However, its size increased constantly. About half an hour later the V-shaped "spot" was only just visible.

In April, a strange meteorite fell to earth in the Kovelskaya Province, the Novoaleksandrovsky district. Local newspapers reported that it was huge, and that it fell near railroad tracks. An engineer stopped his train, and passengers got off to see a strange meteorite. Most of it was buried by the impact, and only its top part protruded from the ground. The object had a stony mass and was white in colour.

In the autumn, yet another meteorite exploded over the Teletsky Lake, and its fragments once again fell to earth. A meteorite was observed flying over the city of Melitopol', in the month of September.

Russian archives reveal that in the summer and autumn of 1908 there was a sharp increase in the number of observed bolides (small meteorites). Newspapers throughout the world published reports about them; there were actually three times as many reports as in previous years. Reports of these bolides came from Russia, Baltic, Siberia, Central Asia, China, and England.

There were more unusual observations. From June 17 through 19, in the area of the Middle Volga in Russia, local residents were astonished to see the Aurora Borealis (northern lights). Residents of the Orlovskaya Province were at loss to explain the silvery clouds in the sky. We will discuss such mysterious clouds in other chapters of the book.

Several days later, the sky over the suburbs of Yuryev city (known as Tartu today) and other areas experienced purple-coloured skies at sunrise, something which they had never seen before.

From June 21, a number of European areas as well as some in the Western Siberia observed very bright multi-coloured skies at sunrise. But during the sunsets people could clearly see these unusual silvery clouds, stretching from east to west. After June 27, a number of the reported sightings of such clouds increased drastically. It was as if nature was preparing itself for something unusual to occur. Not since the 1883 Krakatau Volcanic explosion in the Pacific did mankind witness such exotic heavenly illuminations.

Events on the ground were quite irregular, too. In the spring of that year Switzerland experienced heavy snowfall and floods.

Crews of the ships that sailed in the Atlantic Ocean reported dense dust, moving high above. Then there were the earthquakes. In the Siberian city of Irkutsk scientists at the local Observatory registered over fifteen hundred weak and strong earthquakes. One was also registered on that fateful day of June 30, 1908.

What is more fascinating is that local observers filled out the questionnaires sent by the Observatory. Nobody observed any earthquakes, but people did hear something that resembled a strong thunder; however, the sky was clear and cloudless. A. V. Voznesensky, director of the Observatory, researched some 60 reports, and concluded that the "earthquakes" were related to the explosion over the taiga. P. Amnuel wrote that when in the early morning of the 30th, the Observatory registered the epicentre of the earthquake; its scientists knew nothing about its origin. They registered three waves, each lasting over two minutes. The ground started moving at approximately 7:19 a.m. local time. The Observatory's director and his assistants quickly established that the epicentre of the earthquake was between the rivers Nizhnyaya and Podkamennaya Tunguska, to the north of the Vanavara trading station. Curiously, the seismograph of the Irkutsk Observatory indicated that the last earthquake took place at 7:46 a.m., some half an hour after the explosion over the taiga. Actually, A. V. Voznesenky believed that it was not the movement of the ground that caused the last report, but the movement of air. A sonic wave, caused by the explosion, reached Irkutsk 45 minutes after the explosion, and still continued to move around the globe.

When the authors of this book researched materials about the Tunguska Explosion, they were struck by the fact that the event itself was barely noticed by Russia's scientific establishment at the time. Later, of course, the event generated hypotheses, discussions, and expeditions that still go on today. It behoves all those interested in the Tunguska Explosion to do a thorough research of the year when it occurred, perhaps day-by-day. We might discover reports of even more unusual occurrences that could help us find an explanation.

THE EXPLOSION

The object approached from an azimuth of 115 degrees, and descended at an entry angle of 30 to 35 degrees above the horizon. It continued along a north-westward trajectory until it seemingly disappeared over the horizon. When the object reached an altitude of 2.5 to 9.0 kilometres over the area, there occurred an explosion-like energy release. The trees burned for weeks, destroying an area of some 1000 square kilometres. Ash was carried by global air circulation around the planet. The mass of the object has been estimated to be 100,000 tons, and the force of the explosion at 40 megatons of TNT. That is 2000 times the force of the atomic bomb exploded over Hiroshima (Japan) in 1945.

Perhaps the explosion or whatever occurred in the taiga on June 30, 1908, would not create worldwide attention (Kazantsev, Kulik, Zigel, Korolyov and others notwithstanding), had it not been for one inconsistency. Various experts in the field of ballistics, who researched the phenomenon, indicated that the body, before the explosion, slowly flew from east to west. That is what eyewitnesses who resided to the east of the lake Baikal stated. But thousands of those who lived to the west stated that the body flew from south to north.

In 1969 Felix Zigel, a famous Soviet scientist and UFO researcher, published an article in Tekhnika-Molodezhi (Issue 12, 1969) magazine, and suggested that it was a UFO that flew over the taiga, and that it made a few steep turns before the explosion. Among those who had observed the flight of the body over the taiga were those who stated that it changed its trajectory, and that it turned over Baikal.

And still, there were other inconsistencies. The "southern object" was described as "star-like" and white-bluish in colour; it was flying early in the morning hours. However, the "eastern object" was seen much later during the day, and it was described as a fast-moving reddish flying object. Aleksey V. Zolotov, another scientist and researcher of the paranormal, proffered an idea that two completely different objects flew over the taiga. He supposed that two UFOs, one from the south, and the other from the east, flew to the same point over the taiga, and blew up.

Was it an intercept? Such an idea was discussed in Russia in 1991. Another Russian scientist is of the opinion that the objects (meteorites, in his view) flew over the taiga on two different days. And yet, if there was an explosion or disintegration of the flying object, no fragments of it were found even by modern day researchers. Later in this book we will discuss the Vashka Object, found in 1985 some three thousand kilometres away, and thought by some to be such a fragment.

THE AFTERMATH

Tens of millions of people around the globe witnessed the aftermath of the Tunguska Phenomenon. After all, night had disappeared to the west of the explosion (or whatever it was…) throughout Western Siberia and Europe. The darkness was gone for 72 hours, an unprecedented event. For several nights all over northern Europe, the sky glowed enough to light the streets of London.

The Irkutsk Observatory reported the disturbances in the Earth's magnetic fields 900 kilometres southeast of the epicentre. The local geomagnetic disturbance was similar to some effects following middle-and high-altitude nuclear explosions in the atmosphere, but unlike the latter, it exhibited a kind of delay: it occurred after the explosion. Other anomalies caused by the explosion included strange mesospheric clouds, bright "volcanic" twilights, disturbances of atmospheric polarisation, and intense solar halos.

The trees were felled in an outward motion, in a radial pattern. In the centre, there was an area of trees that remained standing, although all their bark and branches had been destroyed. It is noteworthy to mention that the taiga recovered quite rapidly and there were clear signs of accelerated growth.

Ecological consequences of the Tunguska explosion include genetic impact; remarkably quick revival of the taiga, and accelerated growth of young trees. We do not know much about the genetic aftermath of the Tunguska

Explosion. There is a serious discussion of the genetic consequences by N.V. Vasilyev, MD (member of the Russian Academy of Medical Sciences) in the RIAP BULLETIN (January-March 1995). He mentions a rare mutation in Rh-antigen that has reportedly arisen among the natives of the region (the Evenks) in the 1910s. The mutation originated in Strelka-Chunya, one of the settlements closest to the site of the Tunguska explosion. There are also morph metric peculiarities of certain ant species found in the area of the epicentre.

Russian researchers A. B. Petukhov and L.A. Pankratov published a most interesting finding in the Anomaliya newspaper in 1997. 207 talented, highly intellectual people were born around the world in 1908. To compare, on average, between the years 1900-1907, 139 talented people were born each year; and in the years 1909-1915, 115 people per year. Further investigation revealed that most of the talented people that year were born in Russia (117 persons), and 92 persons were born in other countries. Hence, Russia was akin to a separated territory; most talented people were born there, above the norm, while beyond its borders the number was similar to the statistics of other years.

There were no great events or inventions that took place in 1908. Then it is possible that the explosion of the Tunguska Phenomenon caused a long-term positive influence on the future intellectual development of human civilization.

THE EYEWITNESSES

There were eyewitnesses, too. Their recollections will help in the objective presentation of this incident. Many of the eyewitnesses spoke of seeing an oval-shaped mass moving across the sky, as well as seeing the object change course, and of having a very low speed.

A traveller on the Trans-Siberian Railway set up his camera to get a picture of the train during a relief stop (Kansk, Russia). The date was June 30, 1908. Suddenly he saw a brilliantly luminous object in the sky. He was able to get but a poor picture on tintype: then the object was gone. It headed in the easterly direction, moving right and left, leaving a bright tail behind it.

Eyewitness Okhchin, a hunter, always warned those who went into the taiga after 1908: beware of a certain brook; its water is like fire, it burns people and trees. "I will pray to Agdi to see you back alive" he would say. Twenty years later the rivers over which the Tunguska Object flew, were devoid of fish.

There were many reports, accounts, and stories in the aftermath of the explosion. Soviet and Russian researchers were able to keep many, so that future generations of scientists could continue the study of the incredible event that occurred on our planet over 97 years ago.

LEONID KULIK

P. Amnuel, who has investigated the Tunguska Phenomenon, noted one strange fact: scientists paid no attention to it for over ten years. Well, except, perhaps, for those who comprised a very secretive expedition of the Geographic Society. (See below)

A report about a giant meteorite falling down in Siberia was printed on the backside of a page in a calendar (the date of the page was June 15, 1910). Probably many people read this page, but none really paid attention. But ten years later L.A. Kulik, a scientist at the Mineralalogical Museum, discovered this very page.

Actually, Kulik had been working in the Museum since 1913, when V. I. Vernadsky hired him. By sheer chance, an editor of the Soviet magazine Mirovedeniye D. O. Svyatsky paid a visit to the Museum, and showed Kulik a page from the calendar (various accounts differs as to whether the date was June 15 or June 2, 1910). The report on the page described a meteorite's crash near Filimonovo, some 11 verstas from Kansk (one versta equaled 1.06 kilometre in the old Russia). Well, Leonid Kulik was always interested in meteorites. Kulik was eager to lead an expedition throughout Russia's territories, to search for celestial stones that fell to earth in his country. This was a difficult period. Russia was engulfed in the Civil War, hunger reigned in its cities, the infrastructure of the old Empire was falling apart, and terrors of the new rule were felt all throughout the land. And yet the Academy of Sciences authorised the expedition. It seemed like fate had intervened when Kulik found the page of an old calendar, and read about the Tunguska Phenomenon. He was a man of action, and led his first expedition to Siberia in September of 1921. He talked to numerous people, questioned eyewitnesses, and realised that the Tunguska Phenomenon was an event of enormous proportions. That year he did not make it to the centre of the "explosion", and returned to Petrograd (the city also known as Leningrad and Saint Petersburg).

The second expedition to the area, funded by Soviet Academy of Sciences, was sent in 1927. Leonid Kulik, a truly dedicated scientist, the founder of meteorite science in Russia, again headed the expedition. The purpose of the expedition was to locate and research the alleged site of the Tunguska meteorite crash. Kulik and his assistant Gulikh arrived in Vanavara in March of 1927. It was a tiny hamlet, consisting of a few houses. In April, both scientists and their Evenk guide Lyuchetkan conducted an expedition to the north. On April 13 they observed huge areas of felled trees. The site amazed all who saw it.

The expedition could not locate any remnants of a meteorite. Over the next 14 years Kulik led several more expeditions to the area, but could not find anything. He had a number of highly placed opponents among Soviet scientists, but a strong ally, too: the academician V. I. Vernadsky.

Kulik's life could have been the subject of a thriller novel. It was full of twists and turns. His travels through the taiga were harsh and difficult. To get what he needed, Kulik often resorted to some very strong-armed tactics. Siberian old-timers recalled the bearded explorer and his revolver for many long years. He got what he needed: supplies, guides, boats, carts, and reindeers. He did not tolerate any dissenting opinions during the harsh treks through the mosquito-infested hellishly hot Siberian taiga. Kulik insisted on strict discipline throughout his numerous expeditions.

He doggedly pursued the search for the elusive meteorite that he believed to be the cause of the Tunguska Phenomenon. But those who wanted to see tangible results of the expeditions became restless. Then, a denunciation was sent to Moscow. Kulik was denounced as the enemy of the people who wasted money of the proletariat: there are no meteorites, and the felled trees were nothing but a result of a hurricane. As a dedicated scientist, Kulik wanted to pursue his dream of finding the meteorite. But Moscow did not send funds on time, and whatever it sent was not enough. Kulik was doing his best to convince the authorities that the meteorite consisted of pure nickel. In 1939 Stalin's Russia was preparing for a war, and such strategic metal would be of great use. Kulik assured them the meteorite that crashed into the Yuzhni swamp (as he was certain) was nothing but pure nickel in its content. The last time Kulik visited the area of the epicentre was on August 6, 1939. The next year there were no funds for an expedition. In 1941 Hitler's forces invaded his Motherland, and Kulik volunteered to go to the front line to defend his country.

Kulik died in 1942, as a prisoner of war. While in the Nazi prison camp, he was attending to the wounded fellow prisoners. As he lay dying, delirious Kulik talked about the Podkamennaya Tunguska.

In the autumn of 1944 a Soviet Yak-40 aircraft crashed in the River Chamba area, thirty kilometres to the south from the epicentre of the Tunguska Explosion. The airplane's instruments failed when it flew over the epicentre. Vadim Chernobrov, a noted Russian researcher of the paranormal and a scientist, was able to photograph fragments of the aircraft in 1996.

No officially sanctioned expeditions were sent to the area until 1958. But there were some other expeditions that we will mention later.

The 1958 expedition, sent to the area by the Soviet Academy of Sciences, concluded that there was an explosion of a body over the taiga. The altitude of the explosion was actually higher than the one suggested by A. Kazantsev, a war veteran, engineer, and a science-fiction writer.

Young Russian scientists Viktor Zhuravlyov and Gennady Plekhanov, who led more expeditions to the taiga, found out that the situation is far more complicated than they thought before. They found neither radiation nor fragments of bolides.

For years Soviet scientists have gone to Tunguska, and collected a huge amount of data. But the Tunguska Phenomenon still remains a mystery. After the end of the Cold War, Western scientists have been able to join their Russian colleagues. And such prominent UFO researchers as Vadim Chernobrov have joined the quest.

Chernobrov and his colleagues conducted an expedition in 1996, and they are sure to continue their research in the new millennium. After all, according to an old legend among those who have gone to the Tunguska taiga in search of the answers to the mystery of the Phenomenon, he (or she) who has entered the area leaves there a piece of himself. Instead, he gets some essence that accompanies him for the rest of his life. This essence forces him to go back, time after time.

MAKARENKO'S EXPEDITION
Alexander Leonidovich Kul'sky published a truly fascinating book in 1997 (Kiev, Ukraine). The title of the book is "Na perekrestkah vselennoy" or "At the crossroads of the Universe". The author was able to collect a great deal of interesting, and usually previously unavailable information about paranormal phenomena in the Czarist Russia, USSR, and Western Europe. Among such materials there is a brochure written by A. Voytsekhovsky. Apparently, at the end of June of 1908, a Russian scientific expedition, led by A. Makarenko, worked in the area of the Katonga (the local name for Podkamennaya Tunguska). A brief report about the expedition's work was prepared by A. Makarenko, a member of the Geographic Society, and was discovered later.

The report stated that photographs of the Katonga were taken, its depths and navigating channel measured, etc. But there were no mentions of any phenomena that would be associated with a meteorite's fall. This is one of the strangest episodes of the Tunguska Phenomenon. Russian scientists of the pre-Revolutionary Russia were educated to no lesser degree than their European neighbours. The Geographic Society was a prestigious group of scientific luminaries. Its members would not miss scientific data, observations, and measurements. How could scientists miss an event like the Tunguska Explosion or whatever occurred that morning, or not report it even in a brief account of their expedition? A. Kulsky offers us two explanations: either the report was later changed (for reasons we cannot comprehend); or the members of the expedition did not observe anything because their minds were, well, "turned off".

Whatever faults could be attributed to Czarist Russia, secrecy was certainly not one of them. The press reported anomalous phenomena quite openly. What would the expedition have to observe in the taiga that day in order to force authorities to confiscate its diaries, and change A. Makarenko's report for another one, where the Tunguska Phenomenon is not mentioned at all? A. Kulsky accepts the second explanation: the expedition's members had their consciousness turned off by artificial means.

However improbable this may sound, there were other strange events related to the "expeditions" to the taiga. According to A. Voytsekhovsky's materials, the very first expedition actually to the site (due of the Tunguska Phenomenon and the need to research it) was organised in 1911. The expedition was sent by the Omsk Department of Highways and Waterways. No other than V. Shishkov, at the time an engineer, and much later, a famous novelist, headed the expedition. His book "Ugryum Reka" or "River Ugryum" was a bestseller in the 1960s USSR, and contained very interesting descriptions of the daily life in the taiga, as well as its inhabitants. Some paranormal episodes could too, be found, on the pages of the book (Paul Stonehill has read it many times, and it is in his library). A Soviet motion picture, based on the book, was produced in the 1960s.

But there was still another expedition to the site. Some old-timers in the taiga, some obscure articles in the newspapers of the time, and recollections of the Saint Petersburg (pre-revolutionary) scientists reveal scattered details. All that is known today is that a group of people with unusual equipment visited the alleged site of the Tunguska Phenomenon (actually, a crash site), and observed incredible phenomena. This was sometime in 1909 or 1910. But who those people were, what their equipment consisted of, we have no knowledge whatsoever. It is important to mention here that the Far Eastern UFO researchers from Vladivostok who embarked on their 1991 expedition to find the "Devil's Cemetery" (the alleged exact site of the Tunguska Phenomenon's crash in the taiga) collected persistent reports of strange animals and humans in the area after 1908.

AND ANOTHER SECRET EXPEDITION

Valentin Psalomschikov, a noted Russian scientist and journalist, published an article in NLO Magazine in 1999. He has researched information about a secret Soviet military expedition, sanctioned by Lavrenty Beria, Stalin's trusted assistant and a top Soviet official. He was put in charge of the Soviet atomic weapons project.

The expedition took place one year after the testing of the first Soviet atomic bomb. In the summer of 1949 Beria presented his idea during a high-level secret meeting. He wanted to study the area of the Tunguska phenomenon, but he was not interested in looking for a meteorite. If there was an explosion of a nuclear-powered spaceship over the Siberian taiga, Beria wanted detailed information about it. Kazantsev's name was not mentioned. Beria ruled against participation of civilian scientists, but demanded experts in the field of atomic tests, and ballistics experts. Before the expedition left, Beria demanded his assistants to collect all information about the geophysical effects of the explosion.

Then, with great care, readings of devices of Russian and German meteorological stations from June 30, 1908, were analysed and researched. This project confirmed that the airwave, caused by the explosion, circled the earth several times. It became clear that the energy of the explosion was several dozen megatons, and the explosion occurred at the altitude of 20 kilometres. Information received from the Irkutsk Geophysical Observatory was also confirmed: intensive disturbance of the Earth's magnetic field (recorded several minutes after the explosion) are like those effects that are caused by increased ionisation in the epicentre and accompany powerful nuclear explosions in the atmosphere. The Irkutsk scientists at that time were also able to receive radio waves from Europe, something that had never occurred before.

Even before the expedition left for the taiga, a reconnaissance airplane twice flew over the area of an alleged meteorite fall, and took photographs of the forest, at different altitudes. Each member of the expedition read Kulik's reports, and saw the photographs he took.

And so, in the summer of 1949, members of the secret expedition, disguised as geologists, were flown to the Vanavara settlement, and then a hydroplane flew them, in turn, to the Cheko Lake. They were prohibited from asking questions of local residents, but they were allowed to listen.

Scientific findings of the expedition were never published. They were different from those of the expeditions later sent to the area by the Soviet Science Academy, and Committee for the study of meteorites. Beria's military scientists established that the trees were felled by percussion wave (i.e. from the Tunguska Phenomenon's inner energy, and not by a ballistic wave of a flying object). Hence, the explosion did occur at a high altitude. Even by most modest calculations, the force of the explosion was over one megaton. But there was no radiation of any significance in the area. After an atomic bomb explodes, there is a substantial radioactive presence in the atmosphere. Then, concluded military scientists, it had to be a thermonuclear explosion.

Upon their return to Moscow, the scientists in charge of different field research groups (ballistics, radioactivity, etc.) prepared their reports. They were locked in different rooms, with typewriters and paper. Beria's officials then collected the reports. There were no discussions, no brainstorming. We still do not know what happened to the reports of the secret expedition.

DR. ALEXEY V. ZOLOTOV

He was murdered in October of 1995. Russia lost a fearless researcher, and a daring scientist. Dr. Zolotov was born in 1919. After his graduation (he was interested in radio physics), Zolotov worked in the Soviet Bashkiria, and later, in Kalinin (now, Tver). Dr. Zolotov was a noted geophysicist. He doggedly pursued the ET hypothesis of the Tunguska Phenomenon. He actually sought to provide scientific background for Kazantsev's ideas. Nowadays, his name is inseparable from the history of the phenomenon. Dr. Zolotov was, essentially, a pioneer researcher. That had earned him many opponents, and on occasions, wrath of the scientific officialdom. He was a highly ethical person, a true intellectual, in the best traditions of Russia. Dr. Zolotov was no armchair researcher; he actually visited the area of the Tunguska Explosion, and conducted field research.

His monograph "Tungusskaya Katastrofa 1908 goda" was published in 1970, in Minsk. There was quite a powerful opposition to the book from those in charge of the Soviet astronomical community; they wanted to prevent the publication. The Vice-President of the Soviet Academy of Sciences, V. P. Konstantinov, backed Dr. Zolotov. The monograph is very useful today, too.

BELIEFS, IDEAS, THEORIES, HYPOTHESES...

The Evenks (the Tungus people) are certain that on that fateful day a deity named Agdi descended from the Heavens down into the taiga backwoods. They insist on the fact that Agdi spoke to them, and they had actually seen the deity. For many years their shamans kept the area sealed off from the rest of the world. They were fearful of enraging the deities whose anger had caused the 1908 Tunguska explosion.

As we noted, scientists did not become interested in the Tunguska Phenomenon until 1920s. However, less trained people proffered explanations of the phenomenon that ranged from a repeat of the Sodom and Gomorra event to the start of the second Russo-Japanese war. Then explanations revolved around astronomical phenomena; explosion of several ball lightning's; an aerolite explosion; unusual earthquake, eruption of an ancient volcano.

From 1927 scientists looked for a meteorite in the area, and also explored the possibility that a meteorite turned into streams of fragments and gas. In 1929 they explored an idea of a meteorite that flew by the area; in 1930, an explosion of the comet's centre. In 1932, an impact of Earth with a cosmic dust cloud in 1934, an impact with a comet's tail. In 1945, an explanation that there was a nuclear explosion aboard a spaceship was proffered. In 1946, there appeared a hypothesis about a disaster aboard a spaceship from Mars. Then, in 1947, there was a hypothesis that a meteorite made from antimatter blew up. In 1958, an idea that a meteorite made from ice blew up was also entertained. From 1959, some hypothesised that a fragment of the planet Phaeton fell down to earth. In 1960, there was a hypothesis that there was a detonated explosion of a cloud made of mosquitoes (over 5 cubic kilometres in density). From 1961 on, there has been talk of an exploded flying saucer. In 1962, a hypothesis was proffered that a meteor caused an electric hole of the ionosphere. The following year, a hypothesis discussed that an electrostatic meteor discharged in the taiga, and destroyed areas of it. In 1964, there was talk of a laser ray from outer space hitting the taiga. 1965 was the year when some people suggested that an Abominable Snow Man tried to invade our planet aboard a spaceship. In 1966, there was discussion that a fragment of the super dense White dwarf fell in the taiga. In 1967, there was a discussion of an explosion of the swamp gases because of a lightning's impact. In 1984, scientists Alexei Dmitriyev and Viktor Zhuravlyov from Novosibirsk proffered a theory of the plasma origin of the Tunguska Phenomenon. In 1996 there was a suggestion that Nicola Tesla caused the Tunguska Explosion by the launch of his wireless energy torpedo, during a long-distance test.

Russian scientist Boris I. Ignatov submitted a hypothesis that the Tunguska Explosion was caused by an impact and detonation of three ball lightning's; each lightning was over a metre in diameter.

Siberian scientists V. Zhuravlev and A. Dmitiriyev recently proposed an interesting hypothesis. Using a computer, they analysed numerous accounts of various eyewitnesses kept in the archives, and also documents and reports from newspapers of the period. The computer concluded that there were three bodies at the time, flying in different directions to the same area: one from south, the other from southeast, and the last one from southwest. The epicentre of the explosion corresponded with the site of an ancient volcano, active two hundred million years ago. The East-Siberian magnetic field, also located in the same area, is one of the fourth greatest magnetic anomalies of our planet. This magnetic field, reaching from the bowels of the earth into the space, is something like a gigantic trap. It could have sucked in the Tunguska Phenomenon.

Both Siberian scientists also revealed new facts about the Tunguska Phenomenon. Six minutes after the explosion, the Irkutsk Observatory's devices recorded a magnetic storm that had lasted almost five hours. They have the magnitogram in question.

Most researchers believed that it was a comet that caused the Tunguska Phenomenon. And yet, they could not prove it. And F. Zigel, whose quest to explain the UFO phenomena had irked the Soviet official scientific establishment, and attracted attention of the Central Intelligence Agency, explained, quite clearly, why this hypothesis is groundless (Mif o Tungusskoy komete, Soviet magazine Tekhnika-Molodezhi, Issue 3, 1979).

Listed below are some other hypotheses as to what caused the Tunguska Phenomenon:

* Airburst of an asteroid
* Comet that detonated in the atmosphere
* Black hole
* Antimatter particles
* Nuclear-powered spaceships
* Solar energophore
* Spacecraft travelling faster than light and experiencing time dilation
* Super conductive meteorite

* Powerful electrical charges of a meteorite interacting with
Earth's surface, causing the destruction of the Tunguska object
* Explosion of natural gas.

If there happened to be deposits of natural gas in the taiga, then due to tectonic processes, the gas would be released into the atmosphere, some 2.5 million cubic metres of it to cause an explosion the Tunguska-type force. The gas would have been dissipated and carried away by winds. Once in the upper reaches of the atmosphere, the gas would interact with the ozone, and oxidise. There would be luminescence in the sky. Within a 24-hour period, a huge trail of some 400 kilometres would cover the sky. Once mixed with the air, the natural gas would become a huge cloud, ready to explode. The spark would be caused by a thunderstorm many kilometres away from the Tunguska epicentre; and like a gigantic bolide this fiery trail would race through the sky, to the epicentre. There, in a hollow, the natural would be highly concentrated, and it is there that a tremendous explosion would result in a fireball. The explosion would shake the mighty Russian taiga. The force of the explosion would move the ground below, close the tectonic splits below, and natural gas would cease its movement to the atmosphere. The author of this hypothesis, D. Timofeyev of Krasnoyarsk, reminded readers of Komsomolskaya Pravda newspaper (November 11, 1984 issue) that the Evenks told after the explosion about water in the swamps "burning like fire". There is hydrogen sulphide in the composition of natural gas. When burning, it forms sulphurous anhydride; and the latter, when mixing with water, becomes an acid. By the way, there is a belief among scientists that the atmospheric nitrous oxide created by the 1908 Tunguska phenomenon in all probability caused the 30% depletion in the northern hemisphere ozone shield that was observed in the year following the Tunguska explosion.

Few people know of another episode, related to the Tunguska Phenomena. Soviet astronavigation specialist Shternfeld calculated something very interesting, but rarely published. In the beginning of the 20th century, scientists expected two great oppositions. To astronomers an opposition is the position of two heavenly bodies when their celestial longitudes differ by 180 degrees, especially the position of a planet or the moon when either is on the opposite side of the earth from the sun.

Shternfeld knew about the expectations, and decided to calculate when a spaceship would have to leave Venus, and through the use of the Earth-Venus opposition, get to our planet using the least energy output. The result was quite fantastic: if such a spaceship were to blast off from Venus at the most favourable time, it would arrive on Earth on June 30, 1908. Coincidence? The same applies to Mars, and its opposition to Earth.

Russian engineer E. Krutelev published his analysis of the Tunguska

Phenomena, in the Rabochaya Tribuna newspaper (1991). He is convinced that whatever occurred in the taiga that day was not a breakdown of an alien ship, but rather its take-off. His clues: reports from the locals, dearth of any material traces of an explosion, and the fact that what the locals heard was the sound of a mighty thunderous roar, moving away in the northern direction. Are Krutelev's views credible? S. Privalikhin, an eyewitness from the Kova Village reported that he first heard a "shot from a cannon". The next moment he saw a long, flying object, thick in its fore part. The object flew horizontally over the ground, leaving behind a fiery trail. I. Starichev observed the object from the Kama River. When he and others looked up, they saw "moving fire" in the sky, and inside it some body (its size that of a half-moon). V. Okhchin, a hunter, was at a hut 35 kilometres from the epicentre. He noticed that century-old Siberian trees were instantly uprooted. The upper parts of trees were ablaze. The next moment people saw a giant mushroom-like cloud, rising up on the horizon.

Professor A. Zolotov, who continued where L. Kulik left off, was of the opinion that the Tunguska Phenomenon was an object of artificial origin. However, in his opinion, the object was a UFO-bomb, its power that of 40 megatons. This "bomb" was exploded to get attention from the humans, a sort of a signal from another world. That is why the aliens chose to explode it in a faraway wilderness, so as to minimise the harm.

A hypothesis proposed in the 1980's points to iridium to be proof that a comet exploded over the Siberian taiga in 1908. Iridium is a rare element on Earth, but common in meteorites, comets and asteroids. Iridium anomalies in peat deposits of Siberia support a cosmic impact hypothesis in the minds of a number of Western and Russian scientists.

Soviet expeditions of the late 1950s and early 1960s discovered microscopic spheres of metal and glass in the soil of the taiga. Ramachandran Ganapathy, an American scientist, analysed trace elements in several spheres and discovered enrichments of iridium, (cosmically abundant but rare on Earth). He believes the spheres are extraterrestrial in origin. But his data is not sufficient to determine whether comets or asteroids were the culprits of the Tunguska Phenomenon.

Ramachandran Ganapathy also uncovered a Tunguskan "sign" in the ice of Antarctica (in 1984). He researched ice formed in the beginning of the 20th century (during the first twenty years). A sample (from 1909) obtained, once melted, left microscopic residues rich in meteoritic material (sub micron-size debris sticking to dust grains). If it resulted from the Tunguska Phenomenon, the discovery could mean we have underestimated the size of the Tunguska Object. Ganapathy estimates the object was a seven-million ton, 160 metre diameter monster (per the South Pole, Antarctica, data as evidence to the total amount of atmospheric fallout from the event).

There is another interesting hypothesis. The plasma origin theory of the Tunguska Phenomenon may be explained today by contemporary military research in Russia.

Russian scientist Boris Belitsky was interviewed in a VOICE OF RUSSIA WORLD SERVICE segment on science and engineering (it aired December 23, 1996). During the interview Belitsky was asked about microwave generator development in Russia. His responses were of great interest to those who study the plasmoid theory of the Tunguska Phenomenon.

Powerful microwave generators are of interest, for one thing, because of their possible military applications. They can be used to fire a plasmoid, that is, a blob, of plasma. Plasma is a mixture of electrons and ions. We have all seen it, for example, in electric air discharges and in sparks, it is also a prime factor in thermonuclear reactions, as in the Sun. Space scientists in Russia have a long record of experimenting with it. For example, plasma engines were tested in some of the early Soviet Mars probes, a quarter of a century ago. Very extensive studies of plasma have been carried out under the program of research into controlled nuclear fusion. Research into the military applications has been conducted at some of the leading research institutes of the military-industrial complex, for example at the Research Institute of Radio Instruments. The interest in such generators exists because it could be used to fire a plasmoid, that is, a blob of plasma into the path of an incoming missile, its warhead, or an aircraft.

The plasmoid would effectively ionise that region of space and, in this manner, disturb the aerodynamics of the flight of the missile, warhead or aircraft. Terminating their flight makes such a generator and its plasmoid a practically invulnerable weapon, providing protection against attack via space. During the 1993 Russian-American summit in Vancouver, the Russians proposed a joint experiment in testing such generators - or plasma weapons (as they are called in Russia) - as an alternative to the Strategic Defence Initiative, SDI. In such an experiment, the system would be used to repulse a missile attack.

Aleksand Krivenyshev, a Russian-American scientist, discussed a very interesting correlation of dates that involve the Tunguska Phenomenon (1908), the Sikhote-Alin (USSR) Meteorites and Roswell UFO Crash (1947), and the Dalnegorsk UFO Crash (1986). There is an interval of 39 years between each event.

THE BRITISH DEFECTOR'S TALE

Lieutenant Colonel Anthony Godley, defence expert, was chief of a work-study unit at the Royal Military College of Science. This is the only information that was available about him other than what the Russians stated below. Godley disappeared in April 1983. His father bequeathed him more than $60,000, with the proviso that he claimed it by 1987. Godley never showed up and was presumed dead. He was 49 years old at the time. What does his disappearance have to do with the Tunguska Phenomenon?

There were over 22 British scientists who have died or disappeared under mysterious circumstances since 1982. They were highly trained and skilled in computer use. Each of the scientists was working on a highly classified project for the American Strategic Defence Initiative (Star Wars program). None had any apparent motive for killing himself.

The British government contended that the deaths are all a matter of coincidence.

Godley resurfaced in Moscow in April of 1985. According to the Russians, he was a colonel in the British Intelligence. He revealed to the KGB that the British were involved in the so-called guided comet weapons development. They planned to send a guided comet to annihilate Leningrad. The comet was to approach the Earth from the direction of the Sun. Astronomers would see it at the last moment, and countermeasures would be futile. Modern technology would not allow a comet to be destroyed without complex and long preparatory work. According to Godley, the British and their American counterparts argued over the target; Americans preferred that Moscow be targeted. Destruction of both targets at the same time would arouse suspicions. Leningrad was the largest Soviet Naval base, and more attractive to be a target for the United Kingdom. A scientist, involved in the British SDI research, whose last name was Brockway, presented a secret lecture for the military leaders of the program.

He made fascinating discoveries about comets; according to the Russian sources (we will list them below), comets have been used by an extraterrestrial intelligence. Following his presentation, the British SDI military directors decide to concentrate on the development of the comet weapons, and curtail more promising programs. Brockway commits suicide, and a recently formed British SDI group for the research of the "comet weapons" is disbanded. Like another British scientist, whose name the Russians write as "Drankwater", Godley is convinced that Brockway was killed, not by hypothetical aliens (Drankwater's belief), but by M.I.5. Godley, himself an officer of M.I.5, knew that the agency headed by Dame Stella Remington, then Director of M.I.5, would not forgive him his doubts about general assumption that Brockway died as a result of a suicide. It would be possible to hide from his colleagues behind the Iron Curtain; it would not be a problem for the ETs or "aliens" to get their hands on him anywhere on Earth, but Godley was not really afraid of them.

According to him, the British wanted a limited impact of a comet with a Soviet target. NATO strategists planned their operation using the research of Soviet scientists, mostly, as we know now, enthusiasts, who every year returned to the site of the Tunguska Explosion. Their findings were published in the

USSR, and those abroad could read them without any problems. One hypothesis stated that the Tunguska object of 1908 was a comet. Hence, a comet used as a weapon was able to reproduce the effect of the Tunguska meteorite (20-40 megatons of explosive power). The British were certain that the body that exploded over the Siberian taiga was a comet.

The source for this information is Entsiklopedia Nepoznannogo or Encyclopedia of the Unknown, compiled by Vadim Chernobrov, and published in Moscow in 1998. It looks like he used some information from Yevgeny Merkulov's article published in Znaniye-Sila magazine (Issue 5, 1995).

Just ravings of a lunatic, who for some reasons we cannot understand, left the United Kingdom for the USSR? Or is there something more to it? Did Godley surface in Moscow in April of 1983, or 1985? Was there a connection to other British scientists (involved in the SDI program) who died in mysterious ways after 1982?

Chernobrov asks another question: did those involved in the British SDI 'comet weapons' program base their information on Valery Burdakov and Yuri Danilov's popular book, published in the USSR in 1980 ("Raketi Buduschego" or "Rockets of the future"). Professor Burdakov is mentioned throughout our book. V. Chernobrov thinks that the British read the Soviet book, and used scientific information in it.

It was a very unusual comet and associated phenomenon that contradicted all laws of astronomy that attracted Soviet scientists. Comet Arend-Roland was observed from the Oslo Solar Observatory at Harestua on 25 April 1957. During the latter half of April it was seen from the Northern Hemisphere as an extraordinary object in the north-western sky at the end of evening twilight. On April 15th the head was of zero magnitude, trailing a 25-30 degree tail. Between April 20th and May 3rd the comet displayed a bright, sunward-pointing anti-tail up to 15 degrees long. At the conclusion of April brightness, it had fallen to the 3rd magnitude. The comet traversed Triangulum, Perseus, and entered Camelopardalus during this period. After the middle of May, when the comet had become a circumpolar object, it was finally lost to the unaided eye.

The unexpected long and narrow "anti-tail" showed up quite clearly. In most other images this anti-tail is shorter and points to the side. The tail, pointed toward Sun, disappeared as inexplicably as it appeared. Also, astronomers discovered a strange radio source in the comet. The most powerful signals (still not deciphered) were registered between the 16th and 19th of March, just prior to the appearance of the tail. The comet behaved like an artificially created and guided object; perhaps, like a comet with an artificial object inside. Burdakov and Danilov came to a conclusion that this and other cases of incomprehensible orbital changes; appearances of strange comet tails, and sudden changes of the comets specters, can be explained by activities of extraterrestrial civilizations.

Apparently, Godley told his KGB handlers that the British scientists chose the 'comet weapons' program as their share of the U.S. SDI program. They disregarded ET hypothesis, but liked the idea of a guided comet. The technical solution would involve sending a space probe to a chosen comet, and fixing it on the comet's body with the purpose of changing its trajectory. We will not discuss all technical details; those interested should contact Vadim Chernobrov. He has another hypothesis about the spatial-time aspect of the Tunguska Explosion, based on the findings of A. Zolotov in the 1960s. But that hypothesis is beyond the theme of our book.

KAZANTSEV

Sergei Korolyov, father of Soviet space science, became quite interested in the Tunguska Phenomenon after reading a story by Alexander Kasantsev. In 1946, a Soviet engineer, a former army colonel, wrote a short story. A. Kasantsev stated that a nuclear bomb caused the destruction at Tunguska.

Vadim Chernobrov has his statement, tape-recorded in 1996. We need to mention here that A. Kazantsev was also one of the leaders of the Kosmopoisk Group (to be described in later chapters). Humans did not possess such bombs in 1908, thus it had to be an alien spaceship that exploded over the taiga. The story became quite popular in the Soviet Union, reprinted several times. In 1958 it was published as a popular book "Guest from space".

It was a radio broadcast that originated the idea in Kazantsev's head. He experienced the horrors of World War II; he started as a soldier, and ended up in the rank of a colonel. Returning home from Europe in August of 1945, Kazantsev heard an English-language radio broadcast about the nuclear bomb's explosion. Now, Kazantsev was very well informed about the Tunguska Meteorite. He also knew about Kulik's expedition, and knew the person who headed the rescue expedition of Kulik (actually, Kulik created a subterfuge to gain attention of the Soviet public to his cause, and get Communist Party functionaries off his back. He succeeded in his designs).

Victor A. Sitin became a close friend of the Soviet science fiction writer, and a war veteran A. Kazantsev. The latter immediately got an idea, after hearing the broadcast, that the two explosions, the one of an American nuclear bomb, and the other one in 1908, were quite similar. He discussed all details with Sitin, in Moscow. Kazantsev also became interested in the Evenk legend about their deity Ogdi who descended into the taiga. Kazantsev also sought details about the nuclear technology. No information was available in Moscow at that time, until the future writer met with the Academician Landau, who revealed the secrets of the American atomic bomb. Kazantsev decided to write a science fiction story, and published it in 1946; the title was "THE Explosion" (published in the famous Soviet Vokrug Sveta magazine).

Kazantsev's hypothesis was that the Tunguska Phenomenon was really a disaster aboard a nuclear-powered extraterrestrial spaceship.

The Moscow Planetarium staged a play, based on his story. Not a lecture, mind you, (although that is how they advertised it), but a play.

Never before was a scientific report disguised as a play. The assistant to the director of the Planetarium was no other than Feliks Yuryevich Zigel, in the future a famous scientist, a professor, and a doctor in the Moscow Aviation Institute. This was how Soviet Ufology originated. Zigel would discuss the Tunguska Meteorite, and various anomalous phenomena discovered by Kulik. A "guest" would ask him questions (actually, an actor who played a Soviet "colonel") regarding atomic explosions. Other "guests" would rise up and discussions ensued, with participation of real guests. Not long after that, all of Moscow talked about the Tunguska Phenomenon, and tickets to the Planetarium were at a premium. The powers that be also turned their attention to the phenomenon.

Some Soviet astronomers became outraged, and published articles critical of Kazantsev and Zigel in scientific magazines. They assumed that the lectures were genuine. Then, major Soviet newspapers published articles against the hypothesis that an alien ship exploded over the taiga in 1908. But young people were mesmerised by the idea. The interest grew, and no power on earth could stop it.

And so, in 1960, Sergey Korolyov sent two helicopter expeditions to the taiga, to find out what "aliens" used as materials for their craft. The expedition consisted of well-educated space exploration scientists who searched the unfriendly taiga for anything that would resemble fragments of alien craft and signs of the explosion. But officially they had embarked to the taiga to spend their vacation. Among the engineers in the group was Georgy Mikhailovich Grechko, a future Soviet cosmonaut. He was also well trained as a diver, but had no chance to study the nearby lakes, for Moscow recalled him. That expedition, too, found nothing.

Another curious note about the Tunguska area has to do with the local beliefs and legends. We already mentioned that the Evenks, who reside there, worship Agdi. According to their legends, Agdi ("Thunder") is the lord of thunder and lighting, and it arrives to its spouse, Water, in the warm summer months. The Evenks, Oroks, Orochi, and some other taiga tribes believe that the arrival of Agdi in 1908 caused the powerful explosion in the taiga. And, as we mentioned, the locals were forbidden to visit the area of the explosion, for it was the residence of Agdi on Earth.

YURI LAVBIN

On August 10, 2004, Russian newspaper PRAVDA carried an article about a new scientific expedition in search of the mysterious Tunguska "meteorite". According to Pravda, members of the scientific expedition of the Siberian state foundation Tunguska Space Phenomenon say they have managed to uncover blocks of an extraterrestrial technical device. The press service of the Evenkiya republic administration reported that the expedition had worked in the western part of the region in the summer of 2004. The mission's itinerary was based on the results of the space footage analysis. Explorers believe they have discovered blocks of an extraterrestrial technical device that had crashed down on Earth on June 30th, 1908. In addition, expedition members claimed that they found the elusive stone that had been mentioned by Tunguska eyewitnesses in their reports. The mysterious stone, weighing 50 kilograms, was delivered to the city of Krasnoyarsk for study and analyses. The stone is called "Reindeer Stone" by locals, and is made up of a crystalline matter.

The researcher in charge of the expedition, Yuri Lavbin, who has spent over 12 years trying to solve the mystery of the Tunguska Phenomenon, is the president of the Tunguska Spatial Phenomenon Foundation in the Siberian city of Krasnoyarsk.

They have been leading expeditions to the area since 1994; among the researchers are chemists, physicists, geologists and mineralogists. Yuri Lavbin believes that a comet and a mysterious flying machine (an artificial object) actually collided 10 kilometres above the planet, and the result of the collision was the 1908 explosion over the Siberian taiga. His group, claimed Lavbin, has found two strange black stones (shaped like regular cubes, about a metre and a half in size on each side) in the area of the Podkamennaya Tunguska. The stones, according to the Russian scientist, are not of natural origin, made of a material that resembles alloys used to make space rockets. Tests have been scheduled to find out the composition of the stones.

Yuri Lavbin told MosNews agency that his researchers had traced the possible trajectory of the 1908 object, but now they contend that it moved eastward, not westward as has been believed.

To solve the mystery of Tunguska once and for all, Yuri Lavbin is planning another expedition to the area.

We will again visit the area later in this book, when we discuss the Devil's Cemetery. It is clear that no matter how many scientists visit the site of the Tunguska blast, even with today's modern sophisticated equipment, all attempts to identify what exactly did explode that day in 1908 have failed so far.

CHAPTER 3

UFOs OVER THE EMPIRE

When Alexei's eldest son, Fyodor, died in 1682 C.E. after only six years as Czar of Russia, a struggle broke out for the throne. Ivan the 5th and his half brother Peter the 1st were proclaimed joint Czars, with their older sister Sophia acting as regent. When Ivan died, Peter the Great became sole ruler, the Emperor of all Russia. Moscow, the capital of the Russian Empire for almost two centuries, had to relinquish this title to a new capital, Saint Petersburg.

Reports of UFO sightings came from all corners of the Empire. For example, various declassified documents of the Russian Ministry of the Interior (1997) that inherited documents of the Russian Imperial Ministry of the Interior dating back to the beginning of the past century, shed some light on UFO observations in the Russian Empire. There is, among the documents, a very unusual report to the Tsar from his Third Department of the Chancellery, as the Russian secret police were called back then. The report describes certain extraordinary light effects observed in the sky by the inhabitants, the police and military in the city of Orenburg during the night of December 26, 1830. The observations bear a striking similarity to modern UFO sighting reports.

Still other reports in the declassified files dating back to the 19th century mention sightings of UFOs over the town of Ustyug on January 30, 1844, as well as sightings from 1846 and 1847.

Unfortunately, most of the UFO sighting reports have been lost in the mists of time. But Russian and Ukrainian UFO researchers, journalists, and history buffs have done a tremendous job of finding and publishing some of such reports. We have compiled here the most interesting cases.

FROM ALL ENDS OF THE EMPIRE

Gherman Kolchin, former colonel of the Soviet Army, is a well-respected UFO historian in Russia. We will mention his research throughout this book. In 1994 he published his famous book UFO phenomenon, a view from Russia. In the book Kolchin mentioned two interesting episodes. One is a report kept in the archives of the Navy, USSR (f. 135, op. 1, d. 519, l. 25-26). Baron de Bie, a Dutch ambassador at the court of Czar Peter the Great, wrote a report where he mentioned a sighting (its description was written down pursuant to the orders of Vice-Admiral Kryuys). The date was April 2, 1716, the area of sighting: near Saint Petersburg. At nine o'clock in the evening the sky was clear and cloudless. A strange, dense and dark "cloud" appeared in the northeastern portion of the sky. Its apex was sharp-like, its base was wide, and it traversed the sky with great speed. At the same time, from the north, another cloud, similar to the first one, also appeared; it moved to the east, approaching the first cloud from the west. When the "clouds" approached each other, some sort of a bright "pillar" appeared between them, and lasted for several minutes. Then both "clouds" crashed into each other with terrible force, and appeared to have shattered from the strong impact. A flame formed in the point of the impact; it was accompanied by smoke, and rays of flame in all directions pierced it. Smaller and numerous clouds moved at great speeds and emitted flames. Also, many fiery arrows appeared in the sky, reaching the altitude of 80 degrees over the horizon. Eyewitnesses described a terrible and fearful scene that reminded them of sea and land battles. The report also mentions that at that very same time in the north-western portion of the sky a giant shiny "comet" appeared and rose to 12 degrees over the horizon. The phenomenon lasted for a quarter of an hour.

G. Kolchin mentioned several more fascinating reports. One dates back to 1812. In the sky over Bukovina (Ukraine), people observed a large "star", accompanied by a beam of light. It flew toward Russia. Later it returned; and continued to move back and forth throughout the Russian war against the Napoleonic armies.

Like Mikhail Gershtein, Gherman Kolchin mentions the year of 1892. There was obvious and increased UFO activity in Russia, with numerous sightings and reports of them coming from all corners of Russia. Kolchin mentions that the majority of the reports came from the Baltic and Poland. The Russian government ordered an official investigation, and as a result a report was prepared by staff captain Kovan'ko (a rank intermediate between lieutenant and captain), head of the air training fleet. His report classified the reported sightings to be of three kinds: bright dots, slowly increasing their size and brightness, and later disappearing as slow; disks that emitted rays of electric light downwards; they appeared in the mornings; and air balloons that sometimes moved against the wind.

A PHENOMENON OVER THE KREMLIN

A document found in the Russian State Historical Museum (OPI GIM, f.233, yed. khr. 8, l. 7-8.) describes a phenomenon observed in the sky over Moscow in 1808. The phenomenon performed movements over the city that resembles later reports of UFO movements in other countries. Its physical characteristics, too, resembled descriptions of later UFOs.

The object was able to move through space in any direction; it achieved incredible speed and was able to stop immediately. The object emitted phosphoric illumination, and also flared up very brightly. The drawing that accompanied the document indicates that the object stopped, flared up and took off vertically in the area over the Vagagn'kovsky Hill (between the Borovisky gates of the Kremlin and the Pashkov house).

The sky was clear and starry on that memorable night on September 1st. It was at 8 pm when the phenomenon was observed; it could be seen quite clearly from the University of Moscow. The object was of "awesome size" (we are quoting the actual document). It also emitted "strong cracking sounds". At the very end of its manoeuvres, the object remained as a brightly lit disk, ascended "very smoothly" upwards "to the stars", was still visible among them for a while, and then disappeared.

The document, according to A. K. Afnasyev, who published his report in a 1995 digest "Reka Vremyon", Volume 2, (Moscow) is authentic. The author discussed the document's authenticity very thoroughly, down to the characteristics of the paper, and orthography. The document's author, in Afnasyev's opinion, was an educated person, and probably a student or a professor of the University of Moscow. He also believes that the official censorship would not allow publication of the document for the fear that it might cause public "indignation", and also due to the necessity to explain the phenomena.

The document was a part of the Pyotr Semyonovich Poludensky (1774-1852) collection; this gentleman was a senator, and held high Russian government positions.

KARELIA'S UFO

On July 30, 1880, a giant spherical and bright object flew over St. Petersburg. The UFO was accompanied by two identical craft, only smaller in size. The flight of the UFOs was noiseless, and they were observed over the city for three minutes.

Some of the most interesting reports originated in Karelia, an area located in north-western Russia, east of Finland, not that far away from St. Petersburg. We will have more to say later about this area of Russia and the strange phenomena associated with it.

Lamivaara is a small town in the eastern Finland, not far from the Ladoga Lake. In 1898 Rita Nukarinen, a girl of ten years of age, was walking through the forest. Suddenly she saw an object, similar to a giant sphere; it hovered over the treetops. Inside it Rita saw humanoid beings. Rita never forgot the sighting, and related the story to her children. Russian engineers and scientists built the first air balloon ever tested in the area of the Ladoga Lake in 1913; therefore, they had nothing to do with the sighting.

The description of the object, given by Rita, is similar to that of UFOs sighted over California in 1890, and Kansas over 1897.

The first abduction case in that area took place in 1917, in the Karkiyeki Township located on the shore of the Ladoga Lake. Enni Leitu (1873-1930) observed a saucer-like object that landed near her house in the township. Something resembling a staircase protruded from the object, and small humanoid shapes descended to the ground. Enni thought that they looked like "small devils". Although she was quite scared, the beings insisted on taking her along, and she was taken to their ship. The ship landed in several places on Earth, and even flew into the near earth orbit for a brief period of time. She was in telepathic communication mode with a being she guessed to be the leader of the aliens. Enni stated that she had a pleasant journey, it was warm inside the ship, and she sat in a wonderful and comfortable chair. The beings actually offered Enni to stay with them, but she refused. After this occurrence Enni became a famous soothsayer in the area. She could actually heal people (through ESP). While some considered her to be "strange", she was well respected in the community.

Seventy years later, in 1987, a strange craft called the Monchegorsk Object will be analysed by Soviet military not far away from the Ladoga Lake. We ask the readers to remember Enni's tale when we discuss that case.

B. Grabovsky was a UFO phenomena researcher from the city of Frunze. All his life he collected reports of UFO sightings, contacts, and related phenomena. He began in 1947, and his book contained many interesting facts. In the 1950s Grabovsky interviewed a Siberian woman. Her grandfather died when he was close to 100 years of age. In his youth he was a shepherd. Once he was looking for an animal lost from the herd. His search was futile, and losing all hope, the youth chanced upon a forest glade. There he saw a giant sphere. It had supports underneath which rested on the ground. Nearby he saw "monsters" that looked quite humanoid. Right next to them was his lost cow. It was dead, and its stomach was slit. Yet there was no blood anywhere in sight. The "monsters" bent over the animal, and studied something inside it; it seemed to the youth they were cutting something out. Some time later they noticed the young man, and gestured to him in a strange fashion. He became afraid and ran away.

This incident took place some time in 1860s, and was recorded in the 1950s. UFOs did not become a fashionable subject yet, so it hardly seems that the Siberian woman invented the story.

FLYING MACHINE OF 1892

Mikhail Gershtein published an article in NLO magazine regarding a very curious incident that took place in 1892. The sighting of a very strange flying object took place in March of that year, close to the town of Lutsk, over the

Zmeinets Village, in the Volinskaya Province. As the witnesses were Russian military personnel, an official investigation ensued. Sightings were therefore publicly confirmed.

The craft flew faster than a bird. The flight altitude was compared to that one of a crane. The craft emitted certain noise; peasants were able to hear it in their huts. The craft created an air current as it flew. An official military report presented to the Razvedchik magazine of the Russian Defence Department contained curious details: the craft flew very fast; its colour was bright and metallic. The Commanding Officer of the 33rd regiment who presented the report did not see this craft, but recalled another sighting he had personally observed in the same month: a comet-like object, over the horizon. It had intermittent illumination, and shone brightly from time to time. There was no wind whatsoever, and the moon seemed to emit a dull glow. The sighting created much discussion in the area.

Other published descriptions of the March 1892 object mentioned "loud noise, like that of a moving train in the distance", " a flying machine, its shape and size that of a haycock; something that emitted pillars of light at night". Some observers discerned moving parts and wing-like details. Gershtein noted that the shape was actually that of a dome, a common shape of modern UFOs.

Other descriptions revealed that the craft moved "violently"; that it illuminated the surrounding area. Peasants mentioned that the shape was actually that of a "box"; soldiers described a "haycock". It was seen over several villages between the 22nd and 23rd of March. What was that mysterious flying machine?

Another interesting testimony comes from Russian military artillery officer, Captain Unzhevsky of the 1st Artillery Brigade. We found it in the Sekretniye Issledovaniya newspaper (Byelorussia, March of 2002 issue). They reprinted a letter the Captain published in a Moscow newspaper Moskovskiye Vedomosti. During the night of March 16, 1892, while a passenger was aboard a train travelling from Vyazma to Moscow, he observed aerial phenomena. It was a bright-red dot, high over the horizon. The captain and other passengers saw the outlines of a sphere. After 25 minutes of observation they quite clearly observed violet light to the right of the object, and to the left they saw a bright red line of light. The sphere itself remained of the same red colour. Some fifteen minutes through the observation, the phenomenon moved up and down, vacillating three to four times. After 25 minutes the sphere rapidly departed, at great speed. The Captain added in his letter that such phenomena has appeared over Russia's western borders on occasions, people talked about the phenomena, and he decided to write his letter to the newspaper.

FIERY SPHERES OVER RUSSIA

Once again, Mikhail Gershtein uncovered interesting reports from Russia's past UFO sightings. In a detailed article published in NLO magazine he lists dates and descriptions. The most interesting, we believe, were reports that date back to the days of the Russo-Japanese war. At that time there were actually many reports about mysterious air balloons as far away as a thousand kilometres from the battlefront. There were sightings of illuminated air balloons, which "spotlighted" Trans-Baikal railroad, (July 10, 1904). Another report, from Selenga, described a cigar-shaped object (October 30, 1904). A stream of continuous sparks followed its manoeuvres. There are several more reports that are of great interest to UFO researchers, including the 1909 report of an air balloon over the Minganski coalmines.

EXTRACTS FROM THE FILES OF THE CENTRAL STATE MILITARY HISTORICAL ARCHIVES OF THE USSR

In April of 1991 the Soviet Union still existed. Among its magazines of the period one was entitled SOVIET SOLDIER. Its April issue carried a very interesting article, written by L. Vlodavets.

A UFO OVER RUSSIA? (actual title of the article) described one memorable sighting that dates back to 1915. The author obviously read the documents form the above-mentioned archives.

In the autumn of 1915 Russia was engaged in the bloody First World War. But the sightings of strange craft we are about to reveal actually took place in a faraway corner of Russia, away from the European battlefields. It was over the mouth of the mighty Volga River that the observations of unknown dirigibles took place in September of that year. Reports came from villages and towns some 150 kilometres from each other. Here is what local people saw and heard in the sky over the Kazan Military District: an object similar to a dirigible, a huge balloon, with a motor roaring in the air and with spotlights shining down. Also reported were a cigar-shaped object with a fin that hovered over a village; and six humanoid shapes in a "boat" under the object's "belly".

As the governor of the city of Astrakhan reported to the garrison commander, unknown dirigibles appeared over the Kalmyk steppes west of the Caspian Sea. Yet Kalmyk Prince Iseren Badmayev saw something else. His sighting is dated September 26, 1915; it was on a Saturday.

He observed a puff of black smoke appear from behind a hill. The "puff of smoke" instantly took off and split into two parts; one of them moved southward, the other headed westward. Both parts had an elongated shape; it resembled a gray-coloured boat. The Prince watched these "boats" for three or four minutes. Their shape was initially spherical, and then in the blink of an eye the objects assumed elongated shapes. Their altitude was considerably high above the horizon. The sky was cloudless. Prince Badmayev did see another "boat" some forty minutes later. Here is what else is striking about his report: the vehicle in which he was travelling at the time of the sighting "stood still "each time he saw a "boat" in the sky.

Similar reports came from as far away as towns lying over 800 kilometres north from Astrakhan. One report, dated October 9, from the village of Baranovka, mentioned a landing in the forest. There were also reports from the Urals, a part of Russia where anomalous phenomena dates back centuries.

A search-and-capture expedition, consisting of an officer, soldiers, policemen, and several civilians was sent to investigate, but its mission failed to produce results. Because the unknown aircraft appeared to be harmless, General Sandetsky (Commander of the Kazan Military District) did not pay much attention to the reports. He did inform the Supreme Command General Headquarters and the Russian General Staff, but received no response, and the documents were shelved in the archives for future reference.

At the time of the sightings, Zeppelins were able to fly eight hundred kilometres. What nation would send them to the Russian steppes district? What purpose would such a mission serve? It was not until 1919 that a dirigible crossed the Atlantic, a journey of 5,800 kilometres. However, even today no dirigible is capable of separating itself into two autonomous craft or devices. And yet, throughout this book we encounter similar witness reports and sightings.

Whatever the mysterious UFOs are it is clear from these reports that they have both amazed and baffled the people and authorities of the USSR right up into the 20th century.

CHAPTER FOUR

THE EARLY YEARS

INTRODUCTION

The Bolsheviks won the Russian Civil War, and through the years of social experiments, military Communism and purges transformed the huge country into a totalitarian state. Millions of people perished in the concentration camps and prisons; and the war with Nazi Germany consumed more millions of Soviet citizens. Throughout the bloodiest century of Russian history, UFOs had hovered over the country. Not all those who observed the strange phenomenon in the sky lived to tell their tale. Their reports had been scattered by harsh winds of Soviet history. Numerous documents, manuscripts, observations and written accounts are still hidden in the vaults of the secret police. Throughout the murky period from 1917 to 1941 there has been an unprecedented interest from the Soviet secret police in the UFO and paranormal phenomena and close attention to those engaged in unauthorised research.

Apparently, the strange objects over the Asian sky interested the Soviets back in 1920's. In the 1930s, under Stalin's brutal reign, the occult, paranormal, and related research subjects were forbidden (although Stalin himself had certain interests, as we will discuss in the chapter about the Soviet dictator). Archaeology, too, was not a safe subject after 1920s. Leading Soviet Egyptologists were arrested and executed. Those who studied genetics were punished, arrested, and some of them executed. Cybernetics was saved only because of the Soviet military-industrial complex (but not all of those who studied it). Futurology was a forbidden subject. Of course no literature about paranormal phenomena was available in the USSR, no libraries carried it, and no publishing houses would even consider looking at such books. Who would dare write and show anyone such a book? The Gulag Archipelago would open its hellish gates to anyone who would delve into the research of the paranormal in the bloody years of Stalin's rule.

VYATKA RIVER, 1923

We already mentioned Felix Zigel's book UFO Sightings over the USSR - 1968 (Volume 1), published by Joint USA - CIS Aerial Anomalies Federation in 1993.

39

It contains a number of fascinating reports of sightings in the former Soviet Union. There is a curious one about a sighting in 1923. M. Volosnikov was aboard a steamship sailing down the Vyatka River in July of 1923. One early morning, as the steamship approached the village of Sosnovka, N. Volosnikov (a crew member) observed a "flying moon". He followed its slow flight, and noticed that its course was parallel to the steamship. The man felt superstitious fear as he looked at the object for two or three minutes. The flying object did resemble the Moon, both in size and brightness. Its frontal part was somewhat lighter and the tail was two or three times as long as its diameter. The tail was not fan-shaped, but tapered toward the end. N. Voloshnikov did not see the start of the object's flight. But, as it seemed to the observer, the object either passed over a large radius or, deviating from a straight line, the object turned to the right of their course and disappeared behind a forest. In 1923, as the observer noted, all of those who saw the phenomenon came to a unanimous conclusion that what they observed that July morning was a "flying evil spirit".

There was another sighting over Sosnovka, thirty years later. In December of 1953 (or 1952, for the observer could not recall exactly), D. Kamkin, a Leningrad engineer, returned to the village. The time was around 9:00 or 10:00 pm, and he was outside, when a weak, whistling sound attracted his attention. There was something in the sky, flying toward him, from south to north. The object was dark, without clear outlines, its shape was that of a circle, approximately 15 to 18 square metres in size. There were visible dark red spots over the entire object. They did not have clearly expressed outlines, but their shape was round. The object moved at a rather high speed. There was a noise two or three seconds before the appearance of the body. Kamkin's report was published in the same book.

KONSTANTIN TSIOLKOVSKIY

Konstantin Eduardovich Tsiolkovskiy (1857-1935) became enchanted with the possibilities of interplanetary travel as a boy, and at age fourteen started independent study using books from his father's library on natural science and mathematics. He also developed a passion for invention and constructed balloons, propelled carriages, and other instruments. In 1878, he became a teacher of mathematics in a school north of Moscow. Tsiolkovskiy first started writing about space in 1898, when he submitted for publication to the Russian journal, Nauchnoye Obozreniye or Science Review, a work based upon years of calculations that laid out many of the principles of modern space flight. The article, Investigating Space with Rocket Devices, presented years of calculations that laid out many of the principles of modern space flight and opened the door to future writings on the subject. In it, Tsiolkovskiy described in depth the use of rockets for launching orbital space ships. He completed a series of increasingly sophisticated studies on the technical aspects of space flight. In the

1920s and 1930s Tsiolkovskiy was especially productive, publishing ten major works, clarifying the nature of bodies in orbit, developing scientific principles behind reaction vehicles, designing orbital space stations, and promoting interplanetary travel. He also furthered studies of many principles commonly used in rockets today: specific impulse to gauge engine performance, multi-stage boosters, fuel mixtures such as liquid hydrogen and liquid oxygen, the problems and possibilities inherent in micro gravity, the promise of solar power, and spacesuits for extravehicular activity. But he never did experiment with rockets himself. After the October (Bolshevik) revolution of 1917 and the creation of the Soviet Union, Tsiolkovskiy was formally recognised for his accomplishments in the theory of space flight. Among other honours, in 1921 he received a lifetime pension from the young Soviet state that allowed him to retire from teaching at the age of sixty-four. Tsiolkovskiy devoted full time to developing his space flight theories studies. He died at his home in Kaluga on September 19, 1935. His theoretical work greatly influenced later designers of rockets both in Russia and throughout Europe. Americans became interested in his works after the Soviet Union beat them in the space race sending first Earth satellites into space.

Tsiolkovsiy was very much interested in anomalous aerial phenomena.

Twice in his life he witnessed strange phenomena, and because of his experiences, he urged people to be more careful in relation to any "incomprehensible phenomena around us, for this testifies that about penetration of some sentient force into our minds and interference into human affairs" (Volya Vselennoy or Will of the Universe, Tsiolkovskiy's work).

In 1899, at the outskirts of Borovsk, the scientist observed a very odd cloud, its shape ideal, assuming first the shape of a cross, and later, a human shape as it moved through the sky. He recalled the sighting as a religious experience; for he yearned to find a confirmation of his fate (he was a Russian Orthodox Christian). Tsiolkovskiy wrote that he needed the confirmation, to fend off despair, and give him the energy he sought.

On May 31, 1928, Konstantin Tsiolkovskiy again noticed strange anomalous phenomenon. He was in the city of Kaluga at the time. He was watching the sunset from his glass-covered balcony. The weather was somewhat cloudy. Something caught his eye: close to the horizon the scientist clearly observed three letters, as if printed in the sky: r, A, and y (he saw Latin, not Cyrillic, script). He surmised the letters were formed by clouds, and must have been at a distance of fifty kilometres, for they hung almost over the horizon. As he observed the letters, their shape began to change. Tsiolkovskiy was very much intrigued by the definite shape of the letters, but could not understand what rAy meant. No language he was familiar with had similar words with any meaning. Some time later Tsiolkovskiy went to his office, to write down the word, and the date of his sighting. Then he read the word, as it would sound in Russian, and it hit him, the word was Ray, or Paradise in Russian. Then the scientist recalled that under the word in the sky he saw something shaped like a tomb or a plate, but paid no attention to it, because he was amazed by the letters. What was it? Did he see a message from some entity?

There is more about Konstantin Tsiolkovskiy in Gennady Belimov's book Proyavleniye inikh mirov v zemnikh fenomenakh or Manifestation of Alien Worlds in Terrestrial Phenomena. Gennady Belimov will be mentioned in other chapters of our book. The Volgograd University published his work, where he describes Tsiolkovskiy experiences. Because of Russia's dire economic predicament, such books are published in meaningless numbers; 500 hundred issues for Belimov's book. Yet those who want to obtain it should write to: Gennady Belimov, Post Office Box 193, 404104, Volzhsky City, Volgograd Oblast', Russian Federation.

Tsiolkovskiy's own grandson reported a huge fiery sphere racing through the sky on May 14 of 1934. The area was brightly illuminated as the sphere flew, and a yellowish-red trail followed it, with sparks behind it. The centre of the sphere was bluish-green in colour, and also pulsating, widening, and then again, narrowing its size. The spectacle was easy to observe in the midnight hour, but the observer did not disturb his famous grandfather. Tsiolkovskiy was upset, but nevertheless went on to collect all available data. He thought it was a bolide, or a gigantic meteor. One week later his request to possible eyewitnesses was published in Izvestiya, and he did find others who observed the same phenomenon. Actually, over five hundred reports arrived in his office, with drawings, details, and descriptions. One observer insisted there was an explosion. Others were impressed by the object's brightness. There were reports about its rumbling noise and thunderous sounds. An expedition from the Soviet Academy of Sciences was dispatched to the Borovsk area, where the object was sighted. The expedition was headed by no other than Leonid Kulik of the Tunguska Phenomenon fame. Both scientists exchanged information. Nothing was discovered in the Borovsk Forest, but local peasants told rumours that a huge sphere was embedded in the marshy soil, and was so hot, as to prevent anyone from approaching it. (Gennady Chernenko published this account of Tsilkovskiy's experience in NLO Magazine, 1999).

MOSCOW, 1938

This is yet another report from Zigel's book. N.A. Gosteva sent it to his research group. She was a physician, and wrote that "until today I was completely perplexed concerning what I saw in 1938". One early summer morning she observed an object in the sky, slightly inclined toward the ground. It rushed upward with a whistle and N. Gosteva felt a light breeze. The object resembled a grayish white or yellowish cloud, dense, with slightly diffused outlines, but still outlined in the shape of an oval. The size was larger than that of a zeppelin or an airplane. She was especially intrigued by the whistling sound; she could still remember it years later when the report was sent to Zigel; the whistle intensified as it approached and quickly abated as the cloud moved away. The other thing that intrigued her was the speed of the cloud.

1942, NAZI - OCCUPIED LATVIA

In June of 1941, a bloody Nazi German invasion tore into the Soviet territories, and war broke out everywhere.

In our chapter Soviet Military Encounters With UFOs, a number of sightings during the World War II are also mentioned. There were some sightings of the period that should be covered in this chapter. Y. Platov and V. Rubtsov mentioned, but did not elaborate, a sighting of A. N. Klimenko in August of 1942. According to them, such sightings (and most have been lost...) became known because those who observed them later understood that the military technology of the war period could not produce similar incomprehensible objects NLO i sovremennaya nauka or UFOs and modern science, Moscow, 1991).

Russian scientist and researcher Konstantin Khazanovich, whose opinion we will explore in our TU-134 case chapter, has an interesting UFO observation case in his archives. Ivan Borovikov sent it to him. At the time, Borovikov, age 13, and his family lived in the occupied Latvia. One wintry evening his mother looked in the window, and started yelling "fire!" All family members ran outside, and immediately saw blood coloured snow. There was nothing burning anywhere in sight. The surrounding dark forest, too, was free of any fires. They gazed up, and observed an orange-red disk. It emitted rays throughout the sky; the rays vanished in the distance, not reaching the horizon. They all watched for a long time, but it was freezing cold, and the Borovikov family members went back inside. When they came outside once again twenty minutes later, the disk was still there, but it dimmed. As time went by, the disk "dissolved" in the sky. One hour later everything was back to normal, the Moon was of silvery-yellowish colouration, and the stars shone brightly. According to Khazanovitch, this was a fragment of Aurora Borealis. He wondered whether whatever the family observed that night in 1942 was of artificial nature. During the last twenty years of the XX century, Soviet scientists learned to create artificial Aurora Borealis by injecting electrons. But who created such artificial phenomena during World War II?

A KIEV SPACE ROCKET, 1948

A. Kulsky, author of the popular book Na Perekrestkah Vselennoy or At the Crossroads of the Universe (Kiev, 1997), discussed a most intriguing episode. V. Sukhoveyev was a noted archaeologist, painter, and journalist. His father was a digger in an archaeological expedition. Long before the October

(Bolshevik) revolution in 1917, famous archaeologist V. Khvoika conducted archaeological digs in Kiev.

Vikentij Khvoika was a pioneering Ukrainian archaeologist of Czech origin who discovered, excavated and studied many Ukrainian sites of Paleolithic, Neolithic, Bronze and Iron Ages. Many artifacts unearthed by him are preserved in the Historical Museum of Ukraine.

The site was approximately where Chaykovsky Conservatory is located today. The archaeologists discovered an unusual, gigantic silvery object. A. Khvoika instructed them to carefully excavate around the find, and as deep as possible. It took them one week to complete the excavations. Pails were used to haul the soil up. The Governor of the province was invited to the site. He looked at the find, and ordered the archaeologists to cover the find with soil. He said that it was too early to attempt to excavate out the mysterious machine. According to V. Sukhoveyev, the object was truly amazing: some three metres in diameter, and over fifty metres in height.

In the 90s of the XXth century the outstanding archaeologist V.Khvoika gained fame through the discovery of the ancient Trypillian culture in Ukraine (the civilization that was a contemporary of Sumer, ancient Egypt, and early Minoan Crete). His published works contain no mention of the Kiev "object" (A. Kulsky read them, looking for an explanation). But, according to V. Sukhoveyev, A. Khvoika explained origins of the strange machine in this fashion.

Prior to the Great Flood, as long ago as 70,000 years ago, shores of seas and oceans presented favourable conditions for development of powerful civilizations. Eleven thousand years ago a huge asteroid crashed on Earth, and prosperous city-states were covered and destroyed by waves, reaching as high as a kilometre in height. But traces of the lost civilizations can be found in some areas of the planet. The space rocket, discovered by V. Khvoika, is exactly such a trace.

V. Sukhoveyev also mentioned that his father once again was "involved" in the matter of the object found by V. Khvoika. This time it was after War World II. When, in 1948, Soviet labourers were removing ruins of buildings destroyed during the war, they found the "space rocket" again. The object was removed, cut into several pieces, and placed on trucks. Allegedly, they took the pieces of the object to a secret testing site near Moscow. Sukhoveyev's father by then was an expert in ancient languages. Strange writings were discovered in the "cockpit" of the space rocket. The language was Sanskrit, an ancient language of India.

According to Sukhoveyev's father, the structure of the rocket was very complex. Also, S. Korolyov, who is mentioned throughout the book, headed the research team working with the ancient Indian rocket; he, too, mentioned the complexity of the design. The Soviets were able to solve some of the secrets of the rocket ship, and it helped them when they were in the process of building their own space technology.

Professor Burdakov never mentions this incident, nor does anyone else in the books and reports we have researched. However, professor Burdakov does mention something else that is quite amazing.

In one of his interviews the Soviet scientist revealed that among those classified documents he had access to, there was one, dated mid 1950s that was of a special interest. It was a report, written by Soviet academicians, top scientists, and "serious people", according to Burdakov. The report was about a fragment that contained a crystalline structure, and resembled a blunted rectilinear cone. The object was obviously of artificial origin. Soviet academicians could not understand either its nature or purpose. Their conclusion was unambiguous: the material, most likely, was not originated on Earth. Today, continued Burdakov, the conclusion would be a different one; after all, there are now analogous crystalline structures throughout the world: we know them as silicon circuits.

Could we surmise that if the object discovered and excavated in Kiev in 1948 was an ancient Indian space rocket, there were other things besides writings found inside it? What other Soviet archaeological findings are still kept secret in the archives of modern Russia?

A CHEST IN KIEV, 1953

There was yet another mention of a strange archaeological discovery in Kiev. An expedition was engaged in excavations, on the Reitarskaya Street. They made a discovery that was to be kept secret for the next forty years. Those who were involved in the excavations are reluctant (or fearful) to reveal their names even nowadays. Only one of them talked reluctantly to a Kiev newspaper in 1993. He said that the archaeologists found a burial vault at the depth of twenty metres; it contained a very large chest. Inside the chest they found five hundred books, written in Arabic, Greek, Sanskrit, and Slavic languages. The books contained drawings depicting construction of orbital stations; hangars for spaceships, and scenes from Star Wars - like battles. The book also contained the original manuscript of Slovo o polku Igoreve (Ancient Chronicles of the Exploits of Prince Igor). Within hours the secret police arrived, placed the findings in three covered trucks, and drove off. The archaeologists were warned to keep silent about the incident. And so they did, until 1953. A report about this case appeared in Dzhentry newspaper, Issue 5, 1993, in Vladivostok.

We found an interesting article in the Russian edition of NEXUS magazine (Issue 1, 2005). Ukrainian astronomer and author of numerous scientific articles, Alexey Arkhipov, wrote about two strange scientific stories published in the USSR in 1928 and 1929, by authors who shared the same last name. One story was titled ALIENS and told a story of a meeting in Africa between a shipwrecked Russian scientist and aliens from another galaxy (from a planet with dual suns). The description of the aliens in the story, the extraterrestrial beings, was amazingly similar to the descriptions given by eyewitnesses in UFO contact reports after 1947. The other story told of Bairo-Tun, a Martian (Zeentar) sentient being whose spaceship crashed on our planet. There were highly technical descriptions of alien technology, space flight, atomic fission, effects of nuclear radiation, powerful antennae, lift-offs of alien ships, gigantic disk-shaped flying craft, elements of abduction, and other ufological "trivia" that did not exist in the late 1920's. Who was that enigmatic Soviet writer whose last name was Volkov (the first names of the writers were different, but it was most likely the same person)? Arkhipov could not find out. No one in the West read Soviet science fiction stories of the 1920s, and Volkov certainly had no ufological literature to borrow descriptions of aliens. Again, American Ufologists did not read Soviet sci-fi stories to borrow ideas from an obscure Russian writer in Vladivostok. Arkhipov wonders if the amazing stories published in the pre-Stalinist Russia were actually a reflection of something real...

These incidents are important for the fact that many pre-date the modern era of UFOs which began in 1947 after a sighting in the USA. They also pre-date technology that today might explain them. Like so many official sightings no matter where in the world they are reported, the witnesses themselves are highly educated and respected in their various fields, which surely make them less prone to misidentify known objects and materials. Whether or not these stories of unearthing previously lost technology either from this world or another are based in fact or folklore still remains to be seen, but irrespective of that these accounts are nonetheless fascinating and echo similar ones found in many other different parts of the world.

CHAPTER 5

STALIN, UFOs AND OTHER SECRETS

The Russian Ufology Research Centre has corresponded with Valery Pavlovich Burdakov, mentioned in other chapters of our book, who provided his account of Stalin's interest in UFOs. There had been other accounts of the unusual meeting between the late dictator and a former GULAG prisoner Sergei Korolyov.

Professor Valery Burdakov is a Ph.D. of Engineering Sciences, an associate at the Scientific Geo Informational Centre, and co-author of an immensely popular book Rockets of the Future. He knew personally many of those who created Soviet ballistic missiles and its space exploration program. Originally, he had heard of Stalin's interest in UFOs from Pavel Vladimirovich Tsibin, a scientist who told Burdakov about the meetings between Stalin, Korolyov and himself.

V.P. Burdakov had worked for 32 years in Korolyov's design bureau. He had also participated in the creation of the Energiya-Buran shuttle complex. Korolyov and his colleagues trusted Burdakov. That is why Burdakov learned of Stalin's interest in the anomalous phenomena. He was told about the dictator's interest later, in the late 1950s, when Stalin was already dead.

They lived in the atmosphere of fear under Stalin's rule. Korolyov, after all, could have informed the secret police about Burdakov's nonconformist views. The famous rocket designer received informants' reports that Burdakov presented lectures about "flying saucers" to other employees. Not only did Korolyov not punish Burdakov, he actually sent him to the Pulkovskaya Observatory and gave him a letter of recommendation. In those years, common people told Soviet astronomers of UFO sighting episodes. Burdakov, thus, was able to read UFO sightings reports that were sent to the observatory.

In 1947 Korolyov was summoned, and informed that it was by Comrade Stalin's request and that he was needed at the Kremlin. Korolyov was provided with two female translators to assist him; was given a stack of foreign newspapers, books, and three days to complete the job.

At the time it was rumoured that a "saucer" was captured near Roswell, New Mexico. In the stack of papers, Korolyov saw many published materials, as well as documentary testimonies. Among the materials there were reports of sightings over the USSR, too. Korolyov asked if he could take everything home with him, study the materials quietly, thoroughly, and consult specialists. Stalin rejected the request and instead provided Korolyov with a special apartment for his work at the Kremlin. In a few days he was again summoned before the dictator.

Stalin asked for Korolyov's opinion. The scientist offered his views, stated that UFOs were not weapons of some potential adversary, and did not pose a serious threat to the country. However, the phenomenon itself does exist, added Korolyov. Stalin thanked him, and said that other experts were of similar opinion. S. Korolyov assumed that Stalin asked such Soviet giants of science as Kurchatov, Topchiyev, and Keldish to perform similar analyses.

In October of 1996, Professor Burdakov published his memoirs in Anomaliya Magazine (not the newspaper ANOMALIYA) in Moscow. Signed copies of newspaper issues containing the memoirs were sent to Paul Stonehill. Burdakov wrote that some of the first rocket launches produced interesting visual phenomena.

If the weather was hazy or foggy outside, people observed a white-greenish glow of a launched rocket (not the rocket itself). In the Soviet Union the first rockets were launched from the Kapustin Yar cosmodrome (in the Volga River area). In the United States (and the Soviets knew it) the rockets were launched from New Mexico. The rocket launch sites in both nations were at the centre of attention of the various intelligence agencies, and those who enjoyed viewing unusual aerial phenomena. If rocket launches failed, they left behind incredible spectacles, visible from a great distance. Hence, opportunities were created for intelligence services that protected their countries' secrets to produce hoaxes, to fool the opponents. Obviously, there were conmen who made money on UFO rumours. But there was always a belief that other sentient beings could be the ones watching the launches.

Stalin was informed about "green balloons" in New Mexico. Burdakov knew that the UFO phenomenon was kept secret because it was related to the secret rocket tests in the USSR. Stalin did consult various experts about the anomalous phenomenon. He never revealed anything to anyone; instead he just collected reports and opinions. But Korolyov was also interested in UFOs, Stalin or no Stalin, rocket launches or not. Tsibin revealed to Professor Burdakov that S. Korolyov told him to go through the collected UFO reports at his disposal. Furthermore, he permitted his assistants to subscribe to Australian Flying Saucers Review.

STALIN AND AERIAL PHENOMENA

V. Psalomschikov was able to discover a most interesting fact: Stalin was very much interested in meteorology. The Geophysics Institute of Georgia has kept original certificates of barometer probes, taken by Iosif Dzhugashvili, who later assumed a more familiar to millions of people (both hated and adored) last name. Moreover, as was described in V. Psalomschikov's article in NLO Magazine (1997), there was an occasion when Stalin and his trusted assistant, V. Uspensky, took a stroll outside. The assistant, a general at the time, and the dictator walked in an area outside of Moscow, when they noticed a round aperture in the clouds above the Dmitrovskaya Church. This aperture would not be concealed even when the sky was completely covered by clouds. They tried to find an explanation of this phenomenon, but could not. Uspensky claimed that Stalin was so impressed as to come to the same area regularly to watch the sky.

STALIN AND THE MISSION TO THE MOON

Did Stalin create a secret program to explore the Moon? However improbable it may sound, V. Psalomschikov found interesting clues that convince us to give some credence to this idea. There have been strange rumours that the Soviets had a garrison on the Moon. There was reference in Fedor Abramov's book; a letter to the Soviet Academy of Commission for the Study of Anomalous Phenomena, written by the brother of the man who allegedly served his military duties on the Moon. A well-known Soviet test pilot, S. Anokhin, said on his deathbed that back in the 1940s he piloted a rocket. The 1945 Potsdam Conference, where Stalin prompted his Allies to discuss how they would divide up the Moon among themselves (and his demand that the Soviets be recognised as having priority in this area). The Conference took place between July 17 and August 2, 1945; present were the principal Allies in World War II (the United States, the USSR, and Great Britain) to clarify and implement agreements previously reached at the Yalta Conference. The chief representatives were President Truman, Premier Stalin, Prime Minister Churchill, and, after Churchill's defeat in the British elections, the new Prime Minister Attlee. Six months after this conversation, the Soviet government issued decrees regarding the development of rocket technology in the USSR and the formation of several research institutes dedicated to the issue. Did Stalin just bluff?

V. Psalomschikov researched this issue thoroughly, and learned that it was rumoured at the end of the 1930s that Stalin was engaged in a most secret space exploration project, based on the ideas of Russian scientist Konstantin Tsiolkovsky. Then came the war, S. Korolyov and Glushko were purged, and the Rocket Institute fell out of favour. Who would lead the program (if there ever was any)? Psalomschikov found out that in 1937 a second Ministry of Aviation Industry was created, and that Stalin was directly in charge of it.

A strange military site was being built twenty kilometres from Kiev. Psalomschikov calls this project Kiev-17. This was the site of the future

Chernobyl Nuclear Power Station. The site contained a military town, eight military plants, storage facilities, an airport, and even something else, a strange launch facility. In 1941, the site was destroyed by the Soviets before the Nazis could capture it. Some believed that Stalin was building an identical site in Siberia, next to the concentration camps of the Gulag organisation. Would the new government of Ukraine declassify remaining Soviet-era files pertaining to the project? It is doubtful that the files would even be in Ukraine, for such important matters were handled out of Moscow.

Strange stories indeed, possibly adding more to the myths and legends of one of the USSR's most controversial rulers. It is of course highly improbable that Stalin sent men to the Moon but it is widely accepted that the dictator was indeed interested in UFOs in general and was extremely interested in the alleged recovery of a crashed UFO in New Mexico in 1947, the now famous Roswell crash. If Stalin new more about Roswell or UFOs in general it would seem that he took such secrets to his grave, unless they still remain hidden in some secret archive in corridors of power at the Kremlin.

CHAPTER 6

LEV TERMEN

The story of Lev Sergeievitch Termen reads like a spy novel. In the United States he was better known as Leon Theremin. Professor Theremin was born in the city of St. Petersburg, in the Czarist Russia, in 1896. He became one of the most important pioneers in the development of electronic music because of the instrument called the Tereminvox (commonly referred to as the Theremin). He lived in New York, and had a number of high society patrons who helped him with funds to conduct his experiments. The inventions he created, unusual and fantastic for the time, included a prototype colour television system.

In the late 1920s Termen settled in the United States. His first wife, Yekaterina, and Theremin decided not to return to the Soviet Russia. But they did keep their Soviet citizenship. Apparently, the Soviets were able to pressure Theremin to divorce his first wife (allegedly, because she had ties in with German fascists). In 1937 Theremin was kidnapped from the New York apartment he shared with his American wife, black ballet dancer Lavinia Williams. The operation was carried out by the NKVD (forerunners of the KGB). There are reports that he left the United States voluntarily, but it is not clear why he would do so (NLO Magazine, Gennady Chernenko's article, Issue 45, 2000). Leon Theremin was transported back to the USSR, accused of anti-Soviet propaganda, and sent to the Gulag concentration camps. He never saw his African-American wife again, a woman he deeply loved and shared happiness with. While he spent some time in Magadan, Soviet agents spread the rumours that Theremin was executed. However, the Soviets recognised his talents, and he was put to work on top-secret projects.

Basically, that is why he survived in those terrible years. During the years he spent as a Soviet "scientist-slave" (some of them in a missile design office behind bars, or "sharashka" in Russian) he met such imprisoned scientists as Sergei Korolyov and A. Tupolev. Theremin invented the "bug", a sophisticated electronic eavesdropping device. Theremin supervised the bugging of the American embassy, and of Stalin's private apartments. He was even awarded the coveted Stalin Prize. But when he was released from the Gulag in 1947, few people remembered him in the world outside of prison walls. His research and work has been lost, or stored in secret archives, inaccessible to him.

Years later the highly talented Theremin was also asked to head the UFO research laboratory. Soviet Radio magazine published an interview with Theremin in its Issue 8 (1990). During the early 1960's Lev Termen was offered to head a laboratory, a secret facility designed and built for the research of "flying saucers" apparently captured by Soviets. The scientist believed in neither extraterrestrials nor in "saucers", and he refused.

Lev Termen or Leon Theremin had returned to the United States years later, when the system that had imprisoned him had fallen apart, and there was no more Soviet Union. He died in 1993, at the age of 98.

What was it that the Soviets wanted Termen to research? Did they really possess captured UFOs or was this merely a cover story? No one really knows as Termen never revealed any further information and the search for information on alleged captured UFOs by the Soviet authorities continues.

CHAPTER 7

UFOs OVER RIGA

There have been many rumours about this incident that have circulated in the USSR. In August of 1961, a test flight of the most modern Soviet fighter-interceptor jet was to take place. Local top brass wanted to film everything, so as to demonstrate the might of the Soviet Air Force. A film crew, headed by Victor Dudinsh, was commissioned for that purpose. They set up their equipment in the vicinity of the airplane, next to the take-off and landing strip. According to V. Avinsky, a noted Soviet UFO researcher, the name of the airfield was "Skulte". Over one hundred military officers had been waiting to see the air show. But nothing happened. The jet was in top condition the day before, but now the pilot could not even start the engine. At the same time a sinister sound pierced the air, and a strange object appeared in the sky.

It appeared from nowhere, and everyone was able to see it at once. They started running in every direction. Fear gripped everyone, and panic ensued. Dudinsh, a true professional, fought this fear to film the occurrence. He aimed the camera at the object in the sky, pushed the start button, and ran to the shelter. The object did not descend, but rather moved in a strange fashion. It would disappear, and reappear, but slightly further from its original position. This went on for a few minutes, and then something else took place. An entity inside the UFO stirred and moved around. The object was illuminated by the sun, blue sky in the background, so the visibility was first class. The UFOs shape was that of a triangle and its colour violet. A few minutes later the UFO suddenly lost some illumination. It remained in the sky, but became somewhat invisible. As its brightness disappeared, so did the fear.

Soviet military personnel crawled out from various holes and shelters, and discussed the event. Not one doubted the extraterrestrial nature of the object. Dudinsh ran back to his camera and saw that it was working, but the film had run out. He wanted to take it back to the studio, but the airfield commander confiscated it. The KGB arrived some time later, and took the film away.

Dudinsh, however, convinced the airfield commander to take signed eyewitness statements from the hundreds of eyewitnesses. Most signed it with trepidation. The pilot was the first to sign; he also mentioned that it was probably the UFO that caused the strange behaviour of on-board equipment, and the dead engine of his jet. Dudinsh and his colleagues did find out some time later that the UFO was indeed visible on his film.

Those who witnessed the object had been warned to forget everything and keep silent. Somehow the information about this UFO event was leaked to the West and letters of inquiry followed. So did offers to buy the film. To diffuse the situation, the Soviet media published a report that the object sighted that night was a meteorological probe. For many long years no further information came from the KGB archives.

S. Boyev pursued this case. Gorbachev's perestroika policies were implemented, and Boyev was able to get permission to see the film. He published his account in the NLO magazine (Issue 13, 1996). Boyev was preparing materials for his documentary dealing with the subject of UFOs over the USSR. The KGB, "damaged" by glasnost and changes sweeping the USSR, relented and released everything. Famous Soviet proponent of UFO phenomenon, a scientist from the Academy of Sciences, V.S. Troitsky, assisted Boyev.

Still, even then the authorities asked them not to disseminate the information. The first public showing of the film took place under somewhat strange circumstances. The giant hall of the Institute of High Temperatures was filled by hundreds of UFO debunkers. Exactly at midnight the light was turned off, and the crowd breathlessly watched the long-concealed film of a UFO over the airfield. The film lasted thirty seconds. For the next three minutes the audience sat silently, and then discussions literally exploded and lasted until the morning. Everyone had a UFO story of his own, and everyone there was tired and disgusted by the silence about UFO phenomenon under the Soviet regime. Experts were questioned, and they confirmed: the UFO has nothing to do with weather balloons, probes, or space junk. The object was classified as a cosmic voyager, a phenomenon of extraterrestrial origin, unknown to science. The psychosis and fear experienced by eyewitnesses was probably caused by powerful and directed infrasonic radiation. Other measurements based on the film and interviews indicated that the object hovered at an altitude of 20 kilometres, and its size was more that 200 metres.

The 1961 Riga UFO left a trace in the history of Soviet UFO phenomena, a trace that the KGB could not hide or erase. But not everyone agrees that the mysterious object was a UFO. Mr. Migulin, a well-known Soviet debunker and scientist, described it as a weather balloon (of French origin). A respected Russian Ufologist Mikhail Gershtein shares this opinion. He wrote, in a letter to Paul Stonehill that a portion of the Dudinsh's film was made a part of the documentary, edited by A. I. Mordvin-Schedro (a well-known and respected St. Petersburg Ufologist; more about him below). The documentary, titled "In search of aliens", was aired in the USSR back in 1988. An article about this film was published in the Soviet magazine Sovetsky Ekran (Issue 16, 1988). Later, Russian television re-broadcasts the documentary on a number of occasions. Migulin's voice is always in the background, when the "triangular UFO" appears in the documentary.

According to Eduard Mirov, who published his own account of the Riga sighting in NLO magazine, the Dudinsh's film was shown to Arthur C. Clark. The latter did reply, rather vaguely, that this film did not dissuade doubts about the ET nature of the so-called unidentified flying objects. Eduard Mirov investigated the Riga UFO sighting and the story surrounding the film. He found out, for example, that a New Zealand television program had offered fifty thousand dollars for the film. But dozens of years later Eduard Mirov was able to get a copy of the film, and show it to Vsevolod Sergeyevich Troitsky, that famous Soviet astrophysicist mentioned throughout our book. According to E. Mirov, V. Troitsky (who assisted Boyev in getting the film released) had considered the object to be a UFO, without any doubts.

Arvid Igorevich Mordvin-Schedro, a former colonel of the Soviet Air Force, stated that several Soviet military officials had confirmed the fact that the UFO did appear in the Baltic sky that day. Among them: Lieutenant-General F. Shinkarenko, an air force commander; V. Svetlov, a local military unit commander; V. Zaretsky, a military doctor and others. Among civilians who had sighted the objects were Y. Gromov, the director of a local hydro-meteorological observatory, Soviet academician V. Kalnberz, and many others.

Eduard Mirov repeated that when the film was studied under a microscope, a definite movement was discerned inside the triangular object. But the nature of what that movement was has not been established.

Hopefully, we will be able to examine the film closely, and find more eyewitnesses who were present in Riga that day many years ago.

There is one definite problem with the date of the sighting, rather, the year when that mysterious UFO appeared over the Riga airfield. Avinsky and Mirov stated that the year was 1968; while Boyev and another publication in NLO magazine indicate that the year was 1961. It may even be 1969; according to I. G. Petrovskaya, an enigmatic scientist, more about whom we will learn in a later chapter. Mikhail Gerhstein did not discuss the year in his letter to Paul Stonehill.

Irrespective of the confusion of the actual date, what is apparent is that the UFO at Riga caused consternation among Soviet officials and that the film of the event still exists is beyond doubt.

CHAPTER 8

THE PETROZAVODSK PHENOMENON

The event that broke the Soviet media's silence of UFOs and ushered in the new age took place in the early hours of September 20, 1977. Unusual brightly luminescent flying objects were observed over the vast area of north-western Russia and Karelia. Over 170 witnesses included policemen, Navy personnel, aviators, and scientists observed what has become known as the 'Petrozavodsk Phenomenon'.

Sotzialisticheskaya Industriya newspaper published a detailed report in its September 23, 1977 issue (and the editor was sacked for doing so). Today we know that many of the strange light phenomena observed that night were produced by the Soviet "Kosmos-955" satellite and its carrier rocket "Vostok", launched from the Plesetsk cosmodrome at 4:01 a.m. And yet, we cannot attribute all of the phenomena to that very launch.

Valentin Golts, active member of the Russian Geographical Society, collected eyewitness reports related to the phenomenon. That night pilots of an airplane bound for Riga observed a disk-shaped UFO. G. Lazarev, a crew member, reported that they attempted to contact the UFO on the radio, but no reply came back, and the plane had to be manoeuvred to escape a possible collision.

A spherical object landed along the Petrozavodsk-Leningrad highway. It was about 20 metres in diameter, and as it landed on a hill, it did not damage the pine trees there: they simply vanished from view. Engineer A. P. Novozhilov from the settlement of Kurki-Yoki at the western edge of the Ladoga Lake witnessed a remarkable phenomenon. A bright sphere exited from the rear part of a UFO, and flew in the same direction as the "dirigible"- like craft. After an initial horizontal flight, the sphere landed at the forest, and caused a bright glow. A lens-shaped craft with eight exhaust pipe-like apertures was observed over the Namayevo Village at 3:00 a.m. Two glowing spherical objects were observed over Primorsk as they manoeuvred in the sky at 3:30 a.m.

About 4:00 in the morning, the UFO, resembling a star, was sighted over Lenin Street, the main thoroughfare of Karelia's capital, the city of Petrozavodsk. The object stopped, grew in size, and assumed the shape of a luminescent jellyfish. Thin, light rays of reddish colour fell on the city below. It was as if a rain was pouring down, except it was not rainwater that poured on the astonished city dwellers. The luminescence was local in nature, for the outskirts of the city were not illuminated. The luminescence was actually described as "pulsating". Windows in nearby houses had holes melted in them. Later experiments proved that even laser rays could not make such perfect holes (their diameter was 5 to 7 millimetres). Also, crystalline structures were discovered in the glass, and that, too could not be explained by scientists at the Moscow Institute of Glass. Automobile engines stopped functioning due to the "jellyfish's" influence. Underneath the windows, on the ledges, they found melted glass "pancakes". The UFO was estimated to be over 105 metres in diameter. Then it moved toward Lake Onega, hovered over the cargo ship Volgobalt, flared up, ascended and then vanished out of sight at great speed.

A. Pavlenko, a local resident, reported that along with the "jellyfish", other objects were reported over the city. A spherical object descended in a spiral motion, and hovered over the hotel Severnaya. The object emitted some kind of a rumbling noise, and flickered. Five or seven minutes later the rumble increased, the object flared up and flew toward the lake. Then, moving over the Onega Lake, the "star" stopped, and descended, and the cloud around it increased. The "star" shone very brightly. Then something separated from it, as if a ray of light, and at the end of this ray a "saucer"- like formation appeared. It descended, and then disappeared (analysis of the Petrozavodsk Phenomenon, published in Chetvertoye Izmereniye in NLO newspaper, Issue 8, 1997).

Sotzialisticheskaya Industriya reported that the UFO "played" with passenger trains. Satellites do not function in such a manner. It is important to add that many residents of the city woke up at 4:00 am that morning in some kind of nervous shock, a condition that could hardly be associated with technical experiments, unless whatever the Soviets launched that morning was not a satellite, but something more sinister in nature. The object did not hover at a higher altitude than 14 kilometres; for it was not observed in the areas located forty kilometres from Petrozavodsk.

Reports about sightings of UFOs that fateful day of September 20th came from all corners of the USSR. According to Gherman Kolchin, such reports came from Dnepropetrovsk, Yalta, Ochakov, Tbilisi, Novosibirsk, Vladivostok, and Altai (Fenomen NLO, Vzlyad iz Rosii, 1994). Yuri Gromov, the director of the Petrozavodsk hydro-meteorological observatory, told reporters from the TASS news agency that nothing anomalous was ever observed in nature by his scientists. He underscored that they knew for certain that technical experiments were taking place in the area at the time. But the phenomenon, according to him, was no mirage, for there were many observers.

The Petrozavodsk Phenomenon's impact forced the Soviets to create the Soviet Academy of Sciences Commission for the Study of Anomalous

Phenomena. In 1978 they were still afraid to say "UFO". We are not certain whether the creation of the commissions and programs (military and academic) was to hide away what was truly taking place in the sky over Petrozavodsk, to fool Westerners, or to hide an even more sinister research. Those who indeed know, like General V. P. Balashov or Colonel A. A. Plaksin have not yet revealed everything. Those who talked about the findings of the programs and later changed their stories (like B.A. Sokolov) cannot be trusted. We will discuss their role in the later chapters. V. Migulin, who was responsible for the government-sanctioned academic UFO research in the USSR, came out with contradictory statements. Initially he mentioned the case in Nedelya newspaper (Issue 3, 1979), and stated that the Petrozavodsk Phenomenon is an extraordinary event, and still is not explained. He still could not explain the event in an interview to a French magazine (La Recherce, August 1979), but did mention that he was amazed that nothing was observed in the area of Arkhangelsk, where experiments were taking place at the time of the Petrozavodsk Phenomenon. But in an article published in Sovetskaya Rossiya newspaper on 19th of April 1980, Migulin declares that the Petrozavodsk Phenomenon was expected precisely in the area where it occurred, and it was timed with experiments in the atmosphere. He changed his mind again, and in an article published in Moskovskiye Novosti newspaper on May 25, 1980, Migulin states that despite the facts at hand, Soviet scientists still cannot explain the Petrozavodsk Phenomenon.

Three years later Migulin made a statement in Smena magazine (Issue 4, 1985) that the Petrozavodsk Phenomenon could now be explained. A powerful solar flare occurred that day, September 20, 1977, and it created a complicated geophysical environment. At the same time the Soviet Academy of Sciences was conducting atmospheric exploration equipment experiments to study the magnetosphere. Also, the very same day a space probe was launched, and elements of it burned in the atmosphere; they were very visible on Earth. Hence, a complicated geophysical environment was further complicated by consequences of human technological activities. As a result, the Petrozavodsk Phenomenon took place.

In 1989, once again V. Migulin states in Nedelya his opinion as to what happened in 1977. It was a failed launch of a rocket from one of Soviet Northern testing ranges, visible in Karelia, and in many areas of the Leningrad Region; but the rocket was actually flying far away from Petrozavodsk. Yuli Platov, V. Migulin's assistant, quoted in the Nedelya Issue 8, 1989, provided more information, stating that that was the carrier-rocket of "Kosmos-955" satellite, launched from the Plesctsk Cosmodrome; its trajectory lay to the east of Arkhangelsk.

Yuli Platov goes into more detailed explanation in the book he co-authored with V. Rubtsov (later of RIAP), NLO I sovremennay nauka or UFO and modern science (1991). He explained the jellyfish-like shape of the cloud with bent "rays" (streams of gas dust trails) to be a consequence of specific character of the rocket engine function in the transitory conditions (when the secondary stage engine is switched off, and the third stage engine is switched on). As for different reports and various sightings that escape his explanation of the Petrozavodsk Phenomenon, Y. Platov called them "mistakes in definition of time of sightings, indicated by fortuitous observers".

The April-September 1995 issue of RIAP BULLETIN contains an excellent analysis of the Petrozavodsk Phenomenon (in English). The authors, L. Gindilis and Y. Kolpakov provide a true scientific analysis of the case, with descriptions of sightings, stages of rocket, instrumental observation, area of the observation, and other important details. We urge those who want to see a more detailed scientific analysis of the Petrozavodsk Phenomenon than the one presented in this book to obtain this issue by writing to Research Institute on Anomalous Phenomena, Post Office Box 4684, Kharkiv-22, Ukraine.

The conclusion of RIAP BULLETIN authors is very important. Among other things, they state that it is hard to imagine a technical experiment of so large a scale, with such unique characteristics. They believe that the nature of the phenomenon is still open, for it has not been investigated thoroughly.

Vladimir Ajaja had another interesting piece of information about the Petrozavodsk Phenomenon. He shared it with the readers of NLO Magazine (2000). Eight hours before the launch of "Kosmos-955", residents of Petrozavodsk went to sleep with a gloomy premonition. Nothing similar was experienced before any launches of satellites. Three hours before the launch of "Kosmos-955", during the flight of Kiev-Leningrad passenger airplane, a UFO followed it until the Pulkovo airport. The captain of the aircraft tried to find out from the air traffic controllers who else were in his air space, and they replied that no other aircraft shared it with him. V. A. Krat, director of the main astronomical observatory, described this UFO in the following manner. It was a bright fiery sphere, moving instantaneously through the sky from south to north; the Pulkovo astronomers were observing it, too. According to V. Ajaja, a Finnish UPI correspondent in Helsinki, reported a bright fiery object over the capital two hours before the launch of "Kosmos-955". The object was visible over Helsinki for four minutes. Finnish control tower reported that the presence of the UFO caused intense radio communications over the Soviet territory at the time when radio broadcast was usually quiet.

There might have been yet another explanation for at least some of the sighted objects. Apparently, the Soviets had been experimenting with the so-called "plasmoids": plasma "clouds" to attack enemy's missiles and render them useless. One source for such information is Dmitry Serebryakov, whose article about the research was published in Noviy Peterburg newspaper in November of 2000 (Issue 18). He specifically mentioned the failed plasma experiment; but he does not mention the year. Similar occurrences took place in 1977 and 1985 (UFOs "playing with trains"). Most likely the plasma weapons development (still taking place in Russia, according to Serebryakov, with certain success) has been going on in the area continuously. And its successes or failures might have fooled innocent observers on the ground.

Then there is the phenomenon of the "false suns" over the city. It was reported on December 23 of 1977 by a local newspaper, Leninskaya Pravda. The sighting took place on the 29th of December. The strangeness of the phenomenon among other things, was in its timing: the "suns" appeared in the sky more than two hours before the rise of the true Sun. F. Zigel analysed the sighting and considered the "false suns" to be a UFO. The sighting and analogous sightings (the same day…) over Leningrad have been thoroughly analysed by M. Gershtein and K. Khazanovich in the Issue 1(4) of Russian Nexus magazine. They explained the Petrozavodsk "false suns" as consequences of unidentified Soviet Naval experiments. No coherent explanation of the Leningrad phenomena of December 19, 1977 (one involved a strange, moving disk-shaped UFO emitting thin, fibrous ray; the other sighting involved three oval brilliant objects moving in a triangular formation to the east; the fog they emitted caused some burning in the chests of the observers, and a short-term memory loss) has been found so far.

We do not know what prompted V. Migulin to come up with different explanations, but in the end, it does not matter. Debunkers and officially appointed debunkers could not and cannot stop people from studying UFO phenomena, even in totalitarian states. We have shown here that these phenomena cannot be easily explained, as the authorities would have us believe.

CHAPTER 9

THE DEADLY CASE OF TU-134

This was a very poignant and well known case of a UFO encounter with an aircraft. On September 7, 1984, a TU-134 airplane, Flight 8352, piloted by a crew out of Tallin (Estonia), was flying the Tbilisi-Rostov-Tallin route. The time was 4:10 a.m. The aircraft was not far away from Minsk, when the Second Pilot, G. Lazurin, noticed a large unblinking star. Rather, it was a yellowish spot, elongated at the edges. A thin ray of light appeared from within it, and pointed towards the ground. Then the ray suddenly opened up, and turned into a bright, luminescent cone. Another cone followed; it was brighter, but not as bright as the first one. And the third one was even brighter than the first two.

The TU-134 pilots determined that there was an unknown object, hovering approximately 60 kilometres away from them. G. Lazurin hastily made a drawing of the object. The ray changed its direction, and turned toward the aircraft. Everyone onboard observed a blinding white dot, surrounded by circles. It exploded and in its place appeared a green-coloured cloud. Flight Commander I. Cherkashin thought that the object was approaching the Soviet aircraft at a great speed. He called out to the airplane's navigator to inform the flight control centre. But right after this order, the strange object simply stopped. The greenish cloud suddenly dropped below the altitude of the aircraft, later ascended vertically, moved to the left and right, and finally stopped right across from the TU-134. The "cloud" was obviously following the Soviet airplane.

The airplane's crew observed that the "cloud" contained multi-coloured lights, flaring up, and then dimming. Then, engaged in a horizontal movement, there appeared fiery "zigzags". The "cloud" changed shape. Something like a tail grew out of it, wide at the top, thin in its lower part. The tail then ascended, and the cloud became rectangular in shape. G. Lazurin shouted that the object was "teasing them". Indeed, a sharp-nosed cloud that resembled an airplane was escorting the Soviet aircraft. At that time another TU-134 entered the area under the Minsk air traffic tower control. The distance between the two aircraft was 100 kilometres. The captain of the other airplane did not see the strange object, however impossible it was to miss the gigantic cloud. But when the distance between the aircraft was approximately 15 kilometres, the other TU-134 was able to see the "cloud". Looking back, one can say that it would have been better if the second airplane never encountered the sinister "cloud".

Fate was very cruel to the crew of the Flight 7084, flying the Leningrad-Borispol-Batumi route. They were flying over the Byelorus Soviet republic when they finally observed the "cloud". It was actually in the shape of a greenish, cigar-shaped body. Three bluish rays were directed toward the ground, and two more rays, of lesser intensity, pointed upward. The flight control centre ordered the TU-134 to approach the object, and the crew obeyed. Two or three minutes later the object turned around sharply and stopped. Its frontal ray focused on the TU-134 (Flight 7084), and illuminated it with a bright light. Then the ray pointed downward, and quickly drew lines of a rectangular shape on the ground. After that, the object made zigzag-like movements and lit up the rectangle below. At the time the TU-134 was some 70 kilometres from Minsk. A few seconds later the UFO descended and stayed below the airplane. The ground control informed the crew that Soviet cosmonauts also observed the object from their orbital station. At approximately 5:00 a.m. the UFO turned to the left, and the crew saw its lateral surface with its running multi-coloured lights.

Consequences of the encounter proved to be very tragic. The captain of Flight 7084, V. Gotsiridze, died in 1985, his death a result of electromagnetic radiation. The ray from the UFO "touched" the captain when it illuminated his airplane. The pilot, Y. Kabachnikov, was fired later because he developed a heart disease. A stewardess, S. Orlova, who happened to walk into the crew cabin, was also "touched" by the deadly ray. She developed a complicated skin disease afterwards. The crew of the other TU-134 (Flight 8352) had a flight engineer who had developed ailments similar to the ones experienced by pilots of the Flight 7084. He, too, was later fired.

K. Khazanovitch has a document in his archives. Rather, it is a copy of a medical document, a conclusion of the Soviet Georgian doctors about injuries suffered by crew members of the Flight 7084. It is a sombre document, and we will not cite all of its conclusions. But the doctors do state that Y. Kabachnikov received electromagnetic radiation of unknown physical characteristics. His brain and heart were affected. It was definitely a work-related trauma as a result of the radiation Y. Kabachnikov was subjected to while performing his duties.

S. Orlova, too suffered horribly, and due to electromagnetic radiation, according to another medical document that K. Khazanovitch keeps in his archives.

K. Khazanovitch, a Scientist and Ufologist, whose articles on the subject were published in Russian Anomaliya newspaper, noted that another flight engineer, who was located between the captain and Y. Kabachnikov, suffered no injuries, and was flying even five years later. Could it be that V. Gotsiridze, Y. Kabachnikov, and S. Orlova were subjected to radiation some other time, aboard some other flight, when the other flight engineer, M. Gvenetadze was not with them?

The incident became a hot news item. An article entitled "At exactly 4:10" was written by V. Vostrukhin, and published in the Soviet newspaper "TRUD". The date of the publication was January 30, 1985. Soviet censorship missed the report, and as a result, the country learned of a UFO incident. The deputy chairman of the Commission for Anomalous Phenomena, N. Zheltukhin of the Soviet Academy of Sciences, stated that what the Tallin crew had observed was a UFO. Other competent witnesses confirmed his point of view. Retired Colonel A. Kovalchuk observed the object from the ground. He saw a strange, cigar-shaped object, surrounded by a greenish halo. The object had two powerful lights in the front and rear parts, and a bluish glow fell straight to the ground. As the object moved, a sound could be heard like that of a functioning transformer; a nearby electric line could cause it. The object's speed was around 60 kilometres an hour. Kovalchuk, an experienced pilot, was aware of the fact that the Soviet Union did not have such aircraft. The UFO had a strange and eerie effect on the high-voltage line: when its light hit it, a loud noise was followed by an intensive "crown".

The case remains almost as mysterious now as it was in 1984. Such prominent Russian Ufologists as V. Psalomschikov have established that a rocket was launched from the Plesetsk Cosmodrome, and that it was the cause of the greenish cloud and other light effects. Thousands of witnesses observed the phenomena from the ground. But still no one can explain all other strange details of the case.

Psalomschikov and some other researchers are proponents of the extraterrestrial hypothesis of the object's origin. They believe that a coincidence took place that ill-fated morning: a UFO observed a Soviet rocket launch, and there was an interaction between the two events. K. Khazanovitch, a Scientist and Ufologist, believes that what took place was a sinister, secret experiment; that an artificial "cloud" was created for some classified purpose. He also wants to see clear answers. The military has remained silent. Hence, we still have no credible explanation as to what happened in September of 1984 over Byelorussia. We do know that people died as a result of this encounter with a UFO.

K. Khazanovich mentioned a "grandiose" experiment over the Kola Peninsula. The purpose of the experiment was the formation of an ecologically safe process of creating artificial clouds at great altitudes. He mentions Soviet and foreign experiments involving electronic beams, emitted from spaceships and satellites to study the atmospheric, ionosphere, and magnetosphere processes. Sometimes results of the experiments amazed even those who created them.

Perhaps one of such experiments, or something much more sinister, something we cannot even suspect, caused the death and illnesses of Soviet crews. K. Khazanovitch does not know.

Like so many events in the former USSR, this one remains shrouded in mystery, a mystery that still remains as baffling today as it ever did.

CHAPTER 10

THE VASHKA OBJECT

Years ago, a strange metallic object the size of a man's fist was discovered on the bank of the Vashka River. This tributary of the Mezen River flows into the White Sea. Three workers from the nearby settlement of Ertom found the fragment on a riverbank near the water. The object was shiny, and if it was dropped upon stones, a shower of sparks flew in all directions. The workers retrieved the object and took it to Ertom. There they cut it into three pieces with a saw. As they cut it, fire and sparks sprang from blade of the saw.

The object, according to the Trud newspaper article (1988), looked like a part of a ring, a sphere, or a cylinder with a diameter of approximately 1.2 metres. Its unusual magnetic properties indicated that it was of an artificial origin.

In 1977, a group of geologists arrived from Syktyvkar (then, capital of the Komi ASSR), one of whom was presented with a fragment of the object for further analysis. The geologist sent it to Professor N. Yushkov of the Institute of Geology (Soviet Academy of Sciences, the Komi branch) for his analysis. The Vashka Object proved to be a very unusual specimen indeed. A spectral analysis performed by a laser showed that the substance was an alloy. It consisted of molybdenum, iron, manganese, magnesium, and iron. But this alloy possessed no crystalline structure. No technological method is able to produce amorphous metal films of thickness larger than 1 micrometre.

Soviet Ufologists found out about the Vashka Object and decided that it could be a fragment from an alien spaceship. The piece was cut into six other fragments, and sent to various Leningrad scientific establishments, for further study (among them the Moscow Institute of Steel and Alloys, Institute of Geochemistry and Analytical Chemistry, and others). This time a diamond circular saw was used at the Leningrad Institute of Physical Technologies.

V. Fomenko obtained one sample for the purposes of investigation. He published a report about it in the RIAP Bulletin, Issue 1-2, 1999. Fomenko performed a first-rate scientific analysis of the object, and those interested are urged to write to the Research Institute on Anomalous Phenomena. His conclusion is fascinating: It would be impossible to manufacture such an object using our existing technology. It was probably manufactured by alien technology.

But certainly not everyone agrees with that conclusion. There have been a number of opinions that the Vashka Object was nothing but a fragment of a fallen stage of a carrier rocket, for the area where the object was found has been known to contain numerous pieces of the fallen Soyuz carrier rockets. Among those who share this opinion is Michael Gershtein, who has completed an excellent analysis of the Vashka Object case.

Like many things in the former USSR nothing is straightforward. It is neither black nor white. The same applies to the Vashka Object. Could it really be a piece of metal from an alien spaceship? Or is it more likely that it came from a Soviet rocket? Opinions, as you might well imagine, are equally divided. The Vashka Object is yet another puzzle from the annals of Soviet Ufology.

CHAPTER 11

THE ORDZHENIKIDZE OBJECT

Perhaps a better name for this chapter would be "An Anatomy of a Hoax". But this hoax does deserve a separate chapter because for many years it was a story that duped many in the Soviet Union and the West.

On May 5, 1983, the air defence units of the Trans-Caucasus military region were able to fire upon and apparently hit a cone-shaped UFO. One missile was sent after the UFO after it appeared on the radar screens for some time. Allegedly, the UFO did not land, but managed to slowly fall to earth in the area of Stopover Mountain near Nalchik. The "aliens" allegedly made contact with a local inhabitant, who eventually travelled to Moscow, and reported everything to journalists. At the same time a group of tourists arrived in Moscow, and reported that they actually got inside the UFO, but found no people or aliens. A group of Ufologists left for the area shortly thereafter. At first they could not find anything, but some time later an object was discovered. However, it was a life-size fake. According to Vadim Chernobrov, a number of Polish cinematographers used the fake for the filming of a motion picture, and left it behind.

CONFLICTING REPORTS
But the case became more complicated and the tourists from Moscow became outraged. What they saw was a product of superior intelligence, not a movie prop. They went back to the area, but found only indentations from the fake UFO. The fake itself was gone, although they searched throughout the area of the Daryal Gorge. Ajaja's SOYUZUFOTSENTR concluded that the object on the photographs that had been taken earlier was no alien spaceship.

THE STORY GETS MORE COMPLICATED
In 1994 Vadim Chernobrov, a well-known journalist, scientist, and researcher frequently mentioned in our book, collected some more unusual details about the case. Soviet officers, not soldiers, but senior officers evacuated the original object, the one shot down by the air defence unit. The object was later seen at a secret military base near Moscow. Marina Popovich gave the photographs in

this book to Paul Stonehill in 1991, when she visited Los Angeles. An awkward looking craft is about 8 metres high, and has a large body with visible hatches. There is a staircase, an elevated ramp. Its upper section, resembles a pyramid, and is constructed from corrugated plates. The surface is either burned or dirty. There are some telescope supports, or maybe supporters of the ramp, it is unclear.

Vladimir Lagovsky, at the time Russia's leading UFO phenomena reporter, sent Paul Stonehill his articles about the incident. He was intrigued by the clumsy apparatus, too, and could not find any explanation. The technology of the "fake" was so crude, that only very naive people could suppose that it was an alien spaceship. But Lagovsky was able to determine that an object was hauled off to the secret Mitische base near Moscow. Lagovsky's sources also informed him that the object's engine used the neutrino radiation (Rabochaya Tribuna newspaper, December 3, 1991). There was even a psychic, Victor Kostrikin, who claimed to get in contact with aliens.

Chernobrov has acquaintances in a secret research facility. He published an informative article in Chetvertoye Izmereniye i NLO newspaper (Issue 12, 1996). They knew of his interest in the nature of UFOs, and showed him a curious film. In the waning days of the USSR, the film was delivered to one of the secret facility's laboratories, and the order was to analyse it. It was done, but as the Soviet state disintegrated, no one asked for the report. It remained untouched until 1995. The heads of the facility were changed many times during the years that followed the demise. Finally, the new head of the secret facility requested that the film be returned. It was found, and when scientists viewed it, they were amazed. Chernobrov also found it to be quite unique: he saw a humanoid face, with large, blinking eyes. There was a cylindrical item in the being's hands. His gaze was intensive, looking straight ahead, as if "he" wants to say something. The image flickers, as if someone pushed the operator's hand, and a second later the screen shows a cow lying on the ground. The animal is either sleeping or dying, as can be interpreted by its jerking movements. The camera then shows an object, about a hundred metres away. It either hovers very low, or is on the ground. The camera shows that the humanoid walks away. Between him and the operator someone's back comes into view: the jacket this person is wearing is military in appearance. The humanoid walks through the meadow, and the military officer calmly watches him. It looked as if someone accompanied his guests to an airplane, according to Chernobrov. The film ends this way: "aliens" walk inside the object, the opening in its hull covers by something like a film, the craft slowly rises up. The next film sequence shows an oval UFO in the air, and then it vanished instantly. The next sequence shows soldiers who comb through the meadow. They bend down to pick something up. The film ends. Chernobrov's contacts do not know the origin of the film. There is a possibility, according to him, that the Ordzhenikidze Object was filmed. There are other video films, as reported by one officer from the HQ of the secret military unit-base 67947 that can make one's hair stand up and fall out. Chernobrov received a telephone call from a captain, who knew about the scientist's efforts to uncover the truth. According to the captain, in 1985-87 a number of Hollywood producers had begun to make a motion picture about "evil Russians who join forces with aliens". Some portions of the film were either stolen by Soviet intelligence, or purchased, and sent to Moscow. The Soviets needed to know how well the Americans knew about Soviet special measures, and methods of operations in case of extreme situations. Thus the captain hinted that the "alien film" Chernobrov saw was American-made. The movie was never produced, due to the perestroika warming up the relations between both countries, or for some other reason. Still, there is no final proof as to where the film came from and who made it.

As for the Ordhenikidze Object, there is another, well-informed opinion. Mikhail Gershtein, whose research is described throughout the book, answered an inquiry by Paul Stonehill about this case through the RUFORS Round Table. According to him, nothing was shot down; Victor Kostrikin invented the incident, and others picked up this "story". We tend to agree with Gershtein, but wanted to present all relevant views.

GIANTS IN JULY OF 1983

A curious report was published in NLO magazine (Issue 7, 1997). B. Borisov, a biologist, was in the Caucasus Mountains area in 1983, during the summer. On July 1 or 2, he and his wife chanced upon a clearing, in the area of Alpine-like meadows. The day was bright, the sky clear. Borisov sensed that someone was watching him from behind. He turned around and noticed two giant humanoid figures. He could make out heads, shoulders, and torsos. But he saw no limbs. His wife became agitated, and shouted that they should run away, as the shapes were approaching the couple. And it seemed to Borisov that the beings did make giant jerky steps toward them, and then stopped. The couple ran away, and continued to watch the area for another half an hour. The beings remained in the crevice of the mountain, and sometimes turned around. Both beings were of the same size. In some countries these creatures may have been linked to other sighting of the so-called Yeti, or Bigfoot, but in the files of the USSR they go down as sightings of alien beings.

In this chapter we have seen a rich mixture of reported events, some of which are surely unique to the USSR. For example, where else would you find a movie prop left behind for innocent bystanders to mistake it as a UFO? Surely only the Soviet Union has such a story. Other reports of UFOs being shot down my military aircraft have come from other parts of the world and are well documented, but it seems that giant humanoid figures with no limbs are reserved for land of the hammer and sickle.

These few incidents serve to show the incredible diversity of the UFO subject, which has confronted researchers in the USSR.

CHAPTER 12

UFOs OVER CHERNOBYL

Prior to 1986, Chernobyl (or Chornobyl' in Ukrainian) was but an obscure town on the Pripyat' River in north-central Ukraine. Then came the horrible day when this town lost its obscurity and anonymity forever.

On April 26, 1986, the planet's worst nuclear power accident took place at the Chernobyl Nuclear Power Station in the Soviet Ukraine. A series of operator errors and reactor design deficiencies produced a devastating steam explosion and fuel-core meltdown in Unit 4. Death-carrying radioactivity spread over parts of the USSR, contaminating the land and causing disease, mutations, and worse. The Soviet Union would never recover from this horrible disaster, although its leaders tried to hide the truth for as long as they could. Valery Iosifovich Kratokhvil, a Ukrainian researcher and author of numerous books and articles, has collected information about UFOs over Chernobyl, and published it in his book NLO: gosti iz buduschego or UFOs: guests from the future (Minsk, 1992).

Few people remember that in their ignoble, criminal and irresponsible attempt to conceal the cause of the disaster, the Soviet authorities tried to misinform the public through rumours that UFOs caused the accident. In August of 1990 Kratokhvil located Mikhail A. Varitzky, who was a technician at the power station, and had lived in Chernobyl from the day it was built. He provided the author with written statements. On the night of the accident his sleep was interrupted by alarms, and with another technician, Mikhail Samoilenko, drove to the area of the power station. They were to collect the dose control and change oxygen tanks. They drove the Gaz-51 automobile, its official license plate number 24-28 KIZ. They arrived at Unit 4 at 4:15 a.m. The reactor was ablaze, and the technicians had no protective suits. Their faces were burning, and the technicians who knew the dangers of radiation, turned back.

As the car was turning around, they observed a fiery sphere in the sky. Its colour was similar to brass, and it moved slowly. The diameter was approximately eight metres. Two bright raspberry-coloured rays shot out from the UFO and were directed at the reactor of Unit 4. The object was some 300 metres away from the reactor. It hovered in the area for about three minutes. Then the rays vanished, and the UFO slowly moved away to the northwest, towards Byelorussia. The gauging device used by the technicians was checked when they returned to the base, it worked fine. But one thing is crucial: the first reading they took, just as the UFO appeared in the sky, was 3,000 mill-roentgens/hour. After the rays did something to the burning reactor, the readings showed 800 mill-roentgens/hour. Three hours after the explosion a UFO brought down the radiation level. The Varitzky account does not diminish the brave work of those who battled the fires at the burning reactor: the truly brave young heroes died to stop the death unleashed by Soviet ineptitude. Perhaps his account reveals that mankind was given a hand in its hour of need.

Others observed the UFO over Chernobyl, for instance V.S. Vasilevsky. Their addresses are listed in Kratokhvil's book. There were eyewitnesses who drew sketches of UFOs over Chernobyl and Slavutich, the town where nuclear scientists reside.

Subsequently, UFOs came back to Chernobyl. On September 16, 1989, when another problem occurred at Unit 4 (radioactive material escaped to the environment), a medical doctor reported a sighting. Iva Naumovna Gospina observed a UFO at 8:20 in the morning, a few hours after the accident. The object was amber-coloured, elliptical, and she discerned its top and bottom parts.

Kratokhvil has a photograph taken in October of 1990 by Alexander Krymov, a scientist at the power station. The UFO in the photograph hovered over the apartment buildings where technicians reside. It is a disk-like craft with visible supports. According to Kratokhvil, the scientist is ready to submit the film for expert analysis. His and Gospina's addresses are also listed.

A fire raged the Chernobyl Power Plant (Unit 2) on October 11, 1991. Vladimir Chevran, a reporter for Ekho Chernobylya newspaper, was taking photographs at the Unit's site on October 16, after the fire. One photograph was of the sky, and he saw nothing there at the time. The sky was absolutely clear. When the film was developed, it revealed a peculiar looking object, very similar to the one Doctor Gospina had previously observed. The editors of the newspaper had the film checked by experts whose analysis showed it to be authentic. The address of Ekho Chernobylya: Ukraine, Kiev, ul. Vladimirskay, dom 47, (redaktzia gazeti).

Prior to 1986, UFOs were rarely seen over the areas located in the vicinity of Chernobyl, and some a little further away: the Bryansk area, the Byelorussian areas, and Kiev. For instance, from 1956 to 1986 only four sightings of UFOs had been registered over Kiev. From the summer of 1986 on numerous instances people who were willing to sign their names to the reports have reported UFOs over Kiev. The Kiev military radar stations have also allegedly observed UFOs.

On November 12, 1989, such a radar station reported a UFO, and Lt.

Colonel V. Shavanov checked the reported sighting. The UFO was hovering over the site of the Exposition of the Achievements of Ukrainian Soviet Socialist Republic's Economy (VDNH, the Russian abbreviation). The UFO was a cross-shaped object inside a rectangular, with a fiery spiral inside it. It hovered 400 metres over the VDNH. This incident was reported in Leninskoye Znamya newspaper (November 17, 1989). In the following days, fiery spheres were reported over the Exhibit. Suffice it to say, the Kiev Institute of Nuclear Research is located in the area of the VDNH, and it has a reactor too. Perhaps, the UFOs were there to control the experiments we know nothing about?

Chernobyl and its nuclear disaster are known throughout the world and its legacy will last for many generations yet to come. But the UFO sightings at the time of the disaster are known only to a handful of people. Did the Soviet authorities receive a helping alien hand during the disaster, or is there a more rational, down-to-earth explanation for the sightings? Again, it would seem that these sightings during such a catastrophe are unique to the USSR. Thankfully, no other parts of the world have witnessed such a nuclear accident and hopefully never will.

CHAPTER 13

THE DALNEGORSK CRASH

This internationally famous UFO incident took place in 1986, on January 29, at 7:55 p.m. Some have called it the Roswell Incident of the Soviet Union. The information about it was sent to the Russian Ufology Research Centre by several Russian Ufologists. Alexander Rempel also provided us with the actual report of Dr. Dvuzhilni.

Dalnegorsk is a small mining town in the Far East of Russia. That cold January day a reddish sphere flew into this town from the south-eastern direction, crossed part of Dalnegorsk, and crashed at the Izvestkovaya Mountain (also known as Height or Hill 611, because of its size). The object flew noiselessly, and parallel to the ground; it was approximately three metres in diameter, of a near perfect round shape, with no projections or cavities, its colour similar to that of burning stainless steel. An eyewitness, V. Kandakov, said that the speed of the UFO was close to 15 metres per hour. The object slowly ascended and descended, and its glow would heat up every time it rose up. On its approach to Hill 611 the object "jerked", and fell down like a rock. All witnesses reported that the object "jerked" or "jumped". Most of them recall two "jumps". Two girls remember that the object actually "jumped" four times. The witnesses heard a weak, muted thump. It burned intensively at the cliff's edge for an hour. A geological expedition to the site, led by V. Skavinsky of the Institute of Geology and Geophysics of the Siberian Branch of the Soviet Academy of Sciences (1988), had confirmed the object's movements through a series of chemical and physical tests of the rocks collected from the site. Valeri Dvuzhilni, head of the Far Eastern Committee for Anomalous Phenomena, was the first to investigate the crash. Anatoly Listratov researched it, as did some other Ufologists. Although some Western researchers wrote about the case, nobody has heretofore presented the accurate account of all that has happened.

Dr. Dvuzhilni, a biologist, once witnessed a UFO during a 1980 expedition to Kamchatka, a peninsula in the Russian Far East. He was actually scared when he saw a strange disk landing near a 90 metre deep lake bottom.

Dr. Dvuzhilni arrived at the site two days after the crash. Deep snow was characteristic of the weather at the time. The site of the crash, located on a rocky ledge, was devoid of snow. All around the site remnants of silica rocks were found: splintered (due to exposure to high temperatures), and "smoky" looking. Many pieces, and a nearby rock, contained particles of silvery metal, some "sprayed"- like, some in the form of solidified balls. At the edge of the site a tree stump was found (allegedly, Listratov has it). It was burnt out, and emitted a chemical smell. The objects collected at the site were later dubbed as "tiny nets", "little balls", "lead balls", "and glass pieces" (that is what each resembled). Closer examination revealed very unusual properties. One of the "tiny nets" contained torn and very thin (17 micrometres) threads. Each of the threads consisted of even thinner fibres, tied up in plaits. Intertwined with the fibres were very thin gold wires. Soviet scientists, at such facilities as the Omsk branch of the Academy of Sciences, analysed all collected pieces. Without going into specific details (the Centre has translated the results into English), suffice it to say that the technology to produce such materials was not yet available on Earth...except for one disturbing account.

To give an idea of the complexity of the composition of the pieces, let us look at the "iron balls". Each of them had its own chemical composition: iron, and a large admixture of aluminium, manganese, nickel, chromium, tungsten, and cobalt.

Such differences indicate that the object was not just a piece of lead and iron, but some heterogeneous construction made from heterogeneous alloys with definite significance. When melted in a vacuum, some pieces would spread over a base, while at another base they would form into balls. Half of the balls were covered with convex glass-like structures. Neither the physicists nor physical metallurgists can say what these structures are, or what their composition is. The "tiny nets" (or "mesh") have confused many researchers. It is impossible to understand their structure and nature of the formation. A. Kulikov, an expert on carbon at the Chemistry Institute of the Far Eastern Department of the Academy of Sciences, USSR, wrote that it was not possible to get an idea what the "mesh" is. It resembles glass carbon, but conditions leading to such formation are unknown. Definitely a common fire could not produce such glass carbon. The most mysterious aspect of the collected items was the disappearance, after vacuum melting, of gold, silver, and nickel, and the appearance, from nowhere, of molybdenum, that was not in the chamber to begin with.

The only thing that could be more or less easily explained was the ash found on site. Something biological was burned during the crash. A flock of birds, perhaps, or a stray dog; or someone who was inside the crashed object.

Dr. Dvuzhilni's article was published in a Soviet (Uzbekistan) Magazine NLO: Chto, Gde, Kogda? (Issue 1, 1990, reprint of an article in FENOMEN Magazine, March 23, 1990). In his article Dalnegorski Phenomen V. Dvuzhilni provides details unavailable elsewhere.

The south-westerly trajectory of the object just about coincides with the Xichang Cosmodrome of People's Republic of China, where satellites are launched into geo synchronous orbit with the help of the Great March 2 carrier rockets. There is no data of any rocket launches in the PRC at the end of January. At the same time, Sinxua Agency reported on January 25, 1988, that there was a sighting of a glowing red sphere not far from the Cosmodrome, where it hovered for 30 minutes. Possibly, UFOs had shown interest toward the Chinese Cosmodrome in the years 1989 and 1988. There is another curious detail: at the site of the Height 611 small pieces of light gray colour were discovered, but only in the area of the contact. These specimens did not match any of the local varieties of soil. What is amazing, is the spectroscopic analysis of the specimens matched them to the Yaroslavl tuffs of the polymetalic deposits (i.e. the specimens possessed some characteristic elements of the Yaroslavl, but not the Dalnegorsk, tuffs). There is a possibility that the object obtained pieces of tuff in the Yaroslavl area. Tuffs experience metamorphosis under the effect of high temperatures.

The site of the crash itself was something like an anomalous zone. It was "active" for three years after the crash. Insects avoid the place. The zone affects humans, too, because various systems of the body demonstrated inadequate reactions to it: blood, pulse, sensor failures, and loss of coordination. The zone affects mechanical and electronic equipment. Some people, including a local chemist, actually got very sick.

This Hill 611 is located in the area of numerous anomalies, according to an article in the Soviet digest Tainy XX Veka (Moscow, 1990, CP Vsya Moskva Publishing House). Even photos taken at the site, when developed, failed to show the hill, but did clearly show other locations. Members of an expedition to the site reported later that their flashlights stopped working at the same time. They checked the flashlights upon returning home, and discovered burned wires.

Eight days after the UFO crash at Hill 611, on February 8, 1986, at 8:30 p.m., two more yellowish spheres flew from the north, in the southward direction. Reaching the site of the crash, they circled it four times, then turned back to the north and flew away. Then on November 28, 1987 (Saturday night, 11:24 p.m.), 32 flying objects had appeared from nowhere. There were hundreds of witnesses, including the military and civilians. The objects flew over 12 different settlements, and 13 of them flew to Dalnegorsk and the site. Three of the UFOs hovered over the settlement, and five of them illuminated the nearby mountain. The objects moved noiselessly, at an altitude between 150 to 800 metres. None of the eyewitnesses actually thought they were UFOs. Those who observed the objects assumed they were aircraft involved in some disaster, or falling meteorites. As the objects flew over houses, they created interference (television, telegraph functions).

The Ministry of Internal Affairs officers, who were present, testified later that they observed the objects from a street, at 23:30 (precise time). They saw a fiery object, flying in from the direction of Gorely settlement. In front of the fiery "flame" was a lustreless sphere, and in the middle of the object was a red sphere. Another group of eyewitnesses included workers from the Bor quarry. They observed an object at 11:00 pm. A giant cylindrical object was flying straight at the quarry. Its size was like that of a five-story building, its length around 200 or 300 hundred metres. The front part of the object was lit up, like a burning metal. The workers were afraid that the object would crash on them. One of the managers of the quarry observed an object at 11:30 pm. The object was slowly moving at an altitude of 300 metres. It was huge, and cigar-shaped. The manager, whose last name was Levakov, stated that he was well acquainted with aerodynamics, knew theory and practice of flight, but never knew that a body could fly noiselessly without any wings or engines. Another eyewitness, a kindergarten teacher, saw something else. It was a bright, blinding sphere at an altitude of a nine-story building. It moved noiselessly. In front of the sphere Ms. Markina observed a dark, metallic-looking elongated object of about 10 to 12 metres long. It hovered over a school. There the object emitted a ray (its diameter about half a metre). The colour of the ray was violet-bluish. The ground below illuminated, but there were no shadows from objects below. Then the object in the sky approached a mountain and hovered over it. It illuminated the mountain, emitted a reddish projector-like light, as if searching for something, and then departed, flying over the mountain.

No rocket launches took place at any of the Soviet cosmodromes either on January 29, 1986, or November 28, 1987.

Dr. Dvuzhilni's conclusion is that it was a malfunctioning alien space probe that crashed into the Hill 611. Another hypothesis has it that the object managed to ascend, and escape (almost in one piece) in the north-easterly direction and probably crashed in the dense taiga.

There are opposing opinions. V. Psalomschikov, an expert on aircraft crashes, and a well-known journalist, stated that the object was manufactured in the USSR, the technology to produce it dates back to 1970's, and that he has similar ultra thin filaments in his possession. However, a Soviet probe would self-destruct immediately, whereas the object reportedly did try to ascend several times. Actually, Psalomschikov believes the crashed object was a Soviet-built intelligence mini-craft.

A Russian Ufologist and scientist, Gennady Belimov, presented information in 1993 that a Soviet military probe had crashed at the Hill 611. His proof was based on similar crashes of highly classified Soviet probes, and he concludes that Ufologists misinterpreted the probe which to be a UFO crashed in the Far East. As for the lead collected at the site, Belimov believes it was extracted from the Kholodnensky deposit in the Northern Baikal region.

A new generation of Russian UFO researchers have reached a conclusion that the probe was an aerostatics reconnaissance vehicle possibly equipped to make infrared photographs. The speed of the probe was estimated to be approximately 54 kilometres per hour, which would negate Dr. Dvuzhilni's data. But even among them (we read their opinions expressed on various Internet forums) there is no consistent belief as to the origin of the probe. Vladimir Smoly, for example, does not believe there was a thermite self-destruction device aboard the probe. The self-destruction would be expected to be immediate, unlike what had happened at Height 611 to the crashed object.

Was this a NATO probe? V. Psalomschikov mentioned that previously the NATO reconnaissance balloons did contain trotyl (TNT) self-destruction devices. One such apparatus fell on a house in the USSR and "self-destroyed" it; fortunately, there was no one inside the dwelling at the time. The Soviets raised hell, the scandal was heard even in the UN, and since that time the NATO probes contained only thermite self-destruction devices. Smoly believes the object was aerostatics apparatus created for entertainment purposes. However, M. Gershtein indicated that the object had a clearly defined trail, and could not have been a balloon moving at the speed of the wind carrying it.

Would the military later stage fake "UFO" flights to confuse and mislead ufologists, and the Western intelligence services? The objects observed on November 28, 1987 consisted of different shapes: cigar-like, cylindrical, and spherical. Their flight was noiseless and smooth, at various altitudes. Actually, not one of the eyewitnesses (including the police) mistook them for UFOs. The impression was that they observed some aircraft, or falling meteorites. While in flight, the objects affected power lines throughout the area. Lieutenant Zhivayev of the Interior Ministry troops described the object he observed as a flame with a lustreless sphere in the front and a reddish ball in the rear. And the workers from the Bor Quarry, Bistryancev, Anokhin, Grigoriyev reported a giant cylindrical object at an altitude of 300 metres. Its fore part was illuminated like melting metal. There are many other witness accounts in the Dvuzhilni report. To remind our readers, the area of the crash is not that far away from the Tunguska Phenomenon site.

Something else, heretofore unknown in the West, took place in the region, that could shed some light on both incidents.

Alexander Rempel published his report in Priroda newspaper (Vladivostok) in July of 1991. A fiery object was observed over the Khabarovsk city on August 24, 1978, at night. It was about a metre and a half in diameter. At one point in its flight, it emitted a hissing (or wheezing) sound, like a jet engine does. The area around it became illuminated, like daylight. The object descended slowly, and lit up brightly. The soil, albeit full of water, burned up. Coal-like pieces were found in the area, they had holes and glass-like structures. For ten years thereafter the soil remained unchanged, and nothing grew at the site of the explosion. The eyewitnesses reported that a dark object flew away just before the explosion. It was not found. Ten years later Rempel and his colleagues received numerous reports about an anomalous zone near Khabarovsk. Few explorers who have returned from the area confirmed that the object fell there, and that fantastic things have been observed there. Yet at the time Rempel could not confirm their reports: the military had sealed the area off. But his group was able to research the area of the Dalnegorsk Object alleged fall after it flew off the Hill 611. They found out about unusual animal mutations.

Russian newspaper Komsomol'skaya Pravda in its December 1, 2000 issue published an article about the Dalnegorsk case (NLO svili v Primorje gnezdo). Most interesting was Andrey Pavlov's (the author of the newspaper article) reference to the fact that in the early 1990s Russian generals from the anti-aircraft forces became concerned about the UFO activity in the area, and contacted local UFO researchers. An exchange of information ensued. It is newsworthy when a major Russian newspaper mentions such fact (the author actually quoted Dr. Dvuzhilni, the chief investigator of the Height 611 UFO crash).

According to Alexander Rempel (NLO Magazine, 1999) very few Russian Ufologists recall the crash, or pay attention to it.

Alexander Rempel informed participants of the UFOMIND Russian UFO Forum that fragments of the crashed object have been examined in Vladivostok, Khabarovsk, Munich, Liege and other places. In 2000, four Japanese and Korean expeditions examined the Height 611.

Ufologists from Korea and Japan have made offers to purchase the "balls". The current price for one gram of any fragment is $500.00, and the price has been going up. There are offers of $1,500 per gram, but the demand exceeds the supply. Rempel is aware that there have been numerous conclusions of a number of institutes and laboratories in Russia and abroad, and yet all of them differ from each other. There is no final conclusion that the object was made on Earth, but at the same time, there is no definite conclusion that the object was of extraterrestrial origin. Some peculiarities of the object still cannot be explained. Since 2000 there has not been anything anomalous in the area. But Russians Ufologists show little or no interest in the famous case, states Rempel, except for those in Vladivostok. Two exhibits of the Height 611 incident have been made and are active; one is in the Dalnegorsk museum, and the other in the UFO Museum in Vladivostok. There are hundreds of witnesses, and dozens of the actual eyewitnesses, and many drawings of the incident, but there are no photographs. Numerous "kontaktyori" (those who claim to be in contact with extraterrestrial civilizations) had made predictions that never came true, claimed to be in contact with alien civilizations, wrote books and made paintings of the event. They even claimed that a UFO would land at the

Dalnegorsk stadium. This prediction had attracted attention of a great number of Russians, thousands of them arrived in Dalnegorsk, but nothing happened. Some of those who had arrived to meet the aliens still remain in the Dalnegorsk mental asylum.

The RUFORS Round Table members (Anatoly Kutovoy and others), as well as Vladimir Smoly's UFO Forum participants, have discussed the case, and actively exchanged scientific information about it. As for the Russian media, it has paid some attention to the crash recently, too.

We must mention another interpretation of the Dalnegorsk crash. It was published in Soviet newspaper Ribak Primorya (Issue 14, 1991). The author of the article about the Dalnegorsk Object was Y. Vasilyev. He states several interesting points. According to him, V. Dvuzhilni and a group of his students arrived to the site of the crash. They searched the area three times, quite thoroughly, and found tiny metallic drops. All required measurements were taken, and took photographs. Then they initiated physical and chemical analyses of the findings. The temperature of the melting was 390 degrees. Silvery metal was very soft; it was easy to break it with a pair of tweezers. On February 8, 1986, V. Dvuzhilni and V. Berliozov, a geologist (who had studied the Sikhote-Alin' meteorite) again ascended the hill. The geologist confirmed that the crashed body was of a cosmic origin, and the traces affirmed this. Its luminescence was similar to that of usual meteorites. Five years later, V. Dvuzhilini came up with further details ("fantastic details", according to Y. Vasilyev).

Then the author came up with his own hypothesis. On January 28, 1986, American shuttle Challenger exploded in the sky. The force of the explosion was such that the fragments were thrown all over the Atlantic. It is possible that one of the fragments, flying from the southwest, landed in Dalnegorsk the next day.

There seems to a consensus of opinion that the Hill 611 crash may well have a conventional explanation, but exactly what remains to be seen. It does have its parallel's in the West, the Roswell case being one of them, but there are others. Irrespective of this, it is a fascinating case, which is sure to divulge more information and more theories in the years to come.

CHAPTER 14

UFOs OVER VORONEZH

Voronezh, the centre of the Black Earth Region of Russia, is located approximately 480 km to the southeast of Moscow. The city was founded in 1585 and ever since then it has steadily grown and now has a population of a close to a million. The Voronezh River splits the city into two parts.

During World War II the city was almost completely destroyed. The region has a favourable climate, fertile black soil, and unique iron ore reserves - all these elements provide a basis for the constant growth of industrial potential and agricultural development. Perhaps such elements also attracted the attention of extraterrestrial civilizations in the fall of 1989, when the former Soviet Union was undergoing tremendous historical changes.

THE PLAYERS

Voronezh Ufologists are famous throughout the world. The official name of their group is the Voronezh Committee for the Study of Anomalous Phenomena. Their leader, Genrikh Silanov, head of the Voronezh Geophysical Laboratory, has sent valuable information and materials to the West, including the book NLO v Voronezhe (UFO in Voronezh, written by Silanov and four other researchers), and photographs of various anomalous zones.

What is important to understand is that there have been UFO sightings in and around Voronezh for a number of years, and eyewitnesses have included civilians, military personnel, law enforcement officials, and scientists.

One week before the historic sightings in Voronezh, locals had reported a huge number of UFO sightings. It all started on the 21st of September 1989. Among the objects observed that day were "hat"- shaped craft, orange-coloured disks, cigar-shaped craft, dark-red spheres that emitted rays, moon-like objects and a huge craft emitting crooked rays (this "moon" was shining upwards). Among those who have reported these UFO sightings were adults, civilian and military people, law enforcement personnel, as well as senior citizens, college students, and children. It was later determined that the aliens (who seemed to be of gigantic size), reported by children, were in reality about two metres tall. Most UFOs were of a spherical shape, and their colour was red, yellow or orange. Their presence did effect electrical appliances in most cases. Some people were also adversely affected: loss of sleep, strange conditions developed after observing UFOs. Several eyewitnesses reported that the UFOs had a strange image placed on their hulls (it resembled a Cyrillic letter). But Mr. Silanov and his colleagues were not able to determine what the image was.

Sightings of UFOs in Voronezh continued into October. An even more sinister development involved sightings reported from Novovoronezh, where the nuclear power plant is located.

HOW IT ALL BEGAN

The actual events that drew the world's attention to Voronezh began with a small article written by Alexander Mosolov in a small local newspaper. He was the one who met eyewitnesses to the incident, including a teenager, Vasya Surin. The boy and his friends stated the events as later repeated by TASS, the official Soviet news agency, and the boy's mother recalled that she and her neighbours observed a strange reddish object some days later, as it flew over their building.

TASS, the Soviet news agency, reported strange events in Voronezh. The world and the Soviets were stunned. After all, witnesses claimed seeing a UFO flying into Voronezh on September 27, 1989. Boys, who played soccer in the Yuzhni Park, saw a pink glow in the sky, then a red ball some 10 yards in diameter. The sphere circled, vanished, then reappeared a few minutes later and hovered over them. A crowd that had gathered there saw a "three-eyed alien" through an open hatch. The alien was about 10 feet tall, in silvery overalls, bronze-coloured boots, and wearing a disk on his chest. The UFO landed, and two creatures, one of them a robot, exited. A boy screamed with fear, but when the alien looked at him (the former had shining eyes), the boy became silent and unable to move. The onlookers screamed, and the UFO vanished. Some five minutes later it reappeared. The alien possessed a "gun": a tube of about 20 inches long. The alien pointed this weapon at a 16-year-old boy, and the boy vanished. The alien stepped inside the sphere, and it took off. The boy reappeared at the same time. Names of the eyewitnesses, three children, were reported in the Sovetskaya Kultura newspaper.

SILANOV INVESTIGATES

Silanov cried foul from the very beginning. He and his colleagues had investigated truly remarkable UFO sightings in the Voronezh area for years. He cast doubts on the TASS reports immediately, his views expressed in an interview with the Associated Press. Silanov and his group went to the Yuzhni Park on October 3, 1989, to investigate: the boys told them exactly where the craft and aliens had landed. Everything was videotaped, the site, a possible anomalous zone, and statements of eyewitnesses. Children had reported numerous UFO sightings at the edge of Yuzhni Park, on different dates and times. Interesting details were provided: the UFOs were of different shapes, some had strange looking supports, and holographic images were described, as well as unusual biophysical side effects of contacts with aliens. As the story became a sensation, the Voronezh government officials provided assistance to Silanov and his group.

Ufologists were able to collect soil samples from the alleged UFO landing site in the park. Local air defence units provided their reports (no UFOs registered at the time of the incident). Local police units assisted Silanov, and questioned witnesses. After TASS broke the story on October 10, during the 120 Minutes TV program, Silanov informed the Voronezh residents of his findings, and warned the journalists not to jump to hasty conclusions (during his October 11 TV appearance). But they did. Yuzhni Park became the centre of world's attention. Philip Mantle (co-author of this book) was quoted in Izvestiya about unusual aspects of the case. Reports of sightings flooded the Voronezh UFO study group and editorial offices of Soviet newspapers.

While the Soviet Central television debunked the incident in its October 11 broadcast, thousands of Voronezh residents observed a UFO, as it hovered over the city at a low altitude, vanishing and reappearing in various places. Soviet Ufologists began to find out in September of 1989 that there was a wave of UFO sightings throughout the USSR, from Siberia to the Baltic republics. In many cases, the reports had been identical to the ones in Voronezh. Then Spanish reports, brought to Voronezh by journalist Miguel Bas, turned out to contain descriptions of almost identical beings, as the ones the Voronezh boys saw. The Spanish events occurred before the Voronezh Phenomenon and were well documented at the time. The russian boys and spanish residents of Cadiz saw exactly the same type of beings. At that time, these Russian boys had no access to the Spanish UFO cases in question.

THE URBAN COMMISSION

A special commission, appointed by the city of Voronezh, consisted of physicists, chemists, biologists, soil experts, nuclear engineers, doctors, criminal investigators, and psychologists. The children in question were questioned thoroughly. Apparently no definitive conclusions could be reached. The commission found no physical traces of anything unusual in the Yuzhni Park. And yet, the commission was aware that one could not approach such a phenomenon with modern scientific methods. For example, why would there be radiation in the soil? Would our instruments and devices be adequate to investigate such a phenomenon? The commission concluded that most likely, an anomalous phenomenon did take place in Voronezh in the autumn of 1989. As for the ufologists, they did find an unusual presence of some elements in the soil samples taken from the sites reported. The samples were analysed at the spectral analysis laboratory of Voronezh.

In mid December of 1989, Voronezh Ufologists revealed their findings in a two hour television program titled UFOs IN VORONEZH.

NO EPILOGUE AS YET

There were several photographs of UFOs taken at the time by several eyewitnesses. Soil samples from the landing sites were subjected to quantitative spectral analysis. The samples contained higher than usual amounts of a number of elements. For example, the presence of phosphorus was 100 times more than in the background samples. The weight of one of the UFOs was determined to be 11,500 kilograms. The soil samples also contained radiation. In the opinion of those who had studied the phenomenon in Voronezh, something quite dramatic and utterly unknown had occurred. According to Silanov, it is still too soon to end the investigation, because the UFO observations in the area continue.

Let us understand one crucial fact: the Voronezh commission that studied the phenomenon consisted of scientists, psychologists, criminal investigators, and medical experts. They interviewed the children involved, and understood that there may be a few changes in their stories due to constant re-telling of the events, perhaps with a little children's fantasy thrown in for good measure, and even a few mixtures of information after the ten days of intensive questioning.

But there was more to the story than people in the West realise. A few years ago we received information about a prequel to the momentous events of in Yuzhni Park.

NUCLEAR PLANT SIGHTINGS

On January 5, 1990 some strange circles appeared next to the building # 17 on Kosmonavtov Street (it looked as if someone had created elaborate concentric snow rings). The night before dozens of people saw UFOs on the outskirts of the city, and near the power Novovoronezh NPP plant. The Novovoronezh nuclear power plant is situated on the left bank of river Don 42 km from Voronezh.

Local police came to investigate appearance of the mysterious circles. In the evening of January 4, a local reporter actually observed (through his binoculars) a strange "star"- like object; it emitted a white ray at the end of which one could see a reddish ball of a smaller size.

The Novovoronezh NPP was the first plant with Power Units LWR (a light water reactor is cooled by ordinary water. Heavy water, on the other hand, is water that is rich in the heavy isotopes of hydrogen). At present there are two Power Units with reactors LWR - 440 (3 and 4) and one Power Unit with reactor LWR - 1000 (5) on Novovoronezh NPP. In 1996, new units were planned to be built at existing Russian plants including Kursk, Smolensk, Kola, Novovoronezh and Beloyarsk. As of 1998, Units 1 and 2 were excluded from operation.

On March 4, 1998, a very strange incident took place in the centre of the Voronezh region, just 10 kilometres away from the Novovoronezh NPP. People observed something that resembled a "falling, burning airplane" at approximately 2 o'clock in the afternoon. The local HQ of the Interior Ministry, as well as representatives of the Ministry of Extraordinary Events and other governmental agencies were immediately notified. The search for the crashed aircraft in the vicinity of the Troitsky, as well as the Liski regional centre, produced no results. But just a few hours later, locals observed strange plumes of smoke some 40 kilometres to the south of the first sighting, in the Ostrogozhsky region. Nothing out of place was found there either. However, the RIA-Novosti correspondent V. Kolobov, the official information agency ITAR-TASS, and the central television announced that an AN-26 aircraft crashed in the vicinity of the nuclear power plant. The search areas were declared off-limits, and journalists were not allowed inside it. Later it was announced that all Russian aircraft that day were accounted for, and returned to their airfields. The locals probably saw falling debris from space, pieces of a Russian spaceship. And yet the search went on, under the cover of secrecy; Vadim Chernobrov states that this search had lasted for three months (V. Chernobrov, UFO Crashes, pieces of the unknown, an article in the RUFORS library). The government produced various, sometimes comic, explanations as to why the search was still taking place. A representative of the Ministry of the Russian Federation for Civil Defence, Emergencies and Elimination of Consequences of Natural Disasters (EMERCOM of Russia) stated that soldiers were removing W.W. II mines in the forests of the Podgorenski region. Yet, noted Chernobrov, in 1998 the only entities that deactivated and removed mines anywhere in Russia were private commercial companies, or private enterprises. The EMERCOM would not dedicate itself to deactivate mines in populated areas of the country; why would it then remove mines for free from an uninhabited forest, and even using soldiers to do so? Why do the soldiers from several units surround the forests, and not just an isolated area where the mines are located? Hence, surmises V. Chernobrov, whatever they had searched for were really not mines.

The search area that had lasted for three months in complete secrecy was some 40 kilometres southward from the Ostrogozhsky region. But what could it have been? It is possible that "something", seemingly a falling aircraft, first had appeared in the area of the nuclear power station, then its plumes of smoke were noticed to the south, and it then crashed even more to the south from there. The incident reminds V. Chernobrov of the Roswell crash of 1947 in the USA.

EYEWITNESS REPORTS FROM 1982

The eyewitness was L.N. Shevchenko, an engineer-geophysicist. Date: August 8, 1982. Time: 19:50 p.m. Place: on the highway Voronezh-Kursk (witnessed from a bus). 5 kilometres from the Tim settlement, approximately 500 metres away from the highway, passengers of the bus saw how a fiery pillar slowly descended into a field. The sun above and the pillar looked red-hot. The pillar was clearly visible. Its height was estimated to be 15-20 metres, and thickness some 2 metres. As it approached the ground, at the end of the pillar appeared a revolving end (corkscrew-like), and with it the pillar bored into the ground. The speed of the pillar's movement remained constant, until it disappeared from view. As the pillar descended into the ground, the passengers noticed smoke in the air. The sighting lasted about five minutes.

PROFILE: GENRIKH SILANOV

He was born in 1934, his father a professional military officer. After graduating from high school, Silanov studied in the Riga marine navigation school. Later he worked as a radio operator aboard fishing trawlers, and then was drafted into the Soviet army. There he graduated from an aviation school, and became an aircraft radio communications hardware mechanic. After his army service, he went to work and study in Siberia to be a geologist. In 1959 he was sent to the western Siberian Geological Agency to learn the spectral analysis of mineral resources, and in 1962 he was invited to Voronezh to organise the spectral laboratory; ever since he has headed it and resided in Voronezh. Mr. Silanov has been an ufologist since 1972. In those days Ufology was a banned subject and information was scarce. But 1989 changed everything in the Soviet Union, including the status of Ufology.

VORONEZH RESEARCH TODAY

The Voronezh researchers have collected a great deal of interesting material since 1985 from an anomalous zone in the vicinity of the town of Novokhopersk of the Voronezh region. Their main thrust of the research is to answer the question... why are aliens attracted to the area in particular and to our planet in general? Silanov stated in his letter to the Russian Ufology Research Centre that it is not plain curiosity that drives the aliens here, but definite interests. The answer lies in the area of the Khoper River, as it flows through the Voronezh region (180 kilometres from Voronezh, and 40 kilometres from Borisoglebsk). Where exactly was shown to Mr. Silanov and his colleagues by pilots from the nearby Borisoglebsk Aviation College. That is where they most often encountered disks, saucers, and spheres during their flights. The anomalous phenomena in this area were strikingly recalled by A. Plaksin, an important personality of the secret Soviet UFO research (we will discuss in the later chapters).

The Novokhopersk zone contains tectonic fault lines, and has provided the researchers with a wealth of anomalous phenomena. Their conclusion is that there is a plasma-like life form. There have been telepathic contacts with humans. The reason why extraterrestrials visit the area is simple: they are able to accumulate and transfer the energy of our planet. Earth is like a gigantic generator, continuously generating electrical currents. Experts call them tellurian currents (Earth in Latin is telluris). If humans could harness such energy, we could dispose of nuclear and other power stations. Our planet could be transformed forever. Somehow the aliens who visit the area of the Khper River have learned to do it. The researchers took pictures of bright, shining spheres hovering over the fault lines; there are basalt columns extending into the bowels of the Earth, some 40 kilometres. At certain times plasma-like pillar rises from the ground to a shining sphere.

Another idea promulgated by researchers is that some things happen in our world that is outside our range of knowledge. Things occur which are outside the realm of Human perceptual capabilities with us being similar to a fly on a TV screen. We can see something is happening but we cannot describe it.

The researchers claim to have discovered a way to photograph past events in time. They will soon reveal the results of their studies; the discovery will help explain such phenomena as ghosts and other similar phenomena.

Silanov has written a new book about the Voronezh anomalies. Hopefully, it will be published in the near future, as many people both in Russia and in the West await further revelations from his field research. From this we know that here is a great deal more information to come from Voronezh, information that may yet shed more light on the sightings we have mentioned above, and others that we yet know nothing about.

CHAPTER 15

THE M-TRIANGLE

In 1989 a newspaper in Riga (Sovetskaya Molodezh) published reports of expeditions to the Perm area, to study an anomalous zone that became known worldwide as the "M-triangle." Strange phenomena have been observed in the zone. Respected Russian Ufologists paid close attention to certain properties of the zone, while discounting the obvious fake reports.

Emil Bachurin, a hunter and later journalist, discovered the zone in 1984. He located it in the taiga when he chanced upon a clearing some 62 metres in diameter. He observed a strange flying object over the area shortly before his discovery. Soil analyses revealed, claimed Bachurin, presence of rare elements, characteristic of UFO landing sites.

Initially it was a journalist named Y. Belikov who published reports about the zone in a Perm youth newspaper in 1988. He went there on a solitary expedition, and reported glowing spheres, strange marks in the sand, and malfunctioning watches. UFO researchers from Leningrad decided to verify the reports after Pavel Mukhortov, a cosmonaut in training in 1991, came up with stories of "spiritual" contacts with aliens, who informed him that humans are descendants of extraterrestrial criminals, banished to Earth for a variety of sins. As a result of Mukhortov's "revelations", people from all over the USSR came to Molebka and the zone. Most reported that nothing out of place happened in the zone. "Miracles" reported from the zone turned out to be trivial events, or practical jokes perpetrated by local teenagers.

A. Baturin, of the Leningrad Commission for Anomalous Phenomena, headed a Leningrad research group in 1989. They arrived at the zone in the autumn. The zone was full of "fanatical believers" who would not permit the use of any devices or tools, as the "aliens" did not like such equipment. However, it was permissible to shoot Polaroid pictures, because the cameras would not work anyway. But they did work, as did other equipment too. Nothing was detected in the zone that is out of the ordinary. The only explanation A. Baturin could proffer regarding the glowing spheres is geological. Areas of active geological faults in the earth's crust often produce glowing phenomena: spheres, pillars, rays, objects that are mistaken for UFOs.

According to Gherman Kolchin, representatives of the Perm Anomalous Phenomena Research Group attended the 1989 Petrozavodsk International Seminar, and unanimously rejected Mukhortov's statements. Not a single fact could confirm the statement that a contact with aliens took place in the zone. They did confirm that when photographic film was developed, strange white and black spheres (not registered visually at the time of the shooting) would be seen on the prints, and that video devices would inexplicably jam.

After 1990, Emil Bachurin tried to stop the influx of people to the zone, and warned them of dire consequences.

CURIOSITY AROUSED

What did the Soviet Armed Forces think of the M-Triangle? In the heady days of the perestroika, a curious publication was available in Russian and English languages. Soviet Soldier magazine carried an article entitled Paratroopers and Ufonauts. Senior Lieutenant R. Boikov of the Order of the Red Banner Siberian Military District was the author of this article. According to him, everything that he described took place near Molebka, a village on the bend of the Sylva River on the borderline between the Sverdlovsk and Perm regions of the Russian Federation. Attracted by "hundreds of mysteries and enigmas" of the Molebka triangle, Andrei Tarnopolsky, a cadet of the Novosibirsk Military Political School, read numerous publications about the anomalous zone, and organised an expedition to study it. He became a laughing stock of the esteemed school. However, other future officers, full of zeal for discovery of paranormal phenomena, joined him. Some commanding officers also supported him, as well as a laboratory of the Institute of Clinical and experimental Medicine of the USSR. Young cadets were examined, and instructed by physicians how to operate metres and bio energy frames (dowsing rods). The expedition was supplied with rations; letters of recommendation, warm clothes, and skis. The most experienced person in the expedition was Lieutenant Colonel Nikolai Gotsalo (a senior instructor of military topography). He was a skilled taiga trekker. Five cadets were from a paratrooper company, and one, reluctantly admitted to the expedition, was from an infantry company. Altogether there were 13 people in the group.

They experienced nothing out of the ordinary in the first few days upon arrival in the M-Triangle. The dowsing rod was used extensively; and cadets studied their own feelings. Yes, they did see the bio frame tremble or rise on occasions (or even turn around its axis), and did observe approximately seven bolides.

They were surprised by the M-Triangle later, while investigating the so-called "pyramids" (heaps of stones resembling remains of a basement, arranged in a triangle). The cadets brought with them devices, such as compass; not far from the "pyramids" it stopped working. Then an unknown force forced the compass pointer against the instrument glass, and slightly bent it. Hence, decided the cadets, electromagnetic pulses were not reliable, and cannot be used. Goblin-like tricks beset young explorers; and even members of the Anomaliya club who used to hang out in the area, almost missed the "pyramids". More than once the explorers spent several hours trying to locate a site within a range of 500 metres. They came to a conclusion that an identified field exerted effect on their mind. Later, even reference points could not always help them. An abandoned dwelling, too, had a certain effect on future Soviet officers. Then there were those ubiquitous locals with their strange fairy tales. Eerie pillars of light rising up above Molebka, their point of origin somewhere in the woods; balloons of various colours, and the "black ones" had been observed there, too. When pressured, the locals would describe the "black ones" as demons.

There came a time when the young cadets began to experience certain changes within themselves. They felt totally alienated from their former lives. They lost the feeling of fatigue, and no load was too heavy for them. They could walk with astonishing ease, that is, until they began to feel apathy, as if some voice told them not to move. Vladimir Saleyev, a young paratrooper, armed with a dowsing rod, probed the abandoned dwelling. The bio frame began to rotate like a propeller when he approached the house, and something put him on alert. He tried to proceed, on his skis, when something moved one of the skis forward, leaving the paratrooper behind. He discovered that something cut the fixture of that ski as if with a sharp blade.

Then there were those "soap bubbles". Rather, "balloons" that sprang up out of thin air unexpectedly and in various places. Lt. Colonel Gotsalo put his hand through one of the "bubbles", and felt that it felt warm. After performing movements with this "balloon", Gotsalo realised that it urged him to go to the "pyramids". No pictures were taken of the phenomenon for the film was stuck and ruptured inside the camera. Even the flash would not obey. Films that were taken later would not develop properly.

The very first night young cadets began to see "animated pictures" (they had to close their eyes and turn their heads to the rocks): silhouettes, faces, masks, and flames. To their amazement, the cadets could not approach the rocks (yes, they tried to), nor could they ever come to the fallen trees close enough. Their attempts to penetrate the zone, to walk into its depths failed. On the eve of their departure the cadets made another attempt, but encountered strange balloons that apparently interfered with their movements. Those pesky balloons managed to change their colours from pale yellow to green to violet. Then the balloons disappeared, but Lt. Colonel knew that he could see it with his "second sight". So did another cadet, who knew the direction that the balloon moved to. Finally, brand new military skis suffered inexplicable damage, and the chase stopped. The cadets tried their best to find the "meadow of horrors", but the dowsing rod lost its ring, and Gotsalo got a feeling that they best go back to the base. One cadet pushed on, and was later discovered sleeping in the snow; his comrades had to push and kick him to wake him up.

Anyway, there were warm birch trees that burned the same young cadet who fell asleep trying to reach the "meadow of horrors"; strange readings of blood pressure, the strange shape of some being observed by Gotsalo next to the "pyramids". When the cadets left the area, they experienced nausea. Then it left them until they began discussing the zone in the train, on their way to the military units and the school. Some cadets felt a strong desire to leave their material things behind. Gotsalo threw away a toy he bought for his daughter, as if a voice told him to drop it. Later, when studied by medical personnel, it was discovered that Gotsalo's blood showed poor coagulation for some time to follow. Somehow it was established that telepathic abilities of the expedition members became "very high". But the cadets never did find the aliens or UFO crews.

This is a typical story about the M-Triangle, and we understand why our colleagues roar with laughter when they read similar reports.

EXPERT OPINION

One of Russia's foremost UFO researchers, Yuri Mefodiyevich Raitarovsky, mentioned in other chapters of the book, is of the opinion that the zone contains geological circular structures. There is a smaller ring inside the larger one. It is this smaller ring that is more active and emits more energy. Molebka Village is located right in the middle of the smaller circle. When he was asked by NLO magazine as to what causes the strange phenomena, Raitarovsly replied that there could be two explanations. One is the ET presence. The other is geophysical. In the area of deep faults, energy is often released and causes powerful ionisation of the atmosphere. Plasma-like clots form over such areas.

V. Psalomschikov, a respected scientist, journalist and researcher, considers Pavel Mukhortov's "discovery" of the zone and the strange events that took place there no more than a fairy tale.

Psalomschikov also analysed the photographs that Mukhortov took in the zone. As he stated in his article in ANOMALNIYE YAVLENIYA magazine (Issue 2, 1991), an amateur would make mistakenly misinterpret images on the photos. However, Mukhortov interprets his poor quality photographs as images of "energy balls", "energy thoughts", and invisible fog. And yet, Psalomschikov does not discount all of the reports that come from the zone as poorly recorded natural phenomena or fairly tales. He just wants to know why an advanced civilization would try to contact us through dubious contactees.

Ufologists in Yaroslavl (who have studied UFOs for many years, whether in the underground or in the open) laughed their hearts out when they received a report from the zone. It is too bad that such "reports" are accepted in the West as serious research.

Vladimir Ajaja published an interesting article in NLO newspaper (Issue 1, 1992). The title of it, Ot ufomanii k ufologii or from ufomania to ufology is most appropriate. He finds Mukhortov's reports about phosphorous robots to be a hilariously fake story. In 1990, in an interview to NLO publication, Ajaja, too, blamed Mukhortov for creating stories of "dark" civilization. According to Ajaja, there truly exists the Perm Anomalous zone, one of many geopathogenic zones around our planet. The force of geophysical, geochemical, and other features in the zone is so great that one can observe UFOs, feel some alien presence, and see images of strange creatures when films are developed. However, it does not mean that one encounters "dark" and "light" civilizations.

In 1995 Valery Yakimov claimed to have filmed an orange sphere. He included the shots in his documentary The Molebka Stories broadcast on Russian television.

Emil Bachurin died in February of 2009. He was a field researcher, and author (Bachurin published several books and hundreds of articles on the subject of UFOs). Together with Nikolay Subotin he investigated an alleged UFO crash in the Tien-Shen Mountains in 1998. Bachurin developed a classification system of UFO negative effects on UFO researchers. He was instrumental in promoting Molebka, and helped make it famous around the world. He had spent his last years living alone in a modest house made of wood in Molebka. Bachurin always said that he wanted to be buried in Molebka, next to the zone he considered to be anomalous...

In conclusion, it is obvious there have been no tangible discoveries in the M-Triangle. The international conference that took place in Perm in August of 1996 and its appeal to the coalition of alien observers is a sad testament to what Ufology can become when exposed to dubious "zones". However, we must always keep an open mind when investigating such claims as other such zones are reported in many different parts of the world. The answer to these zones may not lie with aliens from another world, but instead with so far unexplained geophysical forces that somehow can affect the human mind as well as the physical world that surrounds it.

CHAPTER 16

THE SASOVO EXPLOSIONS

We have researched numerous sources to find coherent details of this strange case, or rather, several cases. Among the sources we used were articles published in Dzhentry newspaper (1994), Tekhnika-Molodezhi Magazine (1992), Chetvertoye Izmereniy Newspaper (1992), Komsomol'skaya Pravda newspaper (1992), and NLO Magazine (1998). It is still a little known case outside of Russia.

THE FIRST EXPLOSION
In 1991 and 1992 two powerful explosions shook the ground in the vicinity of Sasovo, a town located 350 kilometres to the southeast of Moscow. The first explosion was more powerful, and was heard at 1:34 in the morning. It was established later that a crater formed at the site of the explosion. The diameter of the crater was approximately 30 metres; its depth was around three metres. In the middle of the crater a hill was formed, its diameter 12 metres, and height approximately 2 metres. All around the crater, covering an area up to 350 metres in distance from the explosion site, one would find huge pieces of frozen soil. The force of the explosion destroyed glass (and some frames) in windows of homes of Sasovo residents, at distances of up to twenty kilometres from the explosion site. A number of houses were damaged, and in some areas the plumbing was broken. Along Vokzalnaya Street tiles flew down from roofs, all doors were open, and furniture shifted in all dwellings. The explosion was accompanied by roaring and whistling noises. But structures closest to the explosion suffered no damage at all.

A petroleum storage facility about 650 metres from the site of the explosion sustained no damages. Neither did the electrical poles in the zone of the displaced soil. One hundred metres from the epicentre there were no broken branches on any of the trees. Destruction in Sasovo creates an impression that the shock wave actually extended to the crater, not away from it. Electrical utility poles were also bent toward the crater. Cracks in the soil, too, demonstrated that some force was pulling the edges of the crater towards its centre.

Over one hundred witnesses described two reddish spheres that flew over the oil storage facility two hours before the explosion.

People who subsequently spent some time in the crater or near it experienced temporal deceleration (their watches slowed down up to five minutes).

There are reports that actually there were no explosions, but thrusts from the ground. It was as if the first thrust came from afar toward the crater, and the second was coming from the crater. There actually was light outside, and some minutes later, after the explosion, one could see over the Sasovo area, a brightly reddish luminescence, shaped like a sphere. Later it dimmed in the distance. A cloud was observed some minutes later; it was shining from inside with white light.

The damages amounted to three million rubles. A criminal investigation was initiated, but led nowhere. A local criminal investigator, Andrei Shirokov, tried to get answers from the Moscow Institute of Court Experts and its specialists in the area of explosives and ballistics. No response to his inquiries was provided, for the Institute did not exist anymore. The Soviet Union was falling apart, and experienced investigators were out of work. Sasovo's residents were impoverished, crime in the area increased, and hopelessness became pervasive.

THE SECOND EXPLOSION

There was another strange explosion, much smaller in magnitude, on May 28, 1992. A new crater was formed, in the same field of the state farm Novy Put. A local farmer recalled some loud popping sound around 2 am that night. Apparently, someone called offices of the regional police to report yet another explosion, and an investigation ensued. The shape of the new crater is perfect, and there are no burned trees around it, and no nitrite anywhere around. It is four metres deep and thirteen metres in diameter. The soil at the bottom of the crater is very strange, as if it was compressed to be as hard as a monolith. There are no mounds or hills inside. Local office of the KGB filmed it, and the surrounding areas; the film was sent to Ryazan, and nothing was heard about it again. This time no generals arrived at the site, and no scientists arrived to take samples from the crater. Some time later a group of wandering preachers arrived in Sasovo, and announced that the crater signified the end of the world.

BEFORE THE EXPLOSIONS

Some twenty years before the explosions, soil deformation was observed in Sasovo and its vicinities. Roads were flooded, houses sunk into the soil, and small rivers were shallow. Also, strange aerial phenomena were observed in the area of the future crater: eerie luminescence, and strange fog-like clouds that seemingly landed there. In 1985, people observed a phenomenon that resembled a rocket launch. About the same time reports of UFOs, and luminescent formations began circulating, too. Sasovo was also subjected to frequent storms and tornadoes from about the same time.

Let us take a close look at the reported UFO sightings in the Sasovo area of the Ryazan region of the Russian Federation.

In April of 1985 a strange trail was left in a meadow of the Sotnitsino Village (49 metres long and 16 metres wide). According to two witnesses, a huge fiery sphere hovered in the area, at about 2 or 3 metres from the ground, projecting a bright ray, as if searching for something in the darkness. In October of 1990 two reddish spheres slowly flew over the Ribnoye settlement, and soon thereafter a hurricane followed, crushing down tree and poles.

Approximately two months before the first explosion a very strange phenomena were observed around Sasovo. Several weeks before, at approximately 3:30 pm, residents of the town observed a gigantic red wall, with a white and blue gleam, moving at the speed of a regular cloud. After the "wall" disappeared, people observed fog in its place, and had a bitter taste in their mouths. Identical "walls" were seen throughout the area that night. One or two days before the explosion, luminescent lights were observed over the area of the future crater. Most of them were observed just before the explosion. Luminous forms were observed just an hour before the explosion, and right before it, two bright blue flares were also seen. Flying luminescent spheres were reported in the neighbouring areas; they were accompanied by humming a noise. Other phenomena, associated with tectonic processes, were also reported. A local radio station reported localised problems. The Sasovo animals behaved erratically, apparently scared by something. Dogs tried to run away. Railroad workers experienced feelings of anxiety. Patients in the local hospital experienced nervousness and sleeplessness.

THE AFTERMATH

There have been several hypotheses to what caused the explosion. One stated that the explosions were caused a rare tectonic process, similar to an earthquake. The second explosion that took place at the end of June 1992, nine kilometres away from the site of the first one, confirmed the tectonic explanation as the cause of mysterious explosions.

Another hypothesis blamed an air crash for the explosion. There were three metallic fragments found next to the crater. They resembled fragments of an artillery shell. A strange oily fuel splashed two houses in Sasovo. There are military airports in the region, and one civilian, too. But local military authorities categorically denied any connection to the explosion.

Other hypotheses included electromagnetic radiation focused on the area through a phenomenon known as caustics; powerful energy emanating from the bowels of the Earth as the causing factor; methane or propane explosion; even nitrate that was lying around the fields in sacks.

In 1992 the crater did not look as it did after the explosion. A small lake formed at the bottom of the crater, and a garbage dump right outside the crater.

To find answers about the nature of the explosions special commissions arrived from Moscow. Experts from several important institutes tried to help solve the mystery. Volunteers from throughout the Russian Federation tried to help find answers, all to no avail. We are still no closer to the answer although years have passed, and Russia has undergone tremendous changes. Could it be like the M-Zone that again unknown geophysical forces are at work in the area? Not only did they produce the optical and psychological effects on humans, but on two occasions actually caused explosions as well. As yet we do not have a definite answer but such unknown forces are considered the most likely explanation.

CHAPTER 17

THE STAVROPOL WINDOW AREA

The city of Stavropol, founded in 1777, is the administrative centre of the North Caucasus Region of southern Russia, and the hometown of Mikhail Gorbachev. It has a rich history of UFO sightings.

IN THE DAYS OF YORE

There is a very fascinating report of strange beings that landed in the Stavropol region long ago. How long ago and who were those mysterious beings? We located two publications that deal with this alleged incident. One was an article written by Andrey Leshukonsky, and published in NLO Magazine (1998). Another article, written by Valery Kukushkin, was published in Anomaliya newspaper, Issue 15, 2000.

The alleged incident in Stavropol goes something like this. In 1957, a letter arrived at the Pulkovsky Observatory, addressed to Professor Mikhailov. The author of the letter reported a story told to her by a person, whose father lived in the Stavropol Province (guberniya, and administrative designation that is translated as province; used in the Czarist times). An unidentified craft flew in and landed in a village where the father resided. Three swarthy and naked men exited, breathing with difficulty. They gestured, trying to show s omething to the villagers. Then the visitors died, because they could not breathe our air. Their craft was taken apart by villagers. Professor Mihailov did not pursue it further, considering it either a hoax, or perhaps, a report of a hot-air balloon landing. In 1960 a correspondent of Yuni Tekhnik magazine discovered this letter. He decided to conduct his own investigation and discovered some interesting facts, and published an article about them. First, he contacted the person who wrote the letter to Professor Mihailov. Olga Vasilyevna Maslennikova had passed away by then, but her daughter replied that the letter from Yuni Tekhnik was forwarded to the son of the person whose father told the story. The name was Mitrofan V. Karpenko. The latter was located, and he did reply to the magazine's inquiry. His father was born in 1861. Karpenko did not remember much except that there were three beings in an unusual craft that landed in the village. They were naked, could breathe with great difficulty, and perished three days later.

The magazine stopped its investigation. Twenty-five years later a letter arrived in the Anomalous Phenomena Commission in Moscow. A resident of Moscow, Irina F. Danilova, was the letter's writer. Her grandfather, Afanasy N. Pugach, who was born in Stavropol Guberniya, told Irina of strange visitors who arrived in their large Cossack village at the end of XIX century. The strangers arrived in a craft that was shaped like an arrowhead of large dimensions. There were three of them, all of whom were described as dark-skinned people. A. Pugach said that they were probably ill, because they could not breathe well. Locals did not approach them, afraid to catch a disease. But they did provide the strangers with water and food; the latter of which went uneaten. Soon thereafter the strangers died, and were buried without any religious ceremony. Local authorities did not make any reports, for they were afraid that there would be an investigation, and local residents could be accused of causing the death of dark-skinned strangers.

Their flying vehicle had many parts made from some metal that resembled silver. The Cossacks took the craft apart, and used that metal to make dishes and samovars.

Were the strangers Hindus or aliens from outer space? It was possible for Hindus to travel to Russia over mountains at an altitude of seven kilometres. If a human being quickly ascends to such altitude, he would die from the Caisson disease. Perhaps, such a craft could be captured by an ascending trail of a powerful storm cloud, and carried away to a distance of thousands of kilometres.

Apparently one of the residents of that Cossack village did send some parts from the craft to the Saint Petersburg Academy of Sciences. The Russo-Japanese war had begun, and no one answered the inquiry. Could it be that the archives of the Academy still have mysterious remnants of the craft that landed in the Stavropol Guberniya?

When did it arrive precisely? Kukushkin calculated that it had to be between 1830 and 1850. Apparently the craft did not have an engine, and used no fuel. Thus air currents apparently moved it. There were no airplanes, helicopters, of dirigibles at the time. It was not an air balloon, too. Then, it had to be a parachute that came from an air balloon. There were already such air balloons with parachutes in the time period outlined by Kukushkin. To fly at great heights one would need to have oxygen. There were oxygen balloons made from alloys that could resemble silver. Oxygen balloons could have been easily used to make dishes or samovars. The nakedness of the visitors could have been explained by tight-fitting costumes.

History did not leave us information about any flights of air balloons that could shed light on the visitors to Stavropol. Was it a secret military mission? Kukushkin researched international situation in the world at the time.

The British Empire was trying to organise world powers to stop Egyptian expansion (1830-1840). After the Turkish defeat in Syria by Egyptian forces the situation exacerbated, for Russia was an ally of the Ottoman Empire. The conflict could have become deadly, but an alliance put together by England prevented a war. Kukushkin is of the opinion that Egyptians, in 1939, were spying on the Turks, and that their air balloon was caught up in the stream that carried them over the territory of Russia. They ascend further, lose their oxygen supplies, and become ill. They have to use a parachute and land in the Cossack village.

There are still questions, and one of them is the most important: did Egyptians possess such apparatus in 1839? And does Valery Kukushkin correctly point out the right time period?

SDI

American magazine Citizens Against UFO Secrecy (CAUS) published an interesting bit of information in its December 1993 issue. It reported that the Department of State released a cable making a remarkable claim. The message (dated June 30, 1987) reads as follows:

> *"(Deleted) reports that Soviet authorities have constructed an SDI research station near the Radio-Physics Institute in the area of Stavropol. The research station apparently is focusing its work on electromagnetic methods of shooting down satellites. When tests are run, scientists working at the Radio Physics Institute can detect the resulting microwaves. Perhaps of equal interest is that this area has the largest number of UFO sightings in the USSR. A phenomenon which our contact says is due to the various SDI experiments conducted there."*

The State Department's source does not elaborate on the nature of technology the Soviets had been using for the "electromagnetic methods". Subsequently, the Soviets developed more "star wars" weapons, and tested them. How did they get the know-how?

In his interview with Vladimir Lagovsky, a well-known Soviet (now Russian) researcher Anatoly Listratov mentioned that Soviet researchers of anomalous phenomena knew that the American SDI had used ET technology for their projects. Apparently, the Soviet military had acquired something equally amazing and powerful, after the Omsk Incident, and begun to use it.

But the Omsk Incident was debunked in the recent years...

Stroganov points to the Monchegorsk Object as a "catch" of the SETKA-MO, and a possible application of the captured technology by Soviet military.

Curiously, after the downfall of the USSR, many of the former Soviet SDI scientists were invited to the United States to continue their research and work.

SUMMER OF 1967

This sighting took place in 1967, in the beginning of August. Friends told the eyewitness that there were UFO observations in the preceding two days. An unusual radiant object looking like a "young moon" was flying over the area. The object moved with its convex portion forward and with its "horns" to the rear. It flew past at around 10:00 pm nightly. The eyewitness, V. S. Zuyev, reported that the UFO did fly the same evening, and he was able to observe its features. Its flares were directed parallel to its movement. The angular dimensions of the object were approximately equal to the angular dimensions of the move. No sounds could be heard that would be associated with the flight.

A barely noticeable "star" moved in front of the object. There were other such "stars", and the eyewitness assumed they were satellites with no relationship to the object. Just as on the preceding days, the object flew from southwest to northeast. Its motion was uniform and rectilinear.

This report came from UFO Sightings over the USSR-1968 (Volume 1), published by Joint USA-CIS Aerial Anomalies Federation in 1993.

Copies of Dr. Zigel's books may be obtained from The Joint USA-CIS Aerial Anomaly Foundation, P.O. Box 880, Los Altos, California 94023-0880.

There was another interesting Stavropol sighting reported in the same book. The date of the report was July 18, 1967, the time 2:45 pm. P.T. Naumenko and his family observed a small bright red band in the sky, approximately 20 degrees east of the settlement Dazhus, in the direction of the Pole Star and at the level of the Pole Star. White bands appeared from the upper portion (and inclined to the east) and grew into a dome-shaped umbrella with an opening inside; the whole process lasted 15 minutes. Stars could be clearly seen through this opening, and this white dome covered the stars. The dome spread out very rapidly and its colour changed sharply to a weak light milky colour. By 3:15 pm the object completely dissipated, and the red band expanded into a large cloud, actually light red in colour.

"RAINBOW OF 1985"

This report comes from a catalogue of reports from UFO eyewitnesses, sent to the Soviet Academy of Sciences (between 1978 through 1992). The Academy received more than 1000 reports, and only 50 were included in the catalogue. We will not analyse why such a small number of reports were included, and whether the criterion used by Soviet Academy of sciences was justified. We do not know if the KGB was looking through the reports; we do not know if Soviet intelligence or other agencies were studying those initial reports. This catalogue was sent to Philip Mantle, and we are grateful that we have even the 50 reports to research.

The date of the report is September 10, 1985, Stavropol region. Actually, there were three reports. Eyewitnesses saw a "rainbow" shaped as concentric circles. It looked like an open umbrella. In the right portion it was possible to observe a small formation of a darker colour. This "rainbow" had an "aura" of diffused light; its borders along the periphery were outlined by a brighter luminescence. As the rainbow approached, the streetlight turned off. The phenomenon turned east along a high voltage electrical line, then to the northeast, and as it departed, the intensity of its luminescence attenuated until it disappeared. The streetlight then turned on again. The phenomenon lasted from 7 to 10 minutes.

Another report described a dome-shaped cloud, of a milky-bluish colour. Ascending upwards, the cloud assumed the shape of a "saucer", its base had rims of dark-violet colour (outside), and blue and turquoise colours. Then the "saucer" dissipated, becoming diffused, but the violet rim continued to outline the shapeless mass. One could see stars soon thereafter through it. The violet rim became an arc, and resembled a rainbow. Then, in place of the "saucer" as if appearing from nowhere, there remained a mass shaped as a "ball of threads". Its colour was initially bright blue, and then turquoise, finally becoming green. Finally it disappeared. Several individuals observed the same phenomenon. The third report, from observers in Stavropol, more or less confirmed the other two. A TV set was reported to experience unusual sounds.

The Soviet Academy of Sciences explained the sightings as a consequence of experiments to create artificial clouds in the upper levels of the atmosphere.

MAGAZALA ENDREEV

In July of 1994 Valery Uvarov, Director of the International Information Centre of UFO Investigation had a very interesting conversation with Magazala Endreev. This gentleman was First Deputy Minister of Internal Affairs, Kabarda-Balkarian Republic of Russian Federation. A number of sightings were discussed. One sighting, reported by Lieutenant Beslan Shogenov of the Regional Department of Internal Affairs, took place on February 13, 1989. At 21:30 he noticed an object (a spacecraft, as he described it), falling from the sky. He thought initially that the object was a burning passenger airplane about to crash. Shogenov estimates he was two kilometres from the object. It flew straight to the Chegem Forest. Shogenov recalls that the object was ten times as big as any passenger jet. It had a pointed nose, a tail, and very short wings. Sparks were emitted, resembling an electrical welding unit. The sparks lit up the wings or whatever resembled the wings. The tail was engulfed in a bundle of fire. It seemed to the eyewitness that some people were firing flares. He was most impressed by windows of the mysterious craft: large, as if covering the entire side of the "spacecraft". The windows were brightly lit up. He counted ten windows. No people were visible through them. The silence was frightening. When the craft flew to the forest, it hovered there, and disappeared in a few seconds. The lights went out, as if dissolved into thin air. The sighting lasted 5 or 6 minutes.

Other accounts established that the strange craft was about 159 metres long. Its diameter was approximately 40 metres. And it flew near the border of Stavropol.

The Deputy Minister informed Uvarov that on Monday, February 13, 1989, no planes crashes were reported in the Kabardino-Balkarian Republic. No asteroids or meteorites were found. The police contacted their colleagues in neighbouring republics of the Russian Federation. And they were informed that a "super dirigible" turned on its lights again near Primalkinkij. It flew in the direction of Chechnya and Dagestan. Soon thereafter the UFO flew away toward Astrakhan.

There were supporting observations of a huge object in the sky that February night. None of those who observed it, police personnel and civilians, doubted the reality of what they saw.

SIGHTINGS OF 1991

This report was published in Chetvertoye Izmereniye Newspaper (Issue 8, 1991). On May 24, 1991, A. Vishnyakov, general director of a local transportation company, was in the Stavropol region. In the evening he looked outside the window of his hotel in the town of Budyonovsk and observed unusual spheres in the sky, falling down at great speed. They had plasma-like colour, each one with a small "tail".

There were small five spheres and one large. He called his colleagues, and all of them observed that the spheres formed one line, and an unusual flying apparatus appeared before their eyes. The object consisted of gigantic "humps" of steely colour, and in the middle of it they could clearly see a cylinder. Its nozzle was huge, as determined by eyewitnesses, and a three-story building could fit inside it. In the middle of this nozzle was a small whitish spot, something like a conical lamp. The object was truly huge, its width as that of a soccer field, but the height was smaller; hence, it resembled a rhombus. The phenomenon lasted for a minute, and then disappeared over the horizon. Its flight was noiseless. It descended toward Elista.

Budyonovsk was an area of a bloody terrorist attack during the first Chechen war in the 1990s. In the early 1990s, when the area was still peaceful, there were other sightings. Soviet newspaper Sovetskoye Prikumye published reports of similar sightings as described by Vishnyakov. A report about an unusual aircraft landing in the area also was described in the same newspaper. At least, those who described unusual circles in the local fields think so. There were no actual eyewitnesses of any landings, but the circles and rectangles. But people in the Kirov region circulated rumours about it. Somewhat more definite reports came from residents of Stavropol called the newspaper and reported a UFO that landed 16 kilometres from Stavropol, in the direction of the airport. All those who called indicated May 24 as the date of the landing. What was the object observed in the Stavropol region that day in May?

STAVROPOL'S SECURITY COUNCIL

Years went by, and the newspaper we knew as Chetvortoye Izmereniye became Chetvortoye Izmereniye I NLO. We have quoted its articles throughout this book. The newspaper's Issue 6 (2000) contained a new report about Stavropol. The gist of it was that aliens probably landed in the area to take soil samples. There were four circles discovered in the neighbouring fields; they appeared during the night of June 12 to 13. The circles were of precise shape, and the one in the centre had a diameter of 20 metres. Representatives of the region's Security Council and special services arrived on the site. The area became off limits.

Experts, who researched the phenomenon, established that the area was not subjected to any radiation or chemical influence. But it was not a product of human activity, either. Also, there were witnesses in the neighbouring village that observed landing of an unidentified object. Vasily Bel'chenko of the Stavropol Security Council commented that it was definitely a landing of an unidentified object. It involved a strange principle of landing, like that of a vortex. Those who saw the landing reported that it landed and took off instantaneously. If it was a craft that landed, its diameter was no less than 200 metres. Perhaps its mission was to take soil samples. Right in the centre of the large circle they found a hole of a cylindrical shape, 30 centimetres deep, with polished sides.

Why is it that certain geographical areas seem to have a concentration of UFO sightings? These are often called 'window areas'. It could well be that Stavropol is one of these areas. In Ufology there are many other such areas around the world, the Pennine Hills of England, the Hessdalen valley of Norway, to name but two. Researchers have tried in vain to explain such concentrations of UFO sighting in these window areas and there are a variety of theories to suit. In these areas all kinds of unusual happenings seem to take place with an abundance of UFO sightings high up on the list. Mythology and folklore also play a large part in such areas and many a strange story arises from them not unlike the story featured at the beginning of this chapter of the three dark-skinned naked aliens landing and dying three days later. Stories of trolls, faeries, demons and much more also arise. For researchers such window areas provide ample material for further investigation and it is our belief that Stavropol will do the same.

CHAPTER 18

THE TALLIN OBJECT

Nikolay Nikolayevich Sochevanov died in 1996. He was an Academic of the Russian Academy of Science and Culture, an expert in geology and mineralogy. He was also senior researcher of dowsing. It is due to his efforts that we have come to learn what we know about the Tallin Object.

Back in 1984, a visitor from Estonia came to Moscow. An inventor and a long-time acquaintance of Sochevanov, he brought along a piece of some dense silvery material, and some amazing facts along with it. Back in the mid 1960's Virgo Mitt, who lived in a settlement near Tallin, was digging a well in his backyard. At a depth of approximately three metres, diggers encountered a metallic obstacle. The object was very solid, and after further excavation, the edge of a plate was located. That plate's edge pierced the well's shaft a little. The thickness of the plate (at the location) was no more than two centimetres. Yet still the drill could not penetrate the metal. A compressor had to be brought to the site. Using a pneumatic pick hammer, the workers were able to break off a piece from a protruding edge.

The piece was delivered to Tallin, where two scientific research institutes came up with very contradictory results. One institute claimed that the piece was an alloy of complex composition, while scientists at the other institute claimed it was made of plain cast iron.

The Estonians asked Sochevanov to organise a program to analyse the acquired sample of the object in top Moscow laboratories. The sample was cut into several thin plates using diamond saws. During the process, two of the saws were apparently broken because of the sample's super-solid state. The sample was determined to have a micro solidity, which varied from 330 to 1500 kg/mm, according to the All Union Institute of Aviation Materials, or Vsesoyuzniy Institute Aviatsionikh Materialov (VIAM).

The sample looked like dense metal of silvery colour. The plates cut from the sample had been analysed at the Moscow Institute of Engineering Physics; at the All Union Institute of Mineral Raw Materials; the VIAM, and several other laboratories. According to Sochevanov, leading Soviet scientists did not doubt the object's extraterrestrial origin (e.g., Professor Mitin, Russia's leading expert on powder metallurgy). Academic Kishkin, after seeing the VIAM's results, stated that he knew of no similar alloys in any application for aviation technology. The alloy of this type must be very heat-resistant, and possess the right resistance in boiling mixture of acids of any concentrations.

Kishkin also told Sochevanov that neither top Soviet labs, nor those in the U.S., Japan, or Germany could produce such alloys. The alloy was subjected to a most thorough testing process in Moscow's labs. The scientists do agree on one point - the material is neither of terrestrial origin, nor is it from a meteorite.

Furthermore, regular researchers at the labs were not informed of the details of the sample; only the leading scientists knew the whole story.

Sochevanov became very interested in the matter after obtaining the first test results, and left Moscow for Estonia. There, using his dowsing techniques, he came up with some answers. There is definitely some object in the ground. The object produces a powerful anomalous zone. The object is approximately 15 metres in diameter and weighs about 200 tons. Most likely, the object is a disk; it narrows toward the edges. In its central section, the object's height reaches four metres. The main body of the object lies in the ground horizontally at a 35-degree angle; one third of the object lies in the ground under the house. Its closest location to the surface is from three to four metres deep; the farthest is 15 metres.

Sochevanov collected results of the analyses, and along with his personal conclusions, sent them on to the Military-Industrial Commission of the Council of Ministers of the U.S.S.R. There, the attitude to the paperwork received was serious: a ban on all related publications was put in force, and a more detailed report was requested. According to Sochevanov, a detailed report was sent to the Academy of Sciences, U.S.S.R. (was that "detailed report" the one requested by the Council of Ministers, and if so, was it sent to the Academy of Sciences by the council, or by Sochevanov?).

From there, the report "descended" to the Geological Institute of Estonia. An order to excavate the object was issued, by whom, it was not disclosed, but no funds were allocated. A year had gone by, and no work had been done.

Then, a local business entity did try to dig out the object. Sochevanov described their efforts as clumsy and misdirected. As a result of the attempt, the house was demolished, the plot destroyed; those in charge refused to use Sochevanov's plan; the upshot is that nothing was retrieved. Local geologists did not want excavations, but made boreholes in the wrong direction. However, several unnamed experts did conduct studies of the site using scientific apparatuses and devices. The results obtained confirm Sochevanov's conclusions. Nobody has ever used the latter findings.

Sochevanov dispelled persistent rumours about the mysterious object.

According to him, the only people to die in connection with the whole matter were the owner of the house (who had been ill for a long time) and an assistant director of the Geological Institute (whose death had nothing whatsoever to do with excavations).

Academic Sochevanov was certain that the alloy could be very promising, if recovered and used in industrial production. But Estonia is impoverished, and few in the West know about the object.

Is some extraterrestrial craft imprisoned by Estonia's soil? Could it instead be a legacy of the end of the USSR and some sinister, yet human artifact, is buried there? The Tallin object has caused a great deal of controversy within Russian Ufology and it is sure to do so for many years to come.

CHAPTER 19

UFOs OVER SOVIET NUCLEAR INSTALLATIONS

Reports of UFOs flying over nuclear installations in the territory previously known as the USSR were relatively common. Such UFOs had vexed the Soviet military, and prompted numerous warning of impending attacks, jet plane chases and general irritation.

A very informative article mentioned a number of episodes of the interaction between UFOs and the Soviet military. Written by journalist and Ufologist Vladimir Lagovsky, the article quotes experienced Russian Ufologist Anatoly Listratov, who conducted a study on the Soviet military and UFOs (UFOs: The Uninvited Guests? It was published in the Molodaya Gvardia digest entitled 'RIDDLES OF THE CELESTIAL ISLANDS', Moscow, 1990).

The Soviet High Command had issued an order to stop shooting at UFOs. Instead the Soviet military was instructed to leave such uninvited guests well alone. Whatever the aims of the UFOs observed over military installations, "they" had shown themselves to be quite peaceful. The subsequent military order regarding these objects could be summed up as follows: There must be no reaction to letayuschiye tarelki (Russian term for "flying saucers"). Let them spy. "They" do not cause any harm unless they are antagonised (by local military responses).

In 1973 a noted Russian Ufologist Vladimir Avinsky was informed of an incident at the Institute for Nuclear Research. The incident involved a UFO. The Institute was located in Dubna, USSR, and scientists who had observed the UFO later told Avinsky what had happened.

The UFO appeared at night, over the most secret installation in Dubna, and hovered there for several hours. The General in charge panicked, and informed Moscow that a metallic apparatus of unknown origin remained immobile in the air over the main building of the centre. He demanded instructions. Moscow replied that "those who are authorised" know what to do, and control the situation. Yet the scientists realised that Moscow controlled nothing in this situation. Rather, the UFO (an alien probe, they theorised) controlled everything. At the time the Soviets conducted the Phasotron space testing there, and the unidentified object was apparently taking an interest. Couriers were sent to Moscow with all photographs and documents made with regards to this UFO event.

There was another UFO incident at a major nuclear centre, which was located in the Volga region: the scientific research institute of atomic reactors in Dimitrovgrad. In the summer of 1991 UFOs appeared over the institute. Some were reported to have descended over the institute. Local residents assured S. Borisov, who collected UFO data for the Institute's newspaper, that such "flying saucers" were frequent visitors of the Brigadirovka area. There was an interesting case of UFOs trying to "net" an automobile with a scientist inside it in 1991. The objects were bright spheres that multiplied into smaller spheres, rotating around, and extending rays to each other, combining into a net. The driver fainted as he opened the car's door. There were independent eyewitnesses who reported a silvery sphere over the area at the time.

The same summer two witnesses reported a UFO sighting: a giant yellow sphere. It hovered over a strange construction that had blinking lights. To the right, another orange-coloured sphere emitted a powerful ray of light. The luminescence was thick, would not diffuse, and inside it was a visible spiral. Along the spirals "pyramids" moved toward the soil. No noise came from the objects. The disk moved right and left. The witnesses observed everything from a distance of 50 metres for some 15 minutes.

Similar UFOs, like the ones observed in the area of Dimitrovgrad, lowered transparent pyramid-shaped objects to the ground in other parts of the USSR. When researchers tried to grab them, the pyramids vibrated and "dug" into the ground, vanishing from sight. Avinsky is of the opinion that such pyramids are devices to deactivate radioactive isotopes in the soil and underlying water. Also, the extraterrestrials may be using such devices to "correct" ecosystems after mankind's nuclear experiments.

Numerous reports in the Russian media mentioned UFOs over the Semipalatinsk area nuclear testing range, and the Novaya Zemlya Island nuclear testing zone. The UFOs were apparently observed there, as a rule, after almost every nuclear test.

Valery Kratokhvil, a Ukrainian UFO researcher and writer, a member of Felix Zigel's research group since 1972, has collected reports on UFOs over Soviet nuclear facilities. His information about Chernobyl will be discussed later. In 1992 Krahotvil published his book UFOs: visitors from the future (Minsk, Byelorussia).

In September of 1988 two objects were observed over the Kiev Nuclear Research Institute's nuclear reactor. The UFOs were bright fiery spheres of approximately 8 metres in diameter. Bright raspberry-coloured rays were emitted from the objects. Almost identical UFOs had been observed over Chernobyl in 1986.

More recently, UFOs have been sighted over a very secret Russian site. It is one of the Russian "Atomic Cities", Sarov, formerly known as Arzamas-16. Numerous buildings and plants of the Federal Nuclear centre are located there. Since 1995, UFOs have been hovering over this secret Russian city. Mikhail Gershtein has collected a number of reports about such cases, and published them in Anomaliya newspaper, Issue 1, 2000.

Back in 1983, a UFO was sighted over the Armenian nuclear power station. It appeared the very same day that a possible breakdown loomed over the station (the cooling system was shut off through unforeseen circumstances). This was reported in Izvestiya newspaper on October 27, 1994.

Again we must ask ourselves what these mysterious things we call UFOs actually are. Are they indeed spacecraft from another world, and if so, are they taking a close interest in mankind's nuclear power and atomic weapons. Similar if not identical reports have also been made over nuclear sites in the USA and the UK. If they are not alien spacecraft then could these mysterious aerial visions be a bi-product of the nuclear industry? As yet UFO researchers around the world hotly debate these and many other questions. One thing we can be sure of is that UFO's, whatever they may be, have hovered and flown over Soviet nuclear power plants and bases, and the Soviet authorities were more than just mildly concerned about them.

CHAPTER 20

UFOs AND BOREHOLES

Alexander Lukyanets, a Russian naval officer, was quite an ardent UFO researcher in the early 1990s. He was stationed in the Far East, and published interesting articles in Dzhentry newspaper. Issue 9, 1993, contained his laudable research of UFOs and boreholes.

In 1992 Lukyanets discovered unusual boreholes in the area of environmental contamination (radioactive in nature) in the vicinity of Chamzha Bay. The boreholes were drilled in the ground, and were obviously fresh, for he knew for sure that since 1985 there was no drilling performed in the area.

Furthermore, Lukyanets was impressed by the fact that the drilling was performed with a definitely meaningless choice of location; and, finally, there was no soil anywhere that could be associated with the drilling. He tried to measure the hole through the use of a three-metre long rod, but could not reach the bottom. Then Lukyanets threw pebbles and found out that he could not hear them reaching the bottom.

One such borehole was drilled in the dirt road, right in the gauge, and not in the roadside, or the in the space between the gauges. That is, whoever did the drilling did not use common sense. The hole was 25 to 30 centimetres in diameter. The second borehole was located at a distance from the road, in the field, and was identical to the first one. There were no traces from an oilrig, no automobile tracks, and no sighs of anything like supports. And no soil present anywhere next to the borehole, although no matter how one drilled a hole, there must have been some soil associated with the drilling.

Lukyanets returned to the same location nine months later, in June of 1993. The first borehole was still visible. The second one presented an enigma of sorts. It was covered by a small mound that consisted of soil that was not present anywhere else in the area. There were no traces of any vehicle that could have delivered the soil to the borehole. There was not that much soil, too, perhaps four sacks of it. Right next to the tiny mound one could see small trees, undamaged in any way. They would have to be damaged either by an oilrig, or a vehicle that would have delivered the soil.

Lukyanets was not able to take a clear picture of the area: when developed, the photograph showed a strange inadvertent exposure, like black commas.

Then Lukyanets decided to search the nearby area, to find something to help him explain strange boreholes. Instead, he found yet another borehole, the strangest of all.

This borehole was drilled straight through a boulder. Its diameter was 20 centimetres. Under the boulder, as Lukyanets was able to determine, the borehole crumbled. He had a measuring device with him, and that enabled him to see that the tape would descend into the borehole approximately half a metre below the base of the boulder. Lukynets found a stick, and with it he could determine: thirty centimetres below his first measured distance, there was soil, more crumbly than the soil next to the boulder. Who would want to mount an oilrig there, or even drill through boulders?

Lukyanets collected more information, and learned that in 1992, early spring, some people did observe a UFO that hovered in the area. There were eyewitnesses who saw that the UFO actually drilled there. He decided to find those who happened to observe this phenomenon. They were workers from the shipbuilding plant, and the UFO was observed in the evening. There were other reports of alleged UFO drilling cases, but we feel that A. Lukyanets is a most qualified researcher to discuss the phenomenon.

Although UFO's have left marks on the ground after landing in many other parts of the world, and indeed in the former USSR, these boreholes seem peculiar to Soviet Union. UFO's have reportedly been observed doing many things including taking water from lakes, taking electricity from power lines, but as far as we can ascertain it is only in the former USSR that they have been reported as drilling apparently useless boreholes for purposes which, like the UFO itself, remain unidentified.

CHAPTER 21

BELGIAN TRIANGLES OVER RUSSIA

We have collected some of the numerous reports of strange triangular UFOs over the USSR. Obviously, Belgium is not the only place where the phenomenon has been observed (there was a huge "flap" of sightings over Belgium in 1989/90 of triangular shaped UFOs).

June 1982, Volgograd region. Vadim Chernobrov and a number of other witnesses observed a triangular UFO. It was an object with bright red lights that increased in intensity during its vertical movement. The sighting lasted 15 minutes. All of the observers were amazed.

August 1987, Sevastopol. Several people on the 11th of the month sighted a triangular object. It consisted of three lights, laid out in the shape of a triangle. The illumination was yellowish around the perimetre, and of bright white colour inside. The lights shined evenly, clearly, and coldly. The object hovered and moved for three hours over the city. Its trajectory changes unpredictably; the object would disappear and appear. Smaller objects would separate from the object (they looked like capsules). They would disappear at great speed. Then the object moved away from the shore, at an incredible speed, increasing instantaneously. People watching the phenomenon were afraid that it would crush them, but the object stopped dead, and in a short while moved in another direction at the same incredible speed.

1988-1990 Triangle-shaped UFOs had been observed over Moscow, St. Petersburg (Leningrad), Zvedny City, Samara, Perm, Odessa, Nalchik, Astrakhan, Saratov, and Volgograd.

Wherever observed, the triangular UFOs were busy observing airplane flights, spaceship and ballistic missiles launches, and activities at the nuclear power stations. Soviet observers saw them over military sites, naval installations, and submarine bases. The main attraction areas had been centres of science, rocket launches, and Soviet Space Forces: Arzamas-16, Moscow, Kaliningrad, Baikonur, Plesetsk, Kapustin Yar, and Samara.

April 10, 1990. Abakan, Siberia. A triangle-shaped object flew over the city, and then turned back. It was observed for 10 minutes. The object had bright white lights and a strange blinking portion. When the object descended, its lights turned red, and then another white illumination joined in. The object was an isosceles triangle with lights around its frame, and dark on the inside. When the UFO turned around, another but smaller frame lit up next to the red one.

June 20, 1990. An expedition of the SAKKUFON research organisation was on its way to the Tien-Shen Mountains, on the Sino-Soviet border. It was comprised of scientists, military personnel, civilians, KGB officers, and Ufologists. Two eyewitnesses, members of the expedition, observed a triangular UFO the Issik-Kul Lake. The object moved at a low-altitude, turned around, and vanished. The UFO had bright luminescent lights. Its altitude was about 20 metres. Later it flew over the main group of the expedition.

July 17, 1990. Sayanogorsk, Siberia. An eyewitness observed a UFO with the help of binoculars. He saw a cone-shaped object, white, and illuminated "from inside". Several people observed for the UFO over an hour. Some of its parts were of different coloured hues. The object remained motionless, and hovered at the same altitude.

July 24, 1992. Dagestan, Izberbash. A giant object flew over the area at night. The shape of UFO was that of an isosceles triangle. The silvery phosphorous lights along the edges emitted cold luminescence. The object was absolutely noiseless and moved slowly. In a distance another object followed: a glowing sphere (as if connected by a "tail").

These are just a few reports of these triangular shaped UFOs. Of course they have been reported in many other parts of the world as well. Like a lot of UFO research the origin of these objects remains a topic of debate, but there seems to be a growing number of UFO researchers who have speculated that these triangular shaped objects are not alien spacecraft, but man-made secret military hardware. Many such sightings were made before the USA unveiled in Stealth aircraft (triangular in shape). Could it be that the USSR too has been developing such secret military aircraft of a triangular shape, but, unlike the Americans, they have not yet rolled them out on the tarmac for the rest of the world to see?

CHAPTER 22

CHRONICLE OF SOVIET UFO RESEARCH

Throughout this book we have presented fragments of the pre-Soviet, post-Soviet, and past-Soviet UFO phenomenon and anomalous research history. We realise that due to tremendous changes in Russia and surrounding countries during the 20th century, huge amounts of data and documents have been forever lost. Still many more have been kept in secret archives of Russian government and various intelligence agencies, both in Russia and overseas. Some documents have been sold to private collectors, for there is a thriving trade in UFO artifacts, as Nikolay Subbotin has informed us. Some Western television programming production companies were able to purchase Soviet UFO-phenomenon related footage that has not been completely analysed by independent researchers.

In this chapter we want to present a chronicle of Soviet UFO research. Some of the information presented here has been discussed in detail in other chapters of this book. This chapter can serve as a reference base for those who need to look up some aspects of Soviet research quickly. We believe that a timeline of the rather fragmented and butchered history of the UFO phenomenon in the former USSR needs to be systematised. To accomplish this task, we have researched published works of Y. Platov and B. Sokolov, V. Rubtsov, N. Glazkova and V. Landa, M. Gershtein, V. Ajaja, Y. Kolchin, F. Zigel, V. Smirnov, A. Kuzovkin, A. Semyonov, L. Chulkov, and V. Golikov. Among them are former military officers, scientists-debunkers, scientists who have researched UFOs and support the ET hypothesis, historians, and people of other professions.

1946 - Soviet science fiction writer and war veteran A. Kazantsev and astronomer F. Zigel begin their summer lectures (and a literally stage play,) about the Tunguska Phenomenon. Tempestuous scientific discussions ensue.

1956 Y - Fomin, senior instructor at the Food Institute, collects information about foreign UFO literature. He posts bulletins in the Institute, to apprise his students.

The same year V. Fomenko, one of Russia's leading Ufologists in the years to come, observed a gigantic cigar-shaped UFO over a secret testing range in Krasnoarmeysk, near Moscow. The object hovered over the sight for two and a half hours, at the altitude of 100 kilometres. There were other witnesses, too. Fomenko was able to measure the altitude. The object was about a kilometre in length, and approximately 100 metres in diameter.

1958 - Feliks Zigel, assistant professor at the Moscow Aviation Institute and a group of enthusiasts start UFO phenomenon study in the USSR.

1959 - V. Makarov and V. Gulikov, engineers, join Y. Fomin in his efforts. All three read lectures in 1960 and 1961 about "flying saucers".

1960 - Doctor of Physics and Mathematics, M. M. Agrest published an article about ancient astronauts, and described his hypothesis about "sons of gods", based on a careful study of ancient myths and legends, geological data, and archaeological findings. Soviet astrophysicist Iosif Shklovsky supported his views, and carried them even further. Carl Sagan and Shklovsky collaborated, and it is quite possible that the latter's ideas were in part responsible for the Phobos project. Another Soviet scientist V.K. Zaitsev conducted lectures and published articles about ancient astronauts.

1961 - On January 8, 1961, Pravda newspaper publishes a now famous article of Academician L. Artsimovich (Mif o letayuschikh tarelkah or Flying saucer myth). It has defined Soviet academic view of the UFO issue. Because of this and other publications Y. Fomin was expelled from membership in dissemination of scientific and political knowledge societies. Fomin abandoned active research.

1962 - Dr. Donald H. Menzel's book Flying Saucers (where he negates such phenomenon, and attributes all UFO observations to optical illusions) is published in the Soviet Union, and creates a stir.

1967 - In November of 1967 Professor Zigel, Air Force General Stolyarov, and Arctic pilot-navigator Akkuratov were given an opportunity to express their views on Soviet national television. Soviet People throughout the huge land viewed the program. Eyewitness reports, drawings of observed UFOs, photographs and data were sent to the address provided in the program. Of course, similar reports also arrived in official Soviet institutions: the Civil Aviation Scientific Research Institute, the Astronomical Council of the USSR Academy of Sciences. But with rare exceptions, the bureaucrats who ran Soviet Institutes and other agencies ignored such reports. Soviet Ufologists were ignored and became subjects of outright hostility toward unauthorised research by civilians. In May of 1967, 45 researchers came together to form the Initiative Group of UFO Investigators. The House of Aviation and Cosmonautics in Moscow became their hangout. Some military officials joined them.

Among them was Major General Reino, who managed the House, and was instrumental in establishing the UFO Department of the All Union Committee of Cosmonautics (under the DOSAAF). Major General Stolyarov (a truly cryptic personality) headed the Initiative Group. The November 10 TV broadcast was their swan song. The Armed Forces (through its DOSAAF, Voluntary Society for Assisting Army, Air Force, and Navy branch) instructed by Communist Party decided to stifle the independent movement. General A. Ghetman ordered the Department disbanded. There were letters of protests to the Central Committee of the Communist Party from some scientists, writers, and military. Notably, Major General G. Uger, editor of Foreign Electronics magazine. In 1968 top Soviet aircraft designers and engineers wrote to Kosygin and tried to reason with the Party boss that UFOs were real and observed globally. Most likely the letter never reached him. By then the Communist leaders and their chief scientists censored seditious articles about UFOs.

1974 - F. Zigel and head of the Moscow Aviation Institute, S. Volokitin, convince the Institute to begin an intramural study of UFOs. The USSR Academy of Sciences began a Research Program of Communication Issues with Extraterrestrial Civilizations.

1975 - Dr. Valentin N. Fomenko, who was a leading and active Soviet Ufologist, a colleague of F. Zigel, and later knew A. Plaksin quite well, had investigated the so-called Black Ball, an enigmatic object, found in 1975 in Western Ukraine. He wrote an article for the RIAP (in 1977), and stated there that a team of investigators had discovered that the Ball had possessed a number of anomalous properties. Reportedly, it had a strange "core" inside it that, (based on results of an experiment) had a negative mass (i.e. properties of antigravity). They had assumed the Ball was a part of the propulsion system of an extraterrestrial spacecraft containing a quantity of antimatter. They were not able to conduct more experiments, because the owner of the object wanted it back. Apparently, as later revealed by Fomenko, the KGB was interested, too. We urge those who are interested in the KGB investigation report to contact our colleagues from the RIAP at riap777@softhome.net.

1974-76 - F. Zigel has conducted a State-sponsored study of primary analysis of main parameters of UFO phenomenon.

1976 - On October 29 of that year the head of the Moscow Aviation Institute made a decision to create a scientific and technical Council for UFO issues. Another decision was to conduct a symposium in the Institute; its name would be NLO-77. This did not come to fruition, because of an article published in Komsomol'skaya Pravda newspaper on November 28, 1976. The article was Tekhnologiya mifa or Technology of a myth. Its author was a well-known Soviet science fiction writer. This article was first in a series of articles in Soviet newspapers, magazines, radiobroadcast programs and television programs. The only purpose behind such publications was to discredit UFO phenomenon in the eyes and ears of Soviet general public. This method was similar to the means employed by KGB to silence dissidents, whose opinion did not follow guidelines, policies, and teachings of the Communist Party totalitarian regime. But at the same time, USSR was no longer Stalin's land of total fear or blissful ignorance about the world outside.

In December of 1976, Soviet Ufologist R. Varlamov an ex-official of the State Committee for Science and Technology, appealed to Soviet leader Alexey Kosigin, and suggested that scientific investigation of UFOs be organised in the USSR. The letter was passed to the Expert Commission of the Department of General and Applied Physics. The answer was basically a bureaucratic promise to increase attacks on those who support and promote UFO research.

1976 - On July 1st of that year F. Zigel was allowed to present a lecture about modern UFO issues. The site of the lecture was Soviet plant Kulon. This lecture caused tempestuous public discussions. Underground copies of the lecture, hastily put together, were prepared and circulated in the Soviet Union. The authorities did not miss this development, and those in charge of the Leningrad Znaniye Society (entity responsible for granting permission for lecturers) forbid Zigel to present further lectures.

1977 was turning out to be an uneventful year, when the Petrozavodsk Phenomenon broke official silence, and caused a number of historical developments to take place.

1978 - In January, the Institute of Earth Magnetism, Ionosphere and Distribution of Radio Waves collected information about UFOs (anomalous phenomena). The person in charge was Vladimir Migulin, corresponding member of the USSR Academy of Sciences. There was no great enthusiasm in this research entity.

At the end of the year, anomalous phenomena research in the USSR Academy of Sciences became the subject of a special scientific research program designated as SETKA-AN. Its functions were distributed among different departments, and a number of Soviet research institutes of the USSR Academy of Sciences received tasks to research various aspects of the anomalous phenomenon issue.

Soviet magazine Nauka I zhizn or Science and life publishes James Oberg's article about UFOs.

On the 18th of October 1978, a meeting took place in the Academy of Sciences, USSR. Those present included Vladimir Vasilyevich Migulin, Georgiy Stepanovich Narimanov, Rem Gennadiyevich Varlamov, Victor Petrovich Balashov, Vladimir Ivanovich Volga, A. N. Makarov, Inna Evgraphovna Petrenko, Evgeniy Pavlovich Chigin, Dmitry Aleksandrovich Men'kov, Zaytsev (a colonel of the Soviet anti-aircraft forces), Lev Mironovich Gindilis, Inna Gennadyevna Petrovskaya, and Yury Victorovich Platov.

By the way, according to Dr. Fomenko, a group of 10 or 15 researchers who later formed the SETKA core regularly met outside their work to discuss the UFO phenomenon.

We know today that at the historic meeting Migulin and Platov represented the Izmiran (the Academy of Sciences USSR Institute of Terrestrial Magnetism and Diffusion of Radio Waves). Narimanov and Petrovskaya represented the Academy of Sciences USSR Space Research Institute. Varlamov represented the Moscow Technological Institute. Balashov and Volga represented the secret military unit 67947. Makarov represented the Department of general Physics and Astronomy of the Academy of Sciences USSR. Gindilis represented the Shternberg State Astronomical Institute. We are not sure who the other participants represented at them meeting. This was the genesis of the SETKA programs, a fundamental research of anomalous phenomena in the Soviet Union. The main agency of the research was to be the Izmiran. Platov was to be the chief executive at the Izmiran for the SETKA-AN. We cannot quote the complete document here (historians should contact the authors for such an arrangement), but we need to mention several crucial points. The Ministry of Defence was worried about the effects of anomalous phenomena; such effects interfered with its work. Balashov mentioned that the priority of research should go to the periodically generated phenomena. He later said that there was no confirmation of sightings by either Soviet or American cosmonauts or astronauts (they observed containers, he added; meaning that the objects the saw were not UFOs). Discussions about the organisational details were, too, very interesting (an HQ is needed at the Academy of Sciences; Platov, the CEO, was to provide it; Migulin promised to "organise" rooms in Moscow; Gindilis mentioned the central archives and the catalogue in one central place). Varlamov mentioned that there are 3000 reports coming in each year from general population. Migulin was against Gindilis's idea of a central storage place of the data. Volga stated that the sources of primary information included the Ministry of Defence, the Ministry of the Interior Affairs, and TASS.

According to Dr. Fomenko, Migulin was chosen to lead the program while he was absent...no one else wanted to touch the dangerous subject.

1979 - Instructions about the procedures to collect information about anomalous phenomena data collection in the atmosphere and space was sent to various Soviet departments and organisations. The order came from the Department of General Physics and Astronomy of the USSR Academy of Sciences. Nedelya newspaper published an appeal by V. Migulin and Y. Platov to those who have sighted unusual phenomena to first determine on site whether the observed object was not an astronomical or another familiar object. If it was not conventional in nature, then to describe the object thoroughly, and send the report to the Department of General Physics and Astronomy of the USSR Academy of Sciences.

As Y. Platov and B. Sokolov state in their History of State-directed UFO Research in the USSR, a decision was made to keep the programs secret. The justification was a necessity to ensure "abatement of public response". There were three reasons for that, according to both apologists for this Inquisition-like approach to UFO phenomena research:

Programs formally belonged to activities pertaining to defence-related subjects; initial assumption that there is a high probability of military-technical origin of the observed strange phenomena; and possibilities that in case of successful completion of the raised tasks some of the UFO characteristics could be used for military purposes.

The Military-Industrial Commission decided to create two UFO research centres, one in the USSR Academy of Sciences, the other in the USSR Defence Ministry. Both centres aided each other's research and exchanged information.

We do not believe that Platov and Sokolov's publication is truthful. For example, look at their insistence that there were virtually no reports of anomalous phenomena from military objects at or next to secret testing areas and ranges. This is simply not true, for Soviet UFO researchers reported a number of such sightings. Y. Platov and B. Sokolov (who had somewhat different opinions when he discussed his work with George Knapp, a noted American journalist in 1993) were official participants and leaders of the programs. Also, both authors admit that because scarce funding was available for their programs, and necessary equipment to research such phenomena as large-sized plasma structures in the atmosphere was not available, their methods could not be foolproof. Basically, information was collected, and analysed, and some physical models of observed phenomena were developed.

But even this assertion seems to be untrue. Their publication was criticised by Russian and Ukrainian Ufologists, and applauded by seasoned debunkers. There is obviously an agenda to denigrate independent UFO research, and not some "secret KGB files", as the authors state in the publication. It would be very decent on their part to inform Russian Ufologists where their archives are located, so that perhaps a joint commission could be formed, and reports researched again. We are not asking that a foreign representation be included, for there may be defence secrets in the archives of reports that spanned over 13 years. But we do not think that Platov and Sokolov should be allowed to dismiss Soviet and CIS UFO phenomenon with their dubious publication. Actually, such prominent participants in the programs as Colonel A. A. Plaksin (liaison between the military and the academic programs) have recently confirmed the UFO incident over Usovo in 1982 (when a nuclear war was almost triggered because the launch codes for the Soviet ICBMs had been bafflingly enabled just as the gigantic UFO appeared over the secret ICBM base in Ukraine). Although Boris Sokolov for years reported the same, he has now changed his story drastically. We believe it is A. A. Plaksin who should be the authority in the cases investigated by the military Setka program; or the head of the program, General Balashov. By the way, Colonel Plaksin nowadays is the leading paranormal phenomena expert of the Russian Defence Ministry.

And he is quite outspoken about the Setka program (September 8 and 15, 2000, REN-TV program titled Voyennaya Tayna or Military Secret). A most curious article was published in Komsomol'skaya Prvada newspaper on 5-31-02. Andrey Pavlov wrote it, and its title is UFOs helped Americans create super weapons. Aleksandr Plaksin, who was interviewed, is called a military geophysicist. In the article Plaksin "reveals" several interesting developments.

1. Many recent achievements of the American military-industrial complex have been generated in the labs dedicated to the research of paranormal phenomena.

2. "Aliens" have nothing to do with American advanced technology (i.e., Stealth).

3. In his 15 years of UFO research A. Plaksin had never obtained direct proof that there are alien civilizations active on our planet.

4. Americans have researched UFOs since 1954 (U.S. Air Force), and since 1974 they have operated a secret scientific research centre to study anomalous phenomena and UFOs through the use of a special Earth-based station. Hence, they (the Americans) were able to create a super weapon. (A. Plaksin goes into scary details, but basically his aim is to denigrate American HAARP, future U.S. policies, etc.)

5. A. Plaksin describes the creation of the Soviet program(s) to study the anomalous phenomena from 1978 on.

6. A. Plaksin goes into fascinating details; the information after all, came from Soviet military branches, the Navy, the border guards, anti-aircraft units, etc. Some of the information revealed in the interview in Komsomol'skaya Pravda contains fascinating details of a sighting from the Borisoglebsk airfield (the immobile black cloud).

This is of great interest; there have been other very strange "clouds" over the former USSR and Russia, as we have described in this book.

7. A. Plaksin mentions the infamous and very dangerous 1982 case (and gives the correct date; Mr. Sokolov, who has changed his story repeatedly, ought to be ashamed. It was the 4th of October, not the 5th; and nothing other than a UFO which almost triggered a nuclear war).

8. A. Plaksin states that there were no UFO crashes in Kazakhstan in 1978; no secret storage for UFO fragments in Mitische (Moscow area), no super secret storage in Novaya Zemlya.

A. Plaksin also mentions that the laboratory he worked with after 1978 was created at the military scientific research institute TSNII-22. He started there as a junior scientist in 1979, and gradually became its supervisor, until 1991, when the program was disbanded due to the lack of funds. It would be great to compare his information to that provided by such respectable former Soviet military officers as Gherman Kolchin, Lev Ovsischer, and others. Gershtein, Subbotin, Chernobrov should also be heard, for their research skills are diverse and vast.

9. A. Plaksin is of the opinion that the unidentified objects ("20 percent", according to him) are of physical origin that is still unknown to us. Our laws of physics cannot explain such objects. The rest of the cases have to do with UFOs that are of the plasma formation, quite natural in origin. The methodology used by Soviet military scientists allowed them to juxtapose the Sun's condition and the timing of UFO appearances. They had determined that under certain conditions a stream of solar radiation penetrates the Earth protective magnetic field and assumes very diverse forms, causing influence on measuring devices and people. He mentions two fascinating episodes (1977 and 1981).

10. Although A. Plaksin states that most likely there are no aliens on Earth, he also mentions that because of military secrecy he cannot reveal everything he knows.

11. Among other projects carried out by the military UFO research lab,

A. Plaksin worked in was the creation of the USSR anomalous zones map. There have been dozens of such zones. The most important ones were in the Ust'-Koksin area of the Altai Mountainous Autonomous region; the Zarevshan area; the Borisoglebsk area; the Plesetsk area of the Arkhangelsk region; the Dzerdzhinsky area of the Nizhegorodsk region; and the Shatursky area near Moscow.

12. The military institute authorised to study UFOs had cooperated with other institutes of the Russian Science Academy to create a number of super sensitive equipment for UFO research. The equipment allowed them to estimate the size of UFOs, density, and their speeds. According to A. Plaksin, the Soviet military scientists also learned to predict UFO waves.

13. They never worked with any contactees. They were only interested in the official reports from Soviet military units; the reports were to be measured by military technological equipment. Plaksin, obviously, is revealing more information, piecemeal. There is more to be learned from him, we hope, in the future.

Scientists in the Novosibirsk "Akademgorodok", a powerful science centre in Siberia, conducted the first data processing of UFO sightings by Soviet computers. The actual calculations were performed in the Institute of Mathematics of the Siberian Branch of the Soviet Academy of Sciences. They used EVM ES 1022 computers. This was done in the framework of the SETKA-AN. Mikhail Gershtein has a copy of this historic attempt to study UFO data; the report consists of 45 pages of graphs and formulas. This is not the last reference to the SETKA programs in our book.

Plaksin never discussed the mysterious "Arkhangelsk Dust" in his interviews, but he knew about it, as does V. Fomenko. Soviet scientists from the SETKA, as well as Novosibirsk came to Arkhangelsk to study the phenomenon. Arkhangelsk Region is situated in the North-West of the European part of Russia. Its shores, three thousand kilometres long, are washed by cold waters of three Arctic seas: the White, Barents and Kara Sea. We could not get more details of the mysterious event. We do know from Mikhail Gershtein's interview with V. Fomenko that Plaksin gave the elderly researcher some notes and information he had kept in his apartment. We need to mention that according to Dr. Fomenko, the most unusual UFO ever observed by him was a gigantic flattened sphere photographed by the American satellite GOES-8. What did Fomenko see?

This was one of the National Oceanic and Atmospheric Administration's (NOAA's) next generation of geostationary satellites. Apparently, the infrared photo was taken by Geostationary Orbital Environmental Satellite (GOES-8) in July 1992. The satellite was 36 thousand kilometres above the Earth.

More detailed information about the case and other photos taken by the satellite years later is available from Skywatch International, and its Chilean director, Dr. Luis C. Sanchez Perry.

1979 (CONTINUED)

The Leningrad Scientific Research Institute of Arctic and Antarctic and the Obninsk Institute of Applied Physics issued special instructions regarding anomalous phenomena to meteorologists, aviators, geologists, and seamen in the area to collect information.

In the same year, the Institute of Space Research of the USSR Academy of Sciences published in 1979, a 74-page statistical analysis of over 256 UFO cases reported in the Soviet Union. After stating that hallucinations, errors, and conventional explanations (aircraft, satellites, etc.) could not account for many of the reports, the study concluded: "Obviously, the question of the nature of the anomalous phenomena still should be considered open. To obtain more definite conclusions, more reliable data must be available. Reports on observations of anomalous phenomena have to be well documented. The production of such reports must be organised through the existing network of meteorological, geophysical, and astronomical observation stations, as well as through other official channels. In our opinion, the Soviet and foreign data accumulated so far justifies setting such studies." (Gindilis, L.M.,Men'kov, D.A. and Petrovskaya, I.G., "Observations of Anomalous Atmospheric Phenomena in the USSR: Statistical Analysis," USSR Academy of Sciences Institute of Space Research, Report PR 473, Moscow, 1979). According to Vladimir V. Rubtsov, contrary to James Oberg's opinion, the famous Gindilis Report was neither sponsored, nor inspired by official organisations (RIAP Bulletin, 1994, Editorial). More about Inna Georgiyevna Petrovskaya in 1981 is stated below.

1980-1990 - The term UFO in the Soviet Union was substituted by two abbreviations: (Aya, anomalniye yavleniya or anomalous phenomena; and AO, or anomal'niy obyekt or anomalous object). This facilitated entrance of psychics and occult members into UFO research organisations.

The Instruction to the Soviet Armed Forces regarding anomalous phenomena is disseminated. The main entity in executing the military SETKA program was one of the central military scientific research institutes, and V. Balashov headed it. He was a top Soviet expert in the area of radiation effect (and other destructive factors) on military technology.

1981 - Kiev, Soviet Ukraine. First Ukrainian conference about anomalous phenomena in the environment took place. Top Soviet scientists participated in it.

1981 - A famous Soviet newspaper, Komsomol'skaya Prvada, published an article about French UFO research (August 8, 1981). The French space agency has conducted a non-military but official investigation into UFO reports. In 1981 phase, the project's name was GEPAN and its focus was first and foremost on UFO reports. It was a very interesting and revealing article, and proved that the Soviet government was truly interested in the unidentified flying objects. The article (titled "UFO" without hullabaloo and publicity) would not have been printed without an official sanction from the censorship watchdogs of the regime. The French scientists involved in the GEPAN were interested in the ability of unidentified objects to "stand" in the air without emitting energy; tried to figure out why there had been breakdowns of automobile engines during appearance of UFOs. The work of GEPAN was controlled by a special council of eight prominent scientists who were worked in the most important scientific agencies of France.

1981 - We did get one interesting commentary regarding the SETKA-AN (Academy of Sciences) reports. It explains some of the reasons why UFO research in the USSR was a forbidden subject. I.G. Petrovskaya wrote this lengthy and detailed commentary on military observations in 1981. Petrovskaya (Institute for Space Studies of the USSR Academy of Sciences), was involved with the Gindilis report (see above; L.M.Gindilis, D.A.Men'kov, I.G.Petrovskaya. Nablyudeniya NLO v SSSR. Statisticheskii analiz, in Russian), and the Black Ball investigation .

Petrovskaya had done an excellent and detailed analysis of the observations, and presented explanation for some of the intriguing UFO sightings (she claims that the case we call "Riga UFO" was actually a French weather balloon carried over into the Soviet airspace by autumn atmospheric streams; the white object sighted over Caspian Sea was explained as a spy balloon launched from Turkey; the explanation of the latter case was helped by a special "expeditionary group" that was dispatched to the Mangishlak Region, and consisted of Soviet scientists and military Ufologists through the SETKA programs).

The commentary is fascinating, and those interested in reading its entire contents should contact the authors of this book. As a minimum it shows how the Soviet science and the Ministry of Defence had cooperated in the field of UFO phenomenon research. What is especially interesting to us is the assessment by I. G. Petrovskaya of the cases to be deemed most perspective for further SETKA research. Such cases fell into several categories. They related to various types of anomalous phenomena: the "nocturnal lights phenomenon; "disk"-like objects, observed in daylight; objects that produce anomalous radar reflection; the objects and phenomena that have an influence on technological means; and the objects that descend to the surface of Earth, leaving traces of physical influence, and causing influence on the biosphere and human beings.

Petrovskaya also mentioned that the results of the executed identification of the manifestation of the phenomena as being those of the military, experimental, and reconnaissance systems of a likely adversary, first of all testify about the timeliness of the decision to regularly and operationally register anomalous phenomena, and about the necessity to continue this work in the future. Such identification continues Petrovskaya, removes the cover of innocent entertainment of extraterrestrial civilization or wonders of nature that cause no danger and do not deserve serious attention from 80% of the observed phenomena. That is why the observations and the transfer of data of appearances of anomalous objects should be dealt with full responsibility. The nearest consequence of light-minded attitude to the issue could be an unimpeded access to the Soviet territories of foreign-type objects, imitating an outside shape of a "saucer". Should we register characteristics of a truly anomalous phenomenon, we get a possibility to progress one more step in the research of this unknown phenomenon. Success in such research is considered throughout the world as a possible guarantee of a genuine leap in both scientific and military knowledge.

Inna Georgiyevna Petrovskaya suffered a family tragedy, became convinced that it happened because she studied the mysterious phenomenon, and forever disappeared from Moscow. She left her archives to her colleagues, and was never seen again. Such notable Ufologists as N. Fomenko (he is 96 now, and although ill, continues his research) tried their best to find her, but were not successful.

1982 - In the beginning of that year, Anomalous Phenomena research groups existed in Moscow, Leningrad, Kiev, Tallin, Vilnius, Gorky, Yaroslavl, Kharkov, and other Soviet cities (some later, after 1991, renamed to their original names).

A play about UFO phenomenon and those for and against it was to be staged by Soviet Big Dramatic Theatre (this theatre was under directorship of famous thespian personality, G. Tostonogov). To promote the forbidden subject, G. Lisov, future editor-in-chief of NLO magazine, was allowed to discuss the phenomenon of UFOs at the end of the play, during the trial performances. The play did not get a permission to be staged in Tovstonogov's theatre, and had a lamented, unsuccessful run in other Soviet theatres.

1983 - The Tomsk Group for the Research of the Anomalous Phenomena in the Environment (abbreviated as TGIAYA in Russian) was created that year as part of S. I. Vavilov Priborprom Russian Scientific and Engineering Society. The group contained chapters dedicated to atmospheric anomalous phenomena, terrestrial and technologically created anomalous phenomena; there was a section to research influence of anomalous phenomena on human beings and biological systems, while another searched for ways to design equipment for the research of anomalous phenomena. In 1990 the section engaged in the research of influence of anomalous phenomena on human beings and biological systems initiated a special school for the study of extrasensory perception. The very first class had 74 students. The TGIAYA conducted scientific well-educated local seminars; participated in the All Union scientific research, presented lectures, published its findings, and built special devices.

1984 - Vsevolod Troitsky, corresponding member of the USSR Academy of Sciences, establishes a commission to study anomalous phenomena. It is established on February 1984, under the auspices of the national scientific and technological society of protection of the nature. Earlier, in 1982 he published an article (Issue 10, Nauka i religiya or Science and religion magazine), where he described complex anomalous phenomena (in atmosphere, hydro sphere, space) that has been observed and verified, but cannot be explained, and need to be researched further, for the sake of science and human society.

1985 - A deep crisis had paralysed Soviet Ufology, as a result of official denunciation of Ufologists following the publication in Trud newspaper of Vostrukhin's article about the TU-134 deadly incident.

1986 - On February 7 and 8, in the city of Gorky, the First All Union seminar designated as Technical methods of anomalous phenomena research takes place. A number of leading Soviet Ufologists and supporters participate in it.

1987 - In January of that year, Yaroslavl UFO research group (then Anomalous Phenomena research group) started to publish its periodical dedicated to anomalous phenomena and UFOs.

1988 - In November, a new organisation is born. A Committee for issues of energy-information exchange in nature was formed at the Union of scientific engineering societies of USSR. Academician V. Kaznacheyev headed the Committee.

On November 20, Felix Zigel died. In 1936 he was a member of the astronomical expedition to Kazakhstan. Not far away from them was another, American expedition, and among its members was D. Menzel. In 1938 F. Zigel was expelled from university studies because his father was arrested by Stalin's secret police (he was accused of attempting to blow up an aviation plant in

Tambov, but was released after serving two years in the Gulag). In 1945 Zigel was able to graduate from a university. In 1948 he became a Candidate of Science of the USSR Academy of Sciences. In later years they exchanged correspondence. He authored over ten large volumes of Ufology; none of them were published in his lifetime. He brought together UFO researchers, organised UFO expeditions, collected information, corresponded with foreign UFO researchers, and promoted study of mysterious and unexplained flying objects in the sky of his country. His legacy lives on, and his works have been published in the United States, as well as Russia. Anatoly Kutovoy in Lithuania and Zigel's daughter in Russia are the best source of information about this remarkable person.

1989 - The Siberian city of Tomsk hosted a conference on sporadic instant phenomena. Over 300 scientists and experts from major scientific centres of the USSR attended this conference. It recommended that the Siberian Branch of the USSR Academy of Sciences draft a comprehensive program for the study of the issue.

The All Union Council of Scientific and Technical Societies (now the Council of Scientific and Engineering Societies) had set up a non-governmental Commission on Paranormal Events, headed by V.S. Troitsky, a Corresponding Member of the USSR Academy of Sciences, was set up in 1984. Here is how members A. Petukhov and T. Faminskaya described some of the activities of the Commission in 1989:

> *'Of special value are the archives set up by the Commission. They contain over 13 thousand reports connected with PEs [Paranormal Events] and with UFOs in particular...'*

UFOs have been seen to hover over ground objects, to chase or fly side by side with airplanes and cars, to follow geometrically regular trajectories, and to send out ordered flashes of light. In other words, such 'paranormals' behave, from the viewpoint of human beings, quite often showing capabilities yet beyond the reach of the machines built on the Earth." (Faminskaya, T. & Petukhov, A., "At 4.10 Hours and After," Almanac Phenomenon 1989, Moscow Mir, 1989.)

On July 5 of that year the Committee headed by V. Kaznacheyev formed the Ufological Commission. Its chairman was V. Ajaja, one of founders of Ufology in the Soviet Union. The Vice-Chairman was Soviet cosmonaut P. Popovich. A split between Ufologists and Parapsychologists took place, but mutual influence remained.

In Moscow, at the Exhibit of Achievements of National Economy, a UFO exhibit was featured. A. Listratov was its prominent organiser.

During the same year, censorship on UFO subject was removed. One of the stimuli for the Council of Ministers, USSR to do so was Y. Smirnov's letter to Soviet authorities (to Deputy Korotich, as well as to Glavlit, the censorship entity in the Soviet Union).

1990 - The very first official public UFO research organisation was formed. Its director was V. Ajaja, and its name was SOYUZUFOTSENTR. It published a Russian and English language magazine; in 1994 it published an article about World War II UFOs written by Paul Stonehill, one of the authors of this book.

In the same year a number of UFO publications appeared in the Soviet Union. Most are gone now. Exchange of information with prominent Western UFO researchers was initiated. Philip Mantle was asked to comment on the Voronezh Phenomenon, and his name became familiar among Soviet Ufologists.

The Tomsk Group for the Research of the Anomalous Phenomena in the Environment was transformed into the Siberian scientific research centre Anomal'niye Yavleniya (at the S. M. Kirov Tomsk Polytechnical Institute). The research centre is not active as of 2002, and its scientists are engaged in private research and development.

1991 - The demise of the Soviet Union rocked the world. Chaos, tremendous changes, opportunities and poverty, crime and local military conflicts forever altered the country, its peoples, and UFO research. Some UFO databases and archives perished, some were locked away, while some were sold overseas. UFO research groups in various Soviet republics in Central Asia ceased to exist. Survival became more important than studies of anomalous aerial phenomena. And yet, in the middle 1990s younger UFO researchers came to the scene. Because of them and their predecessors this book became possible.

Facts: According to the USSR Academy of Sciences, some 90 to 95% of UFO reports are a result of such causes as optical atmospheric effects, flocks of birds, rare astronomical phenomena, meteorites, luminous insects, hoaxes, weather balloons, aircraft, missile and rocket launches, streams of space articles, clusters of light, ball lightning, luminous pollutants, Polar lights, and so on. The remaining share of UFO reports still constitutes thousands of unexplained phenomena.

"Observations show that UFOs behave 'sensibly.' In a group formation flight, they maintain a pattern. They are most often observed over airfields, atomic stations and other very new engineering installations. On encountering aircraft, they always manoeuvre so as to avoid direct contact. A considerable list of these seemingly intelligent actions gives the impression that UFOs are investigating, perhaps even reconnoitering. The important thing now is for us to discard any preconceived notions about UFOs and to organise on a global scale a calm, sensation-free and strictly scientific study of this strange phenomenon. The subject and aims of the investigation are so serious that they justify all efforts. It goes without saying that international cooperation is vital." (Felix Zigel Unidentified Flying Objects, Soviet Life, Issue 2, February 1968.)

Despite all the problems the former USSR currently has, UFO research continues and it looks set to do so for many years to come despite upheavals and transformations in the lands that once formed one huge country.

CHAPTER 23

SOVIET MILITARY ENCOUNTERS
WITH UFOs

FROM THE CIVIL WAR THROUGH THE 1930s

History is mostly silent about sightings and encounters between the Red Army and UFOs that took place prior to the 1940s. Sometimes long-lost accounts are found. Most likely, other reports are still locked away in the impenetrable files left behind after the fall of the USSR.

N.I. Khrenov, director of the Donetzk Centre of Air Travel and an airline captain, recalls a story told him by his grandmother, a nurse in the Red Army during the bloody Russian Civil War. She was a courageous woman, who could tend to, shoot to defend, and protect her patients. The incident she revealed took place in the Crimea. The string of wagons that comprised the military unit's transport was lost in the battle and left behind. There were wounded in the transport, few guards available to protect them, and any skirmish could mean the end of the Red Army soldiers. They moved ahead very slowly, not smoking, and using very little light. A machine-gun cart (tachanka) with reconnaissance personnel, among them Nurse Khrenova, zigzagged the area. They were the ones who noticed a very strange spectacle. In the darkness ahead of them they observed a luminescent "marquee", and around it moving figures clad in "armour", as if covered with "scales". The Red Guards felt something sinister and alien coming from the strangers. After a brief deliberation, the Red Guards decided to approach the "marquee", and open fire on "counter-revolutionaries" dressed in "armour". When they did so, their horses became uncontrollable for no apparent reason, and ran away, pulling the machine-gun cart behind them into the darkness (Almanac NLO-Svyazniye vselennoy, Issue 22, 1995).

In the following years Soviet soldiers and officers would use other, more advanced weapons against strange entities and their unidentified flying objects. The results were almost always the same. We know almost nothing about the 1920s and 1930s, save for the KGB's interest in the paranormal and Gleb Bokiy's (who headed one of the NKVD/KGB's powerful departments) research. We will learn more about that page of Soviet history later in the book.

Stalinist terror and purges took their toll; people were afraid to discuss anything out of the ordinary course of things. Nazi Germany's invasion into the Soviet Union changed the situation.

UFOs OVER SOVIET BATTLEFIELDS

Just as their allies did, the Soviet military, too, noticed the presence of strange flying objects over their troops and battlefields. Germans also knew about UFOs, perhaps as early as 1940. A report on file at the Russian Ufology Research Centre describes a UFO sighting over Poland. The year is 1944. Lev Petrovich Ovsischer, a decorated Soviet pilot-navigator of bomber airplanes, had fought against Hitler's armies through the war. He later graduated from the Military Air Academy of the Soviet Army, and for many years served in the fighter aviation of the Soviet Air Force. A former colonel of the Soviet Air Force, he now resides in Israel, where he is an honorary colonel of Israel's Defence Forces.

In November of 1944 he and other Soviet aviators observed a strange, bright object in the sky over a frontline airfield in the Warsaw area. The UFO hovered at a great altitude, not moving, for about fifteen minutes. Its illumination was incredible. The object ascended at great velocity, and disappeared from view. None of the witnesses had heard anything about "flying saucers" and they could not explain what it was that they saw. This sighting prompted Ovsischer to collect reports about the military and UFOs.

Other sightings had been reported, too. One took place on August 26, 1943, at the Kursk Bulge. This was the site of a crucial tank battle between the Soviet Army and the Nazi panzers. Senior Lt. Gennady Zhelaginov observed the sky after the Soviet artillery shelled German defence lines. The adversary had frequently bombed Soviet positions at that section of the front. Suddenly he saw a sickle-shaped object. It flew at a great velocity in a south-westerly direction, and soon disappeared from Zhelaginov's view. The colour of the UFO was dark bluish, tinted, from front to back. But towards the middle the colour turned to a bright orange. The impression was that of a giant dolphin breathing, because the middle section continually expanded and contracted its size. The object seemed to be something animate, and impressive, because of the volleys of Soviet artillery and explosions in the background. Other military eyewitnesses were listed in the signed report.

There was a report of a huge UFO that hovered over the neutral Kursk Bulge area just before the start of the battle. The Soviet high command feared that the object was Hitler's much-vaunted "secret weapon". An actual drawing of the object was done, and several Soviet colonels, who later took part in the battle, had signed it to prove authenticity. The drawings were kept in Feliks Zigel's archives, but then disappeared. Professor Burdakov, a friend of the late Ufologist, knew the contents of his archives, but did not see any wartime "disc" reports.

Retired Soviet Colonel Gherman Kolchin published an article in NLO Magazine (2000). He mentioned recollections of A. Kovalchuk, a Lt. Colonel during the World War II. A huge, dirigible-like object some 100-150 metres in length, visited the military airfield where Kovalchuk was stationed. There was no gondola, and the object moved at the altitude of 500 metres. Air defence units fired on the "dirigible" from cannons and machine guns: they had to protect the airfield. But they did not harm the object, as it flew over the airfield, and disappeared into the distance.

Sergei Korolyov, and M.K. Tikhonravov, prominent Soviet scientists, vaguely mentioned "German disks". However, at the time young Burdakov did not feel at ease to ask them for details. Unfortunately, both men are now deceased, taking their secrets with them to the grave. They had visited defeated Germany; Tikhonravov went through Pomerania with a group of scientists in the ranks of Marshal Konev's armies. Tikhonravov was the first Russian to see the bases, factories and barracks of the SS forces that guarded and maintained the V-1 and V-2 projects. S.P. Korolyov was later sent to Germany on an official mission to study and select materials directly related to the V-2 program.

Professor Burdakov has in his possession many interesting reports about the V-1 and V-2 programs from those Soviet experts who had worked in Germany during the last months of the war, and in 1945-46. He has materials on the jet-propelled aircraft (tested in the Reich prior to such tests having been undertaken in either the United States or the USSR). However, he has no reliable data on testing of any "flying disks." The Germans, he states, did have diagrams; that is, general intentions, testing of models, calculations, and estimates, but the professor thinks that it would be most difficult to turn all of the above into a viable aircraft.

Nazis did test strange-looking aircraft at the Prague's Khbely airfield, in 1944. Czech journalists from Signal magazine conducted a thorough investigation in 1990. The aircraft, according to eyewitnesses, was spherical, and had a diameter of about seven metres. It had a small, drop-like cockpit, four tall "legs" (supports) with tiny wheels. The aircraft's hull was either made from metal, or covered with silver-coloured fabric. There was something like a jet engine. The craft commenced its flight by gaining an altitude of five metres, flew for a few hundred metres, and then landed. It experienced instability during the flight. When the Red Army liberated Prague, the NKVD removed everything from the airfield. Another report, by a Russian prisoner of war, who survived Nazi concentration camps, tell similar stories of German test flights of experimental aircraft in the vicinity of Pennemunde, in September of 1943. The primitive machine, equipped with the Messerschmidt 262 engine, crashed and burned. Clearly, the UFOs sighted in the wartime Europe were not of German origin.

ENCOUNTERS AFTER THE WAR

Some of the better-known cases of the 1940s involve Soviet test pilot Apraksin. On June 16, 1948, he was performing flights over Baskunchak Lake, and encountered a cigar-shaped UFO. Apraksin chased the object. The response was quick and pitiless: a ray was emitted from the UFO, Apraksin was temporarily blinded, his engine and equipment damaged. The altitude of the encounter was 10.5 kilometres.

One year later, on May 6, 1949, Apraksin had another encounter with a UFO. In the area of Vol'sk, while flying at the altitude of 15 kilometres, Apraksin discovered another cigar-shaped craft. The UFO would not let his aircraft approach closer than 10 to 12 kilometres. Finally, rays emitted by the UFO damaged the onboard electrical hardware, turned off radio communications, damaged protective glass of the cockpit, as well as the heretical integrity of the cockpit. Apraksin was barely able to land his aircraft on Volga's shore, and then he fainted. He spent the next two and a half months in a hospital. The encounters were first mentioned in the underground samizdat publications of the 1980s, and in Vadim Chernobrov's book Nad propastyu neraskritikh tayn, Moscow, 1997.

A STRANGE SIGHTING OF 1953

A very sinister incident took place in the area known as Krasnoyarsk Kray, not very far away from the site of the Tunguska Explosion. The eyewitness to the incident is a highly reliable source. His name is Veniamin Dodin, a writer, scientist, and lecturer. He was arrested in 1940, and spent the next 14 years in prisons, concentration camps, and exile throughout the USSR. Dodin had authored 26 books, and for 20 years he had taught Soviet military engineers.

On a clear night in June of 1953 Dodin walked back to his hut at the Ishimba River. The taiga was quiet, light winds chased away all clouds. All of a sudden Dodin heard a high-pitched noise, seemingly inside his head. Then he saw the object that emitted that noise. It was a long cylinder-like craft, seemingly gleaming, as it hovered over the clouds at a distance of about two miles. Dodin could clearly see its rotating drum-shaped body. The hull was girded with something that resembled a moving staircase with many steps. Completely opened and half-turned toward Dodin was the butt-end of the cylinder. Dodin immediately assumed that the object was a dirigible, but the absence of cabins or cockpit confused the scientist. The object, slowly rotating, moved in Dodin's direction. He noticed that the cylinder had something like a butt-end exiting from its ellipsoid body. The design of the "dirigible" appeared to be technologically incorrect to Dodin. He had no doubts that the object was a dirigible; what worried the exiled scientist was the possible payload it was carrying. There was a top-secret Soviet research centre in the area, the so-called "Box 26". New types of super-powerful weapons were being developed behind the walls of the "Box", and Dodin assumed that now he had entered the testing area. Then he noticed that the "butt-end" was actually a flat, drum-shaped body. It separated itself from the cylinder, and rapidly ascended. The noise Dodin felt in his ears receded, but became even less pleasant, something like a painful squeak. Several more flat drums exited from the dirigible, and flew upward. Then the open end of the mysterious object closed, and the cylinder flew away. Dodin's earache was gone, too; and "flat drums" disappeared as well. The sky was brighter now, as the morning was approaching. Dodin kept observation of the sky from his hut, the view was perfect, but there was nothing to observe.

The "dirigible" returned the following night. As a scientist, Dodin knew perfectly well that no man-made object could travel at such velocities as to instantly disappear from view. Was the object in the sky above him some super aircraft? Dodin was quite worried that those who ran the sinister "Box 26" would come to the area, along with top Soviet test pilots. Even exiles like him, and inmates of local concentration camps heard horrible rumours about the projects of the secret research centre. And yet, Dodin was a scientist and a researcher; hence, he decided to investigate. He took photographs of the object with his camera. Should authorities catch him, his fate would be sealed: an exile taking photographs in the forbidden Oimolon area would be sent back to the GULAG camps, or worse. But Dodin was a brave person, and he observed the UFOs for over 40 hours. The objects continued to "pour out" smaller flat drums. In turn, the "drums" vanished almost instantly. Dodin estimated that each "drum" was approximately 80 feet in diameter. The mother ship-dirigible was approximately 650 feet in diameter. Each mother ship "threw out" eight perfectly and smoothly polished "flat drums". Dodin used a Zeiss theodolite to observe the strange objects, for he had no other tools. The eyepiece he looked through enabled him to discern slight luminescence emanating from the panels of the "drums". The mother ship did not emit any luminescence. Dodin tried, in vain, to reach the site of the nearest cylinder. He failed every time. Moreover, he became ill whenever he approached the site. Prior to the incident Dodin was never ill in the taiga. Now he experienced sharp pains in his joints. The same sharp, painful noises as on the first day he observed the cylinder came back. It was an unbearable pain, and it forced Dodin to turn back. As soon as he came home, Dodin fell asleep for a long time.

The MVD (KGB of the period) arrived in the area in early July, accompanied by Soviet military pilots. The secret police noticed Dodin's camera, and confiscated it and the film. He was questioned extensively; after they took away his camera, Dodin was certain that he photographed some top secret Soviet project. The scientist found out later that he was wrong. The objects Dodin observed troubled Soviet military commanders in the area, too;

they tried to use radars, but discovered that something was jamming their radar station. The radiation, at super high frequencies, emanating from the mother ship, was so great that the MVD and pilots decided to "evacuate". Before fleeing the site, however, they ordered Dodin to continue his observations.

The entire incident is still classified in Russia, but Mark I. Shevelyov, who later headed the Arctic Aviation Agency, knows the reason for the secrecy. It turns out that the Soviet leadership quickly learned about UFOs of the Oimolon area, but decided to refrain from challenging the unknown. Stalin died not that long ago, and the situation in the USSR was not very stable. Finally, however, the Soviets blinked, and on August 7, 1953, their airplanes attacked the UFOs over Ishimba. As a result of the attack, two interceptor-aircraft vanished, along with four pilots. The exploded "air-to-air" missiles (inexplicably turned away from their UFO targets) burned a giant chunk of the taiga. All radar equipment in the 120-mile radius area of the site broke down.

Dodin would never forget that evening of the doomed attack. His radio made a piercing noise and shut down. Then a horrible noise hit Dodin inside his ears, and he fainted. He regained consciousness at night. When he climbed outside his hut, Dodin discovered a world painted in greenish hues. The luminescence in the area remained greenish for over a month. It faded slowly, like radiation after a nuclear explosion.

On July 24, 1957, a UFO appeared over the Soviet anti-aircraft installations on the Kuril Islands. The Soviets fired upon it, but scored no direct hits.

Those ubiquitous UFOs troubled the Soviet military long after Stalin was gone.

ALTAI, 1950-1957

The Altai Kray and Mountainous Altai are located near the Pamir, Himalayan, and Tien-Shen mountainous systems. Mountainous Altai is a sparsely populated area, and the Soviet government had used it and abused it repeatedly. The Baikonur Cosmodrome, mentioned on other pages of our book (and so are UFO sightings over the Altai land and cities), is in the area, as well as the Semipalatinsk nuclear testing range, and the Katunski power station. Because the Soviets had conducted nuclear explosions in Kazakhstan during the period between the years 1950 to 1957, the Altai area was contaminated no less than eight times. Soviet military commanders started reporting to Moscow that UFOs frequented to the Mountainous Altai. A. Plaksin (see Chapter Twenty Two), an important military UFO researcher, mentioned the area in his interview to the Russian newspaper Komsomol'skaya Pravda on May 31, 2002. The Soviet military Ufologists knew the area was one of the most important anomalous zones of the former USSR.

Sergei Skvortzov, researcher of the paranormal phenomena in the Altai, published some rather interesting information in NLO Magazine (1999).

It happened on August 17, 1954, at 8:12 a.m., according to a log entry of an anti-aircraft unit guarding a missile battalion very close to the Chinese border. Their radars registered strange interference. A few moments later there was a visual observation of an object that resembled a rocket, but had no stabilisers, and moved horizontally at low speed. Rather, the movement of the UFO resembled that of a dirigible. Three missiles were fired on it, exploded before reaching the target. The object rapidly ascended, and soon thereafter disappeared.

A commission from the Ministry of Defence was sent to investigate, and arrived the very next day. Its members found no objective reasons for firing missiles under the circumstances, and the commanding officer of the missile battalion was removed from his position.

UFO ENCOUNTER IN 1967: SOLID RAYS

In March of 1993 AURA-Z magazine (Moscow) published an account of a UFO sighting and ensuing encounter.

Lev Vaytkin, Fighter Pilot of the 1st Class, and a Lieutenant Colonel, is an experienced aviator, a graduate of the Yeisk Top Naval Aviation College. On August 13, 1967, he flew his interceptor airplane on a training flight. The night was calm, and the visibility unobstructed. A few minutes after 23 hours Vyatkin ascended the airplane to the altitude of 10000 metres. Below him glimmered the lights of Yalta, a Soviet city on the shore of Black Sea. Readings from the instruments were normal, and the flight conformed to all standard procedures. Then he looked up from the panel and noticed a UFO. It was a very large oval-shaped object that was somehow fixed to the port of his plane. A strange object so close to a military airplane worried the pilot, and he asked the Flight Commander Major Musatov: Who is in the zone? The latter checked the instruments and reported that all other planes had landed, and no one else was in the zone. Vyatkin banked the plane to the right, trying not to lose sight of the UFO. Careful not to approach too close, the pilot tried to determine in what direction it was moving. Several seconds later the UFO's lights gradually dimmed (as if a rheostat switch had been turned off inside).

Meanwhile the airplane made a complete right turn and came back to the starting point. Vyatkin considered his next move and then decided to make the left turn he had planned. He just barely banked the airplane to the left and adjusted the speed and thrust when Vyatkin noticed a flash of bright light from above straight on the course of his airplane. A slanting milky-white ray appeared in front of his airplane. The ray was closing in. Vyatkin levelled his plane out, and escaped running into the ray with the fuselage or cockpit. Still, he hit the ray with the left wing. Vyatkin was approaching the ray at very high speed, not taking his eyes off it, and had time to notice and feel something very strange. No sooner had the wing touched the ray than the latter broke into a myriad of tiny sparkles like those of a spent firework. The plane shook violently and the instruments read off the scale. Vyatkin instinctively thought that the ray was solid. The strange sparkling pillar stretched downwards. Soon the light above and the ray below disappeared.

Flying back to the airfield, Vyatkin kept searching the sky above for more surprises but found none. His flight ended safely. For many days afterwards the surface of the wing that came into contact with the strange ray shone at nights as if to remind him of the phenomenon.

Vyatkin did recall the episode for years to come: the very idea of a "solid ray" seemed outlandish, but he encountered the impossible phenomenon in real life. Then he read an article in Komsomolskaya Pravda newspaper (October 17, 1989 issue). The article, titled Cosmic Ghosts stated that "solid rays" do really exist, and others came in contact with them. The police chief of Voronezh, V. Selyavkin, described an experience when a ray of light fell down on him from above. It was bright, powerful, and pinned the chief down to the ground with its weight. Later it moved away and vanished. Vyatkin collected other accounts, and found out that witnesses reported rays that project themselves from UFOs like telescope supports or probes. Vyatkin is of the opinion that the ray was a pillar of fluorescent, highly magnetised gas, which was concentrated into a "pillar"?

We found another episode of a UFO sighting reported by the same Soviet pilot. The sighting took place six days before, on August 7, 1967. The account was published in Vadim Chernobrov's book Nad propastyu neraskritikh tayn, Moscow, 1997. That morning, at 6:30 a.m., at a military airfield near Sevastopol, Lev Vyatkin was sitting inside the cockpit of his interceptor jet, checking the onboard indicators. A jet maintenance technician interrupted him. Nikolay Yemelyanenko pointed to a luminescent sphere in the sky. Its diameter was not less than 80 metres, its colour that of a burning match. The UFO moved from the north to the south. The sun was not up, yet, and Soviet airmen were able to see the object very clearly, against the cloudless background. Inside the UFO they could see a bluish round centre with its edges brightly green. No noise of any kind was associated with the strange sphere. By then, more witnesses were watching the UFO. But it was not registered by radar. Vyatkin was eager to fly after the object, to investigate it. But after repeated inquiries, the mission control centre would not allow Vyatkin to fly after the UFO. He did find out that his superiors classified the mysterious visitor as a UFO, and were fearful of the consequences. Vyatkin's chase could be interpreted as initiation of an attack. What experience prompted the Soviet air force commanders to stop Vyatkin?

He and five technicians continued their observation of the UFO. It moved at the same altitude, and then stopped. Its luminescence was uniform throughout. Suddenly, from its centre, a small ray appeared and pointed downward, into the ground. The sphere, then, "turned off this ray", and vanished instantly. Some witnesses stressed that the UFO disappeared into thin air. Vyatkin disagrees: he is sure that the sphere rapidly ascended: he heard powerful noise in his earphones, resembling strong hissing sounds. It was estimated that the UFO moved at the speed of 60 to 70 kilometres per hour. The altitude was approximately 300 metres. Initial distance from the airfield: two kilometres.

1974, BOROSOGLEBSK AREA
The area is also named by A. Plaksin (see Chapter Twenty Two) as one of the most important anomalous zones of the former USSR. That year a very interesting case took place at the Povorino airfield. A motionless black cloud appeared over the site. It was hovering at the altitude of seven kilometres. It was approximately a kilometre and a half long. The radar below indicated that it was an aircraft. A jet was sent to intercept it; there were two fliers aboard. A soon as they entered the cloud, a sharp siren pierced their helmet's earpieces. The sound was powerful, above "pain threshold". At the same time their onboard device illuminated the "dangerous altitude" reading, and the aircraft started shaking violently. The fliers were barely able to shut down the power and with great difficulties guided the aircraft out of the cloud. The cloud hovered over the airfield for four hours, and then disappeared. The Soviets were never able to determine what that "cloud" was or consisted of.

THE LOTOS GROUP, ALTAI
Rumours about this military group circulated back in the 1980s. Sergey Skvortzov confirmed the existence of Lotos in his article in NLO Magazine (1999). If true, the Lotos Group was formed in the middle of 1960s. It was created in the Main Intelligence Directorate of the Defence Ministry, USSR. The duties of the secret group included collection of reports and data about all paranormal activities taking place in the Armed Forces of the USSR. The group had a special laboratory where experiments aimed at the creation of cutting-edge weapons, based on use of gravitational and electromagnetic fields. Those unit commanders who sent reports to the Lotos Group signed secrecy oaths. Skvortzov's research concerns the Altai Mountains area, and he established that the Lotos officers paid visits there.

ENCOUNTERS IN THE YEARS 1976 THROUGH 1978
The Petrozavodsk event generated the SETKA programs to be discussed later. Prior to 1977 as a result of the careful observations of the consequences of UFO activities, various orders issued by the Air Force high command absolutely forbid any contact with UFOs. Furthermore, military pilots were not to

approach the unidentified objects any closer than 10 kilometres. Various sources point to 1976 as the year the orders were issued.

STILL CLASSIFIED...

Serious incidents forced the Soviets to act. Colonel Ovsischer and Veniamin Dodin recall the tragic events of the 1960's. Because the incident is still classified, few details are available. It happened in the area of Soviet borders with Iran and Afghanistan. Six modern Soviet aircraft were destroyed, and 12 pilots perished. Apparently it was a UFO attack; but who attacked first? The directive issued by the Supreme Commander of the Soviet Air Defence Forces dated 1965 absolutely forbid to fire on or initiate any military action against unidentified flying objects. The Soviets were faced with the presence of UFOs in the areas of top secret testing of nuclear bombs, missiles, rockets, new technologies and weapons systems. Pesky UFOs hovered over their silos, and secret facilities. To the great irritation of the Soviet aviation, civil and military officials, the UFOs also frequented forbidden Arctic territories. E. Loginov, the civil aviation minister, asked the legendary Soviet Arctic pilot Akkuratov to describe his experiences after four incidents of direct UFO encounters. Akkuratov did, and mentioned in the end that the pilots had many more encounters, but were hesitant to report, because the Soviet press had decreed UFOs do not exist, and those who reported them would be ridiculed. The highly militarised Soviet Arctic has attracted the uninvited guests: in 1972, reddish noiseless disks hovered over a radar unit. When the information was dispatched to the regiment HQ, a reply arrived by radiogram: do not report anymore, UFOs do not exist. Eyewitness Stieglitz and his comrades spent the next six hours observing the non-existing UFOs, while their radar registered the objects.

Soviet Armed Forces, at the time the largest in the world, had their share of bureaucrats, daredevils, vile Party functionaries, brilliant strategists, and dull, bored commanders dreaming about retirement. The UFO Phenomenon was more or less a priority, but just as their Western colleagues, the Soviet military were at loss on how to classify UFOs and deal with them. 1976 was a wake-up year. In the summer, something occurred in the sensitive area along the Chinese border, in the Chita region. The border guards, air defence unit, and civilians reported a very unusual object in the sky. The UFO was elongated; it had portholes, and emitted three rays, directed downwards. It made horizontal moves for three hours. Then it vanished quite suddenly. Despite numerous eyewitnesses, three different types of military radar could not register the UFO.

URKAN, SIBERIAN TAIGA

The source for this information is Entsiklopedia Nepoznannogo or "Encyclopedia of the Unknown", compiled by Vadim Chernobrov, and published in Moscow in 1998. Urkan is an anomalous site in the area of the River Urkan, between Tinda and Zeya. In the early 1970s Soviet Air Force had fruitlessly searched there for UFO landing sites. In the spring of 1970 the Soviets observed frequent UFO flights, not long after the relations between USSR and China were dangerously strained, and warfare ensued over the possession of the Damansky Island. UFO appearances were thoroughly recorded by both sides. Once the UFOs appeared over Mongolia, too, and Mongolian border guards tried to shoot them down in vain. It was the Mongolians who publicly revealed UFO presence in the area. According to them, UFO flight routes were over the Soviet territory, approximately 1660 kilometres to the northeast from Ulan-Bator. Soviet radar operators were able to pinpoint the area more precisely, but all attempts to locate the UFOs ended in failure. The only thing the Soviets were able to establish is that the UFOs appeared and then disappeared over the same area of the remote Siberian taiga not far from Urkan.

Felix Zigel's book UFO Landings in the USSR and Other Countries (Volume 5, 1979) was published in the United Stated in 1992 by Dr. Haines's Federation. There is an interesting entry about Mongolia. Back in 1951, Soviet veterinarian V. D. Petrenko witnesses a UFO landing in the Gobi-Altai Almak area. One evening, at about 7:00 pm, he and his companion observed a blinding flash on a mountain's slope. At a distance of a kilometre and a half they saw an object, shaped as a mushroom cap, of approximately 100 metres in diameter. There were humanoid beings, moving up and down from the object to the ground. It appeared that instead of eyes and stomachs the beings had light projectors. Both eyewitnesses decided to approach the object, but could not go through a force field about 500 metres before the site. Some twenty minutes later, the UFO flashed and departed. The landing site contained scorched ground of 30 metres in diameter. This was the very site where some years later a rich uranium ore was discovered.

"DO NOT FIRE!"

The other incident in 1976 that shook up the Soviet military command took place in Kazakhstan, in the area of Mugojar Mountains. The location was Emba 11 air defence and anti-missile testing range. A huge disk, measuring 500 metres in diameter appeared during the testing of new missiles. The commanding general ordered "open fire", and an antiballistic missile was launched at the UFO. It was blown up by a ray from the huge unidentified object. The insubordinate general was punished (Mark Shteunberg's article reprinted in Anomaliya magazine, April 1992 issue, is one source for this information; Vadim Chernobrov's book Nad propastyu neraskritikh tayn, Moscow, 1997, also mentions the incident briefly, without details).

Soviet Minister of Defence issued a ban on such firings, and mentioned the previous ban that obviously was not obeyed. After 1978 the Soviet military became more efficient when it came to UFO observations and data collection. The order not to shoot at UFOs was disobeyed one last time in the summer of 1981, during the Afghan War. Mark Shteynberg, a Russian-American journalist and a former veteran of Soviet armed forces mentioned in other chapters, reported that in August of that year a giant UFO appeared over the air defence regiment of the Soviet 12th Army of the Air Defence Forces. The area is close to the Iranian border, in the town of Kizil-Arvat. The Soviets were vigilant and nervous, because Saddam Hussein's forces were fighting the Ayatollah's armies. The strange elliptical object hovered at an altitude of seven kilometres. Two MIG-27 jets were dispatched after it. The UFO slowly and noiselessly moved in a northerly direction. The radar registered it without any problem. The captain who flew the leading interceptor told his ground control that he had the UFO in sight. An order from the ground control ordered him to fire two missiles at the target. The UFO disappeared at a great speed. But it was not alone: the leading interceptor and the missiles it fired vanished instantly. No traces of the plane or its missiles were ever found on the ground.

Another confirmation of this incident is found in Vadim Chernobrov's book *Nad propastyu neraskritikh tayn*, Moscow, 1997. The UFO was sighted at the altitude of 7 kilometres. It was shaped like a cigar, its size approximately 100-200 metres. A special commission investigated the incident; it confirmed all facts in the report prepared by the regiment's commander. As a result, he was demoted because he issued orders without asking his superiors (Vestnik, Issue 3, 1992). His arguments that the sighting took place so close to the Iranian border (a mere 100 kilometres) were not accepted. The Soviets knew better than to shoot at UFOs. This was no longer 1976. This time the instruction (see below) was in force.

THE LENINGRAD AREA, 1977

This case was revealed by A. Plaksin (a Soviet military Ufologist we have mentioned before). On June 22, 1977, the Soviets were conducting training flights of the TU-16 jet. The jet was equipped with a so-called "cone" (target for shooting). At the moment when the pilot initiated the "cone", he observed a gigantic fiery sphere in front of the aircraft. At the same time he heard a popping sound, the "cone" was shut down, and the engine of the jet stopped functioning. The pilot tried unsuccessfully to restart it, but after a few seconds it started working by itself.

BALKHASH, 1978

Alexey Valentinovich Smirnov, an engineer and former Soviet military officer, revealed several interesting UFO sightings in an interview with Ukrainian newspaper Nasha Gazeta (December 18, 1999 issue). There are at least ten people who reside in Ukraine, who had served with him, and can confirm his stories.

Smirnov was a patriot of his country (USSR), and like his comrades, military engineers, considered it his duty to develop defence weapon systems. In the 1980s they knew that it would take Pershing just 8 minutes to reach Soviet borders. Smirnov and his colleagues had to create a missile that would be able to shoot down the Pershings during the eight minutes. The problem Soviets faced was that at the supersonic speed, their missile was engulfed by a plasma "hat" while in the thick layers of the atmosphere. The missile's manoeuvrability was lost, and it could not be controlled. Thousands of Soviet researchers had tried to improve their missile's design. Smirnov had access to the Tupolev Design Bureau albums; they contained photographs and technical descriptions of UFOs. Those in charge of the project supposed that such photos and drawings would enhance Soviet designers' creativity.

Smirnov recalls that design engineers shared a story, based on factual events. Pyotr Grushin, another famous Soviet rocket designer, ordered a UFO to be shot down. This took place at the end of 1978, and the UFO hovered over the Soviet testing range Balkhash, at the altitude of 30 kilometres. The missile scored a direct hit. The object burst into many fragments. For one week several large military units searched the area; those soldiers who found fragments were given leave, as a reward. The fragments showed that the UFO consisted of unusual elements. They resembled electronic boards of modern TV sets, except that their elements consisted of atoms and molecules skillfully "mounted" on silica (silicon) base. Mankind does not have the know-how yet to mount elementary particles. But Grushin was able to use this "prompting". Modern Russian anti-aircraft missile's nose and rudder controls are seemingly coated with granite. It is actually silicon, installed through the method of plasma-spray. Because of such technology Soviet designers were able to create a missile able to cross the supersonic barrier in the thick layers of the atmosphere, and shoot down Perhsings over the United States.

1981: A SECOND SUN

Alexey Valentinovich Smirnov, an engineer and former Soviet military officer (see above), served (at the time of the incident) at a testing range of the Soviet anti-air defence forces. The date was July 26, 1981, at 5:10 a.m. That morning Smirnov woke up, and was filled with a sense of dread (he was to observe missile launches later the same morning). He approached an open window. In the predawn sky he observed two suns. One was the usual, the other, a sinister red sphere. The engineer decided that what he saw was an optical phenomenon, and did not take a second look. Soon thereafter he and fifty more officers were in the meeting area before leaving for the testing range. At the same time the crimson sphere, flying at incredible speed, approached them from the south, hovered over their heads for five seconds, and then turned around, and disappeared in the easterly direction.

Soviet engineers were shocked. They knew perfectly well that such a manoeuvre, at the given velocity and altitude was impossible according to terrestrial physics. No human being would survive such turns and the overloads involved. No terrestrial flying craft would be able to fly in such manner. Later, while discussing the incident, Soviet officers recalled strong, causeless fear they all experienced at the time. Smirnov lives in Kiev, and another witness, Yelena Grigoryevna Zaslavskaya, resides nearby, and can attest to his story. She was one of the town's residents (and wife of an officer) who went to the hospital because of the stress caused by the UFO. The town's people discussed the incident, but surreptitiously. They all knew about secret orders that forced unit commanders to report amd collect all information about UFOs, document it in special forms, and send to a designated military unit in Moscow.

For Smirnov's colleagues such orders were quite timely. The airspace over the testing range was divided into sectors. Each sector was observed by special radio telescopes that registered all flight details of launched missiles. Thus visiting UFOs were photographed frequently. Reports about UFOs were then sent to the appropriate place; Smirnov recalls at least twenty such reports.

1981, MUKACHEVO, UKRAINE

Again, we have A. Plaksin to thank for the information about the case. It took place on September 14, 1981. A MIG-23 jet was conducting a training flight. And a fiery sphere appeared from nowhere, right in front of the aircraft. The front part of the jet was destroyed. The pilot had time to eject himself from the cockpit. A. Plaksin claimed that such incidents were never explained by his military UFO research.

1981: STANISLAV MOSKALENKO'S TALE

The U.S. Department of the Navy has a Naval Historical Centre in Washington. The bibliography section of the Centre contains an article published in Soviet Soldier, Issue number 8 (August 1991). The USSR Ministry of Defence published the magazine in English and German. The author, V. Vasilyev, went to great lengths to confirm the episodes told him by Stanislav Moskalenko, military pilot 1st class. The pilot is a well-balanced, clear-thinking man, not prone to fantasies. When he first related the episode to Vasilyev, there was no question the media censorship would never allow it to be published. In 1991, however, times had changed.

In the early 1980's Stanislav Moskalenko served in the Central Asia (we have already described a number of incidents and sightings there). He was the youngest pilot in the regiment. On weekdays he used to fly missions and spent his day's off-duty in a standby flight. The political situation was tense and the neighbouring state continuously resorted to muscle flexing. Its bombers often skirted the Soviet border and Soviet planes had to escort them out.

"Nine zero six" was the call over the loudspeaker, and Moskalenko ran to his airplane. He was ordered to take off soon thereafter. His supersonic fighter gained altitude in a couple of minutes. He made a corrective half-turn and carefully examined the sky. There were no clouds, and the air was crystal clear. In front of him lay the expanse of foreign territory. The fighter airplane sent ahead of Moskalenko could not shoot the target on the first run. His second and third attacks also failed. He could not even detect the target either visually or on the radar sight. "Nine zero five" was ordered back to the base, and Moskalenko was ordered to proceed. The ground aircraft controller could see the target, but the pilots could not. Not visually, not through the scope. Moskalenko's attacks failed. However, the controller ordered him to maintain the heading. The pilot understood he was sent to ram the target. What was he to ram? When the fighter plane pierced the air at the spot where the target supposedly had been, a light fog trapped the canopy for a split second. There were no clouds; there was fog. The controller shouted that the target was right below the plane. Moskalenko turned sharply his plane down and fixed eyes on the expanse below. No target anywhere...But near the ground he saw an object moving left to right. The aircraft controller, Captain Oleg Kazyunin, later stated that the target blip on the radarscope had turned into a thick dot. It flashed suddenly, turned green and began moving quickly towards the scope upper rim. Its movement was so swift that Oleg exclaimed that the target is leaving the zone, at a vertical velocity much faster than a missile. Strange visions came after Moskalenko's own vision became blurred. He saw fires, blurring masks. When he came to himself, Moskalenko levelled the plane, and reported that no target had been detected. His altimeter showed that instead of descending in an inverted flight, he was actually ascending.

For three days their whole regiment was chasing the ghostly target. They flew hundreds of sorties, urgently changed several radar sights, and sent a request to Moscow to allow them to test secret equipment. When it became clear that they had encountered something incomprehensible and inexplicable, it was decided to terminate the flights.

In 1990 Moskalenko recalled the incident to his friend, Major Oleg Belomestnov. What Moskalenko went through next was confirmed by his friend (who doubted the UFO story), and corroborated by Soviet Soldier editors. A sudden, powerful blow in the back knocked him down and flung off the road. Major Belomestnov saw how Moskalenko soared horizontally a few metres, and came crashing down. He helped Moskalenko to his feet, shaken by what he saw.

On his way home, assisted by Major Belomestnov, Moskalenko was in pain, and confused. He had visions, vague and hazy, of some landscapes. Right then he was ordered to stop. A short lean man, clad in black, dishevelled, warned him there might be another "energised strike". The man in black appeared to be telepathic. He paid no attention to Belomestnov, who blasted him with words. He told Moskalenko that this was a warning only. The stranger squatted down and touched his swollen leg with the palm of his hand. It instantly got hot, and the pain vanished. All pain in Moskalenko's body, as well as the delusions that had haunted him from time to time since the attack on the UFO, disappeared completely. The stranger asked Moskalenko questions that convinced the Soviet pilot he knew his thoughts. Apparitions that had haunted Moskalenko for years had been part of the information stored in his subconscious.

Actually, transmitted to him in the form of hallucinations from the UFO he was going to shoot down. The contact established was not quite successful, but not through the fault of the UFO or Moskalenko. Those who are against such contacts distorted the information. And they also knocked down the Major when he talked to his friend and equal in rank. Apparently, he talked too much about the sortie. As to whom the others were, the stranger described them as the "forces of evil". The man in black had disappeared as suddenly as he had appeared behind the pilots. Major Belomestnov, who does not believe in UFOs, confirmed the events of the day to the editors. The story was important enough to be published in a military magazine, and to be kept on file in the U.S. Naval Historical Centre.

IRANIAN BORDER, 1985

Alexey Valentinovich Smirnov, an engineer and former Soviet military officer, revealed several interesting UFO sightings in an interview with Ukrainian newspaper Nasha Gazeta (December 18, 1999 issue). We mentioned several episodes before. Another incident deserves our attention.

It happened on August 17, 1985. At three o'clock at night reports came in to the HQ from the testing areas that numerous objects (crosses, rings, bright dots) appeared in the sky. The officer on duty, Lt. Colonel Valentin Ivanovich Kan, issued orders to photograph the objects. There were all together eleven kilometres of shot film. The orders to the unit were to develop the film, and write a report about the incident. Lt. Colonel Pyotr Sergeyevich Meleschuk was in charge of the project; he resides now in Nezhin, Ukraine. Lt. Colonel Alim Antonovich Ustimenko, responsible for the technical portion of the project, resides in Lokhvitza, Ukraine. There were 30 illustrations in the report. Several types of objects were registered. The main one: a huge white cross against dark sky. It had two crossing bars, each 800 metres long. It hovered in the sky for a long time, and then disappeared, as if into thin air.

The other group of objects consisted of rings. Seven whitish rings visible against the dark sky. They moved all the time. Two of the rings flew parallel course, and then the smaller was immersed into the larger, and there was but one ring.

The third group of objects consisted of bright dots. Strong light emitted from a bright dot in the sky, and diffused, like a cone-like manner. The light was very intensive, and did not abate anywhere along the luminescence.

The report, like other such reports, was sent to Moscow. Smirnov and his colleagues made no further inquiries. The Cold War was in full swing, and they were trying to create new missile technology. Who knows what hovered over Soviet testing ranges and facilities: perhaps UFOs, perhaps enemy intelligence equipment. The Soviets did observe that as a rule, strange objects had appeared right before new missile tests.

When the Ukrainian was asked about his opinion as to the nature of UFOs, Smirnov replied that he is an engineer, a materialist, and he is against anything mystical. He is certain that alien intelligence exists. He also knows that our current level of knowledge does not allow us to communicate with "them". One can fanaticise as much as possible, but that is how things are now. Smirnov often observed rockets piercing the ozone layer of the atmosphere, and harsh cosmic radiation entering the air. It is a spectacular spectacle. Half of the sky is taken by waves of blinding white colour. We feel pride, but do we really understand what happens at the moment? Maybe our experiments cause pain to an alien intelligence that co-exists with us in some other dimension. Similar to how a human being would feel pain, if a nail pierced his skin. So, they send objects to us in order to understand who we are, what we want, and why we do what we do.

THE MONCHEGORSK OBJECT

A highly classified incident, it was researched by Russian Ufologists and some information became available. According to Konstantin Volf and Valentin Psalomschikov, a former Soviet military pilot, Captain N.V. Fedotov, (who had twice personally observed UFOs) was sent to the city of Monchegorsk. Once there, he was told of a UFO captured by the Soviet military. Fellow officers, who knew that the unidentified flying object had been transported to one of the military units in the vicinity of the city, told the story, but they did not know the exact details, nor did they know of the location where the UFO was captured. They had no knowledge of the object's shape and size, but they did know that an explosion destroyed the UFO.

Fedorov could not determine the precise date of the object's delivery to Monchegorsk, but in the approximate period when it happened, the then-President of the USSR, Mikhail Gorbachev, had visited the region, and although it was said his itinerary indicated he was to visit Severomorsk, for some reason, he visited Monchegorsk instead. The press had nothing logical to say about the purpose of the unexpected visit. Is it possible that the captured object had something to do with it?

Yuri Stroganov, a noted Russian Ufologist, personally knows a person involved with the Monchegorsk Object, a man who signed a written statement of non-disclosure of the highly classified information. His name is not provided, and so for our purposes here will be referred to simply as "B." Stroganov sent "B"s diagrams of the object to the Russian Ufology Research Centre.

"B" was silent for five years after being demobilised from the armed forces and the events described below.

In early August of 1987, "B" and four other servicemen from the Leningrad military region (okrug) were sent on an unusual mission to a military unit in Northern Karelia: to guard an "object" of unknown origin and purpose. The object had been recently discovered in the territory of another military unit near Viborg. It was delivered to the vicinity of Monchegorsk by a military transport airplane, placed in the former fuel depot and put under a cover.

The guard detail was given strict orders not to let anyone come near, but the guards had an opportunity to look under the cover more than once. Their commanding officer's gave no explanations to the guard detail, but one of the Leningrad servicemen (who, according to "B", worked in the Leningrad HQ) confided in them that the object was a UFO.

Externally, the object resembled an American "space shuttle." Initially, the object's fore part was mistaken for an aircraft's hull (fuselage). The object was an estimated 14 metres in length, 4.5 metres wide and 2.5 metres high. The body appeared to possess a smooth, seamless, grayish tan finish. When touched, the surface seemed to be somewhat rough, like ceramic. "B" claims that when the guards initially approached the object, each experienced pain.

Three triangles in the fore part were perceived only by their colour hues. No exits or entry doors were visible.

In the rear (after-body), the object looked somewhat chopped off, and there were neither wheeled undercarriages nor any supports. The bottom part of the body was completely smooth. To prevent it from rolling away (the surface was sloped), the object was placed on logs and railroad ties.

About one week after the object's arrival, a special commission comprised of senior officers also arrived on location and at once began to analyse it. Although "B" did not take any direct part in the investigation and research, he was able to observe from a distance. The commission tried to enter the object using autogenous welding techniques, but failed.

After that unsuccessful attempt, the object was moved inside an aircraft shelter (a hangar): an artificial mound with metal gates. Once the object was inside, the gates were immediately welded shut and the servicemen from Leningrad were sent back to their unit.

In early September of the same year, the Leningrad officer who had stayed behind - the only one from the Leningrad group to take part in the actual study of the object - came back. He informed others that the commission was able to penetrate part of the fuselage.

The triangles, visible on the outside only because of their colour tint, were transparent from inside of the object. Most likely, the area entered was a cockpit, or a control room. It definitely was not made for adult humans because two officers could barely fit in.

Inside the cockpit they found two armchairs. What seemed like two steering wheels and a control panel, were located nearby. The control panel looked like a smoothly polished plate; and no buttons, switches or devices were found. According to the officer, it took him half an hour to figure out how to put his hands on the object that reminded him of a steering wheel. No one risked sitting in the armchairs. The officers then attempted to break something off. They succeeded, but only in the stern area.

The officers were able to extract some shiny rods, which varied in size from about twenty centimetres to a metre, some 6 centimetres thick. The officers who had extracted the rods had worn gloves, yet traces of thermal burns were found on their hands.

The incident ended very strangely. A "lieutenant" who arrived in "B"s military unit from the okrug's HQ, told "B" and others that at the end of September the object had unexpectedly disappeared. Allegedly, it vanished after the radio engineering equipment and radars had experienced intense and prolonged interference.

Stroganov cautions us to be prudent. The lieutenant's mission might have been to plant "dezinformatsia" (misinformation) and confuse members of the former special guard unit. One episode is hard to explain: how could a 15 metre long object disappear from a guarded shelter, especially during the malfunction of radio engineering equipment? The military base's personnel knew the 1980 guidelines regarding anomalous phenomena, and, with respect to vigilance, the guidelines are quite specific. What happened to the rest of the commission that investigated the object? Stroganov thinks they had accompanied the object to the SETKA-MO secret laboratory.

SOVIET TOP MILITARY BRASS AND UFOs

Gorbachev's platform for the new Soviet Union was founded on two now quite famous terms: glasnost (openness) and perestroika (restructuring). Glasnost was responsible for the Soviet military leadership revelations about UFOs over the Soviet Union.

The first report, about a sighting dated March 21, 1990, was published in Stalker-UFO (Issue number 1, 1990) newspaper (Leningrad), and other media. The report was made by Colonel-General Igor Maltsev, who at the time was the Chief of the Main Staff of the Soviet Air Defence forces near Moscow. The UFO he mentioned was a disk of about 200 metres in diameter. It had pulsating lights on its sides. The object flew horizontally, and then the line of lights was parallel to the horizon. When the UFO moved vertically, the lights moved in a perpendicular angle to the horizon. The object moved around its axis, and travelled along a zigzag like trajectory. The UFO was registered in the areas of Zagorsk, Pereyaslavl-Zalessky, Fryazin and Kirzhach. The radars confirmed reports of eyewitnesses. Two fighter planes were sent to identify the object (one flown by Lt. Colonel A. Semenchenko). The UFO hovered over an area, and then resumed its movements. Its speed was three times greater than that of a modern fighter plane. The higher its velocity, the brighter became its lateral lights. It was a noiseless craft, and it reached the altitude of 7000 metres. The UFO clearly impressed Soviet generals. They refrained from attacking it because it could have possessed formidable capacity for retaliation (according to Commander in Chief of the Soviet Air Defence Forces and General of the Army Ivan Tretyak, Deputy Minister of Defence at the time). He confirmed Maltsev's statements during his own interview with Literaturnaya Gazeta newspaper (November 9, 1990). What is curious, and supports other UFO military reports, the onboard radars of the fighter planes could not record the UFO. At the same time, Tretyak refused to acknowledge UFOs, yet refused to speculate on the nature of the object.

Colonel-General A. Maximov, Hero of the Socialist Labor, and expert of the Soviet Space program, stated that the Soviet Armed Forces had received special instructions to inform main institutes about UFO sightings. Such institutes were established in all branches of the Armed Forces. Each institute had "working groups" to study the incoming information (Stalker-UFO, Issue 2, November 1990).

In 1993 there was another interesting high-level confirmation of UFOs. This time it came from Colonel-General V. Ivanov, Commander of the Military Space Forces. He was interviewed by a famous and highly respected Russian newspaper Argumenti i Fakti (Issue number 16, 1993). Colonel General mentioned the existence of a military institute for UFO studies.

Former Soviet colonel and one of Russia's top UFO experts, Gherman K. Kolchin, discussed the military interest in UFOs in an interview published in Anomaliya newspaper (Issue 2, 1995). He recalled the conversation with Colonel General Sapkov, who informed Kolchin about the brightly greenish elliptical UFO that hovered over the Kapustin Yar testing range during secret tests of new military technology. The same Colonel-General gave more details in his memoirs. The episode, published in Stalker-UFO (Issue number 3, 1990), was dated November 1979. Sapkov and other officers observed the UFO. It changed hues, and hovered for thirty minutes over the secret rocket testing range. But seven years later, Colonel General Sapkov observed the very same UFO over Kapustin Yar. The officers assured Sapkov that such phenomena are frequently observed over the testing area.

According to General Yevgeniy Tarosev, the reality of UFOs is beyond doubt. He states it in a one page article published in Trud newspaper on August 22, 1992. Trud is a very popular newspaper. Tarosev at the time was the Chairman of the Scientific and Technical Committee of the Commonwealth of Independent States (the entity that replaced the USSR, to a lesser extent). While he did not doubt the reality of UFOs (often chased by Soviet military aircraft), the "physical nature" of the phenomenon was unknown. No overt hostility from UFOs that he knew about, but the pilots had been warned to treat UFOs in a "peace-loving" way.

Colonel-General Gennady Reshetnikov, Chief of the top Command Academy of the Air Defence Forces, is a former Commander of the Air defence Forces of the Soviet Far East. Valery Uvarov, a Russian Ufologist, interviewed him. In his interview, published in Anomaliya (Issue number 3, January 30, 1996), Colonel General mentioned several interesting incidents when aircraft had to be scrambled after UFOs. He investigated a UFO sighting in the late 1970's, over the Arctic area of Norilsk. The UFO was a cigar-shaped craft, with portholes. It visited the area several times, alarming the military.

V. Alexeyev, Major General of the Russian Air Force, an official at the Space Communications Centre made an interesting revelation in ANOMALIYA newspaper (Issue 8, 1997). According to him, some unnamed testing ranges of the Soviet Armed Forces learned how to contact UFOs. Here is how they did it. First, a UFO would appear. For the most parts, they were spherical UFOs. Then the contact would begin. Those engaged in contact would make physical signals, like through spreading one's arms to one or another side. The sphere would compress itself (change its form) into the same direction. If arms were raised upwards three times, the sphere would compress itself vertically, also three times. In the early 1980s, the Soviet leadership allowed conducting experiments with the use of technology (theodolites, radar stations, etc), and as a result, such new equipment would register the unidentified objects.

Alexeyev, in his military capacity, received information from military units throughout the former USSR. He was aware of the existence of the group that conducted actual research, but due to secrecy, his tasks were limited to sending the collected data and information to his superiors. Military people ask no explanations when none are offered. The question was put forth in this manner: we are interested in this and that. Then a chart containing images of UFOs that have been registered would be demonstrated. There were approximately fifty of such images, elliptical, spherical, spaceship-like UFOs, and so on.

Eyewitnesses would be asked what their sighting looked like; then the area would be described, and the reports would be sent elsewhere. When asked to comment on the KGB's research of UFOs, Major General Alexeyev said that interest in UFOs among the military and special services were founded on the desire to determine what the new phenomenon was and what its nature was.

As we shall see later in this book, the military of the states that replaced the disintegrated USSR also pay close attention to UFOs.

THE INSTRUCTION

Information about instructions to the Soviet Armed Forces comes from many sources: Yuri Stroganov, Anatoly Listratov, noted Russian Ufologists, and their colleagues. Of course Colonel-General A. Maximov has already been mentioned. We will discuss the Instruction throughout this book, uncovering more sources and information. Suffice it to say that Vladimir Ajaja provided the exact language of the Instruction; rather, according to many sources, he actually wrote it for the Soviet Armed Forces.

A sharp increase in UFO activity in 1978 had forced appropriate departments within the USSR Academy of Sciences to agree to a research program for anomalous atmospheric phenomena. The code name for this program was SETKA-AN (Akademii Nauk Set' - Academy of Sciences Net, or AS-NET.)

The first act of the SETKA-AN resulted in official sanction of "anomalous atmospheric phenomena" as a descriptive term instead of the forbidden "UFO". The censorship chains on the UFO subject were removed in 1989.

The Ministry of Defence embarked on a similar program, dubbed SETKA-MO (Ministerstva Oboroni Set).

The well-planned tasks of the SETKAs had a terrifyingly effective impact. The "Academic Commission" did its best to prove there are no UFOs, only errors in observation of rocket launches, or at the very least, ball lightning.

SETKA-AN served as a powerful cover, creating a distraction away from the workings of the Ministry of Defence, whose SETKA-MO is said to have been, or is, more serious in its investigations than the academic group (more about the programs is in Chapter 22). Despite the SETKA's nonchalance there had been occasions when "anomalous phenomena" had led to the unauthorised launches of mobile missiles, and on other occasions, the appearance of UFOs during military training exercises had resulted in the breakdown of radio communications and equipment malfunctions.

There had also been reports from military personnel including senior officers, about the strange conduct of UFOs over Soviet missile bases and cosmodromes. Listratov's military sources provide a more vivid picture of apparent unwanted contacts, persistent "visits" and occasional belligerency by the phenomena.

Scientific arguments regarding the nature of UFOs had been the least of the military researchers' concerns; they did, however, pay close attention to the hypothesis that UFOs are manifestations of an ET civilization. Most of all, they have been concerned with UFOs' impact on military technology and on personnel; such impact could be quite unpredictable.

The Russian Ufology Research Centre has obtained several excerpts from the Systematic Guidelines of the Ministry of Defence, implemented in 1980, which apply to UFOs.

The Guidelines for the Soviet Navy had been dated March 7, 1980, and signed by Deputy Commander of the Main HQ of the Navy, Vice Admiral Saakyan.

Stroganov claims the SETKA's activity was successful, and these guidelines are a confirmation. On one hand, the guidelines represent a "treated" statistical analysis of facts that were previously acquired, and on the other hand, can be considered a step toward increasing a net of informants through enlisting the services of the entire military forces in the country.

Each and every serviceman who had observed UFOs had to immediately turn over the information to authorised officials. That particular "step" had resulted in a marked increase of reports of sightings by servicemen. The success of this effort proved to be contagious. In 1984, four years later, the State attempted to increase the ranks of informants through the creation of so-called "anomalous phenomena commissions."

The commissions, according to Stroganov, proved to be another successful effort to pump out information from different strata of the population. Due to the previous debunking efforts directed against the UFO phenomenon by the Academy of Sciences, eyewitnesses were not too eager to contact representatives of any State organisation. The newly born "anomalous phenomena commissions" were seen as "independent action" organisations, however, and that created a certain trust. People largely believed them to be independent, when in actuality such commissions were a cover to conceal an acute interest on the part of the government in the collection of information and research about UFOs.

Stroganov ties these commissions to the SETKA-MO. The commissions first appeared five years prior to the removal of the ban on UFO information in the USSR, and during their existence, the information collected was, according to their members, input into computers. Where the data went thereafter hasn't been explained.

Overall, Russian Ufologists are not certain what had actually been "caught" by the SETKA-MO. Stroganov feels this is because none of the Ufological organisations in the former USSR has done anything that would prompt the declassification of at least some of the results of SETKA-MO research.

The Instructions signed by Saakyan mention two military units where the most serious UFO data collected was to be telegraphed to immediately: Unit 67947 (Mitischi city, Moscow region), and Unit 62728 (Leningrad). "Serious" data concerned the following: physical traces of anomalous phenomena, death of military personnel (as a result of contacts with the anomalous phenomena), and breakdown of technology.

Between the end of 1988 and March of 1989, all Soviet military units, including the one stationed in Yeisk, had destroyed the Instructions of Ministry of Defence, USSR (UFO-related). Units 67947 and 62728 became more classified than before. While glasnost still intoxicated Soviet people, Stalinist secrecy shrouded military collection of UFO data. A military institute empowered to study such data is mentioned later.

THE LABORATORY

Korolyov and Termen, discussed in another chapter, mentioned the "flying saucers research laboratory", and we became curious.

Even during the "perestroika" years it was not possible to locate it. Russian UFO researchers knew that it existed. Finally, the search brought them to the city of Akhtubinsk (not to be confused with Aktuybinsk). The laboratory for "saucer" research has been under the territorial authority of the Kapustin Yar testing range and the Cosmodrome. Although the location of the laboratory had been a State secret, the UFOs were not affected by the Soviet secrecy. "They" had been observed over the lab immediately after its creation.

Stroganov and his colleagues were able to collect interesting and relevant information about the lab. Its main research has to do with antigravity and propulsion (assisted by electric and magnetic fields). Numerous Soviet directors of research institutes would be quite surprised if they had found out that the projects, financed and managed by the military-industrial complex, were actually part of the research of the "flying saucers" mystery.

V. Pupkov, a Lt. Colonel (Retired) added more information about Akhtubinsk. His article was Published in Chetvertoye Izmereniye i NLO newspaper, 1995 He confirms the existence of such a lab in the city. Akhtubinsk is also home to the famous V.P. Chkalov Institute and the flight and testing centre of the Air Force. The centre is better known as Vladimirovka (among Russia's top guns). Vladimirovka is the place where most advanced Russian jet fighters are tested, as well as some other aircraft. The same place is home to the Centre of pilot and pilot-navigator training. One could compare Vladimirovka to the American Area 51. Instead of the Nevada desert, endless Kalmik and Kazakh deserts separate the Vladimirovka from the world. A few dozen kilometres from the Vladimirovka one finds Russian cosmodrome and missile testing range Kapustin Yar.

In 1978 Nilolai Semirek was sent to serve at the Centre after having graduated from the Tambov Military Aviation Technical College. In spring 1979 (before the Instruction was in force) he was operating his radar and noticed several targets moving at impossible speeds: they flew 350 kilometres in 50 seconds. Over all, that night hundreds of UFOs moved through the sky at the same speed. Neither Semirek nor the officer on duty wanted to report the incident to the CO (NLO Magazine, Issue 46, 1997).

WHAT HAPPENED IN 1982?

Details about this remarkable and frightful case are found in the chapter about KGB and UFO files.

We want to elaborate on this case because of former Colonel Sokolov. Reports received from Russia indicate that Soviet Colonel Boris Sokolov investigated the case, and on October 5, 1982, he was sent to Ukraine. Sokolov knew quite a lot about UFOs, as he was involved in the information collection and analysis per the Instruction. The reason he was summoned to the Soviet Ukraine was an urgent report from an ICBM base, sent to the Chief of General Staff. On October 4th, a UFO was observed in the area; it remained there for about four hours. But the control panel indicated that an order came in to prepare launch of the bases missiles. Lights actually lit up on the panel, and launch codes enabled the missiles; there were many officers present that witnessed the incident that could have started a nuclear war. Apparently Boris Sokolov's team came to the conclusion that it was the UFO that bears responsibility for arming Soviet missiles. In the year 2000 Sokolov changed his views, perhaps under direct pressure, and came out against UFO hypothesis in this and other cases. We will discuss this in our later chapters.

SOVIET ASIA

A very interesting meeting once took place between civilian Ufologists and lecturers and Soviet military. The meeting took place in Soviet Kirgizia, in the town of Temga, in 1990. The lecturers were from SAKKUFON, a UFO study organisation. Those present included patients of the Temga military hospital. The town is located in a strategic area. Not all of the officers present had been aware of the Instruction of the Ministry of Defence USSR, which seems to confirm Stroganov's argument. However, not the entire Soviet military stationed in Asian republics (today's sovereign states) had been uninformed. The area of special interest to SAKKUFON was the former Soviet-Chinese border along the Tien-Shien Mountains. The area, on the border with China, has had its share of UFO sightings (as we have mentioned before), and the SAKKUFON had collected many of them. Its expeditions to the mountains had Soviet military and KGB people participation.

One report came from the students from the top-rated Alma-Ata Military All-Branches Command College. It claimed that between May 15 and 18, 1990, the Avoku firing ground range hosted military tactical exercises for second-year cadets. Lt. Colonel Chernov and his assistant were riding in their automobile to the designated area. Upon arrival, the officer quite unexpectedly sighted a big cigar-shaped object emitting a ray of light. Then the UFO separated into four parts that flew in different directions. Ten minutes later the same "parts" formed a sphere. The sphere entered the mother ship located nearby. All students at the exercises observed the incident, as well as their higher-ups. It all took place 48 kilometres to the north of Alma-Ata.

STRANGE HELICOPTER

On March 25, 1990, Izvestiya newspaper reported an interesting UFO sighting. The air traffic controllers of the Nalchik Air Detachment had observed an unidentified flying object for 23 minutes on their screens. A crew of the Mi-2 helicopter observed the same UFO. The commanding officer of the detachment, as well as a flight controller named in the article clearly stated that the object registered by their radar was not one of meteorological nature. The speed of the object equalled 100 to 200 kilometres an hour, and it flew at a low altitude. Hence, the conclusion initially was that the registered object is a helicopter. But their inquiries revealed that no helicopters were present in the area. At that time, a Mi-2 helicopter was in the air, for a training flight. The crew was able to visually observe the UFO in question. Radar screens indicated that Mi-2 approached the UFO. When the distance between them was narrowed to six kilometres, both objects disappeared from the screen for 18 to 20 seconds. Yet the two-way communications between the helicopter and the air traffic controllers did not disappear. When both objects reappeared, ground control noticed that the UFO was flying parallel to the Mi-2. A short time later the object changed its course, and headed towards the helicopter. The Mi-2 immediately changed its course, and headed to the base. Local air defence units also observed the same UFO in the sky.

According to the commanding officer of the Mi-2 helicopter, the pilots noticed a brightly lit object and flew towards it. The Sun was bright; the object flew below the Mi-2, in a haze. When the UFO headed towards the helicopter, as if trying to ram it and sharply increasing in size, Soviet pilots noticed that its diameter was about three metres. The UFO's shape was spherical. To prevent an impact, the crew decided to turn away.

It was an unusual case, because as a rule, UFOs did not register on radar screens. A. Kazikhanov, the reporter for Izvestiya, recorded conversations with the crew.

STRANGE AIRCRAFT

Retired Soviet Colonel I. Tikhonov sighted something so interesting that the experience prompted him to write to Agitator Armii I Flota newspaper. Issue 17, 1990 carried his report of an "aircraft" he observed in the sky one morning not long before the publication. The aircraft had no wings, and flew noiselessly.

The inversion trail was as large as five such airplanes, but disappeared immediately, unlike the ones made by regular aircraft.

RUSSIAN MILITARY AND UFOs

Yuri Stroganov, through his military contacts, had collected some information about mobile UFO-research groups capable of rapid response. Case in point: March 15, 1994, at 14:00 hours, a missile base of the Russia's air defence forces.

A report came into the unit's HQ that some "thing", resembling a flying saucer, landed right in front of the main building. Five minutes later all those not on combat duty surrounded the plaza in front of the building, their machine guns aiming at the "thing". The object stood in the middle of the plaza on three supports. Reporting officers mentioned that they looked at the object from a distance of 100 to 150 metres. It was shaped as a disk, with a dome on the top, three semi-spheres on the bottom, and three landing supports. The size of the "visitor" was reported as 23-24 metres in diameter; the dome was 6 to 7 metres; and the semi-spheres ranged from 4 to 5 metres. Its colour was silvery, with bluish tints. The object created a reflecting mirror effect.

At 14:10 hours, per the Instruction of 1980, the unit's watch officer reported about the UFO to superiors. Their order was not to approach the UFO, and to cease all activities that could render a response from the object. The order also instructed the base to get ready to receive an airplane-laboratory with a group of 15 military specialists onboard. They arrived at 15:20 hours. After filming the object on their approach to the plaza, they split into three equal groups. The specialists were clad in hermetically sealed and shiny suits, and held some instruments. They approached the UFO, and when the distance to it was some 6 metres, the object or the surrounding air "rippled". A sizzling noise was heard, and the soil shook a little. Then the UFO initiated a slow ascent, and at the same time, "pulled" the asphalt-covered surface of the plaza towards itself. The "pull" occurred from the edges, and to the centre of the plaza. When it reached the altitude of 15 metres, the UFO stopped, its supports disappeared. It made a spiral-like turn, and vanished in a blast of bright light. The experts remained in the area for one more day.

Who is in charge of Russia's military UFO research? According to interviews in 1994, the head of the military UFO research program is Major-General A. Savin, commander of one of the units of the General Staff of Russia's Armed Forces.

Russian Ufologists tried to confirm that the military have in their possession captured UFOs or parts thereof. Gherman Kolchin and his colleagues made an inquiry in 1992. Kotenkov, the deputy chief of the legal department of the President of Russia, in charge of the defence and security matters, gave a vague answer: he personally did not hear of any objects kept anywhere for some research and study. Colonel Sokolov, who revealed several aspects of the Soviet and Russian military research to visiting American journalists in 1993, stated that he never had any material traces of the existence of UFOs. But Sokolov also, according to Kolchin (NLO Magazine, 2000) mentioned that three Soviet jet fighters crashed, when they tried to chase a UFO, and one pilot perished.

Listratov confirmed that the Soviets did capture remnants of a UFO (in Omsk area), and used it for their "Star Wars" program. A. Anfalov, who has collected interesting data on alleged UFO crashes, confirmed other reports. Of great interest is his data about the 1981 UFO explosion in the forbidden Kola Peninsula area. We mention the area in other chapters of the book, and it certainly deserves close attention. Soviet military experts collected the fragments of the object. Anfalov's report was published in Chetvertoye Izmereniye i NLO newspaper (Issue 8, 1996), and created a stir. He named the military base from where the Monchegorsk Object was transferred to Monchegorsk: the Veschevo air force base. Anfalov also revealed the date of the Omsk Incident: October 13, 1987. A UFO blew up, and pieces were collected by Soviet military. But in its July 18, 2003 issue, Russian newspaper Pravda revealed that mystery of Omsk UFOs (of June 20, 2003) was finally unveiled. According to the newspaper, it was the Molniya-M rocket and the launching of a military satellite from Plesetsk Cosmodrome into space. The second-stage of the carrier rocket separated and fell to the ground. "The separation of the second stage happens thousands of kilometres far from the cosmodrome. It is possible to see something only during sunset or before dawn hours, when it is night on Earth, but the rocket's tail of gas is lit with the sunlight. In Russia, such events can be seen only in Omsk and on the outskirts of the city", according to Yevgeniya Lifantyeva, the reporter. Most likely the above also explains the Omsk Incident mentioned by Lsitratov and Anfalov.

The Soviet government had assigned the task of creation of their "star wars" to NPO Energia and a group of military-industrial enterprises. On August 24, 1996 RSC Energia of Russia (its current name) celebrated its 50th anniversary as a pioneer in the field of space technology. The legendary Academician Sergei P. Korolev founded what has become today a private Russian corporation. During the 1970's and 1980's Energia was engaged in complicated space warfare projects. Two combat spacecraft were developed, using the same design, but equipped with different types of onboard weapons complexes: laser and missile systems.

In the early 1990's Russia's Space Missile Defence Forces picked up the projects. Victor Smirnov, Colonel General in charge, mentioned several entities engaged in the projects: he Vympel JSC, Kometa R&P Associates, Research Institute for Electronic Devices, and Research Institute for Long-Range Radio Communications Systems ("Space Missile Defence Forces: Yesterday, Today, Tomorrow", 1997). Of course, there are others (such as the mysterious Izhevsk Electromechanical Works) he never mentioned. Whether the technology used for their projects is of extraterrestrial origin is a question that will get no answer any time soon. President Yeltsin had issued a decree in July of 1997, and ordered the Space Missile Defence Forces, Russian Space Forces, and Strategic Rocket Forces to be reformed into one centralised military branch. It would be known as the Strategic Rocket Forces, and consist of rocket forces, military units and facilities for spacecraft launches and control, special defence forces for space defence. This was to be done by January 1, 1998.

In August of 2000, the world learned that Russia intended to cut the size of its nuclear rockets, and merge its armed forces (restructuring of Russia's armed forces that would start in 2001 and result in three branches of the military land, sea and air, rather than four, including the Strategic Rocket Forces). President Vladimir Putin, as has been reported, would cut some land-based nuclear missiles and merge the Strategic Rocket Forces with the air force. Silo-based missiles, which become obsolete in 2003, will be scrapped.

The aim was to put greater emphasis on the navy's submarine-based missile deterrent.

Russia's navy will once again become one of the leading naval forces in the world. And those officers, who have encountered strange, unidentified objects and beings in the sky and under the ocean's surface, may play an important role in the new Russian navy.

Will we ever get to see the priceless paranormal phenomena files of the Soviet Naval intelligence? Will we ever find out what was truly collected by Soviet Armed Forces between 1980 and 1989, when paranormal phenomena became a focus of monumental, comprehensive research? As more former KGB officers assume the reigns of power in today's Russia, the answers to our questions are not clear. Yet President Putin makes it clear in his speeches that he supports democracy in Russia. Meanwhile, Russia and Iran have jointly begun to study UFOS observed over Iran in 2005. There are interesting rumours coming out from Russia that Putin would declassify certain UFO files. The situation is far from being clear.

Russian newspaper "Novaya gazeta" reported on 26 of October 1998, that the Defence Ministry houses a group of specialists studying "paranormal phenomena," such as UFOs and occult practices. According to the newspaper, Major-General Aleksei Savin, who heads the unit, allegedly founded the group in the late 1980s at the behest of former General Staff Chief of Staff Mikhail Moiseev. The unit reportedly conducts experiments on humans, specifically military cadets. Allegedly, it also won support from the highest levels of the Defence Ministry, when some of its staff "predicted" the ascent of Anatolii Kvashnin to Moiseev's position.

A CHRONOLOGY OF SIGHTINGS

1962. June. Lesozavodsk, Soviet Far East. Two witnesses, Nechayev and Sindeyev, were fishing in a river close to the Chino-Soviet border (militarised area). Shortly before midnight they observed a crimson-coloured luminescent sphere. It moved toward them noiselessly and slowly, some four metres off the ground. The sphere stopped at a short distance, hovered for a few moments, and then flew away slowly.

1968 - The Riga area, Soviet Latvia. In May of that year, Soviet soldier Novitzky and three of his comrades observed that three artillery battalions fired on an object hovering high in the sky. Its size was several times less than the visible disk of the Sun. Ten missiles were fired, and all blew up before reaching the object. The object later ascended and disappeared.

1970 - The "Kapustin Yar" Cosmodrome. It happened the night after the secret launches of new rockets. A UFO alarms the sentries, and their shouts awake others. The sky was clear and starry. A giant black object, dirigible-like, hovered over the rockets. The UFO emitted a thin, needle-like green ray. It seemed to grope the positions of rockets. A sentry panicked and fired at the UFO. The ray vanished. Some soldiers immediately screamed in pain: they had developed horrible headaches.

1978 - January. Location: Soviet Arctic areas. Source: Pavel Popovich, Russian cosmonaut. During their flight between Medveziye and Nadim, crew of a Yak-40 airplane, observed a very bright sphere. It approached, and flew right at them. The UFO increased its size. Then, just before an imminent collision, the sphere veered off upwards.

1978 - The "Baikonur" Cosmodrome, Leninsk. A UFO hovered over one of the facilities. Alarmed sentries fired at it. The UFO replied in its own way: all communications were interrupted, ceased to function and the illumination failed.

1978 - Gatchina region, Lenigrad oblast. A military engineer, expert in the missile and space exploration technology, witnessed the incident, in October. Strange looking cone-shaped "sacks" were hanging around power cables. The colour and sizes of the "sacks" changed from transparent to dark; they became bigger. Later the "sacks" ascended, and became smaller, as if sucked out.

Igor Filatov, the eyewitness, then observed three flattened disks, silver-coloured, and with portholes. They hovered over the cables for 30 seconds, and then disappeared in the westerly direction, against the wind. The same witness reported another UFO sighting on the 31st of October, the same year. There were hundreds of other witnesses, too. A ray noticed by Filatov from the train turned into a cigar-shaped object. It hovered for a moment, and slowly descended. Its coloured changed, from grayish to white. The object appeared to be a rocket, but there was a fiery sphere next to it. Later, there were two spheres; the "rocket" was still changing its appearance.

1979 - The incident took place in the Tver area, the town of Toropetz, in September. Aleksandr Alekseyev was serving in the paratrooper troops of the Spetznaz. The order that was announced over the loudspeakers informed the troops that in the area the First Mounted Army settlement's radars and jet interceptor located a UFO. No contacts with the UFO and no actions against it whatsoever stated the order. Increase visual observations. The object returned to the area the next evening. It hovered over Alekseyev's regiment. He was able to see it: the UFO looked like a plate turned upside down, it moved erratically, hovered, rapidly descended, and then rapidly turned sharply left and right. The UFO "played" like that for five minutes, and then flew away in the south-western direction.

1980 - The incident reported by V. Pupkov, a Lt. Colonel (Retired), took place at the Domna airfield, in the Trans-Baikal military district, in December. In the late evening hours, a UFO appeared over the airfield, very suddenly. The object was red in colour, and luminescent. Its shape was that of a ring. The UFO pulsated, and emitted several reddish rays to the ground. A MIG-23 was sent to investigate. Colonel Antonetz, who flew it, reported the UFO to be at the altitude of 4000 metres. The object slowly dimmed, and disappeared. Soon thereafter a special commission arrived in the airfield, investigated, and took signed secrecy oaths. No one found out what happened to the collected information. Colonel Antonetz later, after the fall of the USSR, was appointed Commander of Ukraine's Air Force. Another incident took place in the area two years later (we will discuss it at length later in our underwater UFO chapter)

1980s - Location: Lake Ladoga area, Morye Village. On several occasions UFOs visited the testing-range; they hovered over it for 10 to 15 minutes each time. The air-defence units opened fire, but scored no hits.

1984 - End of October. Location: Sea of Laptev area, Russia's northern territories. Valery Lukin, head of an expedition to the Arctic and Antarctic areas, received a disturbing report. A UFO was reported in the area, and the border guards confirmed that they had observed fire thirty kilometres from the base airport. Lukin and others took a helicopter up. They observed a sphere; it emitted raspberry-coloured luminescence. It was "internal" luminescence, not like floodlights would make. The UFO would not let them come close, and vanished when the helicopter was three minutes away from reaching it. They circled the area for half an hour, but found nothing.

1984 - Two Soviet jet fighters fired on an identified object, moving at the altitude of 2000 kilometres, over the eastern shore of the Caspian Sea. When the object approached the city of Krasnovodsk, a helicopter opened fire on it, but to no avail. The object continued its flight.

1986 - Reported by Sergei Smirnov, an engineer and former Soviet military officer. On August 18, 1986, Smirnov was given orders to guide a column of trucks to a new testing site. He was seated in the front vehicle, next to a driver, a Kazakh, who spoke very little Russian. The weather was quite hot. An arid Kazakh semi-desert lay outside the window. All of a sudden Smirnov felt fear. Then he observed straight in front of him, at the distance of 500 to 700 metres, at the altitude of 3 to 4 metres, a steely disk. Its diameter was some 150 to 200 metres. There were no portholes at all. Smirnov felt very bad, had a feeling of impending death. The Kazakh felt something similar. He screamed something in his language, dropped the wheel, and cowered on the bottom of the cabin. The truck lost direction, ran into a swamp, its vehicle stalled. Smirnov climbed out of the cabin, and got stuck in the dirt up to his knees. At the time the object ascended, at great speed, and across the laws of aerodynamics. It was gone in a mere moment, leaving behind a column of dust.

The Kazakh driver was very ill by then. Smirnov took him to the hospital. Later he wrote a report about the incident.

1987 - The month was April; the area of the incident was the Kizil Arvat airfield of the Turkestan military district. The eyewitness to the incident was Lt. Colonel Ivan Ivanovich Zhdanov. He and other officers walked to the HQ at approximately 24:00 hours. They noticed a strange object overhead. The sky was clear, starry, and across it, noiselessly, slowly, moved this object that looked like white lights, seemingly tied together. They could not determine its altitude, as there was nothing to measure it by except for the lights. The flight might even be in the space. All who observed the flight estimated that the structure (the UFO) was gigantic. The officers decided not to write any reports; they had agreed that what they saw was a satellite.

1989 - Siberia. On October 28 of that memorable year, in the vicinity of Irkutsk for over three hours displays of the Irkutsk, Bratsk, and Zhigalovsk airports, as well as local anti-aircraft military units, registered numerous UFOs. The objects moved at complicated trajectories, crossing the flight patterns of aircraft, and sometimes flying behind the jets. Some objects flew towards the jets. This information was revealed in a Ukrainian newspaper Kiyevskiye Vedomosti (Issue dated December 25, 1997). More detailed information about the strange incident that day had appeared in the Soviet magazine Vozdushni Transport on November 2nd, 1989. The article mentioned that UFOs also followed a Korean aircraft. Among Soviet aircraft the article mentioned An-12, An-24, An-26, and TU-154 airplanes. No UFO approached any aircraft closer than 20 or 30 kilometres, a safe distance indeed.

1990 - It happened in the month of December, in Kuybishev. Long-range radar picked up a blip on its screen at a range of 60 miles. The shape, size, and other readings were comparable with a strategic bomber. The automatic friend or foe system failed, so they couldn't tell if the object was hostile or not. They had it on the screen for 2 1/2 minutes. The UFO separated into smaller objects. The largest object had a triangular shape and heading toward radar post. It stopped and hovered at 300 feet. Soldiers observed a flash and a mobile, short-range radar array was ignited and subsequently collapsed to the ground; it was melted. The craft was described by both enlisted and officers as black and smooth - not reflective. It was about 45 feet long and 10 feet thick.

There were no openings or portholes. It hovered there for about 90 minutes and then took off and disappeared completely in the night sky.

1990 - February 24, six in the morning, near the city of Odessa. A UFO hovered over a border guard frontier post. It had silvery colour, like tin foil. The UFO looked like the Moon, but its upper part seemed cut off. Its bottom part revealed a small semi-spherical cut. The luminescence was like that of a raging fire. It also rotated rapidly. One side of the UFO was illuminated along its length by a powerful light source (not the Sun). The nearby frontier post reported that a module separated from the UFO. Ground radars also registered the UFO. The object hovered for close to two hours.

1990 - Early summer. Port of Loksa, Estonia. A. Maksimovich, Soviet Navy officer, reported a strange bright object. It hovered noiselessly in the clear sky. For four hours he had observed it through a looking glass. The UFO was spherical, its luminescence very bright. The object changed colours. Other crewmembers and their commander watched the UFO. The onboard radar was not able to register it. The border guard vessel in the vicinity also observed but could not register the UFO.

1990 - This happened in the city of Grozny. Major Ryabishev was ordered to fly his fighter jet to the area of a UFO registered by ground radars. He obeyed, but upon arrival found nothing. Flying back he noticed two giant cigar-shaped objects behind the jet. He turned it around to approach the UFOs, but they instantly vanished. Ground radars registered both UFOs.

1990 - At the end of the year Colonel Nikolai Chaga was conducting a night training flight in the area of Lipetsk and Dobriy. The sky became strangely illuminated as the craft was ready to land. The pilot observed an elliptical formation that resembled a dirigible, with a bright star on its "nose". It seemed to Chaga that the object was hovering quite close to him, at the altitude of 3000 metres. The Colonel reported this situation to the flight control centre. They already knew about it, as a civilian pilot who flew the Moscow-Voronezh route, reported the same UFO. Chaga wanted to find out more about the UFO, and he asked the control centre for permission to fly-by the object, but the response was "Nyet!" Meanwhile the dirigible changed into something that reminded him of a whale, but instead of a tail it had white rays steaming into different directions. Later it became known that many military pilots observed the same, but were afraid to report the situation, so as not to be considered mentally unstable (the crude Russian expression used by Chaga was "choknutiye"). UFOs frequented the Lipetsk area for the next two months. Chaga collected drawings of the objects drawn by his colleagues and photos made by onboard cameras. The mysterious objects usually appeared during training flights. "They" were careful, as if not to cause accidents. Most were lentil-shaped, but some were sphere-shaped. Colonel Vladimir Litvin almost collided with such "spheres" during the fake attack of his MIG-29 against a target. Five greenish-blue objects were flying in a formation. The largest one was in the anterior. The distance between each UFO was precise. Their speed was constant. The MIG's onboard equipment did not register anything unusual. The area of the training battle was closed, and only two aircraft could be present there. Yet the UFOs were there, and the MIG was about to collide with the "spheres". The frontal UFO directed a green ray at the pilot. It blinded Litvin. But he was able to activate the colour filter of the helmet protecting him, and cowered. After conducting a manoeuvre the pilot saw that the "spheres" were gone. Litvin decided not to make a report, but checked the craft for damages, and found none. In the morning he learned that his onboard equipment photographed the UFO. Chaga checked the film, and confirmed its authenticity. He wanted to publish the photos in 1990, but advised not to raise hell. One year later he was contacted by Marina Popovich, who asked for the photos. Chaga gave her the photos when he was in Moscow to receive his Distinguished Pilot of the USSR rank. Marina Popovich kept the pictures, and the ones in the flight control centre were destroyed, for the policy was to burn the photographs after one year of storage.

Today Nikolal Chaga is Major-General (Ret.) of Aviation. Marina Popovich turned the photos over to Komsomol'skaya Pravda newspaper, where the story about the encounters was published on April 7, 2005.

1990 - This incident was reported by Vladimir Ajaja in NLO Magazine (1999). The place was Samara, the date September 13. A giant pulsating, triangular UFO was registered by military radar. It "swallowed" the radar's waves at the distance of 5 kilometres. When local officers came to the surface from their underground facility, they noticed the UFO over their heads, flying low, at the altitude of 10 metres. Its bottom part was smooth, but not reflecting. They found no apertures, portholes, or landing parts. Its side of the triangle was some 15 metres long. Its colour was black. The thickness of the UFO was approximately three metres. The object emitted powerful radiation, as was established later. It emitted a forceful ray that destroyed the radar's antenna and set it ablaze. The aiming was precise; the ray went around corporal Dudnik. It also landed, very quietly, for a period of time not exceeding an hour and a half. There was a case of missing time associated with the incident: one corporal and a soldier disappeared for the period that the UFO was on the ground. Both were convinced they were on their posts. The corporal's bayonet and machine-gun had their serial numbers removed by some means.

Pavel Kirillov confirmed the story, and published the information in Tainy XX Veka magazine (Issue # 6). His account is as follows. Shortly after the midnight hour a large object appeared on the radar screen. The UFO was approaching a local Soviet radar station, and did not acknowledge inquiries from the automatic identification control system. Furthermore, the object transformed itself: it dissipated into small fragments, creating a cloud of sorts. Then, having collected all the fragments into one mass, the UFO resumed its movement. Now the displays clearly showed a glimmering isosceles triangle. But at the distance of five kilometres from the station the object disappeared. A group of officers ascended from the underground command centre to the observation deck. And just as they did, an identified object approximately 15 metres long flew right over their heads. Its bottom portion was but ten metres away from the officers. It emitted three light-bluish rays upwards. This mysterious triangle circled over the station, and landed nearby, close to the fence. Next, an incredible occurrence took place: the antenna, located inside the fenced area, caught fire. It fell to the side, and burned as if it was made from wood. Some unknown force shattered the mechanisms of the antenna's drive, and scattered nearby. The wagon where they were kept was melted, and the paint blackened and swelled up like bubbles. The aluminium parts of the antenna literally oozed as drops of melted matter. The energy impulse generated by the triangle (Kirillov believes it to be the source) caused the damages from the distance of 143 metres. The impulse was indeed a powerful concentrated force. The triangle remained by the station for an hour and a half. It is not known what other damages it had caused at the military site.

1992 - Soviet Far East. Radars followed flight of the new Russian SU-27 fighter plane. It suddenly vanished form the screens. The territory's air defence HQ reported that a UFO was sighted in the area at the time of the disappearance. Subsequent intensive search and investigations lasted for one month, and failed to account as to where the aircraft disappeared.

It is not often that UFO researchers reach agreement, but the one thing that most of them do agree upon is that pilots, either civilian or military, along with other trained military personnel, do probably make the most reliable witnesses to UFO events. Because of the huge size of the former Soviet military machine it comes as no surprise that we seem to have an abundance of UFO sighting reports from Soviet military personnel. It is without doubt that such military personnel have encountered the enigmatic UFO in the former USSR in great profusion and as a result, remain as mystified as the rest of us as to the exact nature and origin of these mysterious aerial visitors.

Professor Kulik   Soviet Ufologist Vladimir Ajaja

Mikhail Gershtein

Drawing of the UFO over Riga

Charjou, Summer 1978
No object was observed during the shooting

Настоящая методика предназначена для систематизации и первичной обработки сообщений о наблюдениях аномальных атмосферных и космических явлений путем выделения определяющих признаков каждого или групп явлений.

Выбор перечня определяющих признаков наблюдаемых явлений и их классификация проводились на основе изучения имеющихся отечественных и зарубежных сообщений об аномальных атмосферных и космических явлениях и использования накопленного опыта их обработки.

Схема систематизации и обработки информации в целом включает:
- массив первичных /исходных/ сообщений /документов/,
- журнал регистрации поступления первичной документации,
- учетно-контрольную карточку,
- информационную карточку наблюдения.

I. МАССИВ ПЕРВИЧНЫХ /ИСХОДНЫХ/ ДОКУМЕНТОВ.

К первичным документам относятся:
а/ письма с описаниями наблюдений аномальных явлений, написанные наблюдателями или со слов наблюдателей,
б/ машинописные или ксерокопии писем в соответствии с п.а/,
в/ донесения, рапорты о наблюдениях,
г/ копии записей или выписки из записей в рабочих или оперативных журналах организаций, проводивших наблюдение,
д/ докладные записки о наблюдениях или копии с них,
е/ телеграммы с описаниями наблюдения,
ж/ рисунки, схемы и т.п. графические материалы, присланные наблюдателями,
з/ фотографии, негативы, кинодокументы,
и/ дополнительные письма и документы, присланные в ответ на запрос,
к/ ответы на опросные листы,
л/ записи бесед со свидетелями и т.п. материалы и документы.

Все материалы нумеруются в порядке поступления в данный отдел архива, на них проставляется индекс данного отдела архива, а также номер по архиву центральной рабочей группы в случае, если документ или его копия передан в этот архив.

Все первичные документы складываются в порядке нумерации в специальные папки исходных данных /исключение может составлять архив

One of the SETKA documents - Courtesy of M. Gershtein

UFO over Yaroslavl, 1983

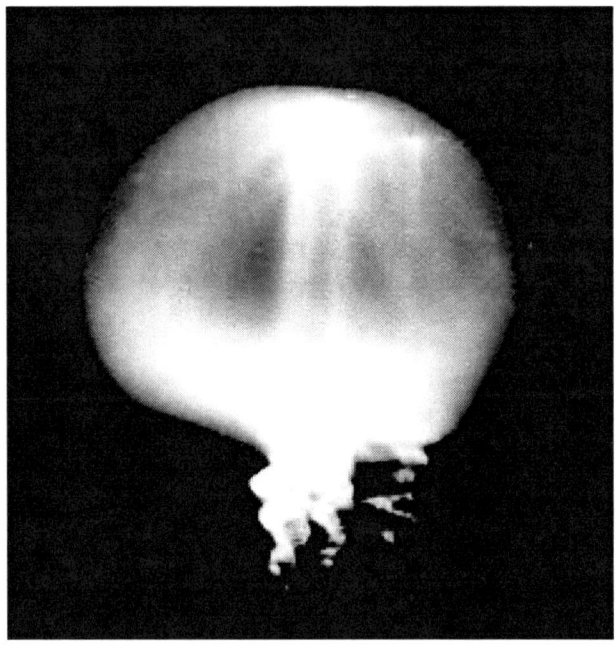

This photo was taken aboard the ship Komsomolets Karelii

UFO over a lake in the Urals in 1976 - Taken by S. Moskoskikh

Crimea, Ukraine, 1988

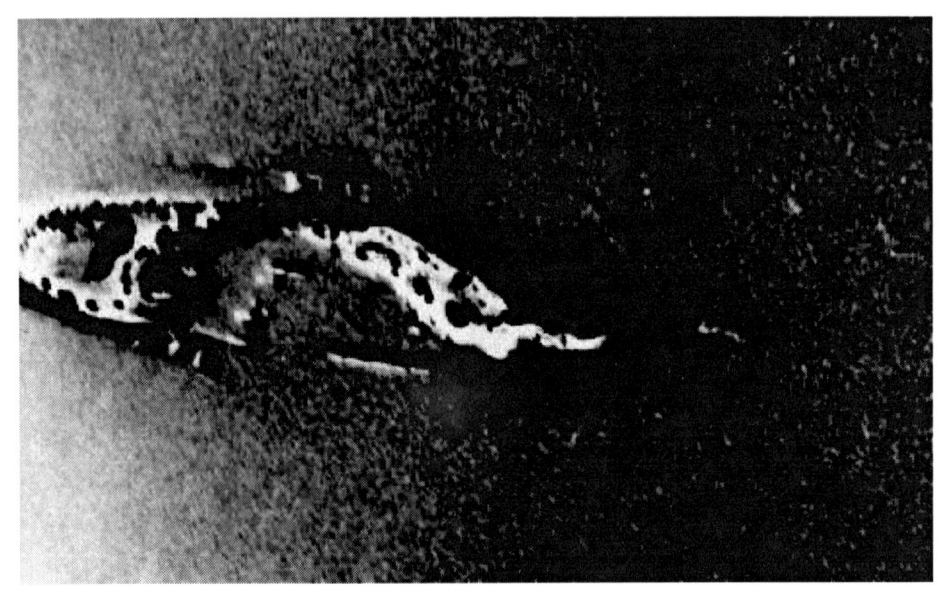

The Norilsk UFO

UFO photographed
near Moscow in 1989

UFO over Murmansk 1978

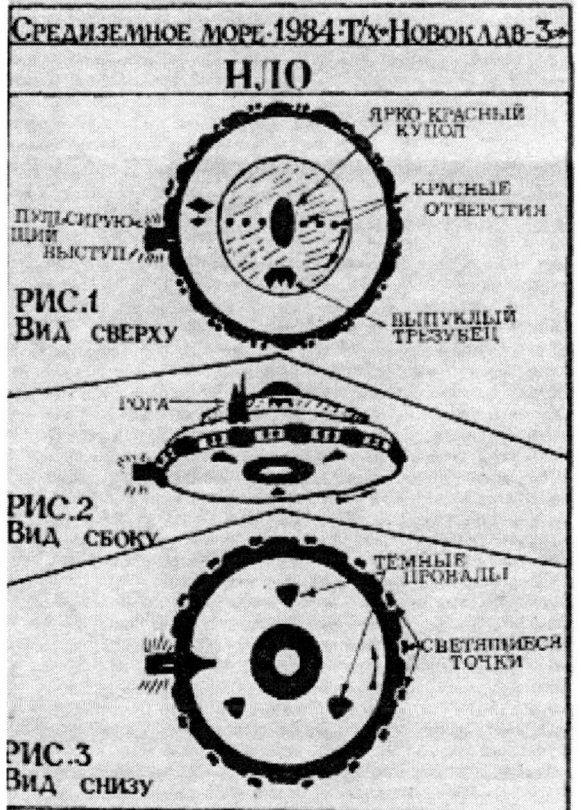

The Gori 1984 diagram

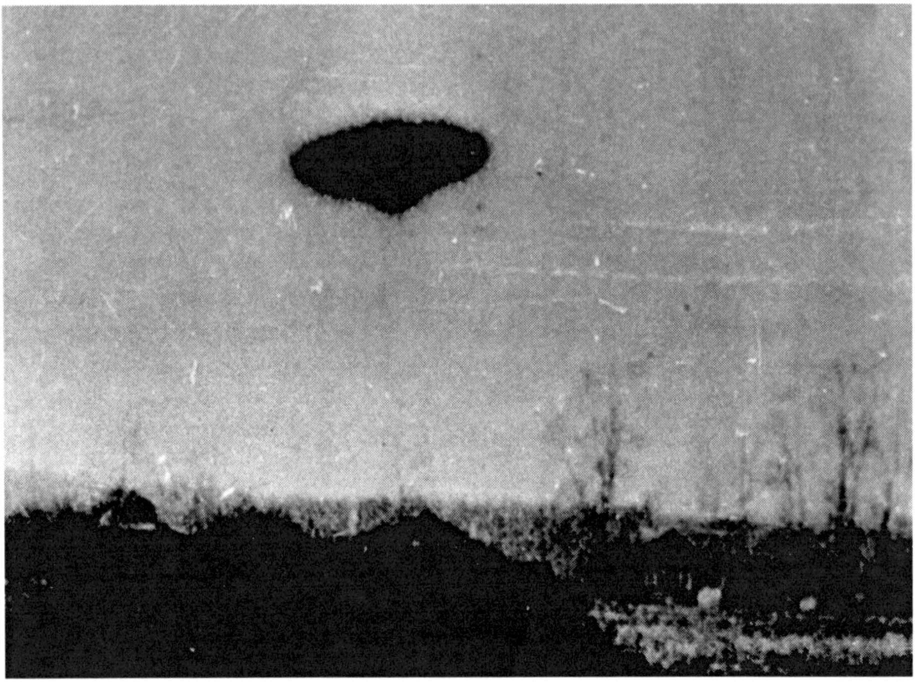

UFO near Tver, 1990

Kosmopoisk's Vadim Chernobrov investigates the Sasovo explosion

UFO sighted in Russia, 1995

The Soviet fake
UFO photo,
Bogoslovsky

Pictures of The
Ordzhenikidze
Object

An eyewitness from Voronezh

UFO landing, Alma-Ata, the road to Medeo. June, 1987.

The Petrozavodsk phenomenon

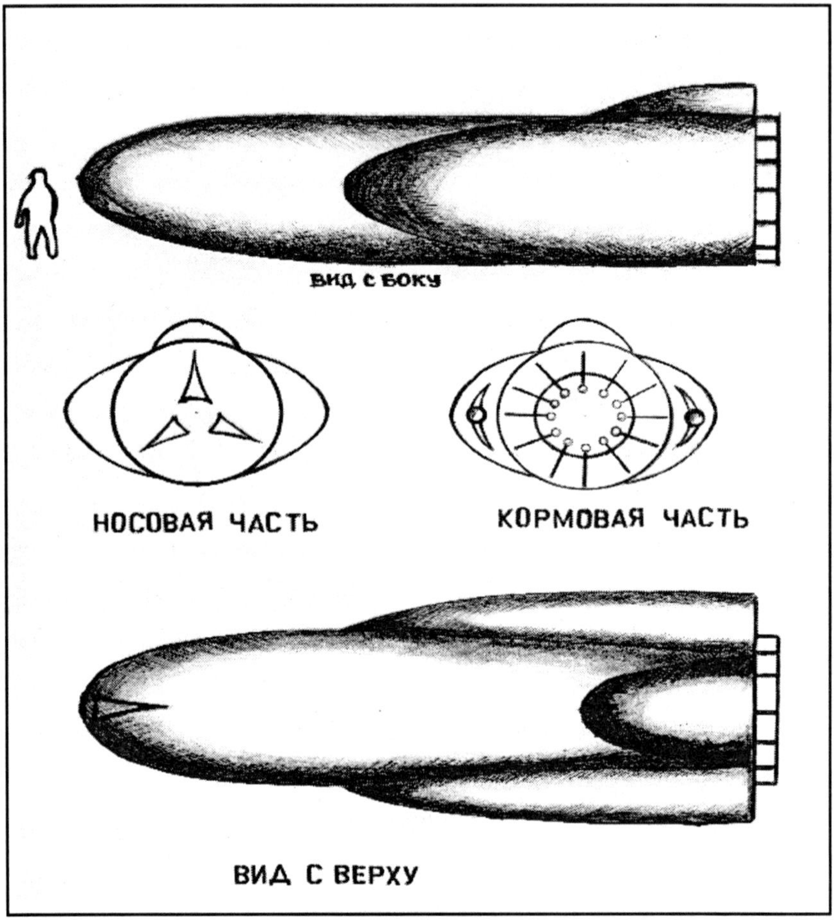

ВИД С БОКУ

НОСОВАЯ ЧАСТЬ   КОРМОВАЯ ЧАСТЬ

ВИД С ВЕРХУ

Drawing of the Monchegorsk object

Vadim Chernobrov,
Coordinator of the
International Kosmopoisk
Organisation, and author,
researcher and scientist

CHAPTER 24

MYSTERIES OF SOVIET AND RUSSIAN SEAS

WHAT LURKS BELOW

Strange sightings of UFOs, anomalous underwater creatures, and powerful vehicles had mystified the Soviet military for years. But even before the Bolsheviks gained control of the revolution-torn Russia, there have been curious reports about very unusual sightings at sea. In 1908, Russian steamship Okhotsk was in the Sea of Okhotsk, in the Russian Far East. F. D. Derbek, a Russian Imperial Navy doctor who was aboard, reported that during the night of October 22, at 11 p.m., a bright and unusual greenish-white luminescence flared up under the ship's stern. The luminescence quickly expanded, surrounding the ship. With the steamship in its centre, the brightly lit surface assumed the shape of an oval. It moved with the ship for a while, and then separated itself and moved sideways, and then forward, ahead of the vessel. The brightly lit and clearly outlined spot rapidly distanced itself from Okhotsk, and two or three minutes later it reached the horizon, where it shone as a bright clear streak, reflecting its light on clouds. This sighting was reported in several Soviet and Russian magazines.

Alexander Gorbovsky, a 72 year old Russian historian, now based in London, who worked for 20 years in the USSR's Academy of Sciences, published a book titled "Zagadki Drevney Istorii" ("Enigmas of Ancient History") in the early 1970's. For many people in the Soviet Union this book opened the door to the forbidden world of Ufology, of paleocontact (a Russian term for the ancient astronaut hypothesis), and mysteries of ancient history. Gorbovsky mentioned an incident that took place in the ancient Mediterranean where people observed a strange underwater vehicle surfacing at high speed. The object ejected itself from the water, and shortly thereafter disappeared.

Tekhnika-Molodezhi magazine published an article of N. Yerokhin, a Siberian engineer, in its Issue 12, 1991. He quotes from a Soviet book, published in 1956 ("Svecheniye Morya" or "Marine Luminescence", Moscow, Nauka Publishing). Its author, N. I. Tarasov, mentioned several interesting episodes of giant underwater "wheels" rotating at great speeds; luminescent lines that crossed the ocean from horizon to horizon; and fluorescent spots, ascending from the depths.

An interesting case took place in early July 1975, in Soviet Uzbekistan. Four young people who were vacationing on the shores of the Charvak Reservoir woke up at 3:00 am from instinctive fear. The reason for this fear was found quickly: a luminescent sphere ascended from under the water approximately 800 metres from the shore. An eyewitness recalled that the light of the sphere was cold and deadly, hundreds times brighter than the light of a day lamp. As the sphere rose up, concentric circles formed around it. The circles were of different thickness and brightness. This luminescent sphere slowly ascended over the lake. They observed this phenomenon for over 7 minutes, in absolute silence. And all the time the observers of the UFO experienced feelings of blinding fear.

MYSTERIOUS GIGANTIC "SWIMMERS"

In the late 1930s, a Russian UFO researcher named Grabovsky conducted an interview with a reluctant witness. That man and his friends had explored a cave near the Issik Kul Lake (Kirgizstan). There they discovered three human skeletons, each more than three metres tall. The skeletons were adorned with decorations that looked like bats (flying mammals) made from silver. The men became scared out of their wits and kept silent about their discovery for many long years. They did melt the silver decorations, but a small piece had been saved. Soviet scientists who had studied the piece said they could not determine its age. Interestingly, a Kirgiz legend does mention a submerged city in the Issik Kul, a deep-water lake in the Transiliysk Ala Tau area. The city's ruler was a creature with "long asinine ears".

The earliest mention of similar gigantic beings dates back to early 1900's. Several boys in Georgia (at the time, part of the Russian Empire) discovered a cave inside a mountain, full of humanoid skeletons. Each skeleton was about three metres tall. To get to the cave, the boys had to dive into a lake. George Papashvili and his wife recall the incident a book published in New York in 1925, St. Martin's Press (Anything can happen).

Many years later a much more sinister incident took place in the Soviet Union. Russian paranormal phenomena magazine ANOMALIYA (issue #4, 1992) contains an article that was written by Mark Shteynberg, a Soviet veteran of the Afghan war. He is an expert on Russia's military, who now resides in the United States. His articles are published in several Russian-American newspapers, and Shteynberg also writes books. In the summer of 1982, Mark Shteynberg, along with Lt. Colonel Gennady Zverev, actively conducted periodic training of the reconnaissance divers ("frogmen") of the Turkestan and Central Asian military regions. The training exercises had been taking place at the Issik Kul Lake.

Just then they received an unexpected guest: Major-General V. Demyanko, commander of the Military Diver Service of the Engineer Forces of the Ministry of Defence, USSR. He arrived to inform the local officers of an extraordinary event that had occurred during similar training exercises in the Trans-Baikal and West Siberian military regions. During their military training dives, Soviet frogmen had encountered mysterious underwater "swimmers", very humanoid beings of enormous size (almost three metres tall). The "swimmers" wore tight-fitting silvery suits, despite the icy-cold water temperatures. At the depth of fifty metres, these "swimmers" had neither scuba diving equipment ("aqualungs"), nor any other equipment; only sphere-like helmets concealing their heads.

Shteynberg stated that the local military commanders in Siberia decided to capture one of the creatures. With that purpose in mind, a special group of seven divers, under the command of an officer, had been dispatched. As the frogmen tried to cover the creature with a net, the entire team was propelled out of the deep waters to the surface by a powerful force. Because autonomous equipment of the frogmen does not allow surfacing from such depths without strict adherence to the process of decompression stops, all of the members of the ill-fated expedition were stricken by aeroembolism, or the Caisson disease. The only remedial treatment available consisted of an immediate confinement under decompression conditions in a pressure chamber. They had several such pressure chambers in the military region, but only one in working condition. It could contain no more than two persons.

Those local commanders had forced four frogmen into the chamber. As a result, three of them (including the CO of the group) perished, and the rest became invalids. The major general was dispatched, and flew to the Issik Kul to warn the local military against similar attempts to capture any "swimmers". Although the Issik Kul Lake is more shallow that the Baikal Lake, the depth of the former was sufficient to contain similar mysterious creatures. The Soviet high command was aware of "swimmers" lurking in the depths. Perhaps they knew much more about the Issik Kul underwater inhabitants than the independent researcher Grabovsky.

A short time later, the staff headquarters of the Turkmenistan military region had received an order from the Commander-in-Chief of the Land Forces. The order consisted of a detailed analysis of the Baikal Lake events and ensuing reprimands. It was supplemented by an information bulletin from the headquarters of the Engineer Forces of the Ministry of Defence, USSR. The bulletin listed numerous deep-water lakes where there had been registered sightings of anomalous phenomena: appearances of underwater creatures analogous to the Baikal type, descent and ascent of gigantic disks and spheres, powerful luminescence emanating from the deep, etc.

B. Borovikov hunted Black Sea sharks for many years. Then something happened that put an end to his hobby. Diving in the Anapa area, he descended to the depth of eight metres. He saw gigantic beings rising up from below. They were milky-white, but with humanoid faces, and something like fish tails. The creature in front of its companions noticed Borovikov, and stopped. It had giant bulging eyes, similar to some vague glasses. The other two joined it. The first one waved her hand (it was definitely a hand with membranes) towards the diver. All of them approached Borokivov, and stopped at a short distance. Then they turned around, and swam away. Borovikov's experience was published in XX vek: khronika neobjasnimogo or "XXth century: a chronicle of the unexplained (Moscow, 1996).

D. Povaliyayev was hand gliding over Kavgolov (Leningrad area) in the early 1990's. There are lakes, and in one of them the skydiver noticed three gigantic "fish". He descended, and was able to discern "swimmers" in silvery costumes. He mentioned the episode in his book Letuchi Gollandets or "Flying Dutchman" (1995). There have been many UFO sightings in the area.

WHILE SPYING ON AMERICANS....

Such documents as the information bulletin mentioned by Shteynberg, were highly classified without exception; and their purpose was to prevent unnecessary encounters. The territory under the military unit jurisdiction where Shteynebrg served had an anomalous water reservoir, the Sarez Lake (in the Pamir area, three thousand metres above the sea level). It is a beautiful, desolate, and hostile place with no vegetation or animal life. Earthquakes and landslides are frequent in the area. Only helicopters are able to reach it during the summer time.

The Sarez Lake appeared in 1911, when the valley of the Murgab River was dammed by the mighty slide, shifted by a powerful earthquake. The kishlak (village) Ussoy with all its inhabitants was buried by the disintegrated rock formations. The waters of the river gathered behind the newly formed dam, resulting in the disappearance under the water of kishlak Sarez, one of the biggest settlements of the Murgab valley. Out of this destruction appeared the Sarez Lake. By blocking the river, the dam caused a new lake to form, currently 60 kilometres long and up to 550 metres deep.

This lake presents a deadly danger to the population of Central Asia: a dam could rupture, and 17 billion cubic metres of water, poised to pour down from the mountains will destroy everything in its path, many areas of Afghanistan included. An earthquake could easily unleash a giant wave that would create a catastrophic flood downstream along the Bartang, Panj and Amu Darya Rivers, perhaps reaching all the way to the Aral Sea.

Sarez was visible to those stationed at a "tracking point" in the Pamir Mountains (the "tracking" was of American SDI satellites by Russians). Super powerful instruments and measuring equipment of the Soviet military subunit (that had been doing the actual "tracking") had repeatedly registered submersion into Sarez of disk-like objects, their ascent through the waters of the lake and subsequent liftoff. What attracted "them" to the anomalous lake? Perhaps it is its imminent demise, fraught with dreadful consequences for Central Asia.

SUBMARINES AND SECRECY

In those years when Soviet Ufologists were persecuted by the all-powerful State, and the very subject of UFOs was a taboo, Vladimir Georgiyevich Ajaja was one of the first Soviets to study the "hydrosphere aspect." At one time in his arduous and tumultuous life, Mr. Ajaja, Candidate of Technical Sciences, served as the head of the underwater exploration expedition aboard the Soviet "Severyanka" submarine. He and the sub's crew had sighted a very strange creature during one of their dives. When his urge to research and discuss the forbidden subject of UFOs got him fired from his job, it was the Soviet Navy that provided Ajaja with employment, and an enviable opportunity to study UFOs. Because as a young man he served in the Navy, and later participated in oceanographic research, he made reliable friends. He was even presented with opportunities to question naval intelligence officers who were responsible for their Navy's UFO studies, and write a monograph about UFOs for Soviet Navy.

In 1976 Ajaja had an interesting meeting at the Department of the underwater research of the Oceanographic Commission of the USSR Academy of Sciences. The date was November 17, and among those present were the Chairman of the Department P. Borovikov, his deputy, E. Kukharkov, and twenty nine other people. They came to hear V. Ajaja's lecture about UFOs and the associated underwater issues. At the time Ajaja was a deputy of Chairman P. Borovikov. After Ajaja's lecture, these present decided to include collection of UFO sightings (over bodies of water, and depths of the hydro sphere) into the planned activities of the Department. Subsequent to collection of data it was to be analysed.

But it is quite possible that Ajaja, too, has not revealed all that he knows about the underwater UFO phenomenon. In 1966, he and other authors published a curious book, titled Submarines in the scientific research (Nauka, 1966). It is briefly mentioned that V. G. Ajaja, N.I. Tarasov, A.K. Tokarev, and E.V. Shishkov performed "intriguing" research in the area of hydrobiology. Ajaja never discussed what that intriguing research was; obviously, some areas of the Russian UFO phenomena remain as secret now as during the Politburo reign.

One interesting episode that has been mentioned by Ajaja several times in various publications (the latest one in 1999 NLO Magazine) took place on October 7, 1977. A floating service base for Soviet submarines in the Barents

Sea was "visited" by nine strange shining disks. The UFOs descended and circled around the base; no radio signal could be sent out or received by frantic Soviet Naval officers. This "dance" had lasted for 18 full minutes, until the UFOs disappeared.

A small Russian newspaper Podmoskovye-Nedelya published a very interesting article in its August 8, 2001 issue. The author was Vadim Kulichenko, a retired Soviet Naval officer, a submariner.

The Soviets had a special name for the anomalous phenomenon that has not been explained to this day. They called the mysterious objects that were detected by Soviet nuclear-powered icebreakers, kvakeri. "Kvakat'", in Russian, means, "to croak". The word also means "Quakers", but there is no connection.

Some Soviet military researchers believed that the kvakeri were underwater UFOs. Yet most of the specialists of the research groups who had studied the phenomenon disagreed with this conclusion.

The mysterious phenomenon in question was discovered in the 1960s and 1970s. Soviet nuclear-powered submarines encountered strange sounds emanating from moving objects at great depths. Listening to underwater sound is known as hydro acoustic monitoring. Soviet monitors heard the strange signals that resembled frogs croaking. They dubbed the objects kvakeri, and the term was officially accepted in the naval documents.

The Soviet Union (later Russia) had built 248 nuclear submarines between 1950 and 2001.

Some of these submarines must have really interested the kvakeri, for the course and bearing indicators of the Soviet Naval vessels demonstrated that the objects circled the subs, changing the frequency and tonality of the signal. It was as if the objects invited the subs to engage in "conversations". The kvakeri reacted especially actively to the acoustic dispatches from the subs, yet never aggressively. They would accompany Soviet submarines until the latter would exit a certain area. Then, emitting the "croaking" sound for the last time, the objects would disappear. There had never been any confrontation with the objects in the long years of their interaction, yet the Soviet commanders and submarine crews had been tense and under stress when the kvakeri accompanied their vessels.

The Cold War was raging at the end of the 1960s, and the strange underwater phenomenon attracted attention of the Soviet Navy's high command. Nuclear submarines drove the Cold War's most furious phase of arms race. Hence, special research groups were created to study the phenomenon. The answers they had to find were not very easy: what underwater objects emit the enigmatic sounds, what is their nature, and are we dealing with a secret American invention that enables them to follow and spy on our submarines?

Several specially equipped vessels were sent to the area of encounters. At the close of 1970s a scientific conference on the kvakeri was conducted in the Soviet Navy, but the participants were not able to reach any definite conclusions.

In early 1980s the Kvakeri program was abruptly shut down. Special research groups were disbanded, and the officers who had worked there received other assignments. All collected information and data were marked Top Secret and locked away in archives of the Navy.

Neither Vadim Kulinchenko nor other former Soviet officers of his rank know why the program was shut down. The reasons why the results of the research have been classified are quite obvious. Former submariner Kulinchenko tried to collect whatever information was available short of opening the secret files. It has been over 12 years since the fall of the Soviet Union, and still, very little information about the kvakeri leaked out. Even those who had researched the phenomenon have very different opinions as to its nature. Apparently, the phenomenon is not being researched nowadays officially, but there are those in Russia who are dedicated to finding out the truth. Still, the kvakeri continue to "croak" and accompany Russian ships, without harming the submarines or their crews.

At the end of the Cold War (1989) there were over 400 nuclear-powered submarines operational or being built.

About 250 of these submarines have now been scrapped and some on order cancelled, largely due to weapons reduction programs. U.S., Russia, Great Britain, France and China possess, in total, 160 such submarines today.

Radioactive contamination from the past industrial and nuclear activities is one of the most complicated uncertain problems in Russia.

The Arctic has become a graveyard for the once mighty and feared fleet of Soviet nuclear-powered submarines.

Perhaps, the kvakeri were attracted to the nuclear submarines because of the unpredictable ecological hazards posed by such vessels to the environment. Nuclear submarines everywhere are extremely disaster-prone. After all, Soviet and Russian nuclear submarines have used enriched uranium for fuel (some as highly enriched as 90 percent). The spent fuel is tremendously radioactive, and contains unburned highly enriched uranium, plutonium and fission products. Russian submarines in the Arctic are corroding and sinking as their reactor compartments fill with water, foreshadowing an ecological catastrophe.

Perhaps the following information serves as a confirmation of the kvakeri phenomenon.

Secret files of the Soviet Navy contain much valuable information on UFO sightings. Soviet military researchers were no nonsense people, and actually, quite thorough. Valentin Vladimirovich Krapiva, a noted Ukrainian researcher, has collected and published information about the "hydrosphere aspect of UFO phenomena."

During the 1960s he attended lectures given by veteran officers who served aboard Soviet nuclear-powered submarines. They had served in the Soviet North, at the secret naval installations and bases. The lectures sometimes veered off the planned presentations, and many spellbinding tales were told.

For instance, episodes when Soviet sonar-operators (military hydro acoustics technicians) were "hearing" (at great depths) strange "targets". Other "submarines" were actually chasing the Soviet submarines. The pursuers changed their speed at will - speeds that were much faster than any other similar vessel in the world at that time. Lieutenant-Commander Oleg Sokolov confidentially informed the students that while he was on duty during his submarine's navigation, he had observed through a periscope an ascent of some strange object through the water. He was not able to identify it, because he viewed it through the optical system of the periscope. This underwater "take off" took place in the early 1960's.

M. Gershtein sent us an interesting observation of a UFO recorded by a crew of a Soviet nuclear submarine in 1965 (it is on file in the G. Kolchin archives). All those who had observed the incident were ordered to report the details and provide drawings to the Special Department (i.e., naval intelligence and security office). The submarine was to rendezvous with a ship in the Atlantic Ocean. They arrived to the meeting place an hour and a half before the time of the rendezvous, and the captain allowed the crew to come to the outside deck. No ships were in the area, and the sky was starry and cloudless. Then the watchman observed a cigar-shaped object moving noiselessly through the sky. Although the submarine was in international waters, they assumed the object was American, and decided to dive immediately. But their onboard radar did not register anything, and the captain decided to stay put, above water. Suddenly three rays shot out from the UFO, and the Soviet submariners noticed something very unusual about it.

It had no gondolas and no horizontal or vertical rudders. The object was about 200-250 metres long, and Soviet submariners were not familiar with such "dirigibles", for those used by American Air Force were much smaller. Then something strange took place: the UFO slowly descended to the surface of the ocean, its searchlights still on, about half a mile from the submarine, and dived underwater. The submarine's sonar had registered a strange and very intensive hissing sound, as the UFO submerged, but the sound was of a very short duration.

On December 26, 2002, Russian newspaper Zhizn published an article about Soviet observations of UFOs. The chairman of the Anomalous Commission of the Russian Geographical Society (Saint Petersburg) made a presentation at the society's meeting that month. The society has studied tens of thousands of cases of UFO sightings, and has reached a conclusion that UFOs are real. The Chairman, Yevgeny Litvinov, recalled that his experience with the UFOs had begun when he was a Soviet Naval officer and did not take seriously any published UFO-related information. Then came the winter of 1979-80, and several incidents had rocked the Northern Fleet, forcing the Soviet General Staff to take UFOs seriously. UFOs had visited a Soviet submarine base at the Western Dvina every week during a six months period. The craft were shaped like disks, and hovered over the weapons preparation sites (mines, torpedoes, nuclear). The UFOs also flew above the classified military town. While the military personnel below freely observed the "flying saucers", the anti-aircraft radars did not register anything. Captain Beregovoy, head of the Naval Intelligence for the Northern Fleet, ordered that photographs of the UFOs be taken, but to no avail, the film turned out to be inadvertently exposed each time. The Soviets were busy trying to find out what the UFOs above their heads were. Initially they suspected NATO, but then it was explained to them that potential adversaries do not possess such technology. To prevent panic, they told their military personnel that the UFOs above were actually Soviet-made craft, and that tests were underway. Of course, high-ranking officers knew better, and felt terrified by the uncertainty. Then a criminal case was opened because four pigs had disappeared from an open-air cage. The investigator was told by sailors that a disk-like object hovered over the cage, and emitted a blue ray. The pigs were lifted from the cage, and placed aboard the craft. The warrant officer responsible for the cage confirmed the story. The investigators were convinced that the sailors were not telling lies because the warrant officer actually contacted his superiors about the disappearance of the pigs; no traces of any theft were ever found; and the sailors were completely sober after the incident. The criminal case was closed. But more serious incidents took place during that winter. The crew of a Soviet Project 671 submarine ("Victor" class sub, per NATO classification) encountered a UFO. The sub's commander was Aleksey Korzhev. The sub was coming to the base; sometimes it surfaced, sometimes it would descend down to two hundred metres. They wanted to be undetected by spy satellites. Then came a report that straight up ahead was an airplane. The commander was surprised, for the weather was absolutely not conducive for aircraft flights. But fifty metres from the sub a silvery disk was hovering, slowly moving with the sub, staying a bit ahead of it. The crew looked at it, feeling mesmerised. Then the UFO emitted a ray of light, and the pillar of bright white light did not immediately reach the surface of the water, but contrary to the laws of physics, it slowly descended. Korzhev immediately ordered a change of course. The disk slowly ascended and disappeared in the clouds. Litvinov said that the Soviets speculated that the UFO wanted to scan the submarine that actually happened to carry newest weapons aboard.

Later, when Litvinov was a part of the special commission of the Soviet Navy's General Staff, he was able to read dozens of UFO reports that came from the intelligence channels. One report described a UFO landing in the Motovsky Bay (located in the Barents Sea). Years later, a leakage of liquid radioactive waste from a spent fuel storage facility took place in the Motovsky Bay and Litza-fiord. In 1996, approximately 130 atomic submarines with unloaded reactors were waiting for dismantling and decontamination. Up to that year, only 12 atomic submarines have undergone the so-called "procedure" (separation of forward and stem parts without core unloading). We do not know exactly what was going on there during the Soviet rule. No radar station in the vicinity registered the UFO. Soviet experts supposed that an ionised cloud enveloped the UFO.

REPORTS AND TESTIMONIES

A few years ago V.V. Krapiva met with Professor Korsakov of the Odessa University. Professor Korsakov told him of a conversation he had with a friend of his, a Soviet Navy officer who had served at the Sevastopol Naval base. Back in the 1950's this officer personally sighted a UFO. The object ascended from behind a battle cruiser. The officer was under the impression that the object surfaced from the depths of the Black Sea. Professor Korsakov has a photograph of the object.

Felix Zigel, back in the mid 1970s, noted that his research included information about "flying saucers" exiting and entering oceans. In his view, there were three types of UFO origin: mountainous, oceanic, and cosmic.

The Russian Ufology Research Centre has a collection of "hydrosphere aspect" sightings.

In August 1965, a crew of the steamship RADUGA, while navigating in the Red Sea, observed an unusual phenomenon. At about two miles away, a fiery sphere dashed out from under the water and hovered over the surface of the sea, illuminating it. The sphere was sixty metres in diameter, and it hovered above the sea at an altitude of 150 metres. A gigantic pillar of water ascended, as the sphere emerged from the sea, and collapsed some moments later.

Soviet magazine Sudostroyeniye published an article by M. I. Girs in 1977. He described an incident that took place in the early 1970s, as observed from aboard the ship Tintro-2. It happened in November, in the Atlantic Ocean. In the evening, as the darkness was descending upon the ocean, the seamen watched a gigantic luminescent cloud. It was slightly over the horizon, and its shape was almost perfectly round. In the middle of the cloud they observed a chaotically moving dot, with a "tail". The cloud grew in size, while the "tail" of the dot constantly moved about. When the first cloud dissipated, another one grew in its place, and then the third one. At one point they covered each other. The clouds were luminescent and resembled the Moon, but not nearly as bright. The radio transmission was not affected, and magnetic compasses aboard the ship were fine, too.

1977 was an interesting year for UFO sightings. Here is one, described in a letter to the Academy of Sciences, USSR, and abridged for this book. The date was July 7, 1977, precisely at 16:00 Moscow time. The motor ship Nikolay Ostrovsky sailed through the Tatarsky Strait from the Vanino harbour and the La Perouse Straight to the Providence harbour. Within the next 32 minutes a very unusual event took place. The weather was cloudy, and the visibility was 5 to 7 miles. To the east of the motor ship, some 300 to 400 metres, the seamen observed a cloud-like formation. The cloud was shaped as a parallelogram. One of the eyewitnesses, head of the onboard radio station, O. M.Dereza, stated in the letter that he shuddered at the thought that whoever was inside the cloud formation (it was moving at the same speed as the ship) must have carefully watched and studied the seamen. He could not see anyone in the cloud, but somehow felt that "they" hear and understand Russian language, and even read the seamen's thoughts from a distance. He thought the perfectly shaped parallelogram cloud formation could have been a spaceship from another world. Whatever it was, the cloud formation disappeared at 16:32 Moscow time.

Some very fascinating reports came from the area of South Georgia Island. Located southeast of the Falklands, the UK-ruled South Georgia is lost in the midst of the Southern Ocean, one of the most remote regions on our planet.

The Antarctic continent is 1,000 miles to the south. South Georgia lies between 35.47' to 38.01' west and 53.58' to 54.53' south within the Polar Front. Glaciers coat more than half the island.

Captains of the Soviet ships reported that a cone-shaped obscure cloud constantly hovered above the island. There was a photograph, attached to the reports, showing an upward fight of a "saucer" from below the ocean's surface. The object resembled neither a missile nor a torpedo. Right after it ascended, the object became invisible for the radars, as if they went blind.

In December 1977, not far from the South Georgia Island, the crew of the fishing trawler VASILY KISELEV also observed something quite extraordinary. Rising vertically from under the water was a doughnut-shaped object. Its diameter was between 300 and 500 metres. It hovered at the altitude of four to five kilometres. The trawler's radar station was immediately rendered inoperative. The object hovered over the area for three hours, and then disappeared instantly.

The testimony of Alexander G. Globa, a seaman from GORI, a Soviet tanker was published in Zagadki Sfinksa magazine (Issue 3, 1992) Odessa. In June 1984, GORI was in the Mediterranean, twenty nautical miles from the Straight of Gibraltar. At 16:00, Globa was on duty. With him was Second-in-Command S. Bolotov. They were standing watch at the left bridge extension wing when both men observed a strange polychromatic object. When the object was astern, it stopped suddenly. S. Bolotov was agog, shaking his binoculars, and shouting: "It is a flying saucer, a real saucer; my God, hurry, hurry, look!" Globa looked through his own binoculars and saw, at a distance over the stern, a flattened out looking object (it did remind him of an upside-down frying pan). The UFO was gleaming with a grayish metallic shine. The lower portion of the craft had a precise round shape, its diameter no more than twenty metres. Around the lower portion of it Globa also observed "waves" of protuberances on the outside plating.

The base of the object's body consisted of two semi-disks, the smaller being on top; they slowly revolved in opposing directions. At the circumference of the lower disk Globa saw numerous shining, bright, bead-like lights. The seaman's attention was centred on the bottom portion of the UFO. It looked as if it was completely even and smooth, its colour that of a yolk and in the middle of it Globa discerned a round, nucleus-like stain. At the edge of the UFO's bottom, which was easily visible, was something that looked like a pipe. It glowed with an unnaturally bright rosy colour, like a neon lamp. The top of the middle disk was crowned by a triangular-shaped something. It seemed that it moved in the same direction as the lower disk, but at a much slower pace.

Suddenly the UFO jumped up several times, as if moved by an invisible wave. Many lights illuminated its bottom portion. The crew of GORI tried to attract the object's attention using a signal projector. By that time Captain Sokolovsky was on the desk with his men. He and his Second-in-Command were watching the object intensely. However, the UFO's attention was distracted by another ship, approaching at the port side. It was an Arab dry cargo ship, on its way to Greece. The Arabs confirmed that the object hovered over their ship. A minute and a half later the object changed its flight's trajectory, listed to the right, gained speed and ascended rapidly. The Soviet seamen observed that when it rose through the clouds, appearing and disappearing again, it would occasionally shine in the sun's rays. The craft then flared up, like a spark, and was gone instantly.

Yerokhin recalls the article published in Soviet Nedelya newspaper in 1977, issue 18. Scientists aboard Vladimir Vorobyev vessel reported a bright white spot revolving around the ship at the depth of 170 metres. Its radius was approximately 150-200 metres; it rotated against the clock, and separated into eight portions. The sonic depth finder registered presence of something at the depth of 20 metres under the keel. The light moved in wave-like manner, in the shape of eight rotating and bending rays (something like turbines' blades).

SOVIET NAVAL OBSERVERS

Krasnaya Zvezda newspaper (the print media mouthpiece of the Soviet Armed Forces) published a curious report in its October 23, 1985 issue. The sighting took place in Soviet Polar Regions. Some seamen reported a very bright, yellowish object low over the horizon' its size like that of a quarter (American coin). Three more similar objects were hovering at an equal distance from the first one. A lieutenant who came from his watch also observed the objects, and stated unequivocally that what he saw were no helicopters. The article ended somewhat usually: without explaining presence of all observed UFOs, the lieutenant was shamed by a flagship navigator who unidentified the UFO as planet Jupiter.

Years went by, and Gorbachev's policies changed the huge country.

Before the fall of the USSR, a Soviet Naval officer published an article about military observations of UFOs. As many other Soviet military officers, Nikolay Dyomin did not consider UFOs to be "optical illusions." The sighted UFOs were the same saucers, balls and rays as seen throughout the ages in other parts of the world, but recorded with the precision and impartiality of a military report. Quite often, naval observers utilised special technical means. In some cases, the objects were observed and recorded from different points in their flight dynamics. The sightings, checking and verification by Soviet fleet meteorological officers had positively established that the sighted objects were not results of human techno-genic activity or optical illusions. A YA. Magazine (Issue 2) Estonia, 1991 published the article that included Dyomin's 1976 sighting of a UFO over Estonia.

It is worth mentioning that the Soviet Navy carefully guarded its secrets, and spoke out against those whose alternative views on the subject of underwater UFOs or USOs (unidentified submersible object) were published in the USSR. Such was a reported reaction of Rear Admiral M. Rudnitsky to an article published in Tekhnika-Molodezhy magazine in Issue 9, 1972. The Soviet Naval official used several arguments, including this one: if intelligent beings have resided underwater for thousands of years, it is doubtless they would have attempted to contact human beings. Yet no such attempts have been recorded in history. Yerokhin, however, is of the opinion that the mysterious fluorescence observed in the sea may be exactly such an attempt to establish communications between an underwater civilization and us.

But such phenomena refuse to be simply dismissed. Nikolai Nepomnyaschy's book Iz sekretnikh arkhivov razvedok mira or from secret archives of the world (Moscow, 1998) mentions a very keen interest expressed by Soviets in 1960 in an underwater object bombarded by Argentinean Navy. Nikita Khruschev, then still the General Secretary of the Central Committee of the Communist Party of the Soviet Union, sent an inquiry to the Soviet attaché in Argentina. But the Argentinean attempt to capture the USOs ended in fiasco.

On August 28 of 1989 a very interesting sighting took place in the area of the Kola Peninsula. This was reported in the Soviet Navy newspaper Flag

Rodini, published in Sevastopol, in the November 11, 1990 issue. The Soviet scientific research vessel Akademik Aleksye Krilov was about five miles away from the peninsula, when its crew observed a UFO (the sighting lasted approximately 4 minutes). The object was a luminescent cloud; inside it there was something flickering. The UFO moved with the speed of an airplane, high in the sky. Suddenly the flickering "something" parted from the UFO, and at a considerable distance from it, simply disappeared. The UFO experienced an explosion and emission of gases, and a few seconds later, another explosion followed.

Another article about the same area appeared in Zhizn newspaper; it was written by Grigory Tel'nov, and titled NLO. He wrote that during the 1980s a large number of unidentified underwater objects were sighted in the northern seas of the Soviet Union. Soviet Ufologists had analysed such sightings, obtained from various sources, and concluded that only during the 1980-1981 period residents of the Kola Peninsula had observed UFOs at least 36 times, ascending from the waters.

At the end of 1982 in Crimea, during the naval exercises, an unidentified target was detected over Balaklava. It would not respond to repeated inquiries. Eyewitnesses recalled that the object, moving at an altitude of a helicopter flight, had a very sharp nose, and sparks were coming from its tail section. Interceptor-jets were sent after it, but the object descended under water at their approach. Soviet Naval vessels could not detect it underwater.

Fascinating sightings have been reported in the Soviet Kuril islands. N.S. Krokhmalev reported the first sighting in an article published in Russian newspaper Chetvertoye izmereniye i NLO, Issue 6, 1997. In August of 1982, Krokhmalev was aboard Nikolai Boshnyak vessel, in the Shikotan island area. The ship was heading to the Yekaterina Strait, between the islands of Iturup and Kunashir. The watch commander at the time invited the crew to observe an interesting phenomenon. An elliptical circle with clearly outlined borders appeared on surface around the ship. The luminescence was like that produced by a TV set. They estimated the size of the luminescence to be 125 metres long and 74 metres wide. No sound except the ship's engine could be heard. There was an object with the ship at the depth of 3 or 4 metres. Also, a perfect round circle appeared around the moon, at the same time. The circle on the surface of the sea accompanied the Soviet vessel for two hours, and then disappeared suddenly. The ship's speed was slow at the time. No onboard devices registered anything unusual. Krokhmalev recalled feelings of depression and perplexity after the sighting.

Another sighting took place in July of 1983, two miles from the Shikotan Island. It occurred during the summertime, in the second half of July, early in the morning. Zenit, fishing vessel from the Sakhalin Island, lay out near the island, and waited for the mooring to load the cargo aboard. Six crewmen stood on the deck. The sun was not out yet, and early haze covered the horizon. All of a sudden they saw a bright orange-coloured sphere. It slowly moved through the north to the south, and disappeared as if it was turned off. The sphere was ten times larger than the visible Moon. It moved for about two minutes. The sea was calm and the fog was light. The sphere moved low over the horizon, between the Shikotan Island and vessel, did not blind those watching it, so that they could easily observe it. The sphere looked like a reddish disk of the setting sun.

This report came from V. P. Krilosov, and can be found in A. Golts archives. M. Gershtein sent it to us.

Five years went by, and another event took place in the very same location. Priroda i anomalniye yavlenia newspaper published an article about it in its Issue 7, 1990. The sighting was dated October 1988, about 21:00. The Soviet aircraft carrier Novorossiysk conducted training exercises. The crew noticed a gigantic body with vague outlines rising from behind the island. There were 36 lights located geometrically throughout the object. As the UFO ascended all electronic systems aboard Novorossiysk went dead. The diesel motors ceased functioning, and even the portable battery-operated accumulator radio stations would not work. A state of the art modern ship, equipped with the modern electronics was turned into a heap of metal three miles off the island. It was completely defenceless. The fishermen at the island, too, observed the object. Forty seconds later the onboard systems came back to life, one after another. The radar did not register any objects. A K-27 helicopter was sent toward the UFO, but the strange object flew away, at a great speed. The whole incident lasted 15 minutes.

In 1989, in the area of the Maritime province, another sighting took place. It was reported in the Tikhookeanskaya Gazeta newspaper (Khabarovsk), October 21, 1989. The report came from the captain of Soviet tanker Volgoneft-161, O. I. Zimakov. The actual sighting occurred on August 2 of that year. The UFO was located in the northern part of the sky, at an angle to the horizon, some 35 degrees. The sphere had pale-yellowish colour, and it had some sort of luminescence around it, like the Moon. The object moved toward the northeast, ascending slightly over the horizon; the observers watched it for about five minutes, and then it disappeared.

NLO Magazine published a letter in its Issue 12, 1997. The author, Nikolai Sadkov from the Russian city of Pskov described an interesting episode about his service in the Black Sea Fleet. He served aboard a naval boat; the purpose of the boat and its crew was to recover Soviet torpedoes that did not explode upon reaching their targets during tests at sea. The torpedoes could stay afloat for up to 48 hours, and then they would sink. Once the crew had to recover a secret "Dolphin" type torpedo. A "special department" representative was with them, as the crew hunted for the torpedo. They located it about two hours later, and in another hour the boat approached it. The torpedo was hardly visible, as the CO guided his vessel toward it. Then, from under the clouds, a bell-shaped "spaceship" hovered over the torpedo. The diameter of the UFO reached 15 or 20 metres. It descended to the altitude of five metres over the torpedo, quite slowly. A voice, emanating from somewhere in the sky, uttered, in clear Russian language, that nothing bad would be done to them, and that everyone must remain where they are now. A round platform extended from the bottom part of the "spaceship", and attracted the torpedo to itself, like a magnet. The boat's sonar technician ran out with a camera in his hands, eager to take pictures. A thin brightly red ray emitted from the "spaceship" and touched the sonar technician's head; he fell down. The voice, unusual, commanding, and at the same time gentle, told the sailors to remain where they are, for nothing bad would happen to them. The UFO disappeared, together with the torpedo; or rather, flew away at a great speed. Two hours later it re-appeared, and hovered over the deck of the recovery boat. The torpedo was slowly descended from the bottom part of the "bell", and placed on the Soviet boat's deck. The "spaceship" disappeared. When the sailors returned to the base, they signed a statement in the Special Department, that they would not reveal the incident to anyone. What was that "bell", assuming that N. Sadkov did not invent the whole story: a UFO, a USO, or an American spy craft?

Two thousand years have gone by since the sighting mentioned by Dr. Gorbovsky, and still UFOs are observed over the oceans, lakes and seas of our planet.

SECRETS OF RUSSIAN DEPTHS

Something very unusual took place in the waters of the North Sea in 1993. This was reported in the February 2 issue of NLO magazine, in an article titled Incredible "Russian" submarines. Unfortunately, we do not have the name of the article's author. On February 6, 1993, during a powerful storm, a NATO squadron encountered three American destroyers. The Americans sent a radio signal, telling NATO's military vessels not to approach closer than three miles. The NATO ships lay adrift. Soon thereafter, sixteen flying craft of bright amber colour appeared over the American ships. They hovered for a few minutes, and then flew away at great speed. A few weeks later there was a report that one of the American destroyers disappeared. Joint NATO and Russian search by naval vessels ensued. On April 15, a Russian vessel reported that they registered an unidentified underwater object. Its approximate speed was 60 knots, and its size was 210 by 120 metres. The American destroyer was never found.

A curious incident is mentioned in Nikolai Nepomnyaschy's book Stranniki Vselennoy or Wanderers of the Universe (Moscow, 1996). Academician E.

Shnyuyukov recalled an expedition that took place in the early 1990s in the Black Sea. He was aboard a scientific research vessel Mikhail Lomonosov. An unidentified submersible object was located at the depths of 1400-1800 metres. Its size was huge (two kilometres by three kilometres); and its shape was elliptic. The sonic depth finder registered the mysterious USO as a dense cloud (up to 270 metres in thickness), but analyses of water taken in the immediate area did not reveal any hydro-chemical anomalies. Here is another fascinating detail: Russian devices that safeguarded barometers against impact with the soil would start functioning immediately upon registering the USO.

Some of the recent events in the area of the Caspian Sea are described in the chapter about the Chechen war. But one incident that took place in 1997 deserves to be discussed in this chapter.

The source of this story is Perekrestok Kentavra newspaper (Issue 13, 1997). On July 21, 1997 (at 10: 20 p.m. Moscow time) an unidentified flying object crashed into the waters of the Caspian Sea. Captain of the tugboat "Schukin" immediately sent a message to the marine rescue services. The crew observed a dark object, its shape like that of a helicopter, moving from the shore. Then the object sharply changed the trajectory of its flight, and crashed into the sea. A powerful explosion ensued, causing a gigantic pillar of water to rise up. Civilian and military land-based search-and-rescue services claimed that no airplane was in the air at the time of the explosion.

Meanwhile, captains of the ships in the area received orders to immediately advance to a specific area in the sea. Its coordinates were in latitude 45 degrees 03 minutes north; and in longitude 48 degrees 00 minutes east. It was there that the alleged crash took place. Russian military patrol boats soon joined the tugboat. They found no traces whatsoever. The sea was becoming stormy, and the divers could not work underwater (the depth of the sea there was 20 metres). The tugboat received a message over its portable radio receiver.

Two meteorologists on watch that evening, not far from the site of the crash (they were stationed on the Tyulenniy Island) did not see any object falling from the sky. The air traffic controllers from the Makhachkala Airport stated that at the hour of the alleged crash, there was only tow Mi-8 helicopters in the sky. But the helicopters were flying far from the area, and both craft safely made it to their bases. Neither the military nor the FSB (Russia's heir to the Soviet KGB) had any information about the UFO. Both entities denied any secret tests in the Caspian Sea area. The media centre of the Federal Frontier Troops issued a press release that the UFO could not have been an aircraft or a helicopter, because all flights over the area of water are being controlled.

Was this UFO a mirage? A. Yakovlev, a Russian scientist, thinks so. But, as noted by A. L. Kul'sky, a Ukrainian author (his book Prizraki Istorii or Ghosts of History, 1998, is quite popular) a mirage is not usually accompanied by sonic effects and gigantic pillars of water.

Alexey B. Blinov, a scientist who headed an Arctic expedition in August of 1995 in the Karskoye Sea, reported another episode in his article published by Anomaliya newspaper (Issue 4, 1996). On August 13, 1995, about 8 p.m., Blinov observed some 100 metres away from the ship an underwater bright object. It moved perpendicularly to his ship Yakov Smirnitsky. Another scientist joined Blinov who went to call attention to the strange object. Initially Blinov thought he saw a beluga whale, but later when they observed it closer, it turned out to be a bright round spot, fluorescent, and approximately three metres in diameter. The speed was even and quite slow for a whale. The object approached Russian ship, went down under the bottom of the vessel, and some fifteen seconds later it ascended from the other side; its speed and direction of movement, even and unwavering under the surface of the sea. A. Blinov believes the object was definitely of non-natural origin, for it moved vertically, and also perpendicular to the current. There were no psychophysical or electrical influence on the humans and seagulls (they flew over the sea surface) in the vicinity of the object.

In all likelihood some of the observations in this chapter are of secret Soviet and/or Western military forces. Other observations may be ascribed to unknown natural phenomenon and even misidentifications of known marine animals. But there are a number of observations that do not seem to fit any of these explanations and still leaved us puzzled as to their nature and origin. The field of research has not concentrated on underwater sightings either in the USSR or anywhere else for that matter, and one thing is for sure (no pun intended) such sightings that we do have on file are indeed the tip of the iceberg.

CHAPTER 25

KARELIA

Karelia is an autonomous republic within Russia, with 172,400 square kilometres, and 800,000 inhabitants. Only 11.1% of them are Karelian. Ethnic Russians comprise the vast majority (71.3%) and there is also a minority of Finns (2.7%). The Vepsian language is spoken in the south.

About 90,000 people speak Karelian (Uralic language close to Finnish) out of an ethnic group of 145,000 in Russia. A number of Karelians live outside the Karelian republic (south of lakes Onega and Ladoga) and around Novgorod and the Tver region.

There have been UFO sightings in Karelia for many years, and we have discussed some of them elsewhere in the book. The Petrozavodsk Phenomenon is perhaps the most famous of such sightings. In this chapter we want to introduce our readers to some other important sightings and events that have taken place in this part of northern Russia.

EARLY SIGHTINGS

In 1928 a cylindrical craft, estimated to be ten metres long, flew over the Shuknavolok Village. Red, blazing fire and sparks were seen to be coming from its tail section. The UFO fell into the Vedlozero Lake, broke through the ice, and submerged. Thereafter the local inhabitants reported a strange, mysterious, one metre tall creature in the area. It had small arms and legs, and an oversized head. The being would jump into the lake every time any human approached it.

In 1932 a thick black cloud enveloped the Shuknavolok Village. After its disappearance, peasants discovered a jelly-like substance on the ground. They collected it, and later used it as a medicine. Many years later there have been unusual interferences with TV broadcasts, and the area affected was limited to the village, but not its immediate neighbours.

In 1943 residents of Karkiyeki township (Charily), once again reported a strange UFO sighting. Two local girls collected berries in the woods, and pedalled their bicycles back home. In the middle of the road they saw an object. It was approximately one metre tall, and a metre and a half long. It hovered over the road, some fifty metres away from the girls. The object was grayish in colour, and resembled a lentil's seed. The girls watched it in amazement for over ten minutes. Then it veered off to the side, and disappeared in to the bushes.

THE LAKE LADOGA'S SIGHTINGS

Lake Ladoga is well known for its anomalous phenomena. This large body of water has been a place of strange mirages. Often people hear a mysterious rumbling sound coming from its depths. Local ship captains recall luminescent lights that accompany their vessels. Tatiana Tyumeneva published an article in NLO Magazine (Issue 9, 1998). She has collected information about sightings and paranormal phenomena in the area of the lake. Once, in the wintertime, a UFO ascended form the waters, breaking the ice, and quickly disappeared in the sky. Sometimes huge, perfectly round unfrozen patches of clear water appear in the Karelia's lakes.

T. Tyumeneva herself observed a strange phenomenon in Ladoga. She was on her way to the Valaam Archipelago that August night. She stood on the deck of the ship; the sky was cloudy, the weather rainy but no storm anywhere in sight. Everything was dark, no stars or Moon visible in the sky. Fifty metres from the ship Tyumeneva observed a gigantic luminescent area. Streams of bluish light ascended upwards from the deep. But they did not reach the clouds. The phenomenon lasted for three minutes, and disappeared as quickly as it appeared; the surrounding area once again turned pitch black.

Valaam is an island in the northwestern part of Lake Ladoga. It is 12 kilometres long and 7 kilometres wide. In the 10th century a monastery was founded on Valaam. The island was basically a piece of granite, devoid of any plant life. The monks turned it into a prosperous place, full of gardens and fertile soil. The island became an attraction for many famous visitors. There have also been sightings of UFOs over it, reported throughout the centuries.

In August of 1989, members of the Fakt UFO research society in Leningrad received a letter from an eyewitness. This woman was on Valaam Island, and observed a fiery sphere of reddish-gold colour. Its diameter approximately equalled two diameters of the Sun. The object descended into the waters of the lake. The Sun itself was visible. K. Khazanovich (see the TU-134 and Petrozavodsk chapters for more information about this scientist) was the Society's chairman at the time. He dispatched Lev Gorokhov and an astronomer to investigate the case. They located a member of the military who observed a similar phenomenon, but would not reveal his name. He actually asked his commanding officers about the sighting, and they informed him that there are descending remote-controlled spherical targets in use in the Lake Ladoga.

Mikhail Gershtein, like Paul Stonehill, has been fascinated by Lake Ladoga's secrets. He wanted to find out whether there is an underwater UFO base at the bottom of the lake. Gershtein was able to uncover interesting information. Russian academic magazine Priroda (Issue 5, 1995) contained an article written by A. Assinovskaya and A. Nikonova, Zagadochniye Yavleniya na Ladozhskom Ozere or Mysterious Phenomena on Lake Ladoga. Researchers of the Institute of Earth Physics studied old manuscripts that described strange rumbling sounds in the depths of the lake. Back in 1914 a letter arrived in the Main Physical Observatory in Saint Petersburg. The Valaam monastery's clerk whose name was Polikarp signed it. The letter stated that in the last five years the monks have observed a phenomenon in the south-western and western parts of the Lake Ladoga: underground rumbling noises that resemble a noise made by canon fire, from a distance. This rumbling noise is not uniform, sometimes it is heard in the distance, as if coming from the depths of the waters; and on rarer occasions, it is heard underground, in the western portion of Valaam. The ground would shake slightly.

Later, Russian and Soviet seismologists asked the monks to record exact date and time when the sound appeared, and the monks did so until 1927. There were 125 reports about this phenomenon. But, as the authors of the Priroda article established, there were no earthquakes registered in the area. They left for Lalaam, talked to local residents, and found out that the rumble was a well-known phenomenon there. The locals have a name for it, barrantida. This rumble reminded them of noises made by a passing train. Another mysterious phenomenon is the sudden boiling of the water in Ladoga. No other than Alexander Dumas, the famous 19th century French novelist who visited the lake reported the "boiling lake, as if in a pot". One local captain informed them that when his ship was on its way to Valaam, it suddenly encountered stormy waters, although there were no weather justifications for it. The rumble originates in the area where Ladoga Lake is the deepest. The authors of the Priroda article suppose opinion that troughs located under Ladoga's waters, formed as a result of the bottom of the lake cracking up, when its descended to different depths levels, separated by crevices.

Gershtein wants to know that if this is the case, why nothing was registered by earthquake measuring devices. He calls for further research of the lake. The February 19, 1997 sightings took place exactly in the area of the origin of the mysterious underwater phenomena. There is also a luminescence that is observed very often in the very same area, and it comes from under the surface of the lake.

Let us look at important sightings took place on February 19, 1997. Bright dots became visible over the Ladoga, but no radar registered them. An air traffic controller called the editorial offices of Anomaliya newspaper to report the sighting. Another witness confirmed the sighting, and reported that a military TV operator filmed the objects. Yuri Mefodyevich Raitarovsky, a noted

Russian Ufologist, and chairman of the Ufological Commission of the Planetology department of the Russian Geographical Society, was able to find the film, and turn it over to the newspaper. Mikhail Gershtein, too, investigated the case, and collected much material. As a result, the sightings of strange objects over lake Ladoga were a subject of discussion of Leningrad Region's Emergency Commission. Tatyana Sirchenko published some information in Issue 13, 2000, of Anomaliya.

Raitarivsky calculated the objects' size, and flight characteristics. There was a cluster of bright lights over the lake, hovering for 15 minutes and 39 seconds, at an altitude of 3.5 kilometres. The local air defence units did not conduct any training exercises at the time.

Russian newspaper Argumenti y fakty published a fascinating account of the Valaam mysteries (September 11, 2002 issue). Besides some other phenomena we have already described, there are strange spherical clouds that move over the lake on numerous occasions; there are also fiery spheres that burst out from under the waters of the lake. What are they? Some try to explain the spheres as consequence of underwater earthquakes. There are other small isles in the area, as strange as Valaam.

An interesting report comes to us from 1967; it was sent to the Russian Ufology Centre in California a number of years ago. Grigory Demyanovich Oleynikov, captain of the fishing boat Kama happened to be in Bay of Viborg in the Gulf of Finland in September of 1967. The day was cloudy. At approximately 1:30 at night the captain noticed a luminescent, milky-white object descending through the cloud. This object hovered, after its descent, at an altitude of 400 metres or so. The witness described the object as a disk with a diameter of about 15 metres. Its outlines were well defined. The bottom portion of the object contained rectangular formations, like nozzles; they emitted flames. For some two minutes the object remained motionless. It was bright, but not blinding, and no components broke apart from the object. No reported influence on humans or devices had been recorded. The object disappeared from sight by suddenly taking off upwards. It emitted no sound. By that time the clouds dissipated, and the witness observed similar object at a distance of two kilometres from Kama. Before the object rapidly ascended, the witness saw that the luminescent in the nozzles highly increased. No consequences, typical for anomalous phenomena, were reported. Only the captain of Kama observed the object aboard the ship. However, the boatswain of the Soviet ship Novorosiysk also observed the same object.

Among reports of sightings sent to Philip Mantle from the former USSR, there is one that pertains to Lake Onega. Reports were compiled by A. S. Savich, and dated February 19, 1982. That day, at 4:54 pm, a strange luminescence was observed in the sky over the lake. The luminescence was pale-blue, and its shape was that of a cloud. Inside this luminescent cloud, moving at a great speed toward the city was a moving bright spot, its shape that of an ellipsoid.

It was as bright as a star. After the bright spot disappeared from the sky (ten minutes later) behind the forest, the luminescent cloud remained in the sky for some time, and then, too disappeared from sight. About 5:00 pm, a little to the right from the place where the first bright spot appeared, two more luminescent spots showed up, moving synchronically in the same direction. One of them resembled the first sighting. It was a luminescent ellipsoid, surrounded by a spherical pale-blue haze, but its size somewhat smaller. Another object was in the shape of a luminescent sphere, moving in a spiral-like motion. As it moved, it left a rapidly disappearing hazy trail. The altitude of the observed objects was like that of aircraft in flight. At 5:15 pm, flying parallel to the ground, right over the observers, a luminescent arrow moved to the city at a great speed, leaving behind a luminescent and short trail. All of the observed objects did not exert any influence on humans, other living organisms in the area, plant life; nor was there any noise associated with the flight.

The report was among a batch of documents of the USSR Academy of Sciences, Institute of Earth Magnetism, Ionosphere, and Wave Distribution. The Institute director was none other than V. Migulin. The address of the Institute where reports were to by other scientific entity was town of Troitsk, Moscow Region, 142092, USSR.

Then there is a no-nonsense but alas brief article written by Senior Lieutenant A. Krishtal in the newspaper Sovetsky Moryak (March 30, 1999). He visited the area of the Gulf of Finland, and collected reports about anomalous phenomena from Soviet Naval personnel. Two sailors told him of strange sightings of a "flying saucer" over the lighthouse on the island where their unit was stationed. It was a grayish disk, shaped like a bagel, with a hollow middle part. It flew at an angle, up and down. Later an officer confirmed the sighting, and Krishtal recorded it. But then later he also obtained confirmations of the sighting from Soviet Naval officers aboard ships in the vicinity of the same island.

KORB OZERO

This is a fascinating Soviet case, but little known in the West. No coherent explanation has been found so far. The source of the case is found in book published by Moldaya Gvardia, 1966 (Mi ukhodim poslednimi or we are the last ones to depart). The author was V. Demidenko, who had investigated the case.

It was in the morning of April 27, 1961, when two inspectors from a lumberyard embarked on an inspection of dams. The same day, in the evening, the dam inspectors arrived at a small lake, known as Korb Ozero, in

Karelia. After their inspection tour of the dam, the inspectors spent the night some 6 kilometres from Korb Ozero. The next morning Vasily Brodsky (one of the inspectors) returned to the lake. He discovered something quite amazing. Whatever traces the inspectors left the day before were gone. Instead, there was a hole, 18 metres in width, 25 metres in length, and 5 metres in depth. The hole had something like a "mouth", an aperture facing the shore's cliff. The aperture had walls that sloped. As for the lake, there was an area devoid of ice.

V. Demidov arrived to the site with a diver, after being summoned by Brodsky's telegram. The diver, A. Tikhonov, searched the bottom of the lake. They found fragments of ice, floating in the ice-free water. The colour of the fragments was that of an emerald. They also discovered grayish foam in the water and in the foam numerous tiny balls. Demidov, who discovered the foam, stated that the balls were black, and resembled burnt millet grain. The balls were hollow inside, fragile, easily crumbling between fingers.

According to the investigator, Major Kopeikin, a strange and inexplicable fibre-like material was discovered on some fragments of the floating ice. An analysis of the material was performed in the Leningrad technological institute. It revealed the presence of magnum, aluminium, calcium, barium, and titanium.

The balls were analysed in the same institute. According to Demidov, when studies under the microscope, the balls had metallic sheen, and possessed structure resembling crystalline, and would not be dissolved in any acid. The conclusion of the experts was quite interesting: the millets were of non-organic origin, and are of origin that is not natural.

The diver discovered that the bottom of the lake was covered with mounds of frozen soil and a layer of pieces of the dropped soil. Broken ice was lying over everything. Apparently, whatever occurred there was so instantaneous, that the ice, pressed down by soil, did not have a chance to surface. That would explain the absence of ice on the surface. Also, the diver discovered a mysterious twenty-metre long track. At the end of the track was a cylinder-like soil formation, about a metre and a half high. It was as if some pipe-like object moved along the bottom, pushing the soil in front of it, and then this something stopped and disappeared. Beyond the unfrozen patch of water the bottom of the lake was quite regular.

As reported by Major Kopeikin, the soil that had fallen to the bottom of the lake, contained a tiny plate, its thickness one millimetre, its length two centimetres, and its width half a centimetre. Its spectral and chemical analyses demonstrated that the plate consisted of iron, silicium, with additives of platinum, titanium, and aluminium. No unusual radiation was detected. When the emerald-covered ice was delivered to a Leningrad laboratory, the experts who conducted the analysis could not explain the colouration.

There is a problem with the volume of the fallen soil. It is less, according to the diver, than the volume of the soil that would be removed from the hole. The ice around the unfrozen patch of water was free of any soil. What happened to the missing soil?

Demidov stated in his book that the local residents did not see or hear anything that night. According to Chernobrov, there are still traces of the mysterious force that changed the lake. He stresses that Yuri Gagarin's space flight took place six months before. From 1961 through 1979 several expeditions worked in the area of the Korb Lake; a noted Ufologist, Y. Raitarovsky, headed one of them. The expeditions proved beyond any doubt that the body that crashed into the soil was neither a missile, nor ball lighting, nor an explosive (Entsiklopedia Nepoznannogo or Encyclopedia of the Unknown, compiled by Vadim Chernobrov, and published in Moscow in 1998).

This is yet another mystery of Karelia, a place of numerous UFO-related mysteries. Perhaps a UFO caused the mystery of Korb Ozero. But let us look at further information.

V. Demidov, former member of the Commission for Anomalous Phenomena clarified a few things in his newspaper article Taina Gluhogo Ozera or Mystery of the remote lake (Na strazhe Rodini newspaper, August 1993. The article was kindly sent to us by Michael Gershtein. Demidov wrote the very first article about Korb Lake to appear in Soviet media (same newspaper, November 27, 1963), and the book we mentioned above. Now that the Soviet-era secrecy is gone, more information seems to surface.

Initially, the phenomenon was investigated by a group of officers and soldiers (pyrotechnics technicians, divers, sappers, and helicopter pilots). No explanation was arrived at as to what happened in the lake located at the border of the Leningradsky and Vologodsky regions. Among the information that was not revealed in 1964 were names of high officials involved, and KGB involvement. Because of such "guardianship", according to Demidov, it was easy to gain access to top research laboratories, and top experts in meteorites, chemistry, ball lightning, and some "secret" subjects. Not one of them was able to determine the exact nature of the event. Professor Aleskovski, of the USSR Academy of Sciences, who headed chemical research of the Academy, recently told Demidov that tiny balls were not of natural formation, and that he could not even imagine a technology that would be able to create such a product.

Demidov was able to determine that neither the Soviet Armed Forces nor scientific establishment were responsible for the Korb Lake event. Even Soviet Cosmonaut G. Titov could not get scientists interested in the story. Vice President of the USSR Academy of Sciences, M. Lavrentyev once told Demidov that Soviet scientists do not have time to dedicate to suspicious "holes". In science, everyone is concentrated in his own narrow field.

Four years later the same newspaper carried a fascinating article (Issues 7 and 8, 1997). N. Kalashnikov hiked to the lake with a group of companions in October of 1993. The lake looked like a cucumber, elongated from north to south. Two tiny huts stood next to the shore (hunters and fishermen use them occasionally). There was also a very old, abandoned and dilapidated chapel made out of wood, nearby.

They could only stay there a short time, but sufficient to allow the author of the article to collect several kilograms of the soil from the area, and find a strange plate, 20 by 30 centimetres, and 3 to 4 centimetres thick. The plate was square and smooth on one side, but the other side was strangely ribbed. He actually had to dig the plate out. Kalashnikov took the plate and the soil sample with him.

Kalashnikov grows ginseng in his dacha, the "root of life". He placed the soil from the Korb Lake in his garden, and forgot about it. Four years later he had to recall it, for when he weighed roots of the ginseng plant grown in the part of the plot where the Korb Lake soil was placed, Kalashnikov was amazed. The root that weighed 100 grams just four years ago now weighed 253 grams. It was a gigantic plant, by the standards of ginseng planting. Radiation was not the culprit, for there was not any whatsoever in the Korb Lake. The root cannot be described, according to the author, for it is truly amazing, and possesses some unusual qualities, too.

Kalashniov hints that other amazing things were found after the soil he brought from the lake, but the author did not go into details, promising to tell more in the future.

A STRANGE SIGHTING

In Karelia, in the summer of 1995 another strange sighting reported by a reliable witness. Not far from the Gorkovsky Station, a UFO was observed in the daytime. It was a sphere, of emerald colour, illuminating the area around it. The UFO consisted of several sections, and each contained three or four "lamps" inside it. The object hovered over the roof, and its size roughly corresponded to 8 to 10 metres. There was a sound, a cloud of grayish colour engulfed the UFO, and everything disappeared.

Again here we see that the former USSR does have many "strange" places within its borders. Anomalous events, sounds and sightings are much localised in such areas and are similar to other such places in many different parts of the world. Like the variety of events reported in such areas there are an equal amount of theories to try and explain them. UFO's, military activity, earthquakes are but a few explanations that have been put forward. Whatever the eventual explanation turns out to be, it is quite clear from the above that such locations have been and remain areas of fascination and wonderment both for the local inhabitants and for the researchers who are trying to find answers to the questions that have so far gone unanswered.

CHAPTER 26

MYSTERIES OF THE URAL MOUNTAINS

LAND OF MYSTERIES

We have discussed UFO sightings in the Urals throughout this book. There have been reports of paranormal phenomena in the Ural Mountains in ancient times, when the land was not a part of the Russian State. We have tried to present some of the most interesting cases in this chapter. It is simply not possible to collect all of the UFO cases reported in the Urals, and we simply do not have information that is in the possession of various governments, intelligence services, and even some Western television producers who were interested in the area's cases. Nevertheless, we believe that the readers of our book will find this chapter of great interest, and will pursue their own research of the Urals and its mysteries. Such Russian researchers as Nikolay Subbotin, who happens to be a resident of the historical city of Perm, will be your guides, should you want to expand your knowledge. You will find out more about such places as the ancient city of Arkaim, the story of the "Kishtim Dwarf", and so much more.

The Urals were "discovered" by the people of Russian city of Novgorod in the XI century during their trips to Pechora and Urga. One could find descriptions of these mysterious mountains in the old Arabian notes and Scandinavian sagas. But the land was no stranger to mysteries and enigmas even thousands of years ago. Take, for example, the Takla Makan Mummies. In the late 1980's, perfectly preserved 3000 year old mummies began appearing in a remote Chinese desert. They had long reddish-blond hair, European features and didn't appear to be the ancestors of modern-day Chinese people. Archaeologists now think they may have been the people of an ancient civilization that existed at the crossroads between China and Europe, perhaps even the southern Ural steppes.

The Udmurts are one of the oldest eastern-Finnish nations in the northwest woodland Urals. In the Russian sources of the 14th - early 19th centuries Udmurts are mentioned under the names ari, arsk people, chud otezkaya, and votyaki. These people called themselves udmurts or udmorts. But legends of the Urals speak of an ancient folk known as chud'. It was a strange, dark-skinned tribe, in possession of "secret powers", dwelling in the ancient Urals. The legends state that for reasons unknown to us, the chud' left the area and descended in the bowels of the earth, where they built underground cities. The chud' still inhabit those mysterious underground cities, away from the eyes of human beings who inhabit the Urals.

The Ural Mountains are the geographical borderline between Europe and Asia.

Ural Mountains (Russian Ural'skiye Gory), is a mountain chain in Russia, extending about 2400 kilometres from its northern boundary at the Arctic Ocean to its southern limits at the steppes of Kazakhstan, traditionally separating the continents of Europe and Asia. The chain is divided roughly into four main divisions: the Polar, Northern, Middle, and Southern Urals.

Geologically, Ural Mountains are remnants of an ancient range that rose toward the end of the Paleozoic Era, some 250 million years ago. The Ural region has extensive deposits of iron ore and coal in close proximity, as well as rich deposits of chromium, manganese, copper, zinc, bauxite, platinum, silver, and gold.

The diversity of flora and fauna is remarkable, varying from mountain pines and fir-groves to rocks, mountain gorges, deep canyons full of strange and mysterious caves, bare steppes and primeval forests. The Urals are not only famous for their mountains but for the rivers and brooks which begin there. There are 821 lakes, splendid glaciers and waterfalls. Unfortunately, ecology of the air has sustained heavy damage during the Soviet period.

Most of the industrial areas are located in the Middle and Southern Urals. The area had experienced a tremendous industrialisation in the former USSR during World War II, when many industries were moved to the Urals, or established to develop armaments production centres far from the battlefields and military zone.

ORENBURG

Orenburg is a city at the southern end of the Ural Mountains, the capital of Orenburg region, Central Asian Russia, located on the Ural River. The city was founded in 1735 as a fortress, guarding Russian rule against nomadic troublemakers. Orenburg resisted (in 1773-74) a siege by Pugachev, a famous Russian leader of an uprising that almost toppled the Czarist rule. It became a centre for Russian trade with Kazakhstan and Central Asia. From 1938 to 1957 it was called Chkalov. It, too, has its share of anomalous phenomena.

On Thursday, October 23, 1997, the short-wave radio show Voice of Russia aired an interview with a noted scientist and engineer Boris Belitsky. The interviewer was Miss Esther Winters. Among the declassified files of the Ministry of the Interior of the Soviet Union, defunct since 1991, there were several files of the Third Department of the old Imperial Ministry of the

Interior, which later became the Czarist secret police known as the Okhranka.

One sighting reported in the Okhranka files has to do with Orenburg. On December 26, 1830, a "certain extraordinary light effect was observed in the sky by the inhabitants, police and military in the city of Orenburg," Belitsky said, calling it "a typical UFO sighting." Apparently, there were other anomalous phenomena in the same city some years earlier.

In late September 1824, people in Orenburg were puzzled when they heard something banging on the onion-shaped roof of the Orthodox Church. They soon discovered little symmetrical pieces of metal falling from the clear blue sky. Months later, on January 25, 1825, the same phenomenon occurred again. Samples of the material were gathered and sent to St. Petersburg, capital city of the Empire.

M. Arago, a scientist, noted that a chemical analysis of the objects had showed them to be 70 percent red oxide of iron, and sulphur, and loss (of mass) by ignition (combustion) 5 percent. What is more amazing, the pieces of metal showed signs of having been manufactured. The Orenburg fragments attracted the attention of Prince Pavel Dolgorukii, the "librarian" of the mystic Brothers of the Inner Order. This was an offshoot of the Lodge Harmonia, founded by Nikolai Novikov in St. Petersburg in 1780. When Empress Catherine II suppressed the Masonic lodges of Russia in 1792 and jailed Novikov, Dolgorukii and two brothers, (Yuri and Nikita Troubezkoi) formed the Brothers of the Inner Order. They then started collecting hundreds of books on alchemy, mysticism and the paranormal, including works by the most notorious occultists of the period.

After Dolgorukii's death in 1838, the collection and perhaps a handful of those mysterious Orenburg artifacts passed into the possession of his daughter, Nadezhda de Fadeyev. In 1846, de Fadeyev's 15-year-old niece, Elena Petrovna von Hahn, spent the summer reading all the mystical books in her deceased grandfather's library.

Thirty years later, as the author and occultist Madame Blavatsky, Elena hinted at the strange happenings in Orenburg in her book, The Secret Doctrine. According to her, a number of Russian mystics travelled to Tibet by the way of the Ural Mountains in search of knowledge and initiation in the unknown crypts of central Asia. And more than one returned years later with a rich store of such information as could never have been given him anywhere in Europe. This trail led from St. Petersburg and Moscow straight through Orenburg. The Dolgorukii collection vanished sometime in the 1890s, after Mme. de Fadeyev's death.

This information was sent to us from Russia; it was obviously taken from an English-language source, and there may be confirmation found in the following sources (The Complete Book of Charles Fort, Dover Publications Inc., New York, NY, 1974. The Masters Revealed by K. Paul Johnson, State

University Press, Albany, NY, 1994, pages 19 to 22.), according to the Russian report.

But there was another mention of Orenburg, in the same report received from Russia and it points out the year of 1842, when small metal objects, perfectly hexagonal, fell out of the sky after a "strange cloud" appeared over the city.

THE PINKEL SAUCER MYSTERY

Back in 1954, Frankfurter Illustrierte, a magazine in Germany, published articles about an alleged development and production of "flying saucers" in the Soviet Union, during World War II.

In 1928, according to the magazine, Horst Pinkel, a German scientist, had participated in an exchange program between the German Army and Soviet officers. Pinkel was an expert in the area of high frequencies. He never returned to Germany. Pinkel shared beliefs of another German engineer, Walter Lemetzow, that there exist rays that could be harnessed and controlled, to produce a colossal and everlasting source of energy. Pinkel was initially assigned a building in the city of Kaluga in 1930, and he set up his equipment there. By 1938 his research into the theoretical rays had advanced significantly, and in November of 1942 Pinkel, along with Soviet scientists, was moved to the Belaya district, in the Urals. There, a secret laboratory was set up, for Stalin wanted Pinkel to construct a new and powerful weapon. But an American intelligence operative was able to escape from the USSR, and brought with him the formula for a special alloy, developed by Horst Pinkel for use in constructing a craft that utilised powerful new rays discovered by German scientists. This intelligence agent reported that in 1948 the Soviets had five flying saucers built; all of them possessed tremendous speeds. We were not able to learn more about Horst Pinkel, and have no idea whether the laboratory did exist, and what it produced. This is but another mystery of the mysterious Ural Mountains.

MOUNTAIN OF THE DEAD

This murder mystery remains unsolved, although top Russian Ufologists used their brainpower to get the answers. The date was February 2, 1959. Ten experienced, well-trained mountaineers departed from the city of Sverdlovsk (now Yekaterinburg). Igor Dyatlov led the team, and their destination was Otorten Mountain. All of them perished under most unusual circumstances. Soviet criminal police conducted a fruitless investigation only to report that an "invincible force of nature" caused the tragedy.

Kholat Syakhel is a snow covered mountain summit, and the name translates as Mountain of the Dead in the language of the Mansi tribe, natives who worship the place as a sacred place where spirits congregate. It was here, in this rugged, desolate area that a search and rescue team found a tent, clearly abandoned in a hurry, because its flaps were cut through with knives, to allow a hasty, panicky escape to those inside. Investigators found footprints, leading from the tent down the slope. And not very far away from the same tent, at various distances from it, corpses, too, were discovered. One mountaineer died from exposure, the rest, as was determined by investigators, died of numerous bodily injuries of unknown nature.

Dyatlov's body was lying 300 metres away from the main group; he crawled to the tent and died. There were no injuries on his body. Another body was found closer to the tent. When the body was autopsied, the doctors found cracks in his skull; the horrible blow was inflicted without any damage to the skin. The female member of the expedition was the closest to the tent. She was lying face down, and the snow beneath her was collared by blood. But no signs of violence were found on her body. The three corpses found at a distance from the campfire presented the largest mystery. They died from horrible injuries, their ribs were broken, heads smashed in, internal bleeding in each body. But how could they sustain internal injuries with their skin intact?

Vadim Chernobrov and his research expedition were in the area in 1999, investigating the same case. They were able to uncover some interesting details.

Mikhail Gershtein, who investigated the same case, reported that the last of the discovered mountaineers died from exposure from cold temperature (Tragediya v gorakh or Tragedy in the Mountains article, published in Perekryostok Kentavra Magazine, Issue 3, 1997). It was also assumed that something blinded them.

V. Chernorov spoke to Maria Solter, one of the doctors assigned to the case. She actually remembered that there were 11 corpses, and where the other two came from no one knew. The bodies were taken to the military hospital in the area, but one body was immediately transferred to Sverdlovsk. During the actual autopsy, a military official that was present, pointed to her, and Maria Solter was told to leave the room. But she had to sign papers stating that she would not reveal any information.

The victims' clothes contained increased levels of radiation, and surrounding tree branches were scorched. L. Lukin, who was one of the criminologists, stated to Chernobrov that the character of the scorching was such as to indicate that a ray, or some other powerful energy inflicted it. This energy was of unknown nature, but obviously directed, for the snow did not melt and the trees in the area were not damaged. Corpses, discovered at the site, had an unnatural, orange colour. The strange orange colour of the bodies was attributed to radiation from a powerful, unfamiliar energy source, possibly an unidentified flying object. Local residents told police investigators that at the time of alleged murders there had been sightings of noiseless orange spheres over the mountain.

People in the Northern Urals still discuss this case. There are rumours that the ten stumbled upon the secrets of the so-called "vacuum bombs" V. Chernobrov points out that no such weapon existed at the time. Researchers believed, at the time, that the tourists were simply killed because they witnessed, albeit inadvertently, tests of secret weapons.

However, according to M. Solter, the colour of the bodies was no different from other corpses. Who "collared" the bodies, as the years went by, and rumours did not die down? For a while there existed a hypothesis that missiles caused their deaths. A metal ring was discovered in the area where Dyatlov's mountaineers died. It was from a Soviet missile. Although reports of sighted missiles in the area at the time were later turned over to Chernobrov's group, there was no official confirmation. There were no rocket launches at the time (the Moscow Aviation Institute Kosmopoisk branch researched all available archives).

Did the ill-fated tourists find something in the mountains that was obviously not for their eyes to see? Was this the laboratory related to the Soviet experiments of the 1940s?

Or was their find or observation related to the tragedies of the 1950s?

The criminologist, mentioned above, recalls that when he submitted facts of the case to the Communist boss of the area (First Secretary of the Regional Committee CPSU, A. Korolenko) he received immediate orders to classify the investigation, bury the corpses in sealed off caskets, and inform their relatives that all mountaineers died from exposure to cold temperature.

There were other strange deaths in the area. Those who had investigated the case also did not die peacefully. V. Chernobrov has eerie details of their deaths, and descriptions of other strange incidents, and those who want to learn more details about the case of the murdered mountaineers and those who died in the following years should contact him. What is important to us, the UFO angle definitely was present in the investigation, and there were eyewitness reports of strange aerial phenomena during the investigation of the heretofore-unsolved murder case. Mikhail Gershtein collected such reports; among them there is a sighting of a large fiery circle that followed one of the rescue teams for twenty minutes.

The region has been a major centre of nuclear weapons production since 1948, when the Mayak complex began operations near the city of Kishtim. Mayak produced the necessary material for the first Soviet atomic bomb, detonated in August 1949. Mayak caused three major incidents of nuclear waste contamination in 1949, 1957, and 1967, which when combined released more than ten times the radiation of the world's worst known reactor disaster near Chernobyl, Ukraine. In the 1950s nuclear wastes from Mayak were diverted into nearby Lake Karachai, and the lake soon became highly radioactive. In the late 1960s workers began filling in the lake with rock and soil and planned to seal it over with concrete by the mid 1990s, but a government commission concluded in 1991 that this might force radioactive isotopes into the groundwater. In any case, containment of radioactive wastes and cleanup efforts continue in the Urals amid public controversy.

Another tragedy took place in the Urals in 1958. Apparently, it was a result of a bacteriological weapons development gone awry. Hundreds of villages disappeared, and thousands of people died from a mysterious illness. Of course, the Soviets kept everything secret, and few details were available until the 1990s.

PERM SIGHTING

There have been other sightings reported in the Urals, but we will describe the one that took place on May 7, 1990. Our source of information is an article in Chelyabinski Rabochy newspaper (August 30, 1990). A number of people reported a bright, luminous object moving through the sky, and emitting rays in a fan-like fashion toward the ground. The UFO flew above Mountain Kamenoi. The object was flying over the expanse of the Katav-Ivanovsk territory. It was a strange object, but of course, no formal investigation was initiated. This was typical of UFO sightings in the waning days of the Soviet Union. Even such prominent paranormal cases as the Sasovo Explosions (where scientists and criminal investigators worked together, at least initially), described in an earlier chapter, basically led nowhere.

ANCIENT HIGH-TECH

The Urals continued to amaze us in the 1990's. German researcher Hartwig Hausdorf recently compiled information about a sensational find that may shed light on whether the area had been visited by extraterrestrials in the antiquity (Ancient Skies, German Edition, 2/1997). Thousands of strange, mostly spiral-shaped objects had been found in 1991-1993 by gold prospectors on the small river Narada, on the eastern side of the Urals, at depths between 10 and 40 feet. The objects range in size from a maximum of 1.2 inches down to an incredible 1/10,000th of an inch. The objects are composed of various metals: the larger ones are of copper, while the small and very small ones are of the rare metals tungsten and molybdenum. We should recall the Dalnegrosk Object, and its composition. Russian and Finnish scientists are engaged in a serious research of the tiny objects. Whatever crated the objects must have been an incredibly advanced technology: there is a remarkable resemblance to control elements used in micro-miniature devices. Scientific tests give an age for the objects of between 20,000 and 318,000 years, (depending on the depth and the situation of the site).

The area itself attracts attention of Russia's leaders. On April 16, 1996, the New York reported on a mysterious military base being inside the Yamantau

Mountain in the Beloretsk area of the southern Urals Times ("Russia Builds Mammoth Underground Complex in Urals" by Michael R. Gordon). The project consisted of a huge complex, served by a railroad, and a highway; thousands of workers were involved.

Russian officials described the underground compound as a mining site, a repository for Russian treasures, a food storage area, and a bunker for Russia's leaders in case of nuclear war. Hence, its ultimate purpose is unknown, but the U.S. government is concerned.

This may be the very site where Russian military UFO researchers allegedly keep the remnants of the mysterious Omsk Object (although it is probably a hoax), and whatever else they had been able to collect in the last sixty years: the ultimate Russian "Area 51".

THE KYSHTYM DWARF

There has been much noise about this weird story in Russia, and more so, abroad. We cannot disregard it, but there has not been much information until 2002. The online Russian newspaper Pravda.RU provided the narrative (it used a number of sources). Its article was entitle 'Archaeologists Puzzled: 'An Alien or Just a Retarded Child?' (2002-10-12)'.

A messenger of a highly developed civilization of Alfa Centaurus, with a head in the shape of a space helmet - in this way, this odd creature looks something from an archive film. It was found in 1996 in a small settlement of the Chelyabinsk Region. Diguci Masao, producer of the Japanese TV Company Asahi TV, offered 200 thousand dollars to the person who could sell him the 21cm mummy.

"Even if we did not have this dwarf, we would have to invent it," stated the article. Asahi journalists even came to the settlement to shoot a film about the dwarf. However, nothing particular was reported to the Japanese. Tamara Prosfirina (who is said to have found the creature and even named it Alyosha), soon wound up in a mental hospital and later died under strange circumstances. In the film, only fragments of her description could be heard. The woman explains that she found the creature while walking through a forest during a storm.

We thank Pravda.ru for its article, and urge the newspaper to cover more stories about Russian Ufology.

Where the creature is (or, as others call it, the mummy of an embryo) now, is unknown. New articles about the "extraterrestrial" appear only as new versions of old descriptions, while accumulating new details. In particular, journalists report that the mysterious creature lived with the woman for about a month and ate exclusively yogurt and caramel.

In the city of Yekaterinburg, discussions were being held as to whether or not to give the mummy over to the foreigners. Leading forensic experts of the

Ural Region, who examined the last tsar's remains, said that the mummy or whatever it is, should first be examined and only afterwards be given to the Japanese.

"It was found on Russian soil, so it should belong to Russia. However, of course, nothing should be concealed in science. And if the extraterrestrial theory is proved, the facts and the mummy should be the property of the whole of humanity," - expert Vladimir Kroptov believes.

Now, regional customs officials are also searching for the extraterrestrial. They say they would not allow the mummy to be smuggled abroad. If necessary, they are ready to send out a description of the mummy to all police stations. Most sensible people in the Ural Region are of the opinion that the customs officials have been fallen prey to the advertising campaign of the Japanese.

Specialists of the Anthropology Institute are skeptical about the case of the extraterrestrial. The chief of anthropology reconstruction laboratory, Tatyana Balueva, said that Alyosha might be a very small, stillborn child. "The creature's arms and legs look like human extremities, while its skull is not completely formed. It could have been a sick child, having a serious pathology. It is most likely a human being" Tatyana Balueva states.

We need to remind our readers about the single largest accident in nuclear waste storage that took place in Kyshtym on September 29, 1957. It was a pressure-related explosion of improperly stored nuclear waste at a large plant that produced the plutonium for Soviet bombs. It spewed radioactive waste over a large area in the southern Urals. The explosion blew apart sections of a mountain and contaminated about 400 square miles of countryside, making it unliveable (70-80MT of waste over a region between 15,000 and 23,000 square kilometres). As a result, whole towns were wiped out from the face of the Earth. The aftermath of this explosion, now known as the "East Urals Radioactive Trace," is one of the radiation sources, originally kept secret, and then denied in the Soviet Union. Was the Kyshtym Dwarf a consequence of the nuclear explosion? It is almost impossible to determine, and probably only military medical researchers could determine the truth. A very informative Russian UFO data collector, whose nom de guerre is Major Thomas, wrote to Paul Stonehill in January of 2003, that there are serious arguments against the mutation hypothesis. The creature's skull is different from human cranial skeletal anatomy. According to this source, it was Vadim Chernobrov who heads the Kosmopoisk research group that had discovered the dwarf's corpse. The corpse is still in Russia, and its new owner is not in a hurry to sell it or donate to science for research purposes. Chernobrov's researchers were able to bring to Moscow a cloth that covered the corpse. They are planning genetic research.

We would like to add that RUFORS is investigating a case of the so-called Kishtim Dwarf.

Mikhail Gershtein was one of the first Russian researchers to introduce the Alyosha case.

The story of the Kyshtym Dwarf is far from over.

Nikolay Subbotin had reported, back in 1998, of a very strange incident over a small port of Zaostrovka (in the vicinity of Perm, Ural Mountains). The date was September 16, 1989. Local denizens watched in amazement an aerial battle between six dark, gray-coloured UFOs who were chasing the seventh unidentified flying object (a golden-coloured UFO). The craft performed incredible manoeuvres at fantastic speeds. They were finally able to shoot it down... A report about the incident was published in a newspaper in the city of Semipalatinsk. The author himself, a former military aviator who fought in Afghanistan is said to reside in Sweden.

Apparently the shot-down craft fell into a swamp, in the territory of A Soviet military unit. When the military tried to collect whatever was left behind of the fallen object, they were badly burned. Russian aircraft flying over the site were reported to have a malfunction of onboard equipment.

There are other somewhat obscure reports of the incident. The UFO battle in the sky had been seen by hundreds of eyewitnesses, and one of the silvery disks was allegedly shot down by the Russian warship Admiral Golovko , crash-landing sixty miles outside of Zaostrovka. A highly classified recovery team was given immediate access to the wreckage. There are very few details available about this case, and we hope N. Subbotin will continue his research to uncover the truth.

The Urals are not just a beautiful mountain range, but a mystifying one as well. It is without doubt that the Soviet military is responsible for a certain amount of the strange happenings in the area, which they are highly unlikely ever to admit to. But the Soviet military cannot be responsible for all the mysterious happenings in this area. As we have seen, such mysteries go back many centuries. Again, we have another mysterious location within the borders of the former USSR that continues to mystify us to this very day.

CHAPTER 27

SAINT PETERSBURG AND ITS SIGHTINGS

GATCHINA

Located forty-five kilometres southwest of Saint Petersburg, Gatchina was first built by Count Grigory Orlov, one of Catherine the Great's lovers. After his death it became an imperial residence and the favourite of Emperor Paul I, who lived most of his life there. Western tourists were not allowed to visit Gatchina for a many years, because an institute for nuclear physics was located here, as well as secret military installations nearby. Perhaps that is why the area is known for its UFO sightings.

The huge park ensemble, originally designed in the English style, is dotted with little gazebos, pavilions, and other small structures. The palace structure and all its furnishings were thoroughly devastated in World War II; about half of the Palace is open for viewing at present.

UFOs appear over Gatchina on a regular basis. In the autumn of 1991 local residents could observe intensive movements of fiery spheres. One of the objects hovered over the Baltic Station, emitting bluish rays. Most often, UFOs are observed over the Uchkhoz and Voyskovitsa settlements, located a few kilometres west of Gatchina.

1991 was marked by numerous sightings of unidentified flying objects. Most often, UFOs sighted had spherical shapes. In the daytime they shined metallically, and at night the UFOs glowed with a red light. Spherical invaders flew along a zigzag-like trajectory, increasing speed instantaneously, and changing flight directions at incredible angles. By the way, there is a Russian air defence unit, located close to Gatchina.

Konstantin Ivanov of NLO Magazine (1998) interviewed officers of this military unit, and they revealed interesting details about UFO sightings in the area. They constantly observe UFOs, and radar devices register the objects more often than the military are able to observe them. One local eyewitness reported just such a sighting. A UFO appeared one evening over the Druzhnaya Gorka (Gatchin Region) settlement. Viktor Mikheyev, who had observed it, said that the object was a giant luminescent ellipsoid body, resembling a cloud. Only its edges were brilliant, the bulk of the body remained dark. The UFO brightly illuminated a large piece of the ground below. A short time later military aircraft took off one after another.

Mikheyev and other observers saw an amazing event: the UFO hovered over the settlement, seemingly undisturbed, while Russian interceptors buzzed around it, like angry wasps. The UFO finally left, reaching incredible speed, and disappeared in the distance. Its size was impressive: the object was at least a few dozen metres long. Later, local observers reported numerous metallic spheres in the area.

There are also reported encounters with aliens on the ground, but there has not been a contact, for local residents flee strange life forms that try to communicate with them.

There is an interesting confirmation of the strange events in Gatchina. A. Serebrov's article was published in Anomaliya newspaper, Issue 18, 1998. In the late 1970s he spent summers in the area. Local residents talked much about the testing range between Gatchina and Viritsa. Strange, sometimes fantastic rumours circulated about the military installation; most people agreed the testing range was a place where secret experiments were conducted, and somehow this was related to UFOs. Serebrov pointed out that there were actually several testing ranges in the area. The first one was located deep in the woods, in the area of swamps and marshes; apparently it was not functioning anymore. Another one was located just beyond the first testing range. That is where Soviet military tested their aircraft. The tests were conducted only at night. Villages in the area heard explosions, roar of engines, and associated noises. Then one day, quite suddenly, there were no more tests. Local rumours mentioned a third, most secret testing range. Sand was delivered to the building site from local sandpits. There is a railroad branch-line deep inside the forest. Trains under heavy guard were also sighted in the area. Locals began to encounter military outposts, and patrols that were comprised mostly of officers. They were informed that this was a forbidden area, and asked to go back to their villages. Rumours had it that whatever was tested now had to do with space research and UFOs. The village where Serebrov stayed was located 40 minutes by foot from the train station. An unpaved road led to it, and a small river flowed nearby. It was not a completely Godforsaken place; some villagers had TV sets, there was a local "klub" where movies where shown to villagers (a common trait of the Soviet existence). There was a store, and even a local medic. Serebrov remembers one thing quite clearly. Horrible noises heard during rainstorms were much more powerful than nature could create, and associated with strange phenomena. A local eyewitness described fiery spheres in the sky, with long luminescent trails. Some time later, amid rumours that the military conducted failed experiments with a captured UFO, all of the testing ranges ceased operations, and equipment was removed.

THE KODUMAA PROJECT

A joint Russian-Finnish expedition of scientists from the Jyvaskyla University (Finland), and Peter the Great Institute of Anthropology and Ethnography (Russia) was completed in the autumn of 1996. Finnish government had invested over 110 million Finnish marks into the Kodumaa Project.

This project was actually initiated before the disintegration of the USSR. In 1986 young Leningrad scientists Vladimir Majdanov and Alexey Knyazev discovered a weak radioactive trace. They established that its path lay through Scandinavia from Helisnki, toward Kronshtadt, and abruptly ended in the Volosovo area (USSR). In 1990, scientists from Finland and Sweden reported that the signal, weakest on Soviet territory, becomes more powerful in the area of the Scandinavia Mountains. Both Soviet scientists came to a conclusion that this was a trajectory of a crashed alien ship.

What happened to its crew, and where are the fragments of the ship? To answer their questions, Swedish and other foreign scientists joined the research. A Swedish satellite performed measurements and studied the trace in the Arctic Ocean. A conclusion was reached that, most likely, a catastrophe occurred before the First Ice Age in Europe (and maybe even caused it). The disaster took place in the outer space, when a huge alien spaceship reached its optimal trajectory, and tried to land in the area of the Scandinavia Ridge. The ship probably touched the ridge, and only a part of the emergency capsule reached Volosovo.

This information comes from an article published in Anomaliya newspaper in its Issue 2, 1997. Knyazev and Majdanov did not have necessary equipment and funds to conduct a comprehensive research. But they think archaeology provides proof of their hypothesis. They attended a painting exhibition of Nicholas Roerich's painting (more about him in the KGB chapter). There the scientists paid attention to a drawing of an ancient burial ground. Locals considered it to be sacred. Roerich's archaeological expedition conducted digs in the area of his Volosovo manor, Izvar. Knyazev and Majdanov, were able to research the documents of Roerich's expedition, and obtain exact description and measurement of the burial ground.

According to them, the measurements were exactly as those of the emergency capsule of American Apollo spaceships. Other interesting details about the burial ground included a sitting "cosmonaut's" position, and strange artifacts found there; their position resembled that of a spaceship controls. Russian scientists believe that those who survived the crash, or early humans, actually buried dead aliens, and then tried to recover fragments of the ship. The Ice Age forced humans to retreat to the Altai and Pamir areas, A giant glacier dragged fragments of the crashed ship to the Arctic Ocean, and partially covered them. It is possible that Nicholas Roerich guessed the same. Many doctors and scientists observed that the Volosovo indigenous people have different anthropological features than residents of Estonia and Finland, as well as Russia. Ancient Russian manuscripts, and directives of Czar Peter the Great, describe magic of "Chud sorcerers". The Russian Orthodox Church and Muscovite princes put down uprisings of the local believers of ancient magic. Yet, there are still legends and ancient knowledge in the Baltic, as well as burial grounds shaped as capsules.

Could it be that the Soviet military did or even still does have a secret UFO research establishment close to Saint Petersburg? It is rumoured that other countries like the USA and Great Britain have such a facility. AREA 51 in the USA has become well known for its alleged UFO studies, and RAF Rudloe Manner in England is also rumoured to have officially investigated UFO's. The theory that mankind, in its ancient past, has been visited by extraterrestrials is know as the 'Ancient Astronaut' theory. It therefore comes as no surprise to us that the ancient lands of the former USSR have such legends of ancient alien visitors, ancient astronauts?

CHAPTER 28

STRANGE PLACES AND ANOMALOUS ZONES

There are many areas of Russia and other parts of the former Soviet Union that could truly be classified as anomalous. They attract UFOs, or perhaps, they emit phenomena that can be mistaken for UFOs. To understand some of the reports discussed in this book, we need to introduce at least some of the areas to the readers.

The Russian Far East has another strange hill (besides the one in Dalnegorsk), and its name is Bo-Jaus. It was there that in 1995 a TU-154 airplane crashed and those onboard perished. During the search, rescuers discovered debris from some ten more airplanes. Researchers proffered a hypothesis that the area itself is a powerful geophysical anomaly; when "active", it brings down aircraft flying in the area. Is this Russian equivalent of 'The Bermuda Triangle'?

The Monchegorsk area has at least one strange site. In 1965 geological expeditions located a geochemical anomaly that contained high percentages of nickel and copper. When they reported the find to their superiors, the joy was short-lived: the centre of the anomaly contained a group of facilities and industrial factories. The ecology of the area was polluted to such an extent, that geological reports were classified until the 1990's. Could it be that UFOs are attracted to the areas of most dangerous pollution: Chernobyl, Monchegorsk, and nuclear power plants? Or do such facilities produce phenomena that become labelled as UFOs?

Kazakstan has a tiny body of water, better known as the Dead Lake. Located in the Taldikurgan region, this lake remains ice-cold even during the summer heat. There is no fish in the lake and no algae either. No research was undertaken, because it is impossible to remain underwater for over three minutes (even for divers with scuba equipment). People drown in the lake, but never ascend to the surface. The Dead Lake is not the kind of place you would want to visit.

The Barsa-Kelmes Island is located in the North western part of the Aral Sea. Its name, translated from the Kazakh language, means "Go there, and you shall not return". There are numerous legends about this island, strange

215

phenomena that concerns the flow of physical time. Those who sought refuge there for a few years found out upon return to their families that they were missing for dozens of years. Some groups of people had disappeared there altogether. The Kazakhs blame a strange creature: a giant flying extinct lizard. Actually, some locals know about its skeleton, and showed a tooth taken from it. Modern expeditions also suffered time-losses at the island. Some members spent half an hour (according to them) in a "white fog"; but upon return found out they were missing a day.

Let us recall that in February of 1955 an underwater nuclear bomb explosion was secretly conducted in the Aralsk town area. This was an idiotic thing to do, but Soviets have committed other idiotic crimes against ecology of Russia, Ukraine, and all other republics that comprised its union. The explosion destroyed a very fragile ground layer, and water from Aral Sea gradually flowed into the surrounding thick sandy layers. That is how the tragedy began to unfold. We do not know how extensively Soviet nuclear tests had harmed the natural environment. Perhaps a criminally negligent arms race related explosion in the post-Stalin's USSR caused the strange phenomenon that is reported nowadays.

Siberia has its share of anomalous areas. The Krasny Greben rock, located in the vicinity of Krasnoyarsk, has been known for its gravitational anomalies. In 1977, for instance, a witness was pulled away from the rock, and an unseen force carried him to the nearby gorge. He hovered in the air for some time, but was finally brought down to the distance of three metres, and then released.

There is a lake in Mordovia, 50 kilometres from Kovilkino. It is well known to the locals, who call it the Lake of Fear. They never swim in it: too many strange phenomena take place in its waters. Quite often at night, a greenish fog engulfs the area, and horrible shrieks are heard at a distance. Many people have perished in the lake through the years. In 1995, two students who went swimming were sucked in by a strange wave. The search produced nothing, and no bodies were recovered. The locals, alerted by other students, would not allow anyone to step into the lake. In the morning the divers arrived, and looked at the bottom. All they found was a sandy bottom and a strange greenish luminescence rising from it, as if an optical mirror effect. The divers could see their own reflections.

Karelia, too, has anomalous areas. It took a group of tourists (comprised of scientists) but a few hours to arrive in Karelia from St. Petersburg, in the summer of 1993. They were in the Vuoksa Lakes area, when a torrential rainstorm engulfed the area. The automobile was forced off the road by lightning, and hit a tree. S. Elbman, an engineer, suffered a concussion, and the tourists had to get help. They found a small hut nearby (it appeared from nowhere, as they recalled); an old hag let them in. She asked no questions, fed them, and washed out the engineer's wound. The tourists were too tired and shaken to ask questions, and the old woman said nothing. They fell asleep, and in the morning woke up under the open sky. There was no hut, no hag, just some ruins of walls made of granite stones. Their search and inquiries revealed that there used to be a mill in the area. But there other similar ruins in the area, so there is nothing strange about old granite walls. The engineer's wound healed rapidly, and even a scar disappeared. But the scientists kept on asking questions, and found out from the highway policemen that back in 1982 a similar incident took place. Did they spend time in a parallel world? Do the UFOs over Karelia come from parallel worlds?

Vadim Chernobrov and his MAI-Kosmopoisk research organisation have been to the Medveditskaya Ridge over 27 times. This is a powerful geologically active area. It is comprised of Rocky Mountains, reaching 200 to 380 metres in height, and located in the Volgograd (former Stalingrad) region. Ancient legends reveal that "cursed" or "bewitched" areas exist in the Ridge, and there have been rumours of strange backwoods dwellers. Curiously, anomalous phenomena (such as UFOs, spheres, and disks) have been observed right where the above-mentioned areas supposedly exist.

Another anomalous zone, Shigri, is located some seven kilometres to the southwest of the Zikeyevo railroad station (Kaluga area). According to Vadim Chernobrov, during the 1990s, sightings of numerous bright atmospheric phenomena and anomalous objects of various shapes had been reported.

Anomalous zones, such as the ones reported above, seem to be in greater abundance in the former USSR than in any other country in the world. It is quite probable that modern day experiments have caused ecological disasters in such areas but this excuse cannot of course be used for all such anomalous episodes reported down the centuries. It is quite clear that in such zones we not only have reports of UFO's, but of reports of missing time, phantom people and places, and even reports of creatures thought to be long extinct. We will delve into such zones in more depth in some of the following chapters, but it is clear for all to see that the former USSR has more than its fair share of such anomalous zones, also termed 'window areas' in other parts of the world. Why this should be remains the subject of much debate.

CHAPTER 29

UFOs OVER THE RUSSIAN FAR EAST

Soviet Far East has been closed off to foreigners throughout the Soviet period. Yet the Tunguska Phenomenon was only a part of the history of anomalous phenomena (including flying objects) to filter through to the West from this area. The natives of Priamurije and Primorije (Russian Far Eastern territories) did not consider anomalous phenomena to be anomalous. They knew and accepted poltergeists, the Abominable Snowman, UFOs, and the Flying Man. The natives have their own names for anomalous phenomena, and some legends, testimonies, eyewitness reports and accounts survived through the ages.

The legends of the taiga dwellers vividly describe heavens opening "doors" between different worlds. The worlds are located in the "outer, original world", "underground", and in the "Great Beyond". The shamans have detailed descriptions of aircraft (as relayed in the ancient legends of their people). They believe that "flying saucers" are nothing other than agd ezen adani, ships of the Sovereigns of the Thunder. The "sovereigns" sometimes took humans with them, regardless of the latter wishes.

Before the First World War, local Udege hunters and their Russian Staroveri descendants of religious dissidents of XVIII century Russia) friends observed some very strange phenomena, while hunting together. In several localities (Annuye, Bikin) they sighted UFOs that moved in the air and mysterious "three bright points" that also moved on the ground. The "goloan", a ball lightning-like object moved through the sky: while in flight it left a smoky or luminous trail.

The elders told stories of the amban khotongon, or "Devil's fiery skull". Apparently it fell down to Earth from a UFO. A "skull", appearing near a dwelling, was able to scare people to such an extent that they could neither move or lie down. To put it in the twentieth century terms, the "skull" exerted adverse biological and physiological effects on human beings. It was observed that lukewarm water in the presence of such a "skull" immediately began boiling.

KHABAROVSK, 1990

As reported by the Northern News Service, bright red spheres flew across the horizon and darted above the ice-bound Amur River. In Khabarovsk in the evening of March 21, 1990, witnesses reported that the objects kept strict distance. The policemen, who observed the UFOs, stated that the objects arrived in force, and tried to videotape them. The video ran erratically and through interference, and that was how Khabarovsk television explained the flickering and flashing images. Witnesses reported strange objects to the military, the police, and the government officials. One city hospital called for help: a cigar-shaped object hovering above it caused panic among the patients and personnel. A patrol car on its way to the hospital caused the UFO to fly off.

Others reported a low-flying "saucer" with a bright surface and running lights all along the hull. The UFO shifted around, its "nose" dipping and rising. The Suvorovski Natisk daily paper, (mouthpiece of the Far Eastern Military District), asked a spokesman of the air defence HQ whether the radars had spotted the UFOs. He informed the journalists that on March 21, the UFO was observed moving 100-120 metres above ground. It was a black cigar-shaped object 50 metres in length. In its rear part, something like a ruby-coloured glow was observed. The orderly officer phoned this information in to the HQ. Yet the radars registered nothing.

Ufologists in Vladivostok reported that in January of 1990, the Tumnin villagers (taiga area, near the Okhotsk Sea) observed a huge spherical body. It slowly drifted in the south-eastern direction. At the time, the sky was cloudless.

Then there was an interesting article in Tikhookeanskaya Zvezda newspaper (January 20, 1990). It referred to an incident that took place on the 14th of January, in the same village of Tumnin. The eyewitness described an object in the sky that slowly drifted from the horizon as a huge egg-shaped body, semi-transparent and hardly visible. The sky was cloudless that day, and it assured visibility of the UFO. As more witnesses came out into the open, the object was described as a silvery sphere that contained inside it something dense. The head of the local meteorological station, Yu. Kwyatkovsky, mentioned that a number of unidentified objects had frequented the area lately. Among them were luminescent balls of red, green, and yellow colours. On November 29 of 1989 another sighting took place: a luminescent body flew from behind the mountains, at low speed, and at a low altitude. The object drifted toward the centre of the village, and hovered over it. Three multi-coloured beams pointed towards the ground. An hour later a similar object was sighted over Vanino, Sovetskaya Gavan', and Zaveti Ilyicha village.

Tumnin Village is located in an area of faults of the Earth core. There are thermal springs. A mighty mountain stands over the site of a magnetic anomaly. Perhaps this is the source of mysterious luminescence that has been reported by local hunters.

As we can see, strange objects have been attracted to the remote area of Russia way before 1908. The question remains: why?

DEVIL'S CEMETERY

In May of 1991 Rempel and his Vladivistok Ufological Association embarked on an expedition to find the notorious and elusive Devil's Cemetery. Allegedly it was the very site of the Tunguska Object's crash (or explosion) in the taiga. They claimed that the site was located in a clearing in the taiga, not far from the Kova River, a tributary of the mighty Angara. Rempel was prompted by persistent rumours that following the 1908 explosion, strange animals and humans had appeared in the Kova River area ("minotaurs", and other beings). The Vladivostok Ufologists knew of the existence of the Devil's cemetery, and they were aware of the fact that animals and humans who wander inside the zone can never leave. They are trapped by some unseen forces, and eventually die, as if "burned from inside". When a human being approaches the area, he or she experiences strange pain all over the body. Prior to the Soviet policy of "forced collectivisation" in the 1930's, locals knew the exact location of the Devil's Cemetery. Stalin's policies resulted in villages being wiped out and their population forced out. The site was forgotten, but its borders had been defined by trees with carved signs on their trunks to warn those who approach. The Simonov brothers, two physicists from Tashkent, had also speculated that the taiga hides the crash site of the Tunguska Phenomenon or Object. According to them the crashed object remains underground, under a clearing, many metres deep. Rempel's expedition did find a site, but no one is certain, for they lacked the much needed equipment. The anomalous zone they discovered possesses very strange and dangerous qualities. They also found the marked trees. Neither animals nor birds were seen inside the zone. According to legends, the Devil's Cemetery should not have any vegetation, but they did see some mutant-like plants. Rempel's group also refrained from the actual entry to the site. They did observe a very strange, eerie, fog-like substance over the clearing, but not in any other nearby areas. Their tools and instruments had been adversely affected, too.

There is another source of information about the Devil's Cemetery. In the Kransoyarsk kray (territory, a Russian administrative designation for a geographic area), in the vicinity of the Kezhma Village, there is a clearing in the woods. The locals call it Devil's cemetery, and shepherds intentionally do not go there. This clearing "killed" animals that wandered in. The first time the Soviet media paid attention to the clearing was before the World War Two, in an article in Sovetskoye Priangarye newspaper. We found out about it in the Soviet digest Tainy XX Veka or Mysteries of the XX Century (Moscow, 1990).

Then there was an article titled Mystery of the Devil's Cemetery in the ever-interesting Komsomol'skaya Pravda newspaper (November 15, 1987). The author of this article, N. Savelyev, initially doubted that the object (he called it meteorite) would be located some 400 kilometres from the explosion. Soviet researchers believed that the object was located in the Kova River valley (Kova is the left tributary of the mighty Angara River). But then Savelyev began reading collected materials and notes of the Boguchansky Hydro electrical power station Tunguska research group, and he changed his opinion.

Savelyev read fascinating testimonies of the locals in the area (Kova River valley). One mentioned an account of a hunter's visit to the Devil's Cemetery before W.W.II. The clearing he discovered was round, some 200 metres in diameter; the clearing terrified the local hunter. The ground was devoid of vegetation, and there were bones and corpses of animals and birds. Tree branches that hung over the clearing were burnt, as if by fire. His dogs, having spent a brief time at the clearing refused to eat, and became flaccid.

Members of the Boguchansky Hydro Electrical Power Station Tunguska research group (they called it a "club") conducted their own expedition in 1984. They left for the Deshembinsky Lake. Old-timers told amazing stories about this lake. According to them, in the summertime (before W.W.II), elderly men would go to the lake, spend a month there, and come back ten years younger. The expedition of the "club" took place in March (they were too busy to go in the summer). It was a very difficult journey over snow, fallen trees, and many other obstacles. But they did find the lake, and took samples. These samples were sent to a local research centre, and revealed that the lake was unsurpassed for the healing qualities of its water.

The head of the "club", Pavel Smirnov, a seasoned taiga explorer (actually, he was a professional land-surveyor) was determined to find the Devil's Cemetery. He and his friends collected information diligently, piece by piece. They were able to find out that the very last dwellers of the area left it in the 1950s. Their grandchildren knew very little. But Smirnov did not give up; his research was corroborated by hypothesis of a young Soviet scientist in Tashkent, a physicist by the name of Aleksandr Simonov (see above).

We decided to find out more about the area, and learned that the Chuktukonskoye deposit of niobium-rare earth deposit is located in the Boguchansky Rayon of the Krasnoyarsky Kray,

120 km of Kondinsk (the Boguchansky Hydro electrical power station). Nizhneye Priangarie (Lower Angara territory) located near the official geographic centre of Russia is comprised of five districts in the Krasnoyarsk Kray: Yeniseisky, Severo-Yeniseisky, Motyginsky, Boguchansky and Kezhemsky. This is the huge area (260 thousand square kilometres) where the Devil's Cemetery is located... but we still do not know where exactly.

And by the way, there is more gold in the area than in two Klondikes put together.

The village of Boguchany is more than 350 years old. Kezhma is probably even more ancient. The area had been off limits to foreigners, because Stalin located there his nefarious GULAG concentration camps.

Not much information is available from these areas but what information we do have is highly suggestive of another anomalous zone. The Devil's Cemetery is a particularly fascinating area for potential research. Not only do such zones have contemporary UFO sightings, but also they are also rich in legend and folklore. It is interesting here that the ancient people who lived in these areas regarded such phenomena as 'natural' or explainable in their culture of the day. Will contemporary sightings of UFOs be viewed by future historians as nothing more than legends and folklore, or will they still be puzzled by anomalous phenomena originating in such areas?

CHAPTER 30

UFOs VISIT CHUKOTKA

STRANGE PHENOMENA OF REMOTE LAND

Chukotka is located at the meeting points of two continents, two oceans, and four seas. The Chukotsky Peninsula is a short distance away from the United States. About half of Chukotka's territory lies above the Arctic Circle.

The Chukotka autonomous region is one of the 89 regions of the Russian Federation. Chukotka is located in the far northeast part of Russia. Chukotka is the Russian territory that is the closest to Alaska. The Bering Strait is the only boundary between Chukotka and Alaska.

Chukotka sits on the second largest reserves of gold in Russia, as well as significant reserves of coal, tin and oil, with plentiful fish stocks off its long coastal areas. Under Soviet rule, when the region was developed to allow the exploitation of its natural resources, the Kremlin encouraged people to move into the region by offering higher than average pay and many other privileges. An expensive program was established to deliver the necessary supplies to the area (it was supplied from Leningrad). After the end of the Soviet Union, it is no longer profitable to live and work there, and life is harder in the North (for Native people particularly).

Today, the entire population of Chukotka is about 70,000 people. The Native (indigenous) population is about only 10 percent of the total.

Permafrost and tundra cover most of the region. Chukotka has a harsh climate. The geographical location of the Chukotka peninsula between two oceans has resulted in extreme temperatures and complex atmospheric weather patterns.

Powerful Russians Air Force Units are stationed in the harsh, rugged land.

When in February of 2001 Russian military forces were engaged in a large-scale exercise involving strategic and conventional military forces that included three long-range missile flight tests, Russian strategic bombers engaged in the manoeuvres included Bear H and TU-22 Backfire and TU-160 Blackjack - long-range nuclear-capable bombers operating in both the eastern and western parts of Russia. The bombers had been flying out of bases in Anadyr, as well as some other important military bases of the nation.

Chukotka, though, has been visited by flying craft that no strategic military aircraft can ever overtake.

Due to the severe and bitter frosts, hellish cold weather and darkness, local inhabitants spend most of their time indoors. But since the dawn of time, when they did venture outdoors, they have seen strange objects in the sky. Local hunters, who dwell along the Arctic Ocean's coastline (the Inchoun village and other places) have observed UFOs for centuries, and claim that there exists a mysterious route where strange objects are seen flying by. The UFOs fly at various heights, under any weather conditions, absolutely noiselessly; and on occasions they display green lights.

A local hunter described a UFO encounter he experienced in December of 1989. It was a large object, with a dim, strange refection. The UFO moved noiselessly. It left a profound effect on the human eyewitness and his dogs. They became sleepy and groggy, almost immediately. But before he completely dozed off, Etinkeu the hunter noticed that the strange object illuminated the dog sled and the surrounding snow cover with a violet-bluish light. Etinkeu was unconscious for a short time. He knew it because his head did not freeze in the icy wind after his hat fell off during the induced sleep. When the hunter managed to get up, his whole body ached, and he felt weary. The dogs hardly moved. Yet shortly before the encounter, they had eaten a hearty breakfast and were full of energy. Now neither Etinkeu nor his dogs wanted to move on. When his story was told to other hunters, no one seemed surprised. Many of them had encountered UFOs in the area. Some experienced painful headaches for days after their encounters with the mysterious objects.

Early in the year is when the people of the North see UFOs. During the "white nights", when the Sun does not leave the sky, such encounters are rare. Yet, there was a noteworthy exception to this rule.

In the summer of 1990 a ship was harboured in the Ust-Belaya Village. Its crew noticed cumulus clouds that suddenly formed a perfect circle. In the centre of the circle one could observe clear blue sky. The watch officer, Aleksandr Polorotov, took pictures of the event unfolding before their eyes. Groups of aircraft exited the circle, and flew away, to disappear in the surrounding clouds. The Soviet sailor, who previously served in the Air Force, knew the types of the aircraft of his country. The "aircraft" he observed in the Chukotka sky appeared nine times. Polorotov was able to take just several pictures before his camera malfunctioned. When the film was developed, a cigar-shaped object could be seen on some of the photos. It had a strange luminescence, and some black dots were visible at a distance. But the mysterious "aircraft", also observed seven other crewmembers, were not on any of the photos. The Soviet crewmembers experienced the same side effects as the native hunter in 1989: general weakness and headaches.

MYSTERIES OF THE LAKE

To add even more questions to the UFO sighting seen in the vicinity of Ust'-Belaya, it was determined that it came from the mysterious El'gygytgyn Lake. El'gygytgyn Lake, located 100 km north of the Arctic Circle in north-east Russia (67° 30' N latitude and 172° 05' E longitude), and was created 3.6 million years ago by a meteorite impact that generated a crater around 20 km in diameter. An international expedition to the lake in May, 1998, successfully recovered sediment cores from the centre of the 15 kilometre wide basin, penetrating nearly 13 metres in 175 metres of water depth using a percussion piston corer from the lake ice surface. They discovered a striking similarity between the El'gygytgyn magnetic susceptibility record and the Bermuda Rise, as well as Bahamas Outer Ridge

Numerous legends exist about this lake, tales of strange disappearances, presence of unknown life forms, and more. According to one local legend, a shaman capable of levitation resides in the area of the lake. From the description provided, the shaman is dressed in something that modern observers could recognise as a spacesuit. A noted Russian UFO researcher and proponent of the ancient astronaut hypothesis, Vladimir Avinsky, has analysed local legends. There is a geographic area of Chukotka where UFOs apparently allow themselves to be photographed; it is bordered by Providence, Lavrenti, and Uelen. In the vicinity of Cape Shmidt, UFOs are invisible to the naked eye. But technical devices are able to register their presence. In the winter of 1991, radar at the Shmidt Airport, as well as the radar of a lone helicopter in the area, registered the presence of a strange object.

The UFO was thirty kilometres from the settlement, and flew at the altitude approximately a kilometre and a half. A helicopter began to approach the object, coming to within a kilometre of it. The indicator on the helicopter's radar clearly showed the object's presence, yet the pilot was not able to see anything outside.

AREA 51 OF THE RUSSIAN NORTH

In the areas of Vankarem, Ust'-belaya, and El'gygytgyn Lake, UFOs adversely affect humans. For some reason, UFOs tend to be quite aggressive there. However, few people inhabit the above-mentioned areas. Yevgeny Rozhkov, who published an article about the Chukotka UFOs in the July 1992 issue of Vostok Rossii newspaper, is of the opinion that there may be secret UFO bases in those areas. Around Shmidt and Anadyr areas UFOs are hardly visible. Are they afraid of the Russian Air Force? Could there be a research base, something like Area 51 in Nevada?

Chukotka lies very close to North America and we believe that researchers in both countries should pay close attention to the strange phenomena in a distant Russian territory.

It is also a beautiful, mysterious land beckoning those who seek areas of paranormal phenomena unspoiled by commercialism.

UFO IN 1993

Vitaly Serikov and his parents resided in Chukotka in 1993, in a small secret and undisclosed military town, some 50 kilometres from Anadyr. The town was located in a gorge, between several hills. Once, returning home with his friends in the evening, Serikov was attracted to an unusual phenomenon. There were three reddish "headlights" over one of the hills. They were located horizontally across the dark sky. The objects hovered over the hill three minutes, and then two of the "headlights" departed, performing an arc-like manoeuvre; and the remaining one just faded away. Serikov reported his sighting on the Kosmopoisk site in April of 2000.

In this zone we mainly have UFO sightings, but not exclusively. Tales of paranormal activity such as levitation are not uncommon. Some of the UFO close encounter incidents seem to have an adverse physical effect on the human and animal witnesses. This again has been reported in other parts of the world. Other UFO 'sightings' seem to be only 'visible' to radar equipment as nothing is seen by the naked eye. Again, such happenings have been recorded elsewhere in the world. Again, like other such zones, we are certain that other UFO and paranormal events will be reported down the coming years and it is hoped that with further research, answers will be found.

CHAPTER 31

MYSTERIES OF YAKUTIA

YAKUTIA

Few people in the West know about Yakutia. The land consists of the thick backwoods of taiga, the seemingly endless tundra, vast mountain chains and the iced Arctic Ocean. Sakha (Yakutia) is a presidential republic and has a constitution. On 27 April 1922 Yakutia was granted the status of an autonomous republic. Since then its name has changed several times. Its present name the country received in 1990 when the Declaration of Sovereignty of the Republic of Sakha (Yakutia) was signed on 27 September 1990.

Yakutia is an enormous country. It covers 3 million square kilometres, which is 5 times the size of France. Yakutia's diverse natural environment ranges from Arctic tundra on the coast of the North Arctic Ocean to the rocky mountains of the Aldan plateau. In between are giant expanses of dense taiga forest and boggy lands dotted with dozens of lakes. Much of the country is flat as a result of the massive glaciers of the last ice age when it levelled everything in their path.

Yakutia borders on the Khabarovsk and Krasnoyarsk territories, Magadan, Amurskaya, Chita and Irkutsk regions.

All are areas of frequent UFO visits. Yakutia has its own paranormal history.

Yakutia is located on the edge of the Laptevyh and East Siberian Seas, and encompasses the Novosibirskie Islands. The major part is taken up by large mountain systems and plateau. The main rivers are the Lena (with its tributaries in the Aldan and Vilyui), Yana, Indgirka, Kolyma, Anabar, Olenek (Arctic Ocean basin).

Long distances, the lack of infrastructure, inaccessibility to the remote areas, dependence on air transport, and climatic conditions are reasons for Yakutia being a place rarely visited by Westerners.

Among the people who inhabit Yakutia are Sakha, ethnic Russians, Ukrainians, Evenks, formerly known as Tungus, and some other nationalities. Reportedly, there are other fascinating life forms in the land.

ULYUYU CHERKECHEKH

In the North-West of Yakutia, in the area of Upper Vilyui, lies the area known in antiquity as Ulyuyu Cherkechekh or Valley of Death. The Tungus tribes who had lived in the sinister hard to reach area full of broken stone pieces strewn around for hundreds of kilometres, for ages told stories of strange sightings. One, deeply carved in their tribal memory, recalls how their land was swallowed by sudden darkness. A mighty, deafening roar shook the area, a powerful hurricane whirled about, and strong blows struck the ground. Lightning lit the sky. When the darkness left, the amazed Tungus saw a giant vertical structure, gleaming in sunlight. It could be seen "from many days away". The structure emitted unpleasant, sharp sounds. It also diminished in size, until it disappeared underground. Those who ventured to the burned-out site never returned. When the land healed, and the plants, animals, and nomadic hunters came back to the area, they found there a strange dome-like "iron house". It had many lateral supports, but no doors or windows on its smooth surface. Nearby there were other metallic constructions, embedded in the ground.

At the spot where the vertical structure had been, the Tungus found a giant vertical "crater". The legends described it in details (and with great awe). The "crater" consisted of three "laughing abysses". In the bowels of the crater located was an underground land, with its own "waning sun". Suffocating stench came from the "crater", and no tribe settled in the area. On occasions, a "revolving island" ascended from the crater. Centuries later the permafrost swallowed the "iron house". An opening was found in its dome. A spiral-like descent led to circular galleries; there were many metallic rooms. The rooms were warm even during the coldest winters; but whoever spent a few days inside, soon perished from strange sickness. The elders had banned any travel to the area.

Numerous legends tell of the Nyurgun Bootur fiery spheres in the area, disk-like "flying objects", and explosions that caused genetic diseases. The second fiery sphere destroyed the area 600 hundred years later. The sphere had a new name then: "Kyun Erbiye", or "bright celestial messenger".

THE CAULDRONS

The last such "explosion" occurred in September of 1880. A famous explorer of Vilyui in the XIX century, R. Maak mentioned giant "cauldrons". One such "cauldron" was of enormous proportions: the explorer saw its edge protruding through the ground, and several trees that grew on it. Contemporary Russian researchers A. Gutenev and B. Mikhailovski interviewed an elderly nomad, who visited the Valley of Death, and saw a metallic "burrow", where he found frozen, very skinny black one-eyed people in iron clothes.

In 1933 Mikhail Petrovich Koretsky of Vladivistok (himself a visitor to the

Ulyuyu Cherkechekh) was informed by a Yakut guide that 10 years prior he discovered several spherical "cauldrons" of perfect spherical shapes. The objects protruded from the ground, and their height was greater than that of a human. The objects looked brand-new. Koretsky described the "cauldrons" he observed himself in 1933-39: six to nine metres in diameter. But their shapes were not spherical. They were from a strange metal; no piece could be broken off. The metallic surface of a "cauldron" was covered with some unknown layer, similar to emery paper. But the layer could not be cut through, too. The vegetation around the objects was very strange, unlike anything growing nearby. It was strikingly more luxuriant; and the grass was unusually tall, twice the size of a human. Koretsky and five others slept one night inside a "cauldron". Three months later one of them lost all his hair. Koretsky developed strange painful spots on the side of the head he slept on, while inside the "cauldron": they were tiny, but no treatment he tried would get rid of them.

The Tungus legends also mention a strange life form: a giant, Uot Usumu Tong Duurai or "Criminal alien who bored through the ground and hides there, and whose fiery torna destroys all around".

Serafim Boyev, in his article published in **NLO Magazine Issue 13**, 1997), described another interesting phenomenon in Yakutia. On the right shore of the Vilyui River, hunters discovered a source of unusual radiation. One curious hunter spent a night there, attracted by superb fauna of the area: gigantic burdocks, trees full of leaves and lianas, velvety high grass as tall as two metres. All this vegetation was completely out of order in an area of permafrost and sparse vegetation. In the morning the hunter screamed in terror, for he lost all his hair, as it fell from his head. But he was determined to find out more about the area. What he found left him dumbfounded: not far from the clearing where he spent the night, the hunter discovered strange, reddish, metallic-looking semi-spheres protruding from the stony ground. He looked inside one, and froze, for inside the hunter saw "very skinny, black one-eyed people in iron clothing".

A strange phenomenon was observed in Yakutia in 1938. It resembled the Biblical story of the Egyptian darkness that lasted three days. The Siberian darkness occurred on September 18 of 1938, and it took the Soviet authorities two years before they issued permission to publish reports about the event. In the beginning of 1940, a Soviet meteorologist V.N. Adreyev published his account. He was able to observe the phenomenon in a settlement Khal'mer-Sede on the river Taz. The sky turned completely black; one could not see anything. The origin of this phenomenon is still unknown.

CRYPTO ZOOLOGY

Although our book describes the UFO phenomena in the former USSR and modern Russia and the Commonwealth of the Independent States, we cannot ignore unusual reports about creatures that inhabit the far away Yakutia. Perhaps there is a connection that is still unclear to Russian researchers.

Vadim Chernobrov, a dogged researcher, collected interesting materials about Yakutia's crypto zoology. He published them in a digest Nad propastyu neraskritikh tayn or Over an Abyss of Unsolved Mysteries (Moscow, 1996). We also researched Gennady Lisov's article in NLO Magazine (2000) for more details.

Both sources describe strange "monsters" and beings in the lakes of Yakutia. Those who want to get all of the fascinating details, should contact Vadim Chernobrov at the Kosmopoisk website:http://kosmopoisk.null.ru/

We will add here that according to Yuri Metelev, a Russian geologist, one of the people in his expedition to Yakutia at the end of 1960s, was able to discover a small herd of buffalos (bisons) in the River Khandiga area. But then this biologist, Boris S. Shlikman, disappeared without a trace somewhere in the mysterious lands of Yakutia.

NUCLEAR REALITY

The wilderness, where the Valley of Death once was present, became a site of Soviet nuclear testing. Something very strange happened there in the 1950's. When a 10-kiloton (the explosive force of 1000 tons of TNT) nuclear device was tested, the explosion registered the reading of 20-30 megatons (the explosive force of a million tons of TNT). What caused an increase of the explosive power of 2 to 3 thousand times, no one knows. Russian researchers suppose that the Soviet nuclear testing damaged one of the mysterious underground structures, releasing the energy contained in it.

In 1993 The Joint USA-CIS Aerial Anomaly Federation published Felix Y. Zigel's UFO SIGHTINGS OVER THE USSR-1968 (Volume 1). It contains a report about Yakutia sent to F. Zigel by S. N Popov, an Air Force reserve officer.

From 1958 through 1965 he worked in the Yakut SSR, at the Ust'-Maya airport, as an aviation technician. In March of 1964, as he and three other men exited a club, he observed two very strange disks. At first the disks moved one behind the other formation, and later they re-formed, and continued their movement in as a pair. Passing almost over the heads of Popov and his comrades, the disks emitted light toward the ground. The intensity of the light was weak. There was indescribable brightness around the disks. It seemed to Popov that the colour was that of a dark bluish-violet, like a discharge of an electric spark. The edge was an exact circle and stationary as if a dull milky smoke tried to go beyond the limits of the circle, and glass walls would not allow it to leave. When the disks passed over their heads, illuminating the men below, Popov did feel something oppressive, as if a natural disaster took place. Curiously, in 1982 a similar feeling was reported by Krokhmalev (see Chapter Mysteries of Soviet and Russian Seas). It was, he recalls, a very unpleasant feeling. Popov thought that the Soviets again launched some "novelty" into the space. However, media reported nothing of the sorts.

Popov also recalled that in March of 1961, "Comrades Orlova and Tirasenko" observed a milky white disk of a perfect shape in the area where the Maya River empties into the Aldan (across from the Ust'-Maya settlement). Then, in 1964, Comrades Orlova, Kozlova, and Sifronova observes three milky white disks at 100 to 110 kilometres from Ust'-Maya upstream, along the Aldan River. The date is 1964, but some other information written by Popov was abbreviated and illegible. S. N. Popov personally heard stories from Soviet aviators who flew to the airport where he was stationed; stories about strange phenomena like "flying saucers" that they had observed. He believed that researchers should inquire the personnel of the Yakutsk Territorial Administration about this issue.

Galina Varlamova, a Russian writer and scientist of the Evenk origin has recently urged Russia's UFO researchers to pay close attention to the mythology and oral traditions of the Evenk people. She has collected Evenk stories for over 15 years, and states that there are numerous stories of encounters with aliens, and ancient astronaut visitation and artificial origin of mankind. The Evenks viewed such phenomena as "protective spirits", and they communicated with the "spirits" (actually, mind or intellect in its various forms) through shamanism, and the tradition of such contacts exists in our times. The word "shaman" was actually an Evenk word, borrowed by other cultures. The Evenk shaman's soul, according to tradition, is able to leave the body and travel to other parts of the cosmos. It travels to a mysterious upper world in the sky and a lower world, located underground. The shaman remains in the control, through the process of kamlaniye.

YAKUTIA'S STRANGE SITES

Ten hours of walking distance from the Bol'shaya Khatim settlement in Yakutia lies a legendary site, where according to local beliefs, people can cure their eye diseases. There is a rock, better known as Bottle Rock, because it resembles broken and compressed bottle glass. If one were to press his face to this rock, and look inside its semi-transparent depth, one's eyesight improves.

Another strange rock in Yakutia contains a cave, where in 1995 sensational archaeological findings were made. The site is known as Yeleneva Cave; the name of the rock is Watch Bull; it is located at the Yenisey River, across from the Ovsyanka Village. One of the findings was an object made from the mammoth tusk; it dates 3000 years ago. Yet, the last mammoth to die in the area did so not later than ten thousand years ago. The object was made for observation, not as a hunting tool. It contains carvings that indicate a lunar calendar; and its base has carvings that correspond to twelve months. The ancients in Yakutia apparently were aware of the calendars for both planets.

The source for this information is "Entsiklopedia Nepoznannogo" or "Encyclopaedia of the Unknown", compiled by Vadim Chernobrov, and published in Moscow in 1998.

Such geographical areas as those we have pointed out in this chapter seem to have a high concentration of all things mysterious. UFO's, unknown animals, folklore and paranormal events galore seem to emanate from them. There are many such areas around the world and the former USSR is not to be outdone. Why such areas have these concentrations is open to debate. Some researchers are of the opinion that natural geological forces cause a type of hallucination, which does seem to be a real event to the people involved. Such geological forces, they add, cause a light phenomenon known as 'earthlights', which account for the UFO sightings as well. Others argue that such geological forces attract UFOs for a variety of reasons. There are many theories to try and account for these areas, but the one thing that we can be sure of is that these areas do provide a wealth of information for researchers who can in turn test whatever theory they like based on this information. Such information and reports have gone on for centuries and it looks set to continue for centuries to come.

CHAPTER 32

CIA, ESPIONAGE AND SOVIET UFOs

That the Soviet UFO phenomenon has attracted attention of various intelligence agencies, from at least 1920's is a fact that few would dispute; and those who would should browse through the recently declassified KGB files of Gleb Bokiy, Barchenko, and Soviet paranormal research (see Chapter 33). We are very much interested to show how foreign intelligence services had viewed reports and sightings of UFOs over the USSR. Although only a few files have been released so far, some files have been declassified in the United States, too, and the information contained there sheds some light on the subject of the CIA research, as well on the Agency (and other services doing similar research) itself. The Agency had a special, very keen interest in Soviet UFOs and those who had paid attention to the phenomenon (whether officially or not) behind the Iron Curtain.

We will examine those CIA documents that have been declassified, released, made available whatever the description; suffice it to say that even the few files available help us learn what the Agency was interested in, in terms of Soviet UFO phenomenon.

Title: USSR AND SATELLITE MENTION OF FLYING SAUCERS
Pub Date: August 21, 1952
Release Date: November 16, 1978
Case Number: F-1975-03653

MEMORANDUM FOR: Deputy Director (Intelligence)
SUBJECT: USSR and Satellite Mention of Flying Saucers

This curious CIA document, released in 1978, was a memorandum prepared for the CIA's deputy Director of Intelligence (DDI). This is full of deletions. It mentions that a search of (deleted) files has so far produced no factual evidence that the subject has been mentioned in the Soviet satellites (countries under Soviet domination-authors) within the past two years. It is believed that a derisive comment was made in a

Russian newspaper in 1948 on this subject, but so far the article has not been found.

But there was one radio broadcast with regard to the subject; the date of the broadcast is June 10, 1951; and the content is attached for the Agency's attention. The summary of that broadcast states that in what appears to be Moscow's first mention of the flying saucers, a "Listener's Mailbag" answers questions on the subject, to the effect that the "Chief of Nuclear Physics in the U.S. Naval Research Bureau had explained them (UFOs-authors) recently as used for stratospheric studies. U.S. Government circles knew all along of the harmless nature of these objects, but if they refrained from denying 'false reports', the purpose behind such tactics was to fan war hysteria in the country".

Curiously, as mentioned elsewhere in this book, top Soviet scientists tried to convince Stalin that UFOs were indeed quite harmless, or at least did not pose a threat to the armed forces and security of the nation. Were Soviet agitprop functionaries helping such scientists? Or was this a signal sent from Stalin to those on the West responsible for UFO phenomenon research?

Getting back to the curious memorandum, we find there a mention of a State Department cable received from Budapest that quoted the August 14th copy of Szabad Nep, as follows: "Flying saucer stories are another American attempt to fan war hysteria". A radar detection of "saucers" is quoted in the article, and it comments on the ridiculous aspects of the source of the mystery. The article concludes that it is but a part of American rulers' propaganda to prove the Western countries are threatening. Perhaps they meant, "threatened". The memorandum concludes that the FBID (Foreign Broadcast Information Department) had been requested to alert field stations to any mention of flying saucers by Iron Curtain states.

Title: ENGINEER CLAIMS 'SAUCER' PLANS ARE IN SOVIET HANDS; SIGHTINGS IN AFRICA, IRAN,
Pub Date: August 17, 1953
Release Date: November 16, 1978
Case Number: F-1975-036

This article definitely attracted the Agency's attention in 1953. We have summarised it below.

GERMAN ENGINEER STATES SOVIETS HAVE GERMAN FLYING SAUCER EXPERTS AND PLANS
Athens, I Vredyni, May 13, 1953

The information contained in this CIA document was obtained by the Agency from a Greek source. The document was analysed in Vienna, by some entity entitled "Special Service". The document states that according to recent reports from Toronto, a number of Canadian Air Force engineers are engaged in the construction of a "flying saucer" to be used as a future weapon of war. The work of these engineers is being carried out in great secrecy at the A. V. Row Company (transliteration from the Greek) factories.

"Flying saucers" have been known to be an actuality since the possibility of their construction was proven in plans drawn by German engineers toward the end of World War II. George Klein, a German engineer, stated that though many people believe the "flying saucers" to be a post-war development, they were actually in the planning stage in German aircraft factories as early as 1941.

Klein said that he was an engineer in the Ministry of Albert Speer (who, in 1942, was Reich's Minister for Armament and Ammunition for the Third Reich-authors) and was present at the first experimental flight of a "flying saucer". During the experiment, Klein reported, the "flying saucer" had reached an altitude of 12,400 metres within 3 minutes and a speed of 2,200 kilometres per hour. Klein emphasised that in accordance with German plans, the speed of these "saucers" would reach 4,000 kilometres per hour. One difficulty, according to Klein, was the problem of obtaining materials to be used for the construction of the "saucers" but German engineers toward the end of 1945 had removed even that obstacle, and construction of the aircraft was scheduled to commence. Klein went on to state that three experimental models had been readied for tests by the end of 1944, built according to two completely different principles of aerodynamics.

One type of the craft was actually in the shape of a disk, with an interior cabin, and was built at the Mite (unidentified transliteration from the Greek) factories, which had also built the V-2 rockets (this statement confirms a report by a Soviet eyewitness who was a POW at the Mite; (see Chapter Twenty Three).

This model was 42 metres in diameter (although this does not confirm the Soviet eyewitness's account; the size he mentioned was much smaller). The other model had the shape of a ring, with raised sides and a spherically shaped pilot' placed on the outside, in the centre of the ring. This model was built at the Habermol and Schreiver factories (identified, stated the CIA, as both names transliterated from the Greek). However, the locations mentioned above, became quite familiar to those Ufologists who had pursued the German "trail", whether in the West and in the USSR.

Both models had an ability to take off vertically and to land in an extremely restricted area, just as helicopters do today. During the last few days of the war, when every hope for Nazi victory had been abandoned, the engineers in the group stationed in Prague carried out orders to completely destroy their plans of the aircraft models, before the Red Army victoriously marched in, after heavy battles (Paul Stonehill's grandfather was one of the Soviet soldiers who battled Nazis to liberate Prague from German occupation). The engineers at the Mite factories in Breslau, however, had not been warned within sufficient time of the Soviet approach, and Soviet forces therefore succeeded in seizing their archives. Captured plans, as well, as engineering personnel, were immediately transferred to the Soviet Union, under heavy guard (coincidental with the departure from Berlin of the creator of the Stuka JU-87 dive bomber, the man who later developed MIG 13 and 15 aircraft in the Soviet Union).

Klein had more to say, but we will stop here. In Chapter 26, we discussed an alleged CIA operation in the Urals, and the German scientists working in the USSR on another secret program. There, too, the American agent involved in the operation who escaped from Soviet Russia, mentioned five flying saucers built by the Soviets.

Title: FLYING OBJECTS SEEN IN SHAKHTY AREA, 1953
Pub Date: August 8, 1955
Release Date: November 16, 1978
Case Number: F-1975-03653
USSR (Rostov Oblast')

The Agency deleted classification status of the report. The date of content was August 1953. The information in the report was obtained in late September of 1954. Source of information was deleted from the declassified report.

Shakhty, which is a small town in a coal mining area, is about an hour and a drive half from Rostov (south of Moscow on the Don river east of Ukraine).

The report states that on a warm starry moonlit evening in August of 1953, three flying objects were observed moving over an Ayuta "camp". The location was 10 kilometres south-east of the southern perimeter of Shakhty, about 600 metres west of the Rostov-Novoshakhtinsk highway, about 2 kilometres south-east of the Ayuta mines and about 3.5 kilometres from Ayuta. The objects were sighted at different times (one hour one after the other, starting at 21:45 hours). The fiery gleam accompanying the object disappeared over the partially lighted installations of the Ayuta mines. The objects moved from south-east to north-west at a deviation of 60 to 75 degrees from the vertical line, and crossed approximately north of the camp. The flight altitude could not be estimated. No sound was heard while the objects were overhead. The speed of the phenomena could not be compared with that of aircraft or Soviet jet fighters. The first object was observed departing toward the Ayuta mines for 5 or 4 seconds. The second body was seen for 6 or 7 seconds after passing the camp.

It also disappeared in the direction of the Ayuta mines. No statement could be made about the third object. The two objects observed had a fiery gleam in a reddish colour which was similar to that of planet Mars. It looked like a comet or a shooting star. The approach of the phenomenon was not observed.
Here's the fascinating part (authors):

On the day following the evening observation, the individual PKs differed considerably in their opinions about the phenomena. Immediately after the observation, source and sub-source believed the objects observed were rockets, similar to F weapons. After the objects disappeared, no detonations were heard.

Field Consent. All previous reports on flying objects observed in the Shakhty area mentioned that loud noise accompanied the action. The description of the noises indicated that the body was propelled by a rocket or fitted with a pulse-jet engine. See (and the Agency deleted whatever followed). The object mentioned in the present report possibly flew at such a high altitude that the sound of the engines could not be heard. Another possibility is that a different phenomenon was observed, which, however appears rather improbable. Another filed consent added that the observation reported agrees with previous information and indicates that a ramjet or a rocket engine propelled the body.

Questions, upon reading the above report:

What came from the Ayuta mines? Who were "PKs"? What was the "F weapons"? What powerful rockets and jets were developed by Soviets in 1953, to propel craft at incomparable speeds? In Chapter Five - STALIN, UFOS, AND OTHER SECRETS we have discussed Soviet super-secret rocket and spacecraft development of the Stalin era (a still forbidden subject; most files or documents have been heretofore unavailable to researchers). Perhaps the Agency was also interested in the same subject 45 years ago. Here's another report that seems to support our view.

Title: FAST-MOVING FLYING OBJECTS OVER STALINGRAD IN SPRING 1954
Pub Date: August 1, 1956
Release Date: November 16, 1978
Case Number: F-1975-03653

The report was taken from someone who, in the spring of 1954, was hospitalised at a Soviet military hospital in Stalingrad (now Volgograd).

On one occasion, the narrator along with other patients had observed the flight of an unknown object from horizon to horizon. The object appeared to be climbing. The narrator could not describe the object, but he recalled that it took approximately one minute for the object to leave the range of his vision. The object caused a great amount of vibration in the air and made a screeching, whistling noise, which was different from the noise made by an artillery shell. The narrator reiterated that he did not see the object itself, but did see the disturbance in the air, which seemed to envelop it.

Title: UNIDENTIFIED FLYING OBJECT OBSERVED ON IRAN/USSR BORDER
Pub Date: August 12, 1957
Release Date: November 16, 1978
Case Number: F-1975-03653

On 12 June at 11:00 a.m. local time, a flying object was seen Iranian Juifa, travelling on a course from Nakhichevan [N 39-15, E. (unclear text-P.S.), USSR. The object appeared to be a ball about one-half metre in diameter and had a tail of half metre in length. It traveled (this is how the word is spelled in the document P.S. and P.M.) at high speed at a height of about 2,000 feet and was visible for only a few seconds. (unclear writing) trail left by the object drifted over Iranian b Juifa from the USSR and (unclear) of a trail about 5 to 10 centimetres in diameter.

Field Comment: (deletion) also reported seeing a flying object at the same time and described it about the size of a football and moving at a height of 2,000 metres. He said the smoke track left behind the object was visible for about 15 minutes.

Once again, as elsewhere in the book, UFOs kept coming to the Iranian-Soviet border. We are yet to learn what has attracted them to the area; obviously, the CIA was (and in light of 2005 news about UFOs over Iran, remains) interested, too. Could the Agency's interest be aroused also because of the oil fields in the area? Maybe. One year before the case mentioned here, there was something else that drew the Agency's attention. Case Number: F-1975-03653, February 7, 1956; Release Date: November 16, 1978. Here the Agency was interested in an object sighted over Baku, capital of the Soviet Azerbaijan. The actual sighting took place on October 4, 1955, and the Office of Scientific Intelligence prepared its analysis of it.

There was another document, declassified by CIA, dealing with the same area.

Title: SIGHTING OF UNUSUAL PHENOMENON ON HORIZON
NEAR IRANIAN/USSR BORDER
Pub Date: September 27, 1966
Release Date: November 16, 1978
Case Number: F-1975-03653

The document, a testimony of a nameless witness, describes an unusual phenomenon, a brilliant white sphere on the horizon, some 25 miles away from the Mehrabad airport. The UFO was on an expanding variety; was clearly visible, and was sighted by another aircraft, too.

Title: MAYBE THERE IS NO UFO
Pub Date: December 25, 1967
Release Date: October 31, 1987
Case Number: F-1990-01473

The Agency is interested in the report about the creation in November of 1967 of the committee for the investigation of the unidentified flying objects. This committee, a part of the DOSAAF (see Part Three of this book, Chapter Twenty Two - CHRONICLE OF SOVIET UFO RESEARCH), is under the command of the Air Force General Porfiri Stolyarov. General Stolyarov recommended that the photographic method be used. The data obtained during the investigation would be correlated to the Pulkovo Laboratory and the Crinca Astronomical Observatory. The observation has been entrusted to a chain of astronomical observatories all over the USSR, as well as civil aviation.

We already know what had happened to the committee (see Chapter Twenty Two - CHRONICLE OF SOVIET UFO RESEARCH). What is interesting is how much time it took the CIA to declassify the document mentioning General Stolyarov and the committee.

Title: FLYING PHENOMENA (UFO'S) - SOURCE - SOVETSKAYA LATVIYA - THE DIRECTOR OF...

Pub Date: December 9, 1967
Release Date: October 31, 1987
Case Number: F-1984-01392

Unfortunately, the CIA document is virtually impossible to read, and seems to contain deletions. But something definitely attracted the Agency's attention to a Soviet publication.

It was Dr. Zigel, mentioned throughout our book, who had attracted the Agency's attention in 1968.

Title: DATA FROM CRS AND FROM FBIS ON ZIGEL, F. YU., DR. OF TECHNICAL SCIENCES WRITES

Pub Date: December 31, 1968
Release Date: November 16, 1978
Case Number: F-1975-03653

Actually, CIA was interested in his articles published in Soviet magazines; his subjects ranged from the Tunguska Meteorite to a "Dialog on Mars".

But, of course, the Agency's fascination with Dr. Zigel's views did not end there. An 11-page document was published the same year.

Title: NOTHING BUT THE FACTS ON UFOS OR WHICH NOVOSTI WRITER DO YOU READ?

Pub Date: April 8, 1968
Release Date: November 16, 1978
Case Number: F-1975-03653

"Unidentified Flying Objects" by Felix Zigel, Doctor of Science (Technology), assistant professor, Moscow Aviation Institute, appeared in the February 1968 issue of Soviet Life (counterpart to USIA), for which APN supplies all materials (APN, the Soviet "unofficial" news agency). The other article, espousing views of Soviet debunkers, was titled "Flying Saucers? They are a myth!" by Villen Lyustiberg, and appeared in the February 16th issue of Moskovsky Komsomolets.

By the way, as we have described elsewhere in the book, the late 1960s had seen crucial battles for openness in the area of UFO studies in the USSR. There was an obvious conflict, and proponents and opponents (among them top military brass) on both sides. The Agency was quite interested, too, and collected whatever information was available.

Villen Lyustiberg's article laughed off UFOs, and accused the United States of publishing accounts of UFOs to divert people's attention from its failures and aggressions. What surprised the Agency was the fact that the Soviets actually published two conflicting views about a subject (any subject).

A truly mysterious document is revealed in the following CIA document. Alas, it is also full of deletions.

(TITLE DELETED) – USSR - UFO SIGHTINGS - SOMEONE MUST HAVE MADE A POLITICAL DECISION

Pub Date: May 7, 1975
Release Date: May 18, 1989
Case Number: F-1985-00010

Yet, what remains is most interesting. Basically, on one occasion someone, whose name is deleted (just as the first two pages of the document were deleted completely), asked whether the U.S. Forecast Centre was ever bothered with UFO sightings. He explained (whom to? - authors) that at one time (deletion) and (deletion) in particular, had been plagued with calls and questions about UFO sightings (sightings was underlined by hand - authors). He said that some of their scientific balloon flights had prompted some of them. Now, he said, he never gets these calls anymore, and half jokingly surmised that someone must have made a political decision that they were not to be sighted anymore (underlined by hand starting with someone must have).

Unfortunately, it is most probable that UFO researchers will never find out what was deleted from the 1975 document.

Title: USSR NATIONAL AFFAIRS SCIENTIFIC AFFAIRS
'UNUSUAL NATURAL PHENOMENON OBSERVE

Pub Date: September 22, 1977
Release Date: November 16, 1978
Case Number: F-1975-03653

In this document the CIA's attention is directed to the Petrozavodsk phenomenon. Moscow TASS information service is the source of the brief mention of the phenomena. Descriptions of a "huge star" and "medusa" were given. We have described the events surrounding the Petrozavodsk Phenomena in previous chapters. Just as we became curious in the late 1980s with all the UFO glasnost developments in the USSR, so did the Agency.

Title: USSR: MEDIA REPORT MULTITUDE OF UFO SIGHTINGS

Pub Date: November 21, 1989
Release Date: July 31, 1991
Case Number: F-1990-00393

Among publications mentioned in the document is one by Anatoly Listratov (Sotsialisticheskaya Industriya, September 30, 1989), whose findings we have mentioned elsewhere in the book.

We will not list here every single declassified CIA document dealing with Soviet UFOs after 1989. Whether statements from top military brass, reports in the Soviet media... the Agency was interested in everything that Soviet/CIS newspapers revealed month after month. Most of the information is covered in other chapters of UFO - USSR.

What needs to be pointed out is that the CIA became interested in the report of a joint Sino-Soviet UFO research.

Title: USSR, PRC SCIENTISTS IN JOINT STUDY OF UFO'S

Pub Date: May 20, 1990
Release Date: May 31, 1994
Case Number: F-1990-01096

We already know that the People's Republic of China has joined the space race, and its astronauts may soon orbit the earth, and go beyond. Here is what worried the Agency in 1990.

The source of the report was Moscow Domestic Service in Russian on May 21, 1990.

A report from Vladivostok: scientists of the PRC and the Soviet Far East have begun a joint study of UFOs. The first meeting of Ufologists of the two countries has ended in the small maritime town of Dalnegorsk. Soviet and Chinese specialists of anomalous phenomena have mapped out a program for investigating incidents that are already known and have also arranged to directly exchange video and photographic materials on new similar phenomena. Dalnegorsk has not been chosen by chance as the place for such meeting.

(There have been a number of cases of visual observation of UFOs over Dalnegorsk and one crash in 1986; see Chapter Thirteen - THE DALNEGORSK CRASH).

Title: 1. OVERVIEW OF THE ACADEMY OF SCIENCES OF THE UKRAINIAN SSR
Pub Date: January 9, 1990
Release Date: August 27, 1997
Case Number: F-1993-02057

We cannot ignore this document. There are a number of deletions in this document, yet even the remaining information is enough to arouse our curiosity.

Someone connected with the Agency paid a visit to the Ukrainian Academy of Sciences (probably, in September of 1989). Someone, a Soviet whose name is deleted in the document, asked about the U.S. research in the area of the unidentified flying objects (underlined). The unnamed Soviet person also said that the Academy has several organisations that follow the subject and that some scientists think this is a serious research.

Who was this unnamed scientist? What happened to the findings of "several organisations"? There are no answers in our possession.

MILITARY INTELLIGENCE

Now, let us look at the information from 1970, and the intelligence agency here is the Department of Defence Intelligence. The report number is 2 723 1209 70, the date is August 19, 1970. The information contained in the report dates back to may 18, 1970. The subject is Soviet Space Development, and the country is Japan. Actually, Yokogama, Tokai University in Kanagawa Prefecture, where Soviet cosmonaut Leonov was giving a lecture at the Shohan Annex. The cosmonaut talked about Soviet experiences in space and future plans of the USSR in space exploration, to include a mammoth space station, which the USSR planned to put into orbit. Leonov also expressed disbelief in UFOs.

Leonov talked about several subjects that day. One had to do with improvement of the Soviet space capsule braking equipment. The other was the confirmation of Soviet moon data by U.S. astronauts. This confirmation interested American military intelligence, and we think we know the reason: like the CIA, they heard about early (and still classified) Soviet attempts to reach the Moon. By the way, it is quite likely that Leonov was instructed to misinform people in the West about UFO sightings in the USSR. As we have described in this book, two years before Leonov's speech in Japan, an organised attempt by Soviet scientists and military researchers to research UFOs independently (including, via television broadcasts and other means) was ruthlessly crushed. UFOs once again became a taboo subject. Leonov had to know about UFO sightings reported by other cosmonauts. But, like other Soviet people, he was not free to express his true opinion; like them, he was a Homo Sovieticus, albeit a privileged one.

Here is what Leonov revealed about Soviet exploration of the Moon:

The Soviet Union has a well-coordinated program for travel to the moon and has compiled complete and detailed data concerning conditions on the moon through its moon station. It has photographs of the moon's dark side and complete data on the make-up and characteristics of its surface, the moon's gravity field, etc. "The US astronauts who landed on the moon only confirmed what we already knew." he said.

Here is what he said about UFOs:

> *The speaker said he does not believe in the existence of unidentified*
> *flying objects (flying saucers). Why, he asked, would flying saucers, if*
> *they do exist, be seen only over the United States, France and Italy? He*
> *said there is no record of any of the Soviet observatories, which are*
> *manned by highly trained technicians, ever having seen a flying saucer.*

Again, this is a crude misinformation attempt. A well-placed functionary of the Soviet space program, Leonov knew what was really happening at the observatories. In this book we have discussed what Soviet astronomers knew about UFO sightings.

The source of the information for the report was a Japanese government agency official.

Question: what happened to the Soviet data about the Moon? Even the data mentioned by Leonov has not become freely available to researchers. Just as the Lunokhod ("moonwalker") craft remains an enigmatic mission (the archives, revealed recently on Russian TV, confirmed our research that special compartments were built for cosmonauts to guide the craft once it "landed" on the Moon), files about Soviet secret exploration of the Moon are still an enigma wrapped in a mystery. Why? Has this secret information become available to other nations?

The more declassified intelligence files we look into, the more questions arise. Apparently, CIA and other intelligence agencies had as many questions but more answers than we do. We can only hope that that more files will be released in the future, which in turn will answer more of our questions.

CHAPTER 33

KGB, TIBET AND UFOs

RUSSIA'S RED REVOLUTION AND THE OCCULT

The Civil War ended, and the Bolsheviks assumed control over most of the former Czarist Empire. The victory was assured by terror unleashed through the use of their Shield and Sword, or the secret police, well known in the West as the KGB. High intrigues, espionage, and research of the paranormal to be used for the aims of the dictatorship of the "proletariat" took place in Soviet Russia early on. We knew little of this until the disintegration of the USSR in 1991. Thereafter some, but by no means all, files have been released.

It was in May of 1921 that the VECHEKA (forerunner of the KGB; the sinister organisation went through many names as its bloody history rolled on) formed a special department specializing in technological activities. Its official name was 8th Special Department of the VECHEKA.

GLEB BOKIY

Gleb Ivanovich Bokiy was born in Tiflis (today Tbilisi, Georgia), in 1897. Gleb Bokiy, who later became the head of the sinister Special Department of the OGPU (forerunner of the KGB), was acquainted with many researchers of the anomalous phenomena. He was also a veteran Bolshevik revolutionary, born to a family of Russian nobles. His genealogy traces back to the days of Ivan the Terrible. Some sources indicate he was a Ukrainian. Bokiy was first arrested at the age of 14, when he battled the Czars gendarmes. He was arrested twelve times until the fall of the Romanov's empire. Yet Bokiy also found time to be a student; Czarist Russia did not liquidate its enemies, or those it assumed to be enemies, unlike the Bolshevik regime he helped usher in.

Later he became leader of the Petrograd (Saint Petersburg, later Leningrad) VECHEKA (aka OGPU). Bokiy operated undercover in the German-occupied Byelorussia, and later commanded VECHEKA troops in Turkmenistan. There, according to an early KGB defector Agabekov (murdered by his former colleagues in 1937), Bokiy proved to be a sinister person, prone to drinking human blood and eating raw flesh of canines, to improve his appetite. Yet Bokiy was well organised, and had tremendous influence in the Central Committee of the Communist Party. Agabekov was not too flattering in his description of other OGPU leaders: most of them, according to him (who knew them well) were sadists, drunks, adventurers and murderers. The only exception was M. Trilliser, who later interfered with Bokiy's plans to go to Tibet. Georgy Agabekov's memoirs were published in the West in 1930, and later in Russia in 1996.

There were conflicting descriptions of Gleb Bokiy. Some people have been kinder when describing this man. He suffered from tuberculosis, and was a workaholic. His Special department was responsible directly to the Central Committee of the Communist party, and was quite independent. This, too, cost Bokiy his life.

Bokiy's Special Department was responsible for the safeguarding Soviet state secrets. His people checked offices of high officials, made sure the safes were impenetrable, and installed secret alarms. There were quite experienced and seasoned detectives and technical experts in Bokiy's Department. Besides assuring safeguards for the dictatorship of the proletariat, Bokiy's people worked with ciphers and codes. Different secret ciphers were developed for Soviet diplomats, the secret police, and Armed Forces. His experts were able to break almost any code. Their other responsibility was eavesdropping and bugging of various Soviet communications. Bokiy's people had such enormous successes in this area of their work that the huge country was shaping to become a society like the one described in 1984 by George Orwell. Stalin knew how to use this omnipresent secret police apparatus for his means. And, finally, the Special Department was in charge of the occult projects in the Republic.

There was a part of Gleb Bokiy's life that the KGB did not find out until later years.

TIBET

Tibet has long attracted attention of the Russian military. Secret missions had been sent there before the Soviet era. Bokiy's colleagues were interested in all areas of the paranormal. Bokiy was recommended to a Martinist lodge in 1909 (a secret order of the Society of Rosicrucian's in Saint Petersburg). Even as a student of a geological institute, Bokiy attended occultist séances. Revolutionaries, staff officers, aristocrats and con men observed mediums at work. Those who belonged to the lodge included Nicholas K. Roerich, a famous Russian painter, author, researcher, guest of Dalai Lama, and philosopher.

Bokiy was very much interested in the paranormal, and became a Mason long before the Red Revolution. One of those who approved Gleb Bokiy's initiation to the Martinist lodge was A. V. Barchenko, a biologist, occultist, and author of mystic novels. Telepathy was his special interest. In 1918 Barchenko was paid a visit by two VECHEKA officers. One of them was Yakov Blyumkin, a terrorist, martial arts expert, adventurer, spy, and person whose life was steeped in intrigues and service to his cause, the Bolshevik Party and the Revolution. Barchenko became a friend of the VECHEKA. It is quite possible that the "Bolshevik professor of the occult" actually was in Paris in January of 1920, when the leader of the anti-Communist military émigré organisation, General Pavel Kutepov, disappeared without a trace. A man was sighted at the Eiffel Tower on 26th of January of 1930. According to a respected Russian émigré, Barchenko protected the OGPU kidnapping operation from French psychics (Nikolay Cherkashin's article in NLO Magazine, 1999, Professor of the Occult Sciences at the KGB Service).

KOLA PENINSULA

In 1921 Barchenko took part in a secret expedition to the Kola Peninsula. There have been UFO sightings for centuries in the remote Russian area. Most of the research that took place there has been classified by Soviet secret police since 1920's. This includes the mysterious "Arctic hysteria", UFO sightings, and other phenomena we know almost nothing about. From the few files that have been released by heirs of the former KGB, we find out that in December of 1924 Barchenko met with top OGPU people, and shocked them with his reports. Kola Peninsula and its mysterious sightings are described in other parts of our book.

In 1996 another expedition left for the area, to the Lovozro Lake. Valery Dyomin Ph. D. (Philosophy) headed this outing to the Russian North. The expedition confirmed incredible findings of A. Barchenko: a paved, two-kilometre long road in the middle of nowhere, pyramid-like stones, and the image of a gigantic black figure on a rock. The expedition (its name was "Hyperborea-97") also discovered ruins of an ancient observatory, and strange structures at the apex of Ninchurg Mountain (Nauka I Religiya Magazine, 1998).

Dyomin tried in vain to obtain the KGB/NKVD documents about Barchenko and his work. He was finally informed that Barchenko's files were burned in 1941, as the Germans approached Moscow. Apparently, this was done to preclude Nazi capture of important files. A RUFORS researcher, Eduard Gozhin, was present at a lecture presented by Dyomin in 2001, and wrote down this information. He also heard Dyomin say that state archives in Russian Buryatiya may contain interesting information about this subject.

BACK TO TIBET

Apparently, the strange objects over Asian sky interested the Soviets back in 1920's.

They, like Nazis, were interested in the mysterious Shambhala, a land allegedly located on the borders of Afghanistan, India, and Tibet.

THE EXPEDITION

Barchenko was getting ready to head an expedition to Tibet, to search for the famed Shambhala, to discover the keys to mysteries of the world. He discussed his plans with Tibetan monks, and a Communist Mongolian official. And then Barchenko was paid another visit by Yakov Blyumkin, a dedicated OGPU officer moving up the career ladder. It did not at all hinder Blyumkin's career that he murdered a German diplomat in 1918. On the contrary, the KGB of the period "forgave" him, and embraced its eager son.

Blyumkin informed Barchenko that his telepathy experiments are necessary for the Soviet defence industry, and the secret police would sponsor him. The scientist was not against cooperating with the secret police, and wrote a letter to its head, the redoubtable Felix Dzerdhinsky.

Bokiy was given the responsibility to research the idea of an expedition to Shambhala. And so, the Soviet secret police chief and a scientist who delved into mysticism became friends. Shambhala figured prominently in their conversations. A laboratory had been created and funded by the OGPU for 12 years, until 1937, when Barchenko was arrested during Stalinist purges. The files of his interrogations have been preserved, and excerpts published in Russia recently. A special "black room" was equipped for Barcheko's research in the OGPU building. Barchenko worked with shamans, mediums, and healers. Sometimes he lectured the OGPU people. One of those who attended the lectures was Boris Stomonyakov, Deputy People's Commissar for Foreign Relations. He was responsible for China and Tibet. Chinese Ufology and ancient history of UFO sightings have been of particular interest to the Soviet intelligence services.

A group of highly placed Communist officials together with Gleb Bokiy and A. Barchenko, formed a secret society they named United Labor Brotherhood. It was a society of mystics whose aims were to discover ways to Shambhala, and establish communications with the mysterious area.

At the same time Barchenko openly promoted an idea of the creation of an International of secret societies, to help Soviet Communists spread their influence. The Komintern leaders residing in the USSR welcomed this idea.

Gleb Bokiy was eager to depart to Tibet to look for Shambhala, but his enemies in the OGPU were able to sabotage his plans. Instead, Yaskov Blyumkin was sent to look for Shambhala, under different guises. While in Western China, Blyumkin joined the Roerich expedition, and travelled through the area under the Star Spangled banner. Roerich's expedition was officially an American enterprise and funded from private sources in the United States. The search for Shambhala was not as important to the Soviets as it later was for German Nazis. No, the Soviets sought to diminish and destroy British influence in Tibet. It was a new Big Game, and the British intelligence was aware of it. Its officers were able to block Roerich's expedition, and stop Soviet move into Tibet.

THE SIGHTING

In 1926, as Roerich travelled in Tibet, his companions and the painter himself provided one of the first detailed UFO reports. On August 5 a gigantic, oval object moved at great speed across the sky. It was shimmering, for the sun reflected off it. Crossing the sky over their camp the object changed its direction from south to south-west. The people below had time to study it through their field glasses. The camp, located in the Kukunor district, not far away from the Humboldt Chain, included well trained mountain travellers and guides. The Soviet secret police asked Dr. Konstantin Ryabinin to join the expedition; he also observed the UFO in 1926. He was arrested in 1930, and his diaries, notes, and Tibetan documents were confiscated. Dr. Ryabinin refused to defame Roerich, and spent years in Stalin's concentration camps, where he had saved many lives, in his capacity as a doctor. The most valuable information and data about "secret knowledge" he obtained in Tibet are still in the KGB archives. Dr. Ryabinin died in 1956 when the subject of Tibetan medicine was still a taboo.

Yakov Blyumkin, a darling of the OGPU, made a costly mistake. He was too arrogant, too sure of his powers. Blyumkin paid a secret visit to the exiled Trotsky, during one of his missions after the Tibet debacle. Upon his return to the Soviet Union, Blyumin was arrested and executed. In 1991 the KGB entertained an idea of awarding him, posthumously, the order of Hero of the Soviet Union. But then, the Soviet Union, too, ceased to exist.

THE END?

Gleb Bokiy was arrested in 1937. Stalin did not forgive him his Bolshevik past and closeness to prominent Soviet leaders, many of them dead or executed during the purges.

Apparently, Stalin wanted possession of Bokiy's secret file, containing compromising materials on Soviet leadership. We do not know whether the file actually existed. Bokiy was executed, along with other members of his Brotherhood. His department was disbanded into other KGB entities. Stalin ruthlessly crushed any dissent, and any potential adversary. He had very practical aims and direct means of achieving them. Mysticism was of no use to him. In this book we learned of Stalin's interest in UFOs; as everything else, it was a practical interest. Bokiy's and Barchenko's paranormal files were confiscated. Some Russian researchers believe that the FSB (modern KGB) keeps them in their archives.

If these files were destroyed it would undoubtedly be a great loss but there is still hope that they may still exist, intact, somewhere in the archives of the KGB. Gathering dust waiting for someone to chance upon them perhaps? Time will tell who is right in this instance.

CHAPTER 34

KGB AND ITS UFO FILES

THE DECLASSIFIED FILES

On October 24, 1991 a batch of documents was given to the President of the All Union Ufological Association, former Soviet cosmonaut, P.R. Popovich. The files consisted of 124 pages. The files contained copies of UFO reports sent to the KGB. Deputy Chairman of the Committee for State Security USSR, N.A. Sham, wrote an accompanying letter. The Russian Ufology Research Centre was able to obtain two copies of the files. The reports consist of handwritten reports, typed testimonies, notes from the KGB informers, crude drawings, and eyewitness reports. Of course, few Russian Ufologists believe that the released documents comprised all of the KGB's UFO files.

The letter, accompanying the released documents, is of an interest to historians of the Soviet Union. It stated the following:

Dear Pavel Romanovich,

The State Security Committee has never been engaged in systematic gathering and analysis of information of anomalous phenomena (the so-called unidentified flying objects). At the same time, the SSC of the USSR has been receiving statements from a number of persons and agencies regarding cases of observations of the above phenomena. We forward you copies of such statements. At an earlier date, the same material was sent to the Central Machine Building research Institute in the city of Kaliningrad.

Appendix: Ref. materials on 124 pages, declassified, to the addressee only.

N.A. Sham
Deputy Chairman of the Committee
October 24, 1991

The cases mentioned in the reports consist of the following:

Sightings occurred all over the immense country: from Kursk City in the European part to Kamchatka in the East and from the Tiksi Peninsula in the North to the resort town of Sochi on the Black Sea coast. They took place over a period of 9 years from 1982 through 1990. We used originals of all documents, though some of them have been abridged.

The first document is the transcript of a radio exchange between air-traffic controller R. Stepanian and the crews of three flights that were in the airport zone at the time. They were scheduled Flight # 138, 397 and 500. The Controller's words are marked "TWR" (for TOWER) and the Flights - "F-1", "F-2", and "F-3" correspondingly. The Exchange started at 11 hrs 31min.

IN THE VICINITY OF THE CITIES OF KURSK, VORONEZH AND YELTS - OCTOBER 17, 1983

Some information was deleted from the report. It was a conversation with Colonel Skrypnik, a duty officer, regarding the visual contact with a UFO on 10-17-1983. The conversation took place on October 24, 1983. Colonel Skrypnik recalled that at 6 am on October 17, 1983, Major Kiselev of a (deleted) CP reported a visual contact with a UFO that was sporadically moving, changing its altitude and brightness, as well as periodically emitting a beam of light, directed downward. The UFO had a round shape, with a bright halo around it and a darker centre. The UFO was moving randomly, and had no clear direction. Observers reported the appearance of periodic light beams, emitted from the UFO towards the ground. When it was closest to the ground, the UFO looked like a polyhedron, invariably with a shining halo. The radar at Georgiu-Dezh could not register the UFO, and provide any valuable data. Those who had observed the UFO are certain that the object they saw was not identical to any star in the observation sector. The UFO was sighted at sunrise, when no stars were visible in the sky. At about 7 am the UFO ascended, and disappeared from sight. Military personnel in Kursk, Voronezh, and Yelts observed the UFO. Colonel Skrypnik reported all of the information regarding the UFO observation through the chain of command to Colonel Galitisn of the Moscow Air defence District.

JULY 26, 1989, SOCHI AIRPORT ZONE

TWR: Go ahead, Flight 138.

F1: Do you observe two objects hanging at our left?

TWR: To the left? What altitude?

F1: Our altitude, right, about 50 or 60 kilometres ahead of us.

TWR: Flight 138, you are clear of traffic now.
Do you observe anything on your left?

F1: There was one object, and then another one appeared nearby. They are flying away from us. The distance is already about 80 kilometres.

TWR: What is their shape like?

F1: One is oblong, like a dirigible, the other's kind of spherical.

TWR: Are they abeam?

F1: Yes, right ahead but they are moving away quickly, the distance is 80-90 kilometres.

TWR: Flight 397, do you observe anything abeam, 30-40 kilometres to the left of you?

F2: 30 kilometres abeam?

TWR: About 40 kilometres from the left to the right.

F1: Flight 397, they must be moving from the left to the right.

F2: No, we do not observe them; I'll look at the radar display.

F1: Flight 397, they are 25 kilometres to the right and behind you.

F2: We do not see them. There are clouds.

F1: Look above the clouds. They are sort of zigzagging.

F2: Flight 397, I've sighted two spots against the clouds.

TWR: Which zone?

F2: About 45 km from Sochi, 30 degrees behind me.

F1: This is Flight 138. One is nearly square; the other is diamond-shaped. They are flying apart now.

TWR: Flight 138; keep us advised on these objects.

F1:   They are hanging close together over there. They are probably about 8 km ahead of us already.

TWR: Are they moving?

F1:   Yes, they were 40 km away, now they are about 100 km away, moving from left to right. Request clearance to climb to 11,100 m.

TWR: Flight 138, climb to level 11,100m and keep us advised on these objects.

F1:   Flight 138, roger, climbing to 11,100m. Control Tower, do you see them on the radar display?

TWR: Negative.

F1:   Right. Now they've made a turn and are moving aside.

TWR: Flight 138, do you still see them?

F1:   They are behind us and to the left. The distance between us is increasing. They have moved away too quickly. One moment they were close to us and the other they were already far behind.

TWR: Flight 138; advise which way they are moving.

F1:   Now they are behind me and to the left.

TWR: Flight 138; is everything all right with you?

F1:   Affirmative, everything is all right.

TWR: Roger, Flight 500, do you see anything?

F3:   Flight 500. There is nothing in sight, either on the right or on the left.

TWR: Roger.

MAY 23, 1985 KHABAROVSK REGION - REPORT

A bomber regiment was carrying out scheduled flights when a UFO was sighted from the Control Tower at 22 hrs 35 min. It was elliptical and of a pale orange colour. The object moved noiselessly at a height of 2-3 thousand metres and a speed of about 600 km/h from West to East. The ellipsis was surrounded with a light halo. Radar displays did not show any signs of the object. No effects on material or personnel were registered. The sighting lasted 13 minutes. Its flight was interrupted with descents and periodical motionlessness. Two hours later a similar object was sighted for 10 minutes. Long-range aircraft passed below it at the height of 800 -1 200 metres. The UFO emitted beams of light up and down. The downward beams were brighter.

Colonel V. Alifanov - Flight Commander

NOVEMBER 3, 1985 VLADIVOSTOK CITY VICINITIES

At 20 hrs 30 min I stopped hunting in the estuary of the river Razdolnaya, jumped into my motorboat "Dnepr" and started the engine

"Vikhr". The engine worked smoothly, trouble-fee. At that moment I noticed a UFO moving at a great speed from North to South at an altitude much higher than that used by planes. It looked somewhat larger than a star and sent a beam of light to the earth at an acute angle. The beam was rather long, yet it did not reach the ground and died away in the air. When the UFO flew up closer, the boat's engine suddenly stopped. I pumped in some petrol, increased the injection and pulled at the starting cord. The engine started. While it was running I noticed some luminescence coming from the basis of the high-voltage coils where they were tapped to the spark plugs of the upper and lower cylinders. The upper plug shone brighter. Five or seven seconds later the engine died abruptly without dropping speed. At that moment the UFO was right over my boat.

After the UFO had moved a little farther to the South in the direction of Vladivostok, my companion A. Khripunov and I noticed a satellite over it. Both the UFO and the satellite were moving at about the same speed and in the same direction. When the UFO approached Vladivostok its beam disappeared, and the object itself was no longer visible. The satellite moved on, it was clearly seen against the sky although it was much smaller than the UFO.

We got into the boat and pushed it away from the bank. Try as I might the engine would not start. The wind and the stream carried the boat to the opposite bank. I stepped out of the boat onto a shallow place and made another attempt to start the engine, changed the plugs but petrol splashed on the first and on the second sets. Changing the second set of plugs noticed that they did not give off a spark. We used oars to row to the estuary and chose a place for rest.

I gave the engine a close scrutiny. I cleaned the contacts of all circuits, changed part of the circuit and the high-voltage wires. A weak spark appeared in the lower cylinder, it showed up periodically at each turn of the flywheel: once, after several unsuccessful attempts. There was still no spark in the upper cylinder. We decided to row, hoping to meet someone. We met some fishermen at 9 a.m. who lent us an old coil. I checked all the contacts once again: nothing had changed in the lower cylinder; the spark was weak but regular. When I changed the coils there was no spark in the upper cylinder at all, yet I felt the spark with my hand when the plug was out..

Then I took a spare booster, which I had already tried at night, put it into a pot, covered it with a lid and heated it for half an hour on a primus-stove. Then I put the booster in position. After the first turn of the flywheel I felt a strong electric discharge in my hand. I adjusted the gaps, connected the plugs, grounded them and saw good sparks on the plugs. I screwed in the plugs, splashed a little clean petrol into both cylinders for an easier start and started the engine at the first attempt. It was 3 p.m. 45 minutes later I was in Vladivostok.

V. Alexandrov - Captain 3rd Rank

NOVEMBER 25, 1986, VICINITY OF THE CITY OF MAGADAN

At 12:50 Moscow time, on November 25, 1986, civilian air controllers and Soviet military air controllers detected an unidentified target at a distance of 80 kilometres and azimuth of 85 degrees. The target's speed was 600 kilometres per hour. At the same time, an Antonov-12 aircraft (Flight 11421) flew at an altitude of 7200 metres. The aircraft was advised about the target on a collision course, and instructed to perform a starboard diversion turn. The crew of this aircraft, at 12:53, observed an identified target (on the flight radar scope) flying along the same course at a distance of 150 kilometres. The target was observed for the second time when the aircraft was over the Tahtayamsk, and reported the fact to the ground control. After the aircraft and the target passed each other the latter also turned to starboard in the direction of the Bay of Shelihov water area, and picked up its speed to 900 to 1000 kilometres per hour. At 12:58, the target picked up its speed (it soon reached 3000 kilometres per hour), heading from the Kamchatka Peninsula. It disappeared from the radarscopes at a distance of 150 kilometres from the coastline. Military personnel of the Magadan Airport photographed the target's path. A written statement was taken from the crew navigator of the Antonov-12 aircraft, who had observed the target.

DECEMBER, 1987 - SEPTEMBER, 1988, VICINITY OF THE SHIVELUCH VOLCANO, KAMCHATKA

The personnel at a variety of observation posts had been systematically sighting ball-shaped UFO over flights. In particular, they looked like small slowly rising fires changing their colour from red to white. The sightings lasted from 30 seconds to 7 minutes. One officer suggested their appearance correlated with the scheduled launching of combat vehicles. He noticed that UFOs did not appear when the launching time was altered.

However, balls the size of a football were sighted without any relation to launching, e.g. on December 16, 1987, an hour after a warhead had fallen to the ground. An orange ball was moving slowly and noiselessly from North to South. It was freezing and there was no wind. On December 21, 1987 the ball appeared at 19 hrs while the launching took place at 22 hrs. The next day there was no launching at all. However, the ball appeared at 18 hrs 35 min. It pulsed, changing its colour from red to blue to white.

On July 26, 1988 a ball with a blurred outline was sighted immediately before launching. The situation was repeated at night, on September 9-10, 1099. This time the UFO appeared 5 minutes before launching. It was a silver ball with a visible dimension larger than that of the Moon. The object disappeared right after the combat vehicle's flight. The radio operator noticed a worsening in the transmission of ultra-short waves. Anti-aircraft facilities and radio instruments of the control complex did not register any unidentified flying objects. Specialists suggested several hypotheses to explain the phenomena observed. They might be:

- ball-shaped concentrations of electric charges in the atmosphere;
- balloons lit by the rays of the setting sun;
- holograms at the crossing of laser beams.

These suggestions are purely theoretical. There are no facts to prove them.
Signed: Unit Commander

JULY 28, 1989 VICINITIES OF THE TOWN OF KAPUSTIN YAR, ASTRAKHAN REGION

Servicemen from two army units sighted a UFO for two hours from different distances at about midnight. Those who were closest to it had a chance to make drawings. We publish extracts from eyewitnesses' reports.

I climbed the aerial support and observed the object from a height of 6 metres above the ground. One could clearly see a powerful blinking signal that resembled a camera flash in the night sky. The object flew over the unit's logistics yard and moved in the direction of the rocket weapons depot, 300 metres away. It hovered over the depot at a height of 20 metres. The UFO's hull shone with a dim green light that looked like phosphorus. It was a disk, 4 to 5 metres in diameter, with a semi-spherical top.

While the object was hovering over the depot, a bright beam appeared from the bottom of the disk, where the flash had been before, and made two or three circles. Then the object, still flashing, moved in the direction of the railway station still flashing. But soon it returned to the rocket weapons depot and hovered over it at a height of 60 to 70 metres. Two hours after the first sighting the object flew in the direction of the town of Akhtubinsk and disappeared from sight.
The light at the bottom of the disk did not flash regularly; it was as if photographs were being taken. Nor did the object move evenly.

Sometimes it rushed sideways or upwards and sometimes it moved smoothly and hovered here and there. I attach a drawing of the UFO's outline and the beam.

Ensign V. Voloshin
Communications Officer-on-Duty.

For two hours Ensign V.Voloshin and I had been observing the object together as it moved and hovered. I confirm everything he reported.

Private D. Tishchayev

Besides the object in the sky I sighted a ball of fire rising toward it from the ground. When the UFO rushed in my direction I physically sensed its approach. The object pulled up suddenly. I saw that a plane attempted to approach the object but the latter gained speed quickly and left the plane behind.

Private G. Kulik

I sighted the blinking UFO from a distance of 3 km. Bright light flashed from the ground over the place where it was hovering. The light moved to the left and right. Another object rose, from there. The higher it rose, the dimmer the light grew. At the end of the second hour of observation I noticed a third object at a height of 300-400 metres. It gave flashes of red light at constant intervals. Then coloured lights ran over it like on a Christmas tree and I could make out that it was cigar-shaped. The "cigar" flew to the first UFO, and together they disappeared beyond the horizon.

Ensign A. Levin

REPORT ABOUT OBSERVATION OF AN ANOMALOUS PHENOMENON IN THE TIKSI PENINSULA AREA

On August 14, 1987, the (name deleted) radar outpost of the air defence commander HQ discovered an unidentified target at the altitude of 3000 metres, its speed reaching 400 kilometres per hour. Six minutes later the target disappeared from the radar screen. Half an hour later the target was again discovered, now closer to the Tiksi. A military helicopter sent to the site did not find the unidentified target. The helicopter's commander, Captain Zikeyev, observed two inversion trails going into the clouds; he then returned to the airport.

An AN-12 airplane on a weather reconnaissance mission was ordered to the site of the target. Colonel Lobanov, the flight commander, upon reaching the altitude of 4000 metres, observed an odd-shaped transparent cloud. Its colour was emerald, with a violet tint. Inside the cloud he saw dark spots. The cloud seemed to move, as Colonel saw two inversion trails behind it. The ground control of the air defence unit registered that when the helicopter and the airplane approached the unidentified target, radio communication with both deteriorated due to interference. The target disappeared from the radar screens shortly thereafter.

(Note: similar strange clouds were observed over the Chukotka in the 1990. The amazing feature of the "clouds" consisted of groups of aircraft that exited from the centre of a circle formed by clouds, and then disappeared into the clouds. The "aircraft" appeared nine times. When the photos taken by observers were developed, they saw a cigar-shaped object, with some black dots in the background. The seamen who observed the phenomenon suffered headaches and became weak after episode. Apparently, the KGB, just as those who sent Soviet cosmonauts Kovalenok and Savinkh (whose adventures are described later in the book) after the silvery clouds, had a keen interest in the "cloud phenomena".

Another curious detail about the Tiksi settlement dates back to 1960. Former head of the operational section of the Yakutsk ASSR KGB, P. S. Pavlov recalled that in the winter of that year he was shown two photographs with the same object on each one. The structure was an Arctic meteorological station, photographed at night. The pictures were taken one after another, seconds later. The photographs clearly show a rhomboid object, moving low over the horizon. The photographer did not see any such objects as he was taking the pictures.

THE BESHTAU MOUNTAIN CASE

December 15, 1987. An airplane on the Volgograd-Tbilisi flight (over Nalchik), reported that shortly after 11 p.m. the crew observed a flying object approaching straight ahead. The object resembled an airplane, its headlights turned off. But the radars could not discover any flying craft in the area. The UFO (note - the term was used by a KGB officer who compiled the report-P.S.) had vanished. Some five minutes later the UFO was observed from another airplane. The crew reported that there was a fiery trail behind it, emitting sparks. The UFO "ceased to exist" after a blast, similar to an explosion. Ten minutes later a call came to the office of the local airport to inform the chief that an airplane was flying and burning over the town. A fiery "train" follows the airplane. Then, a blast (but no noise whatsoever) and the airplane disappeared. The person who alerted the chief of the local airport left to the site but could not find any debris or remnants. The KGB officer checked with the local military and found out that the area restricted for the passenger airplane flight that night was through Guriyev-Astrakhan line only.

An eyewitness, who was questioned and signed his statements as Sergey Sergeyevich Karapetyan, stated that the "airplane" was of gigantic size, much larger than any airplane. Rather, the object resembled a rocket. But it descended very slowly, and went down somewhere at the Beshtau Mountain area. Sergeant-Major Varyutin reported to his superiors that the object he and another sergeant had observed that night resembled an airplane, flew at a slow speed, and had a powerful searchlight illuminating the area in front of it. The object moved noiselessly.

KAMCHATKA

The KGB was also concerned with reports coming from the Kamchatka area, between 1987 and 1988. The objects had been flying over the secret combat field "Kura". The unidentified objects were small spheres, changing their colour from red to white. The officers, who reported the incidents to the KGB, noted that the objects "existed" for close to three minutes. They appeared at the time of the secret testing of "heavy, manufactured articles" and the objects did not come down (as the "articles" would). But a warrant officer and some soldiers observed a fiery sphere, one hour after the tests. It moved through the air noiselessly and slowly; the weather was cold and windless. The same sphere was observed after another secret test. The unidentified object was measured from afar. It flew in a vertical and a horizontal pattern at different times. Sometimes it pulsated, and its colours changed from red to blue to white. Among different objects observed by military, there was one that resembled a silvery moon. A cone-shaped ray pointed downwards from the object. There seemed to be a smoke-like substance around the object. When the "article" was tested, and made its way upward into the air, the object vanished. The radio communication deteriorated, and there was interference. At the same time the KGB agent "Shestakov", who was visually following the "article", observed a luminescent dot in at the slope of a mountain ridge. The dot emitted a reddish ray, narrow at the origin point, becoming wider as it reached the area of the testing. As it precisely reached the separating parts of a rocket, the dot disappeared. Local radars registered nothing unusual.

Thus, the KGB report reveals secret testing of rockets that "separated" into different parts. But just as the testing range experts, who tried to come up with explanations as to the origin of the objects, the report cannot explain who or what flew over the forbidden areas of Kamchatka during secret tests.

ON THE BRINK

A transcript from ABC News Prime Time Live dated October 5, 1995 describes the segment about the KGB files. David Ensor, a well-known correspondent for the network, conducted a five-month investigation of the KGB and UFO files. Dozens of Russian scientists, military and government officials had been interviewed. Ensor found out about forty major incidents, including one that prompted fears of starting an accidental nuclear war. Ensor's team also found out about the Instruction (military study of UFOs we described in the previous chapter). They viewed awesome footage of a huge triangular UFO filmed by a Soviet propaganda film crew. Other reports confirmed by eyewitnesses proved to be important. The incident that almost unleashed a nuclear war took place in 1982, on October 4. The place was Byelokoroviche, Soviet Ukraine. That day a huge UFO of perfect geometrical shape and 900 metres in diameter hovered over a nearby ballistic missile base. Numerous eyewitnesses confirmed the sighting to David Ensor. So did Lt. Colonel Vladimir Plantonev, a missile engineer. According to him the UFO was a noiseless, disk-shaped craft; it had no portholes, its surface completely even. It made turns, like an airplane would. The missile silo at the base contained a nuclear warhead pointed at the United States. It was dismantled in the early 1990's. But in 1982 it was fully functional. Plantonev was in the bunker that fateful day in 1982. The room contained dual control panels for the missile, each of them hooked to Moscow. As the UFO hovered overhead, signal lights on both the control panels suddenly turned on, for a short period of time. The lights indicated that the missiles were preparing for launch. Moscow could have initiated such launch, by its transmission of special orders. But no order came from Moscow, and no one at the base pushed any buttons. For 15 long seconds the base simply lost control of its nuclear weapons. Moscow was very much alarmed, and sent an investigation team to verify the incident. A member of the commission, Colonel Igor Chernovshev, corroborated the 1982 incident to David Ensor.

Finally, it is important for our Western readers to understand that because the Soviet Union was a totalitarian state built on secrecy and lies, the KGB was omnipresent. For example, the USSR Academy of Sciences had a special First Department, actually a secret police outpost that spied and collected information. Every Soviet State institution had such outposts. The files collected by KGB scientists are out of reach of Russian researchers. Without a doubt, UFO reports and observations are hidden in such files. One wonders what secrets they contain and whether they still remain in Russia.

Allegedly, some files and video films have become property of Western television producers. UFO researchers, like the authors of this book, are interviewed occasionally for such programs, but researchers are never given the actual films for independent study. Of course, no documents in the possession of such producers are given to independent researchers. That is why we will abstain from commenting on such "KGB files" productions. But we urge television producers that claim to possess KGB UFO files to turn them over to serious researchers for a comprehensive, detailed examination. There are such entities as MUFON and the J. Allen Hynek Centre for UFO

Studies in the West; and Gherman Kolchin, the RIAP, Aleksandr Plaksin, Mikhail Gershtein and other decent and experienced researchers in the East who could join forces for the task. This is the only way to establish authenticity of the documents and films.

KGB QUESTIONS AN EYEWITNESS

Boris A. is a former Soviet scientist who currently resides in Chicago. He sent me a report of the sighting he had in December of 1992. The UFO he observed was very similar to the ones that caused the famous Greek wave of 1981.

The KGB investigation of the sighting ensued, and reveals how the secret police was interested in the phenomena.

The incident took place in Kiev, shortly before New Year's Day. A's friends invited him to their parents, to Rusanovka, a suburb of Kiev.

The sighting occurred as Boris was leaving his friends' parents' place. Lena had forgotten her cigarettes upstairs, and her husband went back to get them. At that time, a man came running past them at an incredible speed for his large size, pointing at the sky. They looked up and saw it.

The object was passing over Kiev with an unhurried grace, not very high from the ground, and it was stunningly beautiful. It was shaped like a mushroom. As A. recalled later, its length was about 360 metres. The "cap" was located in the "nose-cone," that is, in the frontal section of the object. It seemed to us as if the "cap" itself was the propulsion engine. In any event, the "cap" glowed, and cast some sort of inversion trace. The UFO had a delicately violet colour, and it was luminous. Rather, the violet colour seemed to be iridescent with tints and hues.

Now, the "cap" of this mushroom reminded A. of a glowing cigarette tip; that is, it was brighter and of a somewhat different colour. In any case, he cannot under any circumstances describe the top of the ship as "violet." A. found it difficult to give a verbal description for the frontal section of the UFO. The next day, he met Lena at the Institute of Plant Physiology of the Ukrainian SSR Academy of Sciences, where she worked. They told everybody about their sighting, but nobody would believe it.

There was an unexpected documentary confirmation of their account. Chervonniy Prapor, a local newspaper, published a brief news report that confirmed the UFO sighting. The newspaper also informed the readers that radars of both of Kiev's airports detected the object. And in that report, a telephone number was provided to contact the combined team from the Academy of Sciences whose members were very much interested in talking to witnesses of the UFO. So, Lena and A. called them.

In a few days, a group of people had arrived at the Institute. They were quite interested. A. had to speak with a young man, who looked very fit and who possessed a square jaw, muscular figure and sharp gaze underneath his straight brows. He looked like a classic movie villain, and that's what he turned out to be.

The first question the young man asked had nothing to do with the UFO. He asked Boris what he was doing at the laboratory, since the komandirovochnoye oudostovereniye (warrant for travelling on official business) was issued for another place, and A. had no "secrecy clearance" at the lab. Boris was stunned by this question, and asked the young man whether he was more interested in his status quo or the details of the sighting. The young man tried to convince A. that he was interested in everything. They could not reach an understanding, and Boris told him to go to hell.

For some reason, the KGB representative liked that. He ceased trying to find out whether A. was a spy, and called in a second member of the team, a young woman. And they proceeded with a genuine interview of a witness to a UFO sighting.

It was very tough questioning. They quickly established the direction of the UFO's flight, its speed, and its angles to the horizon. But the colour range A. had described drove them up the wall, for no one else had described the UFO the way he did. Boris tried to explain to them that their task was to collect information, and not whether to believe or disbelieve a witness. Still, they refused to believe him.

At the end of their conversation, the KGB reluctantly agreed that he was somewhat correct, because Lena gave them a description of the colour range.

A. was already aware that the "comrades" from the combined team were KGB people. He thinks that perhaps they had conducted the conversation in a certain manner on purpose; having classified him into some group of those questioned that Ag. was not aware of. He never did see them again, although they promised that they would meet again.

The UFO, he recalls, was a pleasure to look at; that is how he felt at the time. It was quite beautiful. Boris A.'s report is another confirmation of a belief that the government-authorised entities empowered to study the UFO phenomenon in the former USSR had mainly existed to obstruct rather than promote genuine research.

A LETTER FROM THE CZECH REPUBLIC

http://www.michaelhesemann.com - This is the site of a renowned German UFO researcher, Michael Hesemann. It contains excerpts of the footage discussed below.

On February 17th, 2002 Michael Hesemann, received an e-mail entitled "URGENT for Mr. Hesemann, New UFO Videos". It was written by a young Armenian, studying in the Czech Republic, who read Mr. Hesemann's name in the Czech version of Magazin 2000, whose editor he was until the year 2000.

After learning about Michael Hesemann's name and work the Armenian student had visited his website, read his interview with General Alexejev and saw the researcher's picture with Pope John Paul II.

According to what he wrote to Hesemann in this e-mail and further e-mails on the following days, his grandfather, a retired former high-ranking KGB officer had died last year. In his possession, the young man - let's call him "T" - found several videotapes and lots of documents. He took the tapes with him to the Czech Republic, expecting some movies in them. But when he got them out of their covers, he was surprised to find some notes in his grandfather's handwriting and, on the tapes, altogether 13 film clips that obviously show UFOs and military planes.

Since his mother was sick and he needed money, he decided to offer them for sale to a UFO researcher - and eventually contacted Mr. Hesemann at least according to T.'s version of the story.

Obviously he was under some kind of time pressure, since he wrote: "I must go back to Armenia and to the Army as all young men must do and I only want to sell these videos with all the movies before I go to Armenia shortly so that my mother who is not in good health can be OK as I cannot take care of her. I need to do this in a matter of days or I will lose this chance. I think right now I am being watched and time is short."

Since T. promised that "these videos of these movies are very clear and there is no question they are authentic as you will see", Mr. Hesemann asked him to go to a lab, order digital scans from some stills and e-mail them to him. Only when eight images arrived the German researcher knew that he was obviously dealing with a promising case.

Hesemann has always been, according to his own words, extremely careful whenever a witness asks for money. T. requested $ 5000, a fortune for a Russian or Armenian and definitely a temptation. The footage, however, could be genuine. Hence, Mr. Hesemann was not willing to accept his offer to meet him, give him all that money and receive all the films at once, but offered a three-step payment, to which T. agreed.

Eventually Michael Hesemann flew to Prague on February 25, 2002 and met T. at the airport. T. was a friendly young man, obviously of Armenian origin (the German researcher checked his passport and saw his student visa for the Czech Republic), kind, with good manners, although he seemed to be under some stress. He gave Hesemann a tape with seven of the 13 films (promising the rest when the researcher raised the funds for a second payment) plus some notes with times and dates. Furthermore he signed an affidavit and an exclusive license agreement for the footage. The affidavit had the following text:

AFFIDAVIT

To Whom It May Concern

I, T. ..., born on ... in Yerevan/Armenia herewith solemnly swear that the following statement is true and that I indemnify and hold all parties involved free from any damage arising out of misleading or untrue statements from my side:

I am an Armenian citizen. My grandfather was a high-level intelligence officer involved with the former Soviet government and the KGB on a high level. He was a personal friend of Anastas Mikoyan and had access to authentic UFO information.

In my grandfather's files, after his death, I found the papers and the video I am handing over to Mr. Michael Hesemann of Germany. The 13 UFO movies on this video were collected by KGB agents from all over the world. Most is original military footage.

The material is historic and authentic and not the product of computer special effect manipulation to the best of my knowledge.

All information given to Hesemann in my e-mails is true. I do not have any contact with neither Mr. K... or any other agent of the C... in Prague and it is not my intention to spread disinformation for any side. I confirm that I sign this affidavit by free will and that I am fully responsible for my statements."

Flying home on the same day (via Frankfurt/Germany, with the train to Düsseldorf), Hesemann had exactly three days to view this exciting material before he flew to the US on March 1st., to lecture in the United States and present the films to the UFO Congresses in Laughlin/Nevada and San Marino. He organised a confidential background check of this material and the claims of his source.

In the beginning, Hesemann's major suspicion was that he was being set up. But T., Hesemann's source is who he claims to be, according to the German researcher: a nice, intelligent young man, fluent in several languages (and English is his worst) from a prominent Armenian family. Hesemann saw his passport and knows that he is who he claims to be. From his family background, according to the German, it is almost expected that he has or had relatives in highest political and intelligence circles. Hesemann decided to look at his claims (in T.'s words, with Hesemann's corrections in brackets) with an open mind:

Regarding the alleged Gun camera Footage of a rotating disk with a dome on top - probably Vilnius, Lithuania, July 18, 1976.

STATEMENT OF (ON) UFO VIDEOS:

My grandfather dies (died) on ..., 2001. It was in Armenia in Yerevan. I was born in Yerevan. My grandfather work(ed) for the government and I always ask(ed) him all the time about his work because I admire(d) him and he would smile and tell me in Armenian, that it was not my business. He was not being mean, he would smile. Every Sunday he have (had) friends over and he was very busy. I met some of his colleagues in the government, I never pay (paid) much attention to their names, I always remember first names, but my grandfather had many friends in the government. He did some secret work for them and the military. My grandfather was (a) very good friend of Anastas Mikoyan (Politburo member under Josef Stalin, MH). They met when they were young boys. Mikoyan went to Politburo and my grandfather stay(ed) in Yerevan. Mikoyan would call when he need(ed) something from my grandfather.

When my grandfather die(d), I went (back) to Armenia after he died and I finish school for last year. Up in the top floor were (were) boxes of his stuff. There were many papers and files and some video tapes. I did not take time to read many of the papers but I make sure they were put in boxes for me to look at later.

I was interested in (the) videos because I could use the tapes for something else if they were not important. My grandfather record movies on TV and no one like(d) them but him. I get (got) some of these tapes. They have movies on them, and then I find (found) one tape that have (has) military info on it in Armenian and I see these UFOs. This is military film of UFOs. There is a piece of paper that list(s) information about them; place and date, but I do not know which film is which.

When you view them you can see which ones are which. I then go (went) into (a) store later (back in the Czech Republic) to buy food at (the city of) Dejvicka and I see your magazine 2000 and I see (read) about the UFOs.

Then I find (found) your web site and I see (saw) your photo with (the) Pope and I know (knew) you are the right person to sell this to. I only want (the) money to help my mother, which is my family. My father I do not know, he left us years ago when I was a small boy. I was close to my grandfather and he give (left) me everything according to the attorney in his will. I will go back (to Armenia) and (will) go through his documents and learn more about this. I want to be careful so I do not get found out (caught).

I know my grandfather would not talk about the UFOs seen in Armenia in the early 1980s. I was young and do not remember much, but I remember police coming to talk to grandfather about them so this is why I think he was involved. Why would the police come to him if this was not true. I could hear them talk about it, about (a) large object seen near our mountain, Ararat. I later ask(ed) grandfather and he said he could not talk about it.

*Now I have this video I want to learn more and will when I go back to Armenia and also in (the) army I can (will) ask quiet(ly) and try to find out things.*T."

According to T. the footage was taken in the following years:

North Korea 1952
Krakov, Poland, July 7, 1986
Helsinki, Finland, September 12, 1996
Ondrey´s Observatory, CSSR, August 15, 199(?)
Vilnius, Lithuania July 18, 1976
He also mentioned footage from Romania.

To quote from his e-mail, the footage shows "a UFO flying over a MIG in Korea. The plane adjust(s) position to get better see (sight) at (of the) UFO. (The) film was taken from (an) other MIG. Another film show(s) a UFO flying over (an) American plane at a base in the USA. It is a clear disk. Another one show(s) a UFO over (a) Romanian plane. Another show(s) (a) UFO over (a) MIG on the air base and another show(s) a UFO over a MIG sitting on (the) runway only a few years ago.

Another shows a UFO taken at Ondrejov Observatory in Czech Republic. This is footage of (a) famous UFO story. There is another UFO (a) big disk in Lithuania and also at night with night camera that show(s a) big disk and also (a film) from World War II that show(s a) disk over (an) airplane from (a) German base. It is clear(ly) a disk. These were (the) best movie(s) from KGB agents who collect(ed) information and even steal (stole) camera(s) if they need to."

Hesemann thinks that if T.´s story is true, we can suspect the existence of a kind of Soviet MJ12 which ordered the collection of this exciting material. In one of his e-mails, dated February 22, 2002, he mentioned the fact that Mikoyan´s brother "create(d) the MIG and it was under this program that they design or try to make aircraft that was (were) copy (copies) of UFO(s) that was (were) reported. They also study reports and yes, as you know (,) there was a secret group."

Do we indeed face a major breakthrough by this unexpected release of unique, formerly top secret UFO footage from the archives of the KGB? Indeed, surmises Hesemann, if T´s grandfather was truly a member of the Soviet intelligence community or nomenclature, we have to assume that he asked his former comrades for a video collection of some of the best UFO footage from their archives because he was personally interested in the subject.

During the breakdown of the Soviet Union, followed by the independence of Armenia (and with it the end of the control by Moscow), this is very well possible. In these times, personal friendships and connections were more important than old orders and classifications.

Hesemann's conclusion is that it is very well possible that T´s story is true just the way he told it. In the investigation of this case we have to consider that the footage was most probably originally shot on 16 or 35 mm and later during the 1990's - copied on video. On most of the seven films the German UFO expert received, the camera is stable, seems to be fixed, indeed indicating surveillance - or   gun cameras. On the other hand, a suspicious element in the lack of camera movement is that it would make it easier to copy "artificial" (computer-generated) UFOs into pre-existing footage. But then remains the question how a hoaxer would obtain raw footage from airborne and landed MIGs on Soviet Air Force Bases which, without the UFOs, make no sense at all.

On March 26, 2002, Michael Hesemann received some more stills from the six alleged KGB UFO films he is supposed to receive in the nearest future. He posted the stills with the limited information available. Hesemann also published the information revealed by his source, T., an Armenian student residing in the Czech Republic. The source stated:

"For the photo that show(s) the MIG jet you will see these red spots. This is interesting because the Russians used to put their cameras in a box to protect them from the weather and I remember as a kid we used to steal them sometimes in Armenia. And we would open up the box and get the camera and we would laugh because sometimes the Russians (did not) clean the glass the camera sat in from the box and it makes some of the images not high quality. The irony being that the Russians was concerned about their cameras being taken to be sold on (the) black market and would sacrifice image quality! So this show(s) that image video is from (an) old Russian camera and (through a) box to keep (the) camera from heat and snow."

"On the other MIG plane, might not be MIG as it is propellar (propeller) plane, this movie (film) show(s) a pilot in his plane and he stick his hand out when the UFO appear from nowhere and you can see him move around and look up and down and he have (has) headphones on."

"These last photos show a dark triangle (next to the crescent).   Near (the) end of (the) video it show(s) how the triangle) reflect(s the) moon light on the (its) bottom."

It is up to Michael Hesemann to reveal what he has obtained from his sources.

PRAVDA REGARDING THE KGB AND UFOs

The word pravda means truth in Russian. Perhaps there is some truth in the report published in the Russian newspaper PRAVDA in its April 1, 2003. Pravda reports the KGB ordered 4 million soldiers to watch the sky in search of UFOs until the dissolution of the KGB and the Soviet Union in 1990.

Yuri Andropov, leader of the Soviet Union's KGB showed an acute interest in the UFO and ordered the creation of a program that lasted 13 years that forced each soldier to monitor the Russian sky in search of sightings (the SETKAs, of course...). Stunning information came to light in 2003.

Igor Sinitsin, who worked with Andropov for six years (as his aide) in the Politburo, revealed that the Soviet leader maintained a file on the UFOs in his daily agenda. Yuri Andropov, the former ascetic Soviet leader and feared, long-time head of the KGB, had a keen personal interest in UFOs. Andropov kept a file on the UFO phenomena in his desk. Sinitsin, who revealed the information to the Observer, mentioned that one of his responsibilities was to monitor the foreign press and he brought Andropov a Stern magazine piece about UFOs. The year was 1977, and the Petrozavodsk Phenomenon was on the minds of Western observers, underground Ufologists, and KGB officers. Sinitsin was hesitant about presenting the piece from Stern to his grim superior, lest he be considered a lunatic, but Andropov's reaction was much unexpected. Andropov handed Sinitsin the text of an official report he had ordered from the counter-espionage directorate. The text described a UFO appearance in Astrakhan that an officer had seen while fishing.

According to Sinitsin, it was Andropov who was instrumental in the creation of the SETKA programs.

Sinitsin added that the KGB controlled what was published on this subject in many other countries. Both military and civilian UFO research centres were created under its direction.

(http://english.pravda.ru/society/2003/04/01/45389.html)

The KGB files that have so far been released are undoubtedly only the tip of the iceberg, but if nothing else they do provide a fascinating glimpse into the study of UFO's by this organisation. It is without doubt that like their counterparts at the CIA, the KGB has files on US UFO sightings as well. It is hoped once again that greater openness in the former USSR will allow access to all such files and that they will fall into the hands of genuine researchers and UFO research centres.

Added in 2009 (Philip Mantle).

As stated in the beginning of this chapter, On October 24th, 1991, documents were provided to former Soviet cosmonaut Pavel Popovich, the then the President of the All Union Ufological Association in Russia. These files contained copies of UFO reports sent to the infamous KGB. An accompanying letter was written by the Deputy Chairman of the Committee for State Security USSR, N.A. Sham. The files consisted of handwritten reports, typed testimonies, notes from KGB informers, crude drawings and eyewitness reports of UFOs. This cooperation between UFO researchers and the KGB was unprecedented and was a landmark in UFO research in the Soviet Union and possibly the world. Sixteen years later we have managed to catch up with the now former Deputy Commander of the KGB, and published here for the first time is an interview with the man himself.

Translated by Paul Stonehill and reproduced with the kind permission of NTV.

In June 2007 I was asked for an interview by NTV. NTV is one of the largest TV companies in Russia. Apparently they were making a new UFO documentary and wanted to discuss with me my research into the Alien Autopsy film and the book I had co-authored with Paul Stonehill (Mysterious Sky-Soviet UFO Phenomenon).

The journalist Alexey Egorov along with his camera man and translator Elena Volkovaya duly arrived and the interview took place at my home in West Yorkshire. After the interview we discussed many things and Alexey informed me that he had interviewed the former Deputy Chairman of the KGB Nikolay Sham, and discussed with him their release of official KGB UFO files to Russian UFO researchers. Alexey went on to say that he could provide me with a transcript of his interview with Nikolay Sham. This duly arrived via email and was quickly translated by my colleague Paul Stonehill. Nothing has been omitted from the following interview, although Paul Stonehill has inserted a few things in brackets for clarification purposes only.

The full interview is reproduced here with kind permission of NTV in Moscow.

Nikolay Alekseyevich Sham was born in 1940. He was in the KGB from 1966 to 1991. From 1974, he worked in the central administration of the KGB. He was involved with the operational, technical and scientific projects. In 1986 he was with the commission that investigated the Chernobyl Disaster. His rank was deputy chief of the 6th Directorate of the KGB (this is where revolutionary scientific ideas and hi-tech technologies were researched and provided protection from foreign agents; this is also where the Soviet economic espionage against other nations was generated). He left the KGB in 1992, because of health reasons.

In 1999 he headed a private corporation, Greenmaster, involved in the production of various devices using technologies of the defence industry. Later he was the General Director of First Leasing Company (2003). He is mentioned in Russian media in connection with paranormal phenomena.

The former KGB Major-General, Nikolay Sham, who for a time served as a KGB deputy chairman, had turned over to cosmonaut Popovich a 127-page record of anomalous events observed on the territory of the former Soviet Union and in the Russian Federation.

INTERVIEW:

Nikolay Alekseyevich Sham. (NAS)
Alexey Egorov (AG)

AG: "Nikolay Alekseyevich, this document here from the KGB, sent to Cosmonaut Pavel Popovich; did you send it?"

NAS: "Quite right."

AG: "What year was it?"

NAS: "It was in '91; the document's registration indicates so, that is why the year was '91.

AG: "Hence, you sent a complete file of documents from the KGB?"

NAS: "Quite right. I simply (unclear-P.S.) story, why the accumulation of these documents took place specifically in the KGB. There was a special decree of the Government and the Central Committee of the Communist Party of the Soviet Union about the commencement of the research of these phenomena that occur in nature. According to this decree all law enforcement agencies (KGB, Ministry of Defence, Ministry of Interior Affairs, and the border guards) had to inform and report to the Centre about facts they had been receiving regarding all such phenomena in nature. And all the agencies had factually accumulated the information. But the KGB was not engaged in research of such issues; it is just that some administration, some special department, if they would get some eyewitnesses of all that was happening in the atmosphere... they would take explanations and mostly hand-written materials that were sent there, describing how they saw (phenomena-P.S.), what they felt during (sightings-P.S.); describing the background of the event, and so on. All that we had eventually accumulated...accumulated, and by the same decree a few academic institutes were obliged to undertake (measures-P.S.) in order to research all these effects, various phenomena, and come to some conclusion of every incident. The main institute in the Academy of Sciences selected and appointed (to head the research-P.S.) was the Institute of Space Studies. All interesting facts were always addressed. Experts, scientists left for the place of the incident, asked questions, took soil samples, took various measurements, and so on; and reached some conclusion based on the results of the event or a fact (that was being researched-P.S.). This work was conducted for several years, and some time in mid '85-'86, in that area, it was completed, this work… and produced was a report about all the events that were registered through a number of years over the territory of the Soviet Union.

I remember that report; I held it in my hands. Of course, I do not remember all of the details there, but from what I remember now, up to 70 percent of all phenomena that were somehow registered had been explained".

AG: "They were explained from the point of view of classical science?"

NAS: "Quite right."

AG: "And, (remaining-P.S.) 30 percent?"

NAS: "Well, 30 percent…of those 30 percent, half were explained; not just one explanation, but variations of: it could be explained this way, or that way. But not in the sense that again, (it was-P.S.) some extraterrestrial civilization, its manifestation, and so on. No. And some 10-15 percent could not be explained at all…what it was, what effects, manifestations, what kind of phenomena occurred in nature, atmosphere, and so on".

AG: "Do you remember any examples of what could not be explained"?

NAS: "Mostly it…things that could not be explained, when some object materialised. Observed was a materialised object, mostly they were spots, some luminescent points, something else of different configurations and so on. As for materialised objects, that truly, if they were photographed, they had a materialised background in the shape of a saucer, some cylinder, or something similar. All such things, of course, could not have been explained: what it was, how one can comprehend all of it. That is what I remember from everything that took place back then. Moreover, all these sharp increases in public interest, they take place periodically. Time after time, the same question…you are fifth or sixth party that come with the same question. Also, from the West I was approached, why? Because these materials; this digest, travel all over the world".

AG: "All comes from this letter, because after this letter, the KGB secret files were sent to Ufologists".

NAS: "No, there was not any secret document".

AG: "That is, the documents were not secret before?"

NAS: "Of course… quite right. Imagine, some citizen   saw   some luminescent loop, and he wrote about it. The officer on duty of some administration or a special department received this information, registered in the logbook, wrote an accompanying letter, and sent to the Centre. What secrets are here? No secrets at all. On the other hand, the explanation for all such phenomena in most cases…you understand, tests were conducted, launches were performed, airplanes fly about, helicopters fly about, and the space is full of space (manmade-P.S.) objects and fragments of the space objects that periodically descend and enter the dense layers of the atmosphere. That is on one hand. On another hand, so-called "mirage" phenomena, mirages. You know, you have heard of mirages. Things related to crashes, disasters; aircraft crash when (the craft-P.S.) falls apart in flight and falls to the ground and so on. That is, a multitude of things that due to some optic distortions and so on, sometimes create such background, that really it can appear that you are in some fairy tale world, and are surrounded humanoids, that another civilization attacks the Earth, and so on. In all of my life I have never met such a fact or event, or something similar, as a result of which one could with some certainty and credibility say, that this was appearance of an extraterrestrial civilization. In all of my life, regretfully, nothing like that happened. At the same time, if we, for example, will find explanations for all of that…Here in Russia now, for some years there is research, various experiments; at their core lies, to say generally, registration of the Galactic and Universal influence on the Earth. If one can imagine this entire world…

AG: "In this file people write… "I saw a strange object, a luminescent cloud". This is not a hallucination; here he exactly…"

NAS: "And I want to address this point…how one can explain such things. Here, based on the results of the work that is being performed here in Russia. What is the heart of the problem? If we imagine this Earth where we live - it is constantly subjected to the effects of the external environment. In fact, we have…we have gravitational fields. Further…we have the Sun, and gigantic energy of the Sun comes to the Earth. Correct? Then, we have heavy planets, we have galaxy, we have so-called "relic radiation"; we have a tremendous amount of electromagnetic fields with different frequencies, and so on. And human being, it is also such a being that has everything moving inside, shifts. You know, there is some aura around a human being; a human being emits some radiation, and so forth and so forth. As a principle, one cannot exclude that in conjunction with certain factors and creation of certain fields, with manifestation of certain electromagnetic fields with certain frequencies there comes some influence on human beings. And results of these studies demonstrate, really definitely and truly demonstrate, that a human being, entering into the area of influence of such natural phenomena…he starts changing, this human being. That is, in principle, he comes to the point where he ceases to comprehend. That is, entering into the field, into this zone, that can continue for dozens of minutes… he becomes inadequate, this human being".

AG: "Can the same objects often be called hallucinations?"

NAS: "Quite so …in the mind of the human being affected by all that, it can (be a hallucination-P.S.), on one hand. On the other hand, because the Earth, too, is not of one origin, that is, there are so-called break-up lines. What is the break-up line? To speak figuratively, it is electrolyte. In the fissure, there is electrolyte. And as this is electrolyte, and imagine, there is some movement of this firmness, naturally it comes (movement-P.S.), currents are registered, and the mechanism...of the equipment in the cables registers currents up to 27 amperes!

AG: "Can you imagine the power that comes as a result of these waves, radiation that comes from the very Earth?"

NAS: "Neutron streams. Neutron streams, they come from space, neutron streams come from the Earth. And this gigantic energy component in various shapes...and what is a human being in comparison to all this power as such? The water, too...it is the stuff that, as it is said, the original mother of all that exists."

AG: "These accumulated documents the Ufologists nicknamed Blue File... Do you know the fate of the Blue File (name given for the KGB UFO documents PS), what happened with it, after Ufologists were given these documents?"

NAS: "Also, there was some interest two - three years ago in the same subject, in this file. I offered them to just meet, I know some Ufologists, I offered to meet them in order to...and I organised this meeting; I do not know what happened after that, but I did previously speak with these comrades on the subject of all these documents. And they said, generally, with regret, with resentment, they told me that all of the materials that had been accumulated in the institutes and so on, it did, to say figuratively, left Russia.

AG: "They say, for five hundred dollars..."

NAS: "In fact...with such (great-P.S.) resentment I was told of all these things. Indeed, some unscrupulous people used the situation, the lawlessness and uncertainty that exist in the country, and tried to make business out of it. And in fact, these materials left the country".

AG: "I can give this example. The letter was addressed to Pavel Popovich. Three days ago we posed a question to Popovich, and he said: let me go through this file, I want to understand, what is there, because he (Popovich-P.S.) did not see.

NAS: "In this case, it was, so to say, the enthusiasts of this field (Ufology - P.S.), they are in the world, enthusiasts of this field, because a human being in its essence is such, he needs something that is always certain, that is why people have sorts of hobbies..."

AG: "How seriously can we take these here shots of the flying saucer?"

NAS: "Firstly, I know absolutely nothing about this. This is the first thing. I can only comment that in the Soviet Union during the period of, so to say, blooming of the rocket-space system industry here, every year more than 100 satellites of various types had been launched. We had that main spacecraft that is still with us, the piloted Soyuz craft, and its descending capsule. At the same time, our other organisations developed completely different systems, including (those for-P.S.) evacuation of the crew, and landings. These systems had been tested, and really they were in their essence, unique, these systems. It seems to me, one of the emergency breakdown situations connected to the experimental work to develop these systems, is depicted in this film. This is most likely. Usually, when there was an emergency breakdown situation, naturally, the site would be sealed off, and experts would arrive there. In principle, all these developments were conducted in the interests of the Ministry of Defence, interests of the Armed Forces. They were not the only developments; they were done in the interests of the Ministry of Defence.

AG: "And that, precisely, is what could have taken place?"

NAS: "Quite right. That very "Buran" (This was a Soviet attempt to create a space-shuttle like vehicle PS) that we created, the orbital craft, it was preceded by a bunch of experiments, connected with tests of various models and so on and so forth. That is, we had a massive volume of undertakings in that direction; various undertakings. Long-term orbital stations, like Mir, this currently international...All of this was preceded by military developments, they were completed these military developments, they were in use and so on"

AG: "If this here autopsy took place, would you be informed?" (Most likely TNT TV show The Secret KGB Files broadcast in the USA in 1998).

NAS: "Of course, naturally...Such event, it just could have gone unnoticed, could not have. Why? Because the KGB, counterintelligence, it was concerned with all our military-industrial sites, that is why...such event, if it truly took place, of course the KGB would have been in the know. I have no doubts about that whatsoever. That is why here, whatever is taking place (in the film-P.S.), and I do not know what it is. Why? Because, in reality, experiments did take place...

And then, we had lots of programs for the study of the planets of the Solar system. If you look at all the apparatuses, which descend, be it on Mars, be it Venus, or our moonwalkers and so on. And there, imagine, how many experiments were conducted here on Earth to supply this or other Martian program, or a program connected with launch of our apparatuses to Venus? These apparatuses were of various shapes. Mostly, of course, they were spherical. Why? Because, for example, it lands on Venus with a parachute, naturally, the best is the spherical shape. As for the strategic weapons that we had created... Strategic weapons, before they are added to the armoury, they (weapons-P.S.) go through a whole series of design experiments. When it flies, the missile, one part separates, the second part separates, the third...There are emergency landings, with breakdowns, and the missile has these disks, these parts...There can be anything, in fact...and in all the cases, you can imagine, you prepare for turning over for utilisation of some strategic complex. And suddenly, in the final stage, an emergency breakdown takes place. The chief, general designer, he has to understand the reason for this breakdown, which is why all fragments had been always collected. And always, special units were dispatched..."

AG: "Nikolay Alekseyevich, in 1991, with this file, at that moment, what was your position in the KGB?"

NAS: "From September '91 I was Deputy Chairman of KGB and remained at that position until June of '92. And, then left because of health reasons".

AG: "In your service, what did you oversee or control that is connected with what we now call UFO; what units and projects were under your control?"

NAS: "That subject of UFO appeared in mid '70s. I already mentioned...From mid -'70s there was a sharp increase, related to these unidentified flying objects. There was a resolution of the government and Central Committee of the Communist Party of the Soviet Union to conduct related projects to bring clarity to these phenomena that took place in the country. This resolution was made, and all law enforcement agencies - Ministry of defence, KGB, Ministry of Interior Affairs - were obliged to receive information from citizens regarding such events and send this information to the centre.

Thus, this system was created, worked out, and from all the corners of the nation, wherever something happened, related to such events and phenomena, all this came to us, to the Centre. And from the Academy side, several institutes were obliged to conduct research of the phenomena that were registered on Earth.

The Institute for Space Studies was designated to be the main one. And for several years this work had been conducted; it was completed some time in mid '80s; a report, a fundamental report was produced, where, generally, all collected matters, related to the events in this or that corner of the country, all were put on shelves, systemised, materials were related to every (appropriate-P.S.) event, location of the event, time of the event, what eyewitnesses, what did they observe, what did they feel at the time, what effects and what shape the thing had - all this was systemised; they even made tabular shapes, shapes and silhouettes (outlines-P.S.) of UFOs that had appeared in the atmosphere.

In most cases, experts went to the most interesting sites. Performed appropriate measurements, conducted questioning of eyewitnesses, and conducted various researches of sorts, and so on. And as a result some conclusion was made for every event.

I remember, around seventy percent of the events were provided with real and objective explanations. What were they connected with? Tests of aviation technology, missile technology, launches of space objects, parts of spacecraft objects falling into the atmosphere, aircraft technology disasters, some cataclysms in nature connected with something being discarded and so on. That is, everywhere they found an explanation.

But in thirty percent of cases, it is as if half of an explanation was given, but not a single one, meaning that yes, something took place, but facts that certainly confirm what is, are not sufficient. And in some instances, simply due to lack of information and due to dearth of any material proof at the incident site, no conclusions were made.

The annual report was completed somewhere in mid '80s. The KGB itself, naturally, did not research these issues; we did not have such direction. There simply was collection, gathering; and periodically the materials, as they say, were dumped into the Institute of Space Studies or other departments, depending again on the contents of an event, as they say. That is what took place".

AG: "Who took the lead in the government to issue resolutions; was it Brezhnev himself; did it fascinate him, was he interested in it? Why all of a sudden in the mid '70s this resolution came about, and who took the lead?"

NAS: "I do not know about taking lead. After all, at the time we had a military-industrial commission, and in cat, many things were originated there. But who specifically at the military-industrial commission all of a sudden took the lead, I do not remember…Most likely it (the initiative-P.S.) could had been the military-industrial commission, or, let's assume, we had the rocket-space technology field; the Ministry of General Engineering Industry, it could have come from there. Or, for example, from the same Academy of Sciences. That is, where would the initiative come from? Well, the initiative came about because the media, as they say, began to play up with things, as such. And since it began to play up, our government and Party always reacted to such things. I cannot say who took the lead with the release of the resolution. The topic was named, I recall, Setka AN (A sharp increase in UFO activity in 1977/78 had forced the appropriate departments with the USSR Academy of Sciences to agree a research program for anomalous phenomena. The code name for this program was SETKA AN-P.S.), the name of this subject, the Setka AN program. And since then…"

AG: "Why Setka AN?"

NAS: "I do not know why it was exactly Setka AN. I cannot say. That did not interest us; what was interesting was why? Because…As a matter of principle, all these things, (unclear)… that take place in the atmosphere, and that assume such various forms, all this, generally, first of all are connected with, of course, power engineering, with electromagnetic fields, with massive radiation that surround us. This radiation…just the enumeration, as they say, God knows how much there is, starting with… (unclear)…was given a Noble Prize for discovering this relic radiation. This scientists had discovered first, launching a specialised satellite, and see how the Americans had developed that topic, and received a Noble Prize for it. And our program was terminated, did not get to be developed.

End of interview.

You don't have to be Einstein to see that Sham is still a little guarded all these years later. It is nonetheless interesting to note that he readily admits that a large percentage of things did remain unidentified and he did clarify what western researchers had speculated about for years, the fact that the Soviets used UFO stories to mask weapons testing. The reason for this is that they were breaking a number of international treaties at the time.

CHAPTER 35

SOVIET COSMONAUTS AND UFOs

EARLY VISITORS

When the first Soviet satellite (and the world's first artificial satellite Sputnik) was launched from the Baikonur Cosmodrome (a designated space-vehicle launching site) by a Sputnik (R-7) rocket, nothing out of the ordinary was reported. Perhaps ET life forms missed the historic occasion, or the earthlings were too preoccupied and stressed to look around them for unusual phenomena. But beginning with the second launch in November of 1957, the unexplained observations came at full force. On November 3, Sputnik 2 was launched from the Baikonur Cosmodrome with the dog Laika aboard.

Eyewitnesses recalled that on that day, about an hour before the launch at some distance from the cosmodrome's facilities, there suddenly appeared a strange, immovable luminescent object. Its shape was spherical, and it hovered at a low altitude. A few days later L. Corrales, a scientist in Venezuela, took some photographs of the Soviet satellite in flight, and observed that an unidentified object flew alongside the craft. It distanced itself, and then again approached the Soviet craft. The strange object was definitely not a stage-rocket. Was it Soviet dog Laika aboard the craft that stirred up curiosity of aliens?

UFOs OVER THE COSMODROMES

Ever since, almost every launch of Soviet space vehicles was accompanied by reports of appearance of UFOs in the vicinity of Soviet cosmodromes. The USSR was by no means the only place where such sightings took place. But in the USSR, people were not allowed to discuss such sightings. Then when thousands of people witnessed sightings of unusual objects, the authorities began publication of reports and commentaries that debunked any unauthorised explanation of this anomalous phenomenon. To preclude unhealthy conclusions by Soviet populace, scientific officialdom attributed each and every incident to ball lightning, fragments of stage-rockets, Aurora Borealis...you name it. What could the officials do when scientists would observe UFOs? In 1982, M.L. Gaponov was a noted Soviet scientist involved in the geophysical and medico-biological research; a participant in international geophysical scientific expeditions to the North Pole. That year Gaponov was working in the Dubna Cosmonaut Training Centre. He personally observed how a gigantic, cigar-shaped UFO hovered over the Star City. Gaponov was by no means the only Soviet scientist to gaze upon anomalous phenomena, as we have seen throughout the book.

While trying to persuade Soviet population that UFOs and aliens are inventions of the hostile bourgeois propaganda, under a regime of complete secrecy, the Soviets had researched all anomalous phenomena that came their way. We have yet to see the most secret documents and findings of the research, ten years after the collapse of the USSR.

But the objects dubbed as UFOs do not care about terrestrial political regimes. The 1990s were no different to them than the 1950s. As reported by former Commander of the Russian Military-Space Forces, General Vladimir Ivanov, not that far away from the Baikonur Cosmodrome, at a high altitude, three objects were registered by radar. This was in the early 1990s. It could not be determined what the nature of the objects was. Definitely, they were not aircraft.

SIGHTINGS IN SPACE

Throughout the history of the Soviet space program its cosmonauts had observed interesting and unusual phenomena. Sometimes they even talked about it. Vladimir Lyakhov once remarked about a very unusual phenomenon he observed from his spaceship looking down on Earth: two gigantic waves ascended from the waters of the Indian Ocean, and crashed onto each other. The mass of water resulting from the crash seemed to be a giant mountain that had vanished in an instant (published in Tekhnika-Molodezhi, Issue 3, 1980). Vladimir Kovalenok reported a very similar water pillar of over 100 kilometres in height in the Timor Sea near Australia (NLO magazine, 10/11, 1996). Yevgeniy Khrunov, a scientist and cosmonaut, remarked back in 1979, in an article published in Tekhnika-Molodezhi (Issue 3) that thousands of people observe UFOs. The properties of unidentified objects simply astound the imagination (he was as outspoken in another interview, a year later, see below). This was in the pre-perestroika times, and Khrunov could not speak freely. Aleksei Gubarev went a step further: he admitted that he believed in aliens. Interestingly enough, he mentions the information that the Americans had at their disposal information to confirm his belief (Tekhnika-Molodezhi, Issue 1, 1980,). Valery Rozhdestvensky, a cosmonaut who does not believe in the presence of extraterrestrial civilization anywhere in the close neighbourhood to us, at the same time reveals knowledge about secret rumours or information those outside of special circles could not know. In the article in Tekhnika-Molodezhi (Issue 10, 1980,) he states that he does not believe that a "green (small) man" actually knocked on the porthole of a Soyuz spaceship.

Russian researchers managed to collect more information about cosmonauts and strange phenomena. An article published in Spektra newspaper (Issue 8, Leningrad, 1992) lists several incidents. In 1976 Vladimir Kubasov told a reporter that he and others have numerous facts that prove existence of UFOs. This was after the famous Teheran Sighting. In 1978 Vladimir Kovalenok observed a strange object on August 15 from the Salyut-6 space station: it approached and distanced itself repeatedly. Valery Ryumin and Leonid Popov, aboard the same station in 1980 (June 14 to 15) had observed a school of white luminescent dots that took off in the area of Moscow, and flew into space above their station. They reported it to the ground control.

Here is a sighting that took place on September 2,1978. Soviet cosmonauts Kovalenok and Ivanchenkov observed the shadow of Salyut-6 orbital station over the clouds. The shadow had very strange orange-reddish colour. What's more amazing, it changed its size. The same year, on August 25, both cosmonauts observed iridescent clouds: green, purple, reddish, blue, and even violet. Other Soviet cosmonauts (V. Sevastyanov, P. Klimuk) had reported silvery clouds. Their origin remains unexplained. Sevastyanov was mesmerised by their dull, occasionally pearly-white, cold, glitter. The structure of such clouds was either very thin (or bright) on the edges of the pitch-dark sky, or porous, resembling a swan's wing.

These clouds are said to be a magic spectacle. Russian astronomer Vitold Tsesarsky first reported them in 1885. The clouds are the highest in the Earth's atmosphere, located at the altitude of 70 - 90 kilometres. They consist of diffused particles, its nature still unclear.

Cosmonaut Georgy Grechko was able to photograph an "ice-floe" over the clouds; it was moving through the air. He was shocked; later Grechko was told that under certain conditions of the atmosphere, an optical phenomenon, such as "ice-floes", was possible.

But so far no one can explain away the effect of enlargement of Earth-based objects, as seen from space. Cosmonaut Vitali Sevastyanov reported that when he flew over the city of Sochi in his spacecraft, the weather was clear and sunny. He observed the city's harbour... and his own home. Hard to believe, but he did clearly see, from space, the small two-story building he grew up in. Cosmonaut Yuri Glazkov, while in space over Brazil, discerned a tiny highway, and a second later, saw a blue bus moving along the highway. He could not explain how was able to see that, but insisted that he saw it.

Georgy Grechko and Yuri Romanenko had also reported to the Tsentr (ground control centre) that while in their orbital station over the Falkland Islands they had actually observed huge letters. The photograph was delivered to Earth by visiting cosmonauts Janibekov and Makarov.

In his interview with Vechernyaya Moskva newspaper (1978), Romanenko recalled that in December of 1977, he and Grechko had observed an object that chased the Salyut-6 orbital station. It was a small, metallic body, its size difficult to estimate. Romanenko was even able to draw it. Later he denied his own conclusions, and said the object was nothing other than a waste capsule. Grechko, too, first discussed UFO observations during his flight, and later denied any.

As for Kovalenok, he reported seeing other strange phenomena in 1978. Thus on October 2, he observed a shadow from his Salyut-6 over the cloud below. The clouds were of eerie orange-reddish colour, and the shadow changed its dimension inexplicably. This was reported in NLO Magazine in the October/November 1996 issue. The source is G. Lisov, a noted researcher and journalist, whose connections are enviable. Georgy Grechko reported a strange being of gigantic dimensions over Mongolia. Later Grechko and Romanenko reported to the ground control about the gigantic letters they observed over the Falkland Islands. Vladislav Volkov, who perished in 1971, recalled the inexplicable noises he had heard in space, in his intercom headset. Dogs barking. Babies crying. The earth was below, and he was in orbit, yet he heard strange noises. To his death Volkov was not able to explain what he felt. Gagarin and Leonov heard music that the former explained as "not of this Earth". Not everything could be explained by sensory depravation. Nor did everyone involved attempt to seek explanations (NLO, 1999).

The very same year, on July 12, Soviet cosmonauts Anatoly Berezovoy and Valentin Lebedev were able to observe on the monitor's screen of the Salyut-7, an unusual drop-shaped object. It flew between the orbital space station and: Progressor-14" craft, from somewhere above. They reported about it to the Tsentr.

An interesting interview was published in Sputnik magazine. The theme was UFOS through the eyes of cosmonauts. It contained stories by ten Soviet and American space explorers. Only one did not refute the possibility of UFOs coming to our galaxy. Yevgeny Khrunov actually mentioned that it is not possible to deny their (UFOs) presence in our galaxy. Thousands of people have observed them. Maybe they are but optical illusions, but some of their characteristics, for instance the change of their flight course at 90 degrees, boggle imagination.

Pavel Popovich became a cosmonaut in 1960. He participated in a number of important space flights. This was a cosmonaut who reported a curious sighting he had in January of 1978. This happened over Cuba. An object shaped like a triangle approached the airplane he was in. Its colour was white. Popovich alerted other passengers and crewmembers that also observed the UFO. No one knew what it could be. Its velocity was greater than the plane's speed, and the UFO passed them by. This account was first published in a book of Soviet debunkers in 1988 (Kak rozhdayutsya mifi XX Veka or How the XX Century Myths are born, Lenizdat Publishing). The debunkers could not find any explanation for his sighting. Then Popovich himself repeated it in an interview with ANOMALIYA newspaper (Issue 7, 1993).

In February of 1991 an interview was published with Vladimir Aleksandrov, who was one of the directors of the Cosmonaut Training Centre. He showed a photograph to the journalists; on it they saw a UFO enveloped by a bright cloud. He said that the picture of the flying object was taken on June 14, 1980, by Soviet cosmonauts Valery Ryumin and Leonid Popov. Aleksandrov also explained that the cosmonauts were at the orbit, and were able to observe this UFO. A pillar of light, according to Aleksandrov, ascended toward the near earth orbit from Moscow, and stopped its ascent over Salyut-6. At midnight the two cosmonauts saw the UFO. The Soviets tried to convince the cosmonauts that what they had observed was a satellite launch. But Aleksandrov refuted their explanation using the same photograph. There one could see that the object depicted had nothing to do with any satellites. One could see a saucer-like dark shape inside the bright cloud. The cloud itself was plasma trails emitted by the mysterious object.

SOVIET LUNAR SECRETS

An interview, published in 1991 in Megapolis Express newspaper (Russia), sheds some light on the subject that remains secret even today. The interviewer was journalist Alexander Sidorko. The person he interviewed was an ex-KGB officer by the name of Vadim Petrov. Mr. Petrov was responsible for the safety and the secret identities of Soviet test-cosmonauts (as compared to test pilots). There are test pilots in any nation that makes its own planes or has an air force. But few people, according to Petrov, knew about the Soviet test-cosmonauts. Those who possessed the knowledge included the General Secretary of the Communist Party; the chief of the KGB; Petrov; and a very limited group of medical doctors, spaceship designers, and operators (close to 15 people). The very existence of the test-cosmonauts was one of the most guarded secrets of the Soviet Union.

The detachment of test-cosmonauts had been created even before Yuri Gagarin's flight. The chief of the KGB at the time, Semichastniy, came up with the idea. The KGB was sure that the automatic equipment on unmanned stations was reliable. But the prestige of the Soviet Union depended on the success of its space program. Soviet unmanned space stations could not fail, and their missions had to be completed. Hence, the decision was to equip some of the stations with pilot modules. The cosmonauts could control the flight through manual control and subsequently report all collected information upon their return. The reasoning of Semichastny was that when actual control would be in human hands, the safety of the flights would be assured.

Only the KGB volunteers were accepted for the secret detachment. Acceptance followed a screening process. Even those who did not make it to be test-cosmonauts were sworn to secrecy.

Vadim Petrov began his career with the detachment in 1969. The Lunokhod (Moonwalker) project was in progress. Lunokhod, pride of Soviet science, was a moon exploration vehicle.

The two test-cosmonauts in training for the flight to the Moon were known as Number 13 and Number 14. Petrov told Sidorko that in his opinion, prior to the Lunokhod project there might have been a dozen other flights. And the true names of the test-cosmonauts remained a State secret.

It was common knowledge of those involved with the Lunokhod project that the men behind the faceless numbers would never return to Earth. They were to stay in a separate module. Once they would descend to the lunar surface, they had to locate the Lunokhod vehicle. Then their mission was to repair the chassis, align the tuning of solar batteries, and finally, provide the corrected directions for television cameras. Apparently, the lateral shots of the Lunokhod were made by the test-cosmonauts.

According to Petrov, the KGB officers in charge of the program actually wept. The volunteers were heroes who guided the station to the Moon and carried out the Lunokhod program projects. Whether drugged "zombies", or psyched-up heroes, their death was a tragic episode in the history of Soviet space exploration.

FLYING SAUCERS WILL HELP YOU

UFOs and aliens were not forbidden subjects for Soviet cosmonauts, as long as they - the cosmonauts - were utterly circumspect. Yuri Malishev, a highly decorated veteran of the program, revealed that thousands of people had observed the UFO phenomenon. It is the nature of UFOs that remains elusive, not the objects themselves. Even though there may not be aliens in the vicinity of Earth, their visit will take place, and they will not immediately establish contact. We, Earthlings, will become the objects of unilateral observation, and there will not be mutual interaction. This was stated by Malishev in Tekhnika-Molodezhi, Issue # 11, 1981 (after the Fifth Expedition had landed and brought their film to Earth, see below- authors). Then he added something quite revealing. Aliens and their "flying saucers" have long ago entered the world of space exploration. Every space flight is completely imitated on Earth using the space simulator. Whatever happens on the simulator may happen in the orbit. The training becomes more complicated, on purpose: even rare incidents are simulated. Sometimes an instructor fails to enter the data necessary, and a system of the simulator fails. Malishev hastens to add that such occurrence never took place in real life, but just in case, the crew has to react as it is real. When the information needed to correct the mishap remains elusive or unavailable, the instructor remarks, in a sarcastic fashion: A flying saucer is on its way, and you will receive all that you need. A hatch opens up (the one cosmonauts use to enter the simulator), and the required information ("a parcel from aliens") is given to the trainees. How touching. In light of all that we already know, the remarks are more sinister than hilarious.

SECRETS OF THE FIFTH EXPEDITION

Soyuz T-4 Soviet spaceship was launched into orbit on March 12, 1981. Vladimir Vasilyevich Kovalenok, Commander, and Viktor Petrovich Savinikh, Flight Engineer, piloted it. On March 13, 1981, the spaceship successfully docked with Salyut-6.

Salyut-6 was the second generation of space platforms built by the Soviets, launched on September 29, 1977. The first crew of cosmonauts went aboard Salyut-6 in December 1977, and the final crew departed in May of 1981. Soviet spaceships, Soyuz and Progress class, came in frequently, as Salyut-6 was involved in the most eventful program of space flights: replacement craft went into space to support longer and longer stays aboard the station.

Professor A.I. Lazarev designed the expedition's programs for scientific research. The watch crew of Kovalenok and Savinikh was given the special task to confirm unusual findings brought back by the watch crews of the Second, Third, and Fourth Expeditions. The "silvery clouds" irked Soviet scientists. That much is admitted in a book written by Professor Lazarev, Kovalenok, and S.A. Avakyan (a Soviet astrophysicist), Issledovaniye Zemli s pilotiruyemikh kosmicheskikh korabley or Study of Earth from manned spaceships (Leningrad , Gidrometeoizdat, 1987). What is indeed very strange, all information of the research aboard Salyut-6 from May 14 to 18 is missing from the account in the book. The last entry states that on May 3, 1981 the crew observed "a ray-like structure" to the South-West of Australia.

Several strange incidents had been reported aboard the Salyut-6 in 1978, 1989. By far, the strangest one took place during the Fifth Expedition piloted by Kovalenok and Savinikh.

Allegedly, from May 14 through May 18, 1981, the two cosmonauts had observed an unidentified alien spaceship. Information about the sighting appeared in at least one Soviet publication in the 1990's, O zagadkah NLO, Issue 1 (Estonia, 1990). Lt. General Georgy Timofeyevich Beregovoy (1921-1995) headed training programs for Soviet cosmonauts at the Yuri Gagarin Cosmonaut Training Centre between 1972 and 1987. He was a highly decorated military pilot, and himself a cosmonaut. His role was prominent in a high-level secret meeting in Moscow, in the Gosplan building, after

Kovalenok and Savinikh came back to Earth. Beregovoy, as the articles stated, presented the report as to what had occurred aboard the Salyut-6 to the crowd of two hundred Communist Party leaders, scientists, space exploration experts, and members of the official UFO Study Commission (headed by Pavel Romanovich Popovich, famous Soviet cosmonaut, and husband of Marina Popovich). And Beregovoy showed the film made by Soviet cosmonauts to the astonished gathering of Soviet top brass at the meeting organised upon their return. The film made by Soviet cosmonauts showed that the aliens left their spaceship without any protective suits, and seemingly had no breathing apparatuses. They floated next to their craft, and later floated further away. Information about the contact leaked to the West. There are other interesting accounts of the May 1981 sighting, also some other observations by Kovalenok.

It is noteworthy that Kovalenok tried to present another account to Italian interviewers some years ago. Beregovoy, before his death, was instrumental in the Russian military space program. He also edited the English-Russian dictionary on advanced aerospace systems (Moscow, Military Publishing House, 1993).

Another Soviet publication, Informatzionniy Byuleten NLO (October 1, 1990) contained an account of the conversation between the crews of Salyut-6 and Souz-4 on May 5, 1981. Kovalenok reported seeing an explosion from space. A brightly burning sphere, moving perpendicularly to the ship, elongated like a melon, and then exploded, twice, in its frontal section, and in the rear section. The location was somewhere in the area of Cape Town, South Africa.

THE SALYUT-7 INCIDENT

This happened in 1984, aboard the Soviet orbital station Salyut-7. In view of the dominant ideology, the incident, quite embarrassing to the Marxist-Leninist regime, was hushed up for years. Russian NLO magazine (Issue 9, 1998) carried one account of the incident.

The crew, at the time of the incident, consisted of six people, Leonid Kizil, Oleg At'kov, Vladimir Solovyew, Svetlana Savitzkaya, Igor Volk, and Vladimir Janibekov. The incident began on the 155th day of the station's flight. The crew was busy with planned experiments, tests, and scientific observations. They were about to start medical experiments. All of them were experienced, skilled cosmonauts. Then, something that was out of their experience, knowledge, and understanding had occurred. In front of the Salyut-7 station, out of nowhere, suddenly appeared a large, orange, gas cloud, its origin unknown. The cosmonauts immediately informed the Soviet Mission Control Centre (Tsentr upravleniya poletom, or Tsentr). While the astonished Earth centre analysed the report, Salyut-7 had entered the cloud. The crew had a brief impression that the orange cloud entered their station.

They were all engulfed by the mysterious orange glow, blinded, out of contact with their comrades. But their sight, however, was restored quickly. The cosmonauts stumbled to the station's portholes. What they saw left them speechless: seven gigantic shapes could be easily discerned inside the orange cloud. Their political ideals, their faith in Marxist-Leninist postulates were gone in a flash. None doubted their eyes. None questioned that the shapes turned out to be seven heavenly angels. They (the angels) looked so much like humans, and yet they were different. Yes, the angels possessed huge wings, and blinding halos. The main difference, however, lay in the angels' smiles. When they gazed upon the Soviet crew, they smiled. What wonderful smiles the angels had! recalled Soviet cosmonauts. Smiles of joy, of rupture... No human could smile like that. Ten minutes had gone by quickly. As the clock ticked away the time, the angles disappeared, along with their cloud. The crew of Salyut-7 felt devastating loss. But Earth was demanding explanation. When the Tsentr received the report, it was immediately classified as secret. A special team of doctors was formed to study cosmonauts' well-being. Hence, instead of carrying out further experiments in space, the crew was ordered to measure its own health, physical as well as mental. The tests indicated that the cosmonauts were well and of sound mind. The incident took place before the perestroika period, and in order to create unnecessary furore, the Politburo made sure that the report remained secret. The crew of the Salyut -7 was warned to keep silent. No angels could exist inside or outside the Soviet Union.

WHISPER IN SPACE

There are still episodes of the Soviet space exploration that are not discussed in today's Russia. Such are the accounts of the so-called "space whisper". One former cosmonaut (Cosmonaut X) did reveal some information, but demanded that his name remain anonymous. He recalled that Soviet cosmonauts heard hushed up rumours about the "whisper", but did not share definite information among them, nor reported anything to the doctors. They were afraid that the latter would remove them from the space program. Cosmonaut X and his colleague believed the rumours to be a legend created by the first team of Soviet cosmonauts, to scare the greenhorns. He was wrong.

They were aboard a Soviet spacecraft, flying over the Southern hemisphere, when the Whisper came to them. The narrator said that he suddenly felt as if someone else was next to them. The feeling he had was that some invisible being stared into his back; it was a hard gaze. The cosmonaut had no doubt he was being observed. A second later his comrade, the flight engineer, who was looking into the porthole, sharply turned around and looked about him. Both were quite prosaic people, far removed from any mystical believes. But they were good friends, and knew each other long before the Star City training. That is why they were not afraid to compare their impressions after the episode ended. They received different "texts"... But their initial reaction to the Whisper was identical: both became mute and dumbfounded. The Whisper came from the debts of Cosmonaut X's consciousness. ... You arrived here too early, and you did it in a wrong fashion. Trust me, for I am your ancestor on the maternal side. Do you remember, she told you; back when you were a child, about your great-grandfather, who had founded the D-s plant in the Urals? Sonny, you should not be here, go back to Earth, do not violate the Laws of the Creator...Sonny, you must return, return, return...

The Whisper also told the cosmonaut a very private story, as if to prove his knowledge that had been circulated only inside the family; it concerned the same great-grandfather.

The two cosmonauts were back on Earth two days later. The Whisper came back to them one more time; the "texts" of what it said were the same as the first time; and both felt the alien presence throughout their time in orbit.

The two cosmonauts faced a dilemma: to report the incident or not. If they did, their career could end immediately. They could be considered impressionable people, their psyche too unstable for further flights into space. Other cosmonauts kept somewhat silent about the Whisper, at least nothing was reported to their superiors.

Cosmonaut X and his comrade spent endless hours trying to determine what it was that they had experienced. They were atheists, and both liked science fiction. This led them to a conclusion that alien intelligence, using some king of hypnosis, is determined to prevent the mankind from exploring the outer space. To convince the mankind that its sons and daughters in the outer space are not experiencing hallucinations, hard facts are presented, facts picked up from probing human brains, memories and subconscious. How long have "they" researched our civilization? Perhaps for thousands of years.

But are the aliens so naïve as not to understand that we would see their ploy? Then, if it was not an alien Whisper...then whose? Did the departed relatives truly visit Soviet crews in space? This conclusion shattered the cosmonauts' convictions, their atheism, and their view of the world. Does it mean that there is life after death, and that the consciousness (not the physical body) continues to exist on some other stages of existence? There must be a hierarchy to such stages, and on the top of the hierarchy would be the Creator, as the great-grandfather had informed the cosmonaut.

Their sense of duty told both cosmonauts that a report has to be made. They did not listen to that sense. But some other cosmonauts, who had heard the Whisper, did make reports. As a result, special medical teams were introduced into the training program, top-rated medical hypnotists began to explore cosmonauts' psyches, and the whole fight-training program had undergone changes.

Cosmonaut X, who has since retired, does not know how the Whisper is treated nowadays, and what conclusions Russian scientists have come to (Press-Extra newspaper, Issue 135, 1997). He did say that his whole outlook on life had changed. The outer space is full of intelligence, is much more complicated than we imagine it to be. Our present knowledge does not allow us to understand the essence of most processes taking place in the Universe. Our abilities are still quite limited. But for those who had heard the Whisper one thing is clear: the future exists, and it is endless, just as time and space are endless.

RUSSIAN SPACE PROGRAM AND UFOs

Russian Ufologists Valery and Roman Uvarov interviewed Musa Manarov and Gennady Strekalov, two Russian cosmonauts, for ANOMALIYA newspaper (Issue 13, 1996). The cosmonauts were quarried about the film Marina Popovich showed to Russian Ufologists. Manarov filmed a strange object while he was in space. On 16th of May 1996, Manarov provided more details.

During a routine filming of another Russian craft through the porthole (to record the docking procedure), Mansarov noticed an unusual detail. Something like an antenna was visible at the bottom part of the spaceship, except it was not supposed to be there. It separated from the ship. By that stage, no part of the spacecraft was to separate: Mansarov is a highly experienced cosmonaut, and knows his work. The strange object rotated; its size was hard to ascertain. It was not close, but Manarov did determine that the object was not a screw nut, or anything of the sort. It remained somewhere behind the craft. Mansarov thinks it appeared from behind the spacecraft, and did not shield it from the cosmonaut's view. The object remained in view several minutes. Mansarov is hesitant to determine the nature of the object filmed: he does think its size was close to a metre. Were it of a large dimension, the Americans and the Russians, who track large debris, would have reacted. Mansarov knew that they would follow an object that approached them so close. However, there are cases when radar is not able to register UFOs.

Mansarov revealed interesting information about Russian space training for cosmonauts. Before embarking on a space flight, they signed documents promising that any video films they shoot in space would not be used against the interests of the State or their service. Mansarov entered the cosmonaut service in 1978, and by then, the UFOs were never mentioned, not even once. Mansarov is personally interested in the UFO phenomenon, but does not pursue any research because of many dishonest people who misuse the whole issue. As for the cosmonauts, only the true realists make it to the program: very few of them are prone to imagine things, or have visions. He personally never had a chance to speak to American astronauts about UFOs: there simply was no time to do so. Mansarov tried to assure the interviewer that he personally had not been admonished not to reveal any secrets about UFOs, nor would anyone kill him if he did.

Gennady Strekalov mentioned that he saw strange phenomena several times, but is hesitant to classify it as UFOs. But his colleagues did see "flying saucers", and he envies them. Strekalov did not provide details about their sightings. He described the phenomenon he observed in 1990, during his flight: a sphere over the Newfoundland. The atmosphere was clear and visibility perfect. The sphere was beautiful, and changed colours. It remained visible for ten seconds, and vanished instantly. Strekalov remembers that it had a perfect shape. He reported the incident to the Mission Control Centre, but did not classify it as a UFO (cosmonauts must be cautious, he said). Gennady Manakov was with him, and observed the same. Vladimir Dezhurov observed the other strange phenomenon Strekalov mentioned in 1995. Perfectly shaped clouds, with even edges, as if someone intentionally carved them that way… Mansarov, too, observed such clouds during his flights.

Another respected source of information about Russian space observations is V. M. Trankov. In 1995 he was interviewed by ANOMALIYA newspaper (Issue 13). At the time, an official at the Coordinating Centre of the Russian Space Forces, Trankov revealed that throughout the years, while at the controls of space communications systems (video TV signals from cameras aboard space stations) he had observed strange phenomena. He specified strange pulsation, luminescence, fog-like zones thickening in the middle part; saucer-like shapes. Everything was recorded on magnetic tape. All such materials are kept in the Central space science archives (Russia). He mentioned that the objects recorded at the ground controls were also frequently recorded from space, by cosmonauts; all such materials "are kept". He would not elaborate further. Trankov stated that there had not been contacts with the Americans about anomalous phenomena, but he hoped that it would change. As for the UFO reports, Trankov said there had been several UFO reports by cosmonauts. Overall Trankov was quite cautious during his interview, but did say that there are numerous unidentified phenomena in nature, and that some day researchers will get to study them. Unfortunately, there are no instruments, on many occasions, for the needed research.

UFOs AND THE ABORTED MISSION OF SOYUZ 18-1

Oleg Makarov, a cosmonaut, scientist, writer, and twice decorated Hero of the Soviet Union, died in Moscow in 2003 from a heart attack. His colleague who had flown two space missions with Makarov, a scientist and a cosmonaut Vasily Lazarev, died of alcohol poisoning in 1990.

The secrets of the aborted Soyuz 18-1 mission still remain unsolved. This author has been following the story for years, and collected some fascinating facts about the unusual 1975 mission to the Salyut 4 station.

The mission is referred to in the literature as Soyuz 18-1 (sometimes, Soyuz 18a) since the following Soyuz mission (in May of 1975) received the name Soyuz 18. In the Soviet Union, only successful missions were given numbers…

That year the Soviets wanted to compete with the U.S. Skylab missions, and establish their own space station program. Cosmonauts Lazarev and Makarov were selected for the Spyuz-1 mission. Both were distinguished personalities. Makarov, a graduate of the Bauman Moscow Higher Technical School, had worked in Special Design Bureau Number One, under the legendary Sergey Korolyov. He was selected to be a Cosmonaut in 1966. Makarov was engaged in the Soviet lunar program (later cancelled), and was training for the circumlunar flight. He participated in the Soyuz 12 spaceflight (1973); Vasily Lazarev was the mission commander. This was the first Soviet manned mission in the wake of the Syuz 11 tragedy (three cosmonauts were killed during re-entry). Makarov and Lazarev returned to Earth safely, after two days in space.

In the later years, Makarov had worked for RSC Energia (former Special Design Bureau), for the MIR space station and also the Buran shuttle development.

Lazarev, a colonel of the Soviet Air Force, a fighter pilot, a surgeon and a PhD in medicine, remained a Cosmonaut until 1980s, but did not fly again after the abortive Soyuz 18-1 launch he commanded…They were tough, those two cosmonauts. And they knew how to keep secrets, too.

UFO SIGHTING: APRIL 5, 1975 - UFO AT THE BAIKONUR LAUNCH

The Vostok-1 spacecraft with the world's first space traveller was launched from the Baikonur Cosmodrome, the world's oldest and largest operational space launch facility, fourteen years earlier. So much has happened since then…1975 was an important year for space exploration.

On the morning of April 5, preparations were underway for the launch of the Soyuz-18-1 spacecraft. The weather was clear, the cosmonauts that comprised its crew felt great. Their mission was to reach the Salyut-4 orbital station, relieve the crew of Gubayov and Grechko, and work at the station for 60 days.

According to the retired Soviet colonel Kolchin, a respected author and researcher who has excellent connections, a few minutes before the Soyuz 18-1 launch, Lt. Colonel V. Ilyin had observed a cross-like object of a transparent-grayish colour, hovering at a great altitude in the sky, over the launching area. While he and his chauffeur watched the peculiar object, the rocket was launched. The officer recalled that the weather over Kazakhstan is usually clear some 270 days a year and he could clearly observe all phases of the rocket flights. At the 120th second, the "bokovushki" (boosters) separated in a proper fashion, and flew off to the sides, in a cross-like manner. Lt. Colonel recalled that after that, one can could observe (without using any optical means) a luminescent dot; it was the engine that was working; and then the dot disappeared, too. At the 150th second, the nose flailing (golovnoy obtekatel) separated. But this time, after the "bokovushki" separated, the rocket made some very strange trajectory that was clearly discerned by inversion trail.

So, this was only minutes into the flight, when the separation problems occurred with the Soyuz booster.

Ilyin remembered the "grayish cross "he had observed in the zenith. But the object was not there anymore. His chauffer, Gena, confirmed that he, too, saw the grayish cross.

Vladimir Ajaja, Russia's eminent Ufologist, mentioned this episode in his book Inaya Zhizn' (Moscow, 1998). He added that we would probably never find out whether the ill-fated UFO had any role in the failure of the mission.

But there are other questions about this doomed mission that we may never find out.

THE DOOMED FLIGHT

The four strap-on boosters separated, followed by the nose flailing and the escape rocket. At 261st seconds after their lift-off, the time came for the third stage to break away from the second stage. It was then that the cosmonauts encountered a violent swaying motion that was followed by a loud siren and a red avariya nositelya "booster failure" warning light on the control panel. The lower stage had only partially separated (the third stage had ignited right on schedule), thus threatening to send the spacecraft crashing onto the taiga below. The crew sent repeated requests to the mission control to initiate the abort sequence. Finally, Syuz-18-1 was separated from the wayward booster. Hence, the spacecraft's main engine engaged and pulled clear. The spacecraft's descent module separated from the rest of Soyuz at an altitude. Following a ballistic trajectory, Lazarev and Makarov were subjected to a horrifying 20g re-entry (twice the normal g-load). The cosmonauts most likely suffered injuries as a result. But then the deceleration forces decreased, their spacecraft's parachute system was activated, as well as soft-landing rockets. And so, the Soyuz command module containing the exhausted crew, was separated from the booster, and having plunged back to Earth, came to rest on an Altai mountainside.

According to Ajaja (and the official report) the suborbital flight had lasted 21 minutes and 27 seconds, reached the altitude of 192 kilometres, and flew 1574 kilometres altogether.

VADIM ILYIN'S INFORMATION

Russian journalist Vadim Ilyin (probably, no relation to the Lt. Colonel Ilyin mentioned above...) published an article in issue 16 of NLO, a popular St. Petersburg magazine, in 2004. Kosmonavtov spas NLO (Cosmonauts were rescued by a UFO) was the article heading. He claimed to reveal heretofore unavailable information.

Vadim Ilyin stated that at the 260th second the voice of P. Klimuk, the communications operator at the mission control station was cut off, and the crew heard, for a moment, noise interferences, and then they heard Klimuk's voice again, but it was weak. It sounded as if someone (or something) unsuccessfully tried to imitate human speech. The cosmonauts thought that such noises could be produced by a computer that would try to relay some information through the use of vocal chords. They could not understand the contents of the transmission. A few seconds later they heard the siren and saw the warning light on the control panel.

According to Vadim Ilyin, the cosmonauts heard the same strange sounds again after the 270th second of the flight. The communications with the control centre were sometimes normal, and at other times died down. Then they heard the sounds of awkward imitation of human voice. They could not understand the meaning of the transmission, and wondered how could an outsider could connect to the radio communication channel designated exclusively for the crew's and the mission control centre's use.

THE LANDING SITE

There have been questions as to where exactly the two cosmonauts landed. It was near the town of Gorno-Altaisk (1600 kilometres from Baikonur) not far from the border with Red China. The cosmonauts (according to some sources) believed that they actually landed in China, at that time their country's adversary. When they opened the hatch, the cosmonauts found out that they were surrounded by snow-covered landscape, that their capsule was held by a parachute (caught in a tree according to some sources, and caught by a rock ledge according to others) over a ravine 500-600 metres deep. Makarov managed to fix their whereabouts, and calculated that they landed in the Altai Mountains (some two thousand kilometres from Baikonur). And yet, to be sure their secrets did not become Red China's prize, according to some sources, he and Lazarev burned flight documents. The cosmonauts, feeling the consequences of their landing, nevertheless managed to crawl outside. Vadim Ilyin stated that they were so exhausted that they could not move. Some time later the cosmonauts could move. They put on their thermal clothing, and after burning the documents, switched on the distress signal. They crawled in the deep snow, gathered some twigs, and were able to light a fire. The temperatures that night were sub-zero.

UFO SIGHTING

Vadim Ilyin states that not long after the cosmonauts lit the fire, the night fell, airplanes (not just one...) flew over them signalling that the landing site was found, and flew away.

The wind chased away clouds that arrived in the evening, and calmed down. All of a sudden Makarov and Lazarev heard an increasing audible whistling sound, and at the same time they saw among the stars some luminescent object, hovering right above them. They could neither determine its shape nor its altitude. They observed a bright spot, glittering with violet colour. The object hovered over them for about half a minute, and then, as if confirming that all was in order, it disappeared as suddenly as it had appeared. According to VadimIlyin, Vasili Lazarev told German journalists in 1996 (while in London on a private visit) that he has since been certain that not only had they observed a UFO that night, a UFO tried to contact them using their communications channel. He added that he thinks it was only because of the object's interference that they had landed in the Altai Mountains in one piece and without harm; in the area that resembles the Moon more than the Earth. Asked by journalists as to why neither he nor Makarov did not say anything about the UFO upon their return to Baikonur, Lazarev replied that in those times, should the cosmonauts reveal that they observed unknown objects in the sky or some supernatural phenomena, they would be excluded from any future flights. He added that the tape containing recordings of all their communications with the mission control centre was carefully studied. He never knew about the results of the study, but did learn the tape had disappeared under unclear circumstances.

There is one very clear circumstance that negates Vadim Ilyin's story: Vasili Lazarev died in Moscow, December 31, 1990, of alcohol poisoning...

Oleg Makarov died in Moscow, May 2003, of a heart attack.

Was it a typo in Vadim Ilyin's article in NLO magazine, and the year of Lazarev's visit to London was actually 1986? If so, who were the German journalists who had interviewed him? Who did he visit in London?

THE GEOLOGIST

L. Smirenniy, a scientist at the Research and Technical Centre of Radiation-Chemical Safety and Hygiene, Moscow, Russia and academician at the International Academy of Astronautics, was once a cosmonaut himself. Excerpts from his memoirs were published in Nauka I Zhizn'website (Issue 5, 2007). He recalls speaking with a distinguished and legendary Soviet test pilot, Hero of the Soviet Union, S. N. Anokhin. He worked in the S.P. Korolyov design bureau, and headed a team of the "test-cosmonauts". Anokhin revealed to Smirenniy that having analysed all of Makarov's actions that fateful day, he found that the cosmonaut behaved exceptionally courageously.

Smirenniy who had trained at the centrifuge (at 10-g) realised that after the 20-g re-entry the cosmonauts would bear consequences to their health. Makarov told him that the mission commander Lazarev was not able to find out from the mission control centre about the landing site. It seemed that the centre did not hear their inquiries. Lazarev asked his engineer to determine where they would land. "It would be China or the Pacific Ocean" came back Makarov's sarcastic reply, who added some strong Russian expressions about the failed mission. They did not know that their conversations were transmitted; the centre heard them, but they could not hear the mission control centre...Makarov's opinion about the engines' emergency performance enraged V. P. Glushko, who was the general designer of the mission (and chief developer of the engines). He ordered the transmission of communications to be limited, and stated that Makarov would never fly again. He was wrong.

Smirenniy added that the cosmonauts were initially discovered by geologists. Their small helicopter flew to the slope, and a young man jumped out. He trudged through deep snow, reached the cosmonauts and offered his help. The rescue helicopter arrived in the evening hours, and because of the darkness, could not take the cosmonauts away. The three of them spent the night in freezing temperature. The next morning their rescuers had returned, and the helicopter commander said he could not take a stranger. Makarov firmly stated that they would not leave without the geologist, and the rescue helicopter took all of them aboard. Lazarev would have mentioned the geologist in his recollections...if he ever did speak to German journalists about that alleged UFO they sighted at night.

CONCLUSION

We probably will never find out what really had happened in April of 1975 during the failed Soyuz 18-1 mission. That mission was the only case of a manned booster accident at high altitude.

Vasili Lazarev never flew again aboard Soviet spacecraft. He was discharged from the cosmonaut corps due to illness, and remained a colonel in the reserves.

Oleg Makarov had two more flights into space, the last in 1980. The aborted Soyuz mission was dubbed the April 5 anomaly, and the Soviet government did not acknowledge it until April 7, 1975. Both cosmonauts were eventually awarded the Order of Lenin for their conduct (despite efforts by those officials who sought to deny them the honour), and because of the personal intervention of Leonid Brezhnev they were given monetary compensation for the use of the emergency escape system.

Rumours have persisted for years that American astronauts have encountered UFOs during their various space missions, a great many of which have gone unproven. It would seem, for whatever reason, we have more solid fact-based information on Soviet cosmonaut sightings that there counterparts in the west. It is obvious from the accounts featured in this chapter that Soviet cosmonauts have observed unusual atmospheric phenomenon, perhaps suffered from the ill effects of space travel, but not all of the observations can be discarded so easily. There are a number of sightings made by Soviet cosmonauts that certainly must still remain as unidentified, and like most things in the former USSR, there will undoubtedly be more to learn about such incidents in the future when yet more files are declassified or when more cosmonauts speak up.

CHAPTER 36

RUSSIAN ASTRONOMERS AND UFOs

Astronomers are trained observers. Soviet-trained astronomers are no different, but their observations remained largely unavailable until the 1990's. We already know that S. Korolyov sent Professor Burdakov to the Pulkovskaya Observatory with a letter of recommendation, as a "punishment" for his unauthorised UFO lectures. In those years people reported their UFO sightings to the astronomers, and Burdakov was able to learn of fascinating reports.

What is fascinating is the extent to which the Soviets went to hide the facts that the astronomers did see UFOs. We also discussed a declassified Department of Defence Information Report (U.S.), dated August 19, 1970. The Americans followed Soviet cosmonaut Alexey Leonov during his visit to Japan. The esteemed cosmonaut gave a presentation at the Takai University in Kanagawa Prefecture on May 18, 1970. Leonov said he does not believe in the existence of unidentified flying objects. He stated categorically that there is no record of any of the Soviet observatories, manned by highly trained technicians, ever having seen a flying saucer.

Soviet newspaper PRAVDA stated on February 29, 1968, that astronomers who carefully observe the sky day and night, never see "flying saucers". Both the cosmonaut and the newspaper concealed the true state of affairs; we do not know why, for there were reports of UFOs clearly of interest to astronomers, and reported by astronomers of the Soviet Union.

Back in the 1960's Robert Vitolniek reported something quite unusual. He headed the radio observation station of the ionosphere at the Radio-Physical Observatory of the Academy of Sciences, USSR (Latvia branch). On July 26, 1965 he and others studied the ionosphere and silvery clouds from the observation centre at the city of Ogra. The astronomers saw an unusually bright "star" moving in the westerly direction quite slowly. They used a powerful telescope, and observed a UFO. The object was a lens-shaped disk, its diameter around 100 metres. In the centre there was a clearly defined thickening, like a small sphere. Next to the disk, at a distance of approximately two hundred metres, they saw three spheres, similar to the one in the thickening. They rotated slowly around the disk. The objects were becoming smaller, apparently moving away from the Earth. Twenty minutes later the spheres distanced themselves from the disk, flying in different directions. The sphere in the middle of the disk also separated. Their colour was greenish-pearly and dull. Vitolniek and other astronomers were certain that they observed neither space rocket nor satellite: such objects would have moved at much greater velocities. Of course, no rocket or satellite consisted of different objects, unlike the mysterious objects observed by Soviet astronomers in June of 1965.

Mikhail Gershtein, writing for ANOMALIYA newspaper also collected information about Soviet astronomers and UFOs (Issue 20, 1996).

On July 18, 1967 the Pulkovskaya astronomer G. Poter had observed a strange blast near Kislovodsk. It formed a reddish cloud-sphere, surrounded by waves of white luminescence. His colleagues informed him that several hours before they observed a flying sickle-shaped object. One month later, another astronomer, A. Sazanov saw one more sickle-shaped body in the area. A star-shaped object flying ahead of it accompanied the UFO. The "sickle" finally changed its shape to a disk, and vanished. On September 21, 1968, L. Tsekhanovich, astronomer and lecturer of the Moscow Planetarium observed another "sickle", for an hour. So did many other local inhabitants. Gershtein was able to obtain a statistical analysis of the UFO observations, produced by the Institute of Space Research of the Academy of Sciences, USSR. The report, published in 1979, stated that 7.5% of the UFO observers were astronomers. This was after the Petrozavodsk Phenomenon, when the military research was in full swing. The astronomers could not be silenced (not even when Stalin ruled the Soviet Union), and they talked.

Donatas Myaziyauskas, a Lithuanian astrophysicist, mentioned in an interview to Komjaunimo tiesa newspaper that it is not "random observers" who see UFO and similar phenomena most frequently. Astronomers and meteorologists observe much more, and as experts, are able to classify the object. On numerous occasions Lithuanian astronomers had observed phenomena they could not identify. So did Myaziyauskas, while working in the Moletsky Observatory: he took photos of a "jumping star", an object he could never explain.

In 1978 Lithuanian scientist Dr. Vitautas Straijis published an article in Mokslas ir givanimas magazine. It was titled Anomalous Phenomena in the Atmosphere and Space, and mentioned some thirty UFO reports in the Vilnius Observatory. The most fascinating one, dated August 20, 1974, actually came from different localities at the same time. It described a triangle of 140 metres in size. The UFO hovered over Raseinyai for 12 hours, at the altitude of 20 kilometres.

Then there is Felix Zigel's book UFO Sightings over the USSR-1968

(Volume 1), published by Joint USA-CIS Aerial Anomalies Federation in 1993. It contains a fascinating report, sent to him by astronomers. Surely a prominent personality of the Soviet space program, Soviet cosmonaut Alexey Arkhipovich Leonov must have read Zigel's books, available throughout the black markets of the Soviet Union, and other, more sinister places. But it is not right to blame Leonov for his statements in Tokyo, for he was but a Soviet citizen, and had to "observe the rules"; he was not the one setting the rules.

The place was Soviet Azerbaijan, the year was 1964, and the date was November 30. Observers at the Shemakhinsky Astrophysical Observatory of the Soviet Academy of Sciences in Pirulki observed an unusual celestial object. It moved from west to north, its maximum altitude approximately 30 degrees. The observation of the object began at an altitude of 3 to 4 degrees above the horizon, and they followed it until it attenuated. Its speed was approximately one degree per minute. The path passed seven to ten degrees below the constellation Aquila, a little below the head of Draco, and disappeared two or three degrees to the right of Ursa Major. Two parts of the object were easily distinguished: its head and tail. The head looked like planetary mistiness with a sharp internal edge and a diffused outer edge.

Located in the centre was a star-shaped object of a third or fourth stellar magnitude that was a point even in an AT-1 astronomic telescope. No sound effects were noted.

We have in our possession a copy of the report filed by S. N. Komlev, a Soviet scientist, regarding a UFO sighting he had in September of 1981. Komlev, a trained meteorologist, had professional experience in observation of the atmospheric meteorological phenomena, flights of weather balloons, and more. We thought it would be prudent to include his testimony in this chapter. Komlev sent his report to a Commission for the study of anomalous phenomena (we described such "commissions" elsewhere in the book) in 1985. He read about this Commission in Soviet newspapers.

The night of the observation was at the end of September 1981 (he did not recall the exact date, even during the interview with a member of the Commission), about quarter after midnight Moscow time, that S. N. Komlev, a passenger aboard TU-134 flight from Balkhash to Moscow observed an unusual phenomenon. The airplane at that time was in the vicinity of the Vnukovo Airport, at the altitude of approximately 8 thousand metres, its speed 800 kilometres per hour. The object was seen by almost all of the passengers, who observed it through the portholes. The object was cigar-shaped. Komlev estimated that its size was similar to the size of an airplane hull (if viewed from a distance of 2-3 kilometres). Apparently, the object flew about 30 kilometres above the TU-134, its speed similar to that of the airplane. They could not determine the direction of the flight. The colour of the object was white-yellowish. The observers did not see any sections or components of the object. None of them could identify the object. They saw no residue or inversion. No effect on humans or onboard equipment was detected. The atmosphere at the time was transparent; one could see the stars, and the ground. The sighting lasted about two minutes. Then the airplane changed its course, and they did not see the object again. The airplane was not allowed to land for an extended period of time. Komlev believed this was a consequence of the appearance of the anomalous phenomenon they had observed.

We still do not know why the Soviets attempted to mislead their citizens and Westerners about astronomical observations in such a clumsy fashion. We also may not find out for some time why the U.S. intelligence report mentioned above dedicated a whole paragraph to Leonov's views about UFOs.

One thing is for sure, just like their counterparts in the West, Soviet astronomers have observed and recorded UFO sightings. And like such observations made by anyone else, many of these sightings have gone unexplained despite the obvious academic qualifications and observational expertise held by the various Soviet astronomers who made such observations.

CHAPTER 37

THE PHOBOS MYSTERY

WHAT IS PHOBOS?

In 1959, Iosif Shklovsky, a Soviet scientist and a famous astrophysicist, who co-authored with Carl Sagan a book entitled Intelligent Life in the Universe, expressed an opinion that Phobos was of artificial origin and quite hollow inside. He tried to explain the incredible rotation speed that the moonlet has in relation to the orbit of Mars.

Phobos is a moonlet of Mars. The two Martian moons, Phobos and Deimos, orbit Mars nearly in the plane of its equator. Phobos goes around once every 7.7 hours, and Deimos goes around every 30.2 hours. Mars itself rotates on its axis once every 24.6 hours; Phobos rotates around its orbit much faster. Planet Mars has the highest orbital eccentricity of any planet in our Solar System except Pluto.

Phobos (meaning "fear" in Greek) is the larger of the two tiny moons of Mars. It is but 13.8 miles (22.2 kilometres) across and has a mass of 1.08×10^{16}. It orbits Mars at a mean distance of 5,600 miles (9,000 kilometres). Its major known feature is a large crater, named Stickney, which is 6.2 miles (10 km) wide. American astronomer Asaph Hall discovered Phobos in 1877. It is also very probable that Jonathan Swift knew about the tiny moonlets, and described them in his literally work.

Shklovsky reached a conclusion that Phobos has to be hollow inside. The Soviet scientist went even further, and hypothesised that Phobos is a gigantic space station.

RACE TO THE MOONLET

Those involved in the Soviet space program, as well as their Western colleagues, had been very much interested in Phobos. On July 12, 1988, the Soviets launched two unmanned probes, Phobos 1 and Phobos 2, in the direction of Mars. The probes were actually a joint creation of Western scientists and their Soviet counterparts. It is an important point to remember for anyone doing research of the space probes sent to Mars: the project had international participation from its very inception. Soviet Izvestiya newspaper on March 3,

1989 (S. Leskov's article) reported that data from the probes is transmitted to the European Mission Centre, to France, and to NASA. Nothing was done by Soviets without the input and recommendations of their colleagues. It looks that the JPL in Pasadena was directly involved, too. Leskov was amazed at the level of mutual participation. Just as equally amazed were authors of this book, after reviewing TASS documents regarding the failed Phobos mission. Whatever Phobos the moonlet contained was of the utmost importance to all. The Americans eagerly transferred all their Phobos astrometrical observations to Soviets. American radio telescopes stationed throughout our planet were to aid the Soviets (March 11, 1989, Uchitelskaya Gazeta newspaper, quoting Y. Kolesnikov from the Flight Control Centre). The Swiss and the French provided a special measuring device they created jointly with the Soviets.

Each probe was a complicated set of devices: three television cameras, spectrometer, guidance system, and video recording system. Also, the Phobos 2 probe contained a strange laser device dubbed LIMA-D. Specialists in the Leningrad Institute of Precision Mechanics, together with East European and Finnish scientists, created this curious machine. The device was to emit a laser ray at the surface of the moonlet, to cause a mini-explosion, and gather data on evaporated substance*. Apparently, this was the most important experiment that the probe was to conduct, according to G. Lomanov, a reporter (Sotsialisticheskaya Industriya newspaper, March 26, 1989 - one day before the failure!) By the way, the technical name for Phobos 2 was Videospektrometricheskiy kompleks (VSK), and its personal name was "Fregat".

DISASTER

Phobos 1 was lost in September of 1988, on its way to Mars. The Soviets claimed a radio command error. Phobos 2 was also lost, but before it did, images and information were sent to Earth. The probe arrived at the Martian orbit in January of 1989. This was the beginning of the mission that included a transfer to an orbit that would make the probe fly in tandem with its namesake moonlet. Furthermore, Phobos was to be explored, and certain equipment had to be placed on the surface of the moonlet.

The problems began when the probe aligned itself with the moonlet. On March 28, 1989 TASS (official Soviet news agency) made an announcement that Phobos 2 failed to communicate with Earth as scheduled after completing an operation around the Martian moon Phobos. Scientists at mission control have been unable to establish stable radio contact.

In April of 1989 Lt. Colonel Baberdin published an article in Krasnaya Zvezda newspaper (Enigmas of Martian orbits, April 4). He mentions the unidentified spot on Martian surface, photographed using the infrared wave range. Soviet Vremya program mentioned it in its broadcast, and the military had to respond, albeit late. Baberdin states that astrophysicists and planetologists carefully studied the image. Most likely this was a shadow from some space object. This shadow was able to sharply lower Martian atmosphere, and the on-board device of Phobos 2 was able to capture the image. But what the space object was remained unclear.

SENTINELS OF THE RED PLANET

In 1991 Marina Popovich, who visited Los Angeles, showed Paul Stonehill a photograph that Phobos 2 made before its demise. It depicts a gigantic cylindrical object approximately 25 kilometres long. After that last frame was radio-transmitted back to earth, the probe disappeared.

AVIATION WEEK & SPACE TECHNOLOGY magazine had more interesting information in its April 10, 1989 issue. A controller at the Kaliningrad control centre reported that the limited signals received after conclusion of the Phobos 2 imaging session gave him an impression that he was tracking a spin-stabilised spacecraft (a "spinner", in his words). Phobos 2 was in orbit around Mars on March 27, when it failed to re-establish communications with earth. The probe was commanded to change its orientation for an imaging session. Its cameras had to be aimed at the moonlet, and later it was to resume its Earth-pointing orientation to downlink the data. But that never happened. Something struck the object, and sent it into a spin. In the October 1989 issue of Nature, Soviet scientists published several technical reports regarding the few experiments that Phobos 2 actually conducted. Just one paragraph dealt with the loss of the space probe. But that report did confirm that Phobos 2 was "spinning", either because of a computer malfunction...or because the space probe was "impacted" by an unknown object. Alexander Dunayev was the Chairman of the Soviet Glavkosmos space organisation, who talked to Leskov on March 29, 1989 (Izvestiya newspaper) about the probe's failure. According to him, a special commission was created the day before, right after the failure, and it included top space scientists. They came up with seven reasons as to why the probe was lost. The commission was to issue a conclusion. Dunayev later reported that the loss of the probe was not a complete failure, because a range of scientific data was collected during the cruise phase and the time Phobos 2 was in the Martian orbit. Images of the moonlet and Mars were being studied on Earth. One image, according to Dunayev, included an odd-shaped object between the spacecraft and Mars. He supposed it was either the debris in the orbit of Phobos or the Phobos 2 autonomous propulsion subsystem that was jettisoned after the spacecraft was injected into Mars orbit.

But Marina Popovich told Paul Stonehill that the Glavkosmos knew all along that whatever it was that destroyed the probe was created by artificial intelligence. There was another article by S. Leskov published in Izvestiya

(November 1, 1990). Professor N. Ivanov, head of the Ballistic Service of the Flight Control Centre mentioned the rumours the JPL in Pasadena "captured" signals from the lost probe contrary to all physical laws. Ivanov did not directly contradict the persistent rumours. He stated that by this time the lost probe would have ceased all communications and become frozen. The only other possibility - not a serious one, he hastened to add-would, be that Phobos 2 was dragged away by extraterrestrials and they kept it functioning. Doctor Selivanov of the Glavkosmos, who was also interviewed by Leskov, adds that he contacted the American scientists in Pasadena, but they claim that no signals from Phobos 2 were received.

We admire the ease the Soviets and Americans handled direct communications about space probes, but there is another scientific opinion that is no less important than that of Ivanov's or Selivanov's.

Professor Burdakov, mentioned in other chapters of this book, made direct inquiries about the loss of Phobos 2 probe, and discussed the matter with the original designers of the project, as well as those who had tested the spacecraft. Suspicious of official explanations, Professor Burdakov questioned the series of strange events that led to the destruction of Phobos 2. He knew nothing about the photo images taken by Phobos 2, and was unaware that certain individuals in the West discussed possible reasons why the probe perished. The Professor came up with a hypothesis: if Mars is inhabited, the intelligent beings who exist there would not like the idea of a device placed on the surface of their moonlet for purposes of constant observation. Consequently, in his opinion, they did something about it. Burdakov's views were expressed in an article published in 1992 in a Russian magazine Quant.

Vyacheslav Kovtunenko was the official head of the Phobos project. In his interview with M. Chernishov of Krasny Voin newspaper (a military publication) dated May 24, 1989, he reveals some details about the probes. The apparatuses were able to solve complex problems. Apparently the designers found out about certain failures and design shortcomings during the flight, but were eager to proceed with new "expeditions". Roald Sagdeyev, who now resides in the United States and could shed much light on Soviet secrets, mentioned in the same interview that the work on the project was going well, except for the reluctance of "financial organs" in the West to help his Western partners complete the project. And yet, 13 countries had participated in the project. What was the haste involved? Why all the secrecy even today?

Roald Kremnev of the Babakin Space Testing Centre, another top scientist involved with the project, mentioned a "swarm of small bodies" around Phobos during the incident. Did they cause the failure? Or, he added in his interview with Chernishov (see above) was the reason the alien body registered by the Phobos 2 on-board device? Kremnev again talked to Leskov on April 14,

(Izvestiya) and stressed that the most discussed version of the failure is the gigantic object registered three days before the accident. And still, there was no official conclusion.

According to Leskov (Izvestiya, April 16, 1989), who talked to top scientists involved in the project, the Soviets spent 272 million rubles for the project, and Western partners spent 51 million rubles. The probes cost 51 million rubles - an enormous amount of money for the time. It took five years (according to official information) to build the probes. What of the weapons aboard?

The probe was to be a long-time automatic station on the surface of Phobos. Among the equipment it was to use was a special "jumping probe" or a "hopper", according to Leskov (Izvestiya, March 24, 1989). The hopper, which looked a little like a mechanised ladybug, would unfold its spindly legs and literally hop around the moonlet (actually, through gigantic strides of about sixty feet). Each time that the hopper would land, it was to use its X-rays to study the soil's chemical composition. It also had a device ("penetrometer") to study the moonlet's physical properties and the underlying geological structure. The hopper, according to the Soviets, was also to carry a magnetometer to measure magnetic fields and a gravitometer to measure the moonlet's mass. Most likely this little ingenious "ladybug" had to carry out some other missions, too, and probably was designed to carry some other, more sinister devices. We simply do not have enough information, even years after the demise of Phobos 2.

NO WEAPONS ALLOWED
We already know that a new type of laser weapons was to be used on Phobos. Perhaps this was the reason why it was destroyed before it could complete its mission. Perhaps Man is not the master of the Solar system yet. Perhaps those who have left mysterious and deep tracks on Phobos are the true masters.

Phobos has mysterious long parallel grooves across a large part of its surface; they are a few hundred metres wide and a few tens of metres deep and may have been formed by the same impact that caused the crater Stickney or by an alien intelligence. Our scientists are unable to explain the nature of the grooves.

Can they explain how could tiny Phobos generate heat and conventional volcanic activity to account for the presence of numerous craters on its surface?

It took the Soviets ten space probes, none of which carried its program to conclusion, to realise that Mars is very inhospitable. Just two Soviet space probes actually made it to the Martian surface. We know about the past failures and recent successes of America's Martian exploration program. We are certain that new space probes will be sent to Mars in the near future. Does it mean that our governments know more than we do and are more than eager to reach Mars and its moonlets? Decide for yourself.

Ten years go by, and another (American Mars Polar Lander) spacecraft is sent to Mars. And onboard it contained a strange device, better known as the Light Detection and Ranging (LIDAR). It was created in the Space Research Institute (IKI) of the Russian Academy of Science, under the sponsorship of the Russian Space Agency (RSA). This was the first Russian instrument to fly on a United States planetary spacecraft. The LIDAR instrument was to look "for ice and dust clouds". The LIDAR system was a laser sounder located on the Mars Polar Lander deck. It was composed of a sensor and electronics assembly. The LIDAR transmitter used a gallium-aluminium-arsenic laser that emits energy in pulses at a constant rate and wavelength. The LIDAR had two sounding modes - active and acoustic:

1. During active sounding, the instrument sends out pulses of light and then times their return in order to locate and characterise ice and dust hazes to a level of two to three kilometres.

2. An acoustic device, the Planetary Society's Mars Microphone, was part of the LIDAR assembly.

Engineers designed the LIDAR to operate in the temperature range from -100 to 50 degrees Celsius (-148 to 122 degrees Fahrenheit) under lower pressure, near one millibar. It was connected to the board by an RS-422 interface and generated science data up to 25.6 Kb per day for standard operation scenario, which is a limit from the spacecraft. The LIDAR also had a high-pressure variometer for studying correlation of optical atmospheric characteristics with very low frequency sounds (infrasound) and changing pressure. The laser transmitter was gallium-aluminium-arsenic pulses laser diode emitting one micro Joule in 20-nanosecond long pulses at 890 nanometer wavelength. The laser beam had a linear polarisation and a 2 milliradian divergence with the output 54x34 mm2 clear aperture. The laser operated with repetition rate of about 20 to 25 kHz. Outside daylight background irradiance was the main source of noise inside the receiver channel. The background irradiance was reduced by an optical interference filter having a bandwidth of 10 nm (FWHM), at 890 nm with 50 percent transmission and a 15 millimetre clear aperture only. One of the receiver channels had a polariser. Its axes were coincident with the LIDAR beam polarisation.

Full sounding distance was 750 metres (2,461 feet) with 5 metres resolution along the trace or the 32 second total integrating time. The single cycle had 10 minute duration.

How powerful can such laser device be? It was not, as far as we know, powerful enough to threaten anything substantial on Mars or Phobos. Similar devices are being used by military for the purpose of precise aim, or to measure distances accurately. Much more powerful systems are needed to pierce a structure (for example, a metallic hull. And yet even such a weak laser device is able to penetrate a surface. Once it penetrates a surface, it can interact with a system below, destroy its equilibrium, and damage whatever mechanism lies within it and consisted of three active measurements by each channel simultaneously and 12 passive measurements of sky brightness.

A Russian scientist who is also a participant of the RUFORS Round Table, actually worked with the creators of the LIDAR (but on other projects). They were the same scientists who had designed all of the devices aboard Soviet spacecraft sent to Venus. "Top experts" is how they were described. Their invention was original and exquisite: two "radars", one acoustic, one laser, function together. Wherever laser is not capable of operation (fog, clouds, smoke), the sound starts its work, for it can penetrate further. Where the environment is denser (for example, water), only acoustic "radar" is capable to provide orientation and communication. Laser needs an ideal, optically transparent environment.

The story of the Polar Lander's failure is well known; although we will probably never learn the true causes of its demise...Maybe we should be more careful when planning to send lasers to the Red Planet and its strange moonlets.

We must be cautious when dealing with the planet Mars as it is the one planet that has fascinated mankind for centuries. We must not read too much into mankind's attempts to explore the Red planet especially when such attempts seem to malfunction. Mars is a most perplexing place without a doubt, and many of the answers we seek about it will only be answered when man finally lands on its surface. Having said all that, it could well be that there is more of a mystery here than just trying to explain Mars and its planetary formation. It would seem that our efforts to study the planet at close quarters are constantly dogged by either our own technical inadequacies or by circumstances that yet remain a complete mystery and quite rightly once again fall into the unexplained category. Such a category must account for the Phobos 2 mission and the perplexing photograph it sent back to Earth shortly before it was lost in space.

CHAPTER 38

PROMINENT RUSSIAN UFOLOGISTS

NIKOLAY SUBBOTIN AND RUFORS

Nikolay Valeryevich Subbotin was born in 1974. He resides in Perm, Russia. Nikolay is one of the directors of the Russian Ufological Research Station (RUFORS), and editor of Russian Ufological magazine Dialog: Zemlya-Kosmos. He is a well-educated young man and a graduate of the Perm State Pedagogue University. Nikolay teaches elementary grade classes, and is a pedagogue of alternative educational methods. But he is also an experienced computer-programming engineer, journalist, teacher of information technologies, and a school administrator. Nikolay has authored over 150 articles, from 1990 until present. He has been published throughout the former Soviet Union, as well as in Europe, Japan, and the United States. His interests include research of UFO phenomenon and anomalous zones, computer programming and creation of special, applied programs as well as poetry and journalism.

RUFORS

RUFORS (Russian UFO Research Station) is an international Ufological organisation, founded in October of 1989. Its main goals are:

. Integration of Russian Ufologists into a united information space
. Research and analysis of UFO issues and anomalous phenomena
. Sponsorship of effective information exchange among researchers
. Cooperation with scientific and State research entities
. Creation of the unified information databank

RUFORS has an immense archive of 100,000 articles; 300 hours of video recorded interviews with eyewitnesses; films about anomalous phenomena; 20 gigabytes of photo documents of anomalous phenomena objects, as well as hoaxes; the largest Russian archive of anomalous phenomena, UFO photographs, and fake photographs; over 500 books in the RUFORS personal library; a database of 150,000 anomalous phenomena websites; and more.

In May of 1997, the RUFORS Round Table was created, and Russian, Ukrainian, Georgian and other researchers began information exchange through electronic mail.

RUFORS has produced several documentaries about UFO cases and is active in the Perm regional radio programming (a series of broadcast programs about anomalous phenomena), and is very much involved in promoting unity and cooperation among Ufologists of Russia and CIS. Among UFO cases researched by Nick, as his friends call him, is the Shaitan Mazar ("Devil's Grave) case. The alleged location of this incident is in the Mangishlak Peninsula, Kyrgyzstan (USSR). Those interested in getting further details about Nick's work should contact him:

Russia, 614010, Perm,
Post Office Box 5172

His email address is: Nikolay.Subbotin@psu.ru
The RUFORS website URL is:
http://ufo.psu.ru/

VLADIMIR SMOLY

This young and very capable Russian UFO researcher has created a website full of tremendously useful information for UFO researchers in Russia and the West. The address is:

http://ufo.metrocom.ru/

Smoly's contribution to the study of UFO phenomenon is great, and his efforts to promote Russian UFO research are to be lauded.

KOSMOPOISK

Kosmopoisk (Space search), in Russian: Космопоиск; its full name is Общероссийская научно-исследовательская общественная организация Космопоиск, (abbreviated as ОНИОО), is perhaps, the largest international public scientific research organisation today: it consists of 200 permanent members and approximately 3000 volunteers from a number of Russia regions who either participate in the expeditions on their own or assist the group in a number of ways. The Kosmopoisk database consists of about seven thousands researchers and explorers all around Russia. The organisation consists of 178 research groups and also chapters throughout the world (Europe, Middle East, the Americas, Asia, and Oceania; in over 20 countries).

Kosmopoisk has existed since 1980. Initially (from 1988 to 1989) it had operated under the Ordzhenikdze Moscow Aviation Institute auspices. Since then it is an independent civilian field expeditionary and research entity engaged in the study and research of anomalous phenomena (Ufology, Crypto Physics), borderline and futuristic scientific breakthroughs for the subsequent application of the gained knowledge to the benefit of all Mankind.

As a self-styled all Russian public scientific organisation (registered as such in 2004), and an International Movement (since 2001), Kosmopoisk has tirelessly studied Ufology, Cryptozoology, and has conducted other anomalous phenomena investigations.

From 1994 to 2002 the honorary chief (and one of the founders) of Kosmopoisk was Alexander Kazantsev (1906-2002), mentioned throughout this book. A former Soviet WWII veteran, this famous Russian writer had been engaged in Paleoufology (ancient astronaut hypothesis; extraterrestrial contacts in past of humanity's history) research since 1945, well before a number of other international researchers.

Another prominent personality that has been mentioned in this book, and who was an organiser in Kosmopoisk was Georgiy Beregovoy (1921-1995), a famous Soviet cosmonaut.

Kosmopoisk is headed by Vadim Chernobrov, its Coordinator.

This Russian scientist, aerospace engineer, inventor, author of numerous books and encyclopaedias, researcher and theorist has been mentioned throughout this book. Other organisers are such notable personalities as Marina Popovich, Cosmonaut Grechko, as well as active and tireless researchers Sergey Aleksandrov, Yelena Chulkova, Yekaterina Golovina, Maksim Golubev, and others too numerous to mention here, but no less dedicated to the goals of Kosmopoisk.

Since 1997, Kosmopoisk has conducted regular annual meetings, in the month of May, in various Russian areas conductive to the open-air gathering of a large number of participants. The annual meetings, according to Kosmopoisk by-laws, are the highest legislative body of the organisation.

Since 1982, Kosmopoisk had carried over 550 expeditions and organised reconnaissance field research in different regions of former USSR and Russia, including Moscow region, Ural, Volga region, Caucasus, Siberia, Yakutiya, Magadan; Baltic countries, Kazakhstan, Ukraine; Poland, Greece, Turkey, China, India, Indonesia, Malaysia...

Expeditions consist anywhere from 2 to 70 persons; and may contain professionals with academic degrees, as well as schoolchildren. The Kosmopoisk members and volunteers search for UFO sightings and observations and meteorites.

They engage in archaeology, ethnography, astronomical observations, and related research. As we have learnt in other chapters of this book, the Kosmopoisk people, among them the multi-talented Vadim Chernobrov, conducted an expedition to the Podkamennaya Tunguska area, to research the 1908 Tunguska Phenomenon. They were in the Kursk area, too, looking for answers to mysterious explosions. Six expeditions in search of meteorites had been conducted in Tver, Ulyanovsk, and Kaluga regions. More expeditions to other areas are planned.

Since early 1980s, dozens of expeditions have been sent to the anomalous area known as the Medveditskyaya Ridge. During this time, those in the expeditions have observed close sightings and landings of a "three-star" UFO, and have observed it at a distance over twenty times. There are video films and quality photographs. Also some twenty sites of UFO landings have been researched thoroughly. Strange artifacts were found around the landing sites (and turned over to various instituted for research). Expedition members who have conducted interviews with locals also discovered ancient sites and tunnels.

And since 1998, Kosmopoisk has led expeditions to the mysterious Kola Peninsula. In September of 1999 they researched the famous 1959 case in the Urals. Also in October and November of 1999 the group, together with a Russian newspaper, conducted a cryptozoological expedition to Yakutia, to search for strange, gigantic animals rumoured to exist in its lakes. Kosmopoisk has reached the forbidden areas of the Ararat Mountain, the alleged site of the Noah's Ark.

Kosmopoisk conducts annual "monitoring' expeditions in Southern Russia (mostly in Krasnodar Region) to detect and research new crop circles (and preserve the information before the descent of tourists to the area). Kosmopoisk has deployed UfoSETI system to collect and analyse the reports about UFO sites and crop circle in Russia.

Kosmopoisk has conducted crypto oological field research expeditions, including the 1999: an expedition to the remote Labynkyr Lake in Yakutia (Sakha Republic), and in the years 2002 and 2003 there had been expeditions to Brosno Lake in the Tver region. For centuries, local denizens believed that an underwater creature (the Brosno Dragon, or Brosnya) had lived there. According to the legends, Mongolian Golden Horde invaders discovered it for the first time in 1240. Complete sonar underwater scan and coastal monitoring was performed. The resulting theory of "hydrate bottom" explained the Brosno dragon phenomenon as the probable result of massive gas eruptions from the bottom of lake. Kosmopoisk had also undertaken several expeditions in the years 2002, 2003 and 2004 in the areas of reported population of Bigfoot-like creatures (i.e. Verkhoshizhemye in the Kirov region).

We have described Kosmopoisk and Vadim Chernobrov's involvement in the Kishtim Dwarf investigation in the chapter Mysteries of the Ural Mountains.

Here are a few examples of data provided by local residents and collected by Kosmopoisk in their Kaluga expedition. The so-called Korenevo event, that took place in October of 1996 in Kaluga region, was the behind the decision to conduct a series of expeditions to the area. The event was thought to be a meteorite fall. Two expeditions were conducted in 1997, and in the years 1998 through 2003 Korenevo was the site of the annual all-Russian conference of Kosmopoisk, each May.

LYUDINOVO (Kaluga region). At 10.40 p.m. from north-northwest to south, a white and yellow coloured object was observed, with 0.2 to 0.3 degrees linear dimensions. Its flight time was estimated as 2 to 10 seconds. According to the information provided by three witnesses, the object was considerably stretched in the longitudinal direction. Its disappearing "tail" was reported to be up to 2 degrees in size. The object flew silently. The object vanished at 2 to 5 degrees altitude. The illumination was sharp. The pause before the explosion was estimated to be from 3 to 25 seconds. One of the witnesses noticed the sparks. According to another, the boom came first, followed by the humming flight of the ball. All of the Lyudinovo witnesses had noticed the same loud noise followed by a roar, similar to one produced by an airplane.

KALUGA. The white and blue sphere was noticed at 10:42 pm at 40 to 50 degrees altitude, the azimuth 300 to 330 deg. The object's angular size was 0.1 to 0.2 deg. During the flight the colour had changed to yellow and red. The disappearance was reported at 215 to 220 degrees azimuth at a one-degree altitude. During the flight the re-converging tail was reported to be up to 2 degrees in length.

During the disappearance stage, the object reportedly separated in 2 or 3 fragments. No sounds were reported. Flight time was reported to be from 5 to 10 seconds. One of the witnesses noticed white and blue sparks in the beginning of the sphere's flight. Totally, 4 witnesses had been interviewed.

Beginning in the 1980s, the Kosmopoisk researchers have conducted speleological expeditions, looking for underground cities, monasteries and other structures in Russia and the former Soviet territories. Special attention is paid to investigation of ancient tunnels, as well as other unusual ancient structures in Russia, Ukraine, Moldavia, Azerbaijan, and other areas.

Kosmopoisk has, according to its website, the largest UFO and anomalous phenomena sightings database in Russia. Thousands of articles have been written about the Kosmopoisk expeditions and its research projects; and over thirty books dedicated to anomalous phenomena research have been published and re-published.

Kosmopoisk has collected and updates scientific databases; as well as encyclopaedic database of 1800 anomalous sites.

Kosmopoisk has its continuously updated news site at:

http://kosmopoisk.org/news_detailed/index.html/

Kosmopoisk has organised and participated in a number of international physics conferences, Ufological, Paleoufological, SETI seminars and meetings. The organisation is opening various museums throughout Russia. The Kosmopoisk website is also the official website of the Zigel Scientific Conferences that take place in Moscow annually.

Kosmopoisk has engaged in the space-time continuum physics experiments since 1988 (and experiments in chronotravel). Its researchers have been working in the RD of experimental models of aerospace prototypes and time machines.

Between 1990 and 2005 Kosmopoisk had investigated causes of disappearances and deaths of the people who had vanished or perished in anomalous zones in Russia, Belarus, Kazakhstan and Ukraine. If a Kosmopoisk member gets lost during an expedition, the organisation immediately begins rescue and recovery missions.

Kosmopoisk conducts research and recovery of space objects (and its findings helped in the research of the Tunguska Phenomenon). Its researchers also look for traces of ancient global and regional disasters. Some of Kosmopoisks meteorite recovery and paleoufological expeditions fall under the description of "disaster expeditions", as their main goals are to find causes of regional and global catastrophes. But it is not only the past that Kosmopoisk has concentrated its attention on: its members have studied the consequences of the 2005 Indian Ocean tidal wave disaster (as part of the UNESCO project). A documentary film had been produced in 2005 about this direction of Kosmopoisk research (Katastrofniye Ekspeditsii Kosmopoiska).

In 2004 and 2006 some of the Kosmopoisk groups had searched for the "Chinese ET pyramids" in China, but found neither the pyramids nor rumours about them. But Kosmopoisk also did not find any of the "ancient pyramids" (claimed to exist by media) in Russia (in the Krasnodar, Stavropol areas, in Crimea…).

In 1998-2003 Kosmopoisk had been engaged in the search for the legendary "Khruschev airplane". Leonid Khrushchev, son of the Nikita Khrushchev (<u>General Secretary</u> of the <u>Communist Party of the Soviet Union</u> from 1953 to 1964, following the death of <u>Joseph Stalin</u>) flew it in a battle mission, but the crew and plane disappeared, and it was rumoured that he betrayed his nation and defected to Nazi Germany. After six years of intensive and difficult search, Kosmopoisk was able to find the site of the airplane that went down in 1943 near Zhizdri, and learned that Nazis recovered the dead body of the brave Soviet pilot who died in battle.

There are many capable, dedicated, experienced young scientists and others in the ranks of Kosmopoisk, and we are certain that they will discover more fascinating objects and sites in the former lands of the former USSR.

Kosmopoisk and its researchers, enthusiastic and tireless, plan a number of new expeditions. Those who are interested in reaching Kosmopoisk and Vadim Chernobrov have several options, listed below.

http://kosmopoisk.ru
(Kosmopoisk official website)
http://kosmopoisk.org
(Kosmopoisk international site)
kosmopoisk@kosmopoisk.org
(Kosmopoisk email address)
http://chernobrov.narod.ru
(Vadim Chernobrov's site)

Or write to:

Космопоиск (115533, Москва, ул.Нагатинская, 19-а, Космопоиск)

Russia, Moscow 111553, Nagatinskaya, 19-A, V.Chernobrov, Kosmopoisk

MIKHAIL GERSHTEIN

Mikhail Borisovich Gershtein was born in Leningrad in 1972. He observed a very mysterious phenomenon in 1985, and was convinced for quite a long time that what he saw was a UFO. Ever since he has been interested in UFO research. But it was not until the Soviet censorship was removed from UFO documents that he understood what he observed in 1985. The day of his sighting was also the day when a launch was conducted from the Plesetsk Cosmodrome, and the launched Soviet apparatus was reflected by super refraction in the upper levels of the atmosphere.

He was not discouraged, but even more determined to solve the mystery of UFOs, real "flying saucers" that have visited our planet. From 1988 on his articles have been regularly printed in the Saint Petersburg and national media. From 1988 through March of 2000, Michael Gershtein was a reporter and leading UFO expert for ANOMALIYA newspaper of Saint Petersburg. He graduated with honours from Russian State Pedagogue University, and is educated in geography and biology. In July of 1995, Michael Gershtein has received a Master of Science degree in information technology. From October of 1995 through 1999 he was a full member of the Russian Geographic Society (Bureau of Planetology), but resigned due to disagreements with their methods of UFO and anomalous phenomenon research. But nowadays he is the Chairman of the Ufological Commission of the Russian Geographical Society. He is an author and a well known journalist. Mikhail is also the Chief Editor of Nexus (Russian edition).

Those who want to contact Mikhail Gershtein, should go to his website:

http://www.ufonav.spb.ru/
ufo_miger@chat.ru
Or write to him at:

Mikhail Gershtein
Post Office Box 4
Saint Petersburg 190008
Russia

ANATOLY KUTOVOY
Anatoly Kutovoy is the deputy director of RUFORS. He graduated from a university with a degree in radio electronics; Anatoly is an expert in cybernetics. He was inspired to study anomalous phenomena by Vladimir Ajaja's lecture presented to Soviet officers of the Rocket Forces in 1978, at one of the garrisons of the Trans-Baikal military district. Anatoly represents RUFORS in Lithuania

INCREDIBLE WORLD
Alexander Bogdanchikov is a writer, playwright, journalist, and founder of one of the first Russian publications about the paranormal, Neveroyatny Mir (Incredible World, in English) magazine, and Liter BM newspaper. In the early 1990s he wrote a bestseller Stars of our Destinies. More recently A. Bogdanchikov wrote a motion picture script titled Russian Secret Materials. He also wrote radio and TV programs. Incredible World has published a number of materials about Soviet and Russian Ufology.

The magazine's website can be found at this address:

http://www.incredible.spb.ru/

EDUARD GOZHIN
Eduard Gozhin is director of the Tomsk branch of RUFORS. He is an active researcher, and created his own UFO research group. Eduard graduated from the Tomsk Polytechnic University. He has created a website dedicated to research conducted by Tomsk scientists.

YAROSLAVL UFOLOGISTS
The Yaroslavl UFO Centre was formed 29 years ago. Yuri Smirnov, one of its founders, publishes a wonderful and informative newspaper Chetvortoye Izmereniye i NLO.
http://www.yarosufo.boom.ru/

NLO MAGAZINE

Throughout our book we have referred to this wonderful and informative publication. Prominent Russian, Ukrainian, and international anomalous phenomena and UFO researchers, historians, scientists, military and naval officers and rank and file personnel, artists and inventors published their articles, reports, and memoirs in its issues since the inception of the magazine in 1996. So much of the arcane, forbidden, and hidden for year's pages of history of the Soviet Union and Russia came to light because of this magazine. Its editor-in-chief is Tatyana Viktorovna Kamchatova.

To see sample issues of the magazine, and to contact its editors, go to its website at: http://212.46.207.138:8000/

ufo@ks.ru

ANOMALIA NEWSPAPER

This wonderful and informative newspaper, located in Saint Petersburg, has been providing information about Russian and international paranormal phenomena for many years. Its editor is Tatyana Sirchenko, a very capable journalist. To reach the newspaper, go to its website at:

http://www.shaping.ru/anomalia/

anomalia@shaping.org

VLADIMIR AJAJA

Vladimir Georgiyevich Ajaja has been a prominent personality on the Russian UFO scene. But he was not always an Ufologist, and when he became one, he gained enemies as well as a tremendous following. With the help of his highly placed Navy buddies, he was able to write a piece about the Bermuda Triangle for Nauka I Zhizhn, a respected Soviet scientific magazine. After all, he was a marine researcher, who, on numerous occasions, studied the depths of the Atlantic Ocean from aboard a Soviet submarine (its many features designed by him). Other mainstream Soviet oceanographers would not touch such a "questionable" subject. In his search for the information, two sources helped him: Charles Berlitz's The Bermuda Triangle book that mentioned UFOs (he could find no other books in the libraries), and Vice-Admiral Y.V. Ivanov, head of the Naval Intelligence Directorate. Ajaja found out that the Naval Intelligence had long considered UFOs to be a subject of serious investigation. But his newly found conviction put him on thin ice. Ajaja's efforts to study and promote Ufology made him a target of the science officialdom, and the Party functionaries. His name was smeared in the Soviet media. Ajaja's works were blacklisted. His lectures were outlawed. He was fired from several jobs, and basically, silenced.

Again, his Navy buddies helped him land a job, and write about UFOs for their practical use.

In his brochure ATTENTION: UFOS he stated that the UFO wave of 1989, still in progress in 1991 when it was published, had swept away ideological and censorship barriers which were placed against Ufology in the USSR. But because of the years of silence, the country has been rendered totally unprepared for UFO phenomena. So he helped organise the SOYUZUFOTSENTR to promote scientific study of UFO phenomena. It broke away from its cradle, the USSR Academy of Sciences, because as did many others, Ajaja was convinced that those responsible for the UFO research within the Academy actually hampered any true research.

Vladimir Ajaja has sent a number of letters and documents to the Russian Ufology Research Centre in the early 1990s. One of them described the demise of his SOYUZUFOTSENTR (2/14/1992); it was forced to close down because of absence of financial incentives. At the time the SOYUZUFOTSENTR became an institute, and published works about Ufology. A new entity was born, the Ufotsentr (or Centre of administration of Ufological Association of Commonwealth of Independent States).

Chetvertoye izmereniye i NLO newspaper published an interesting article written by Vladimir Ajaja as a response to criticism that he has kept secret UFO data from the public, among other issues (Issue 2, 1998). Ajaja noted that he was never a Captain of the Soviet Navy, and that in the 1980s he was pleading with the Soviet government to assist him in the area of UFO research (and they showed him the door). Also, his work for the Soviet Navy (the hydrosphere aspect of UFO phenomenon), according to Ajaja, was done for free, because as a former submariner Ajaja wanted to help his Navy to discern UFOs that resembled strike force military objects. Then he mentioned that for over twenty years he was considered to be a persona nongrata, and a target of numerous verbal attacks.

He wanted to clarify his view about secret UFO data in the possession of Russian government. In his opinion the government does keep such data secret, because such data comprises of military and official State secrecy. As long as States and their attributes (armed forces, intelligence services, defence industry and related areas exist, such secrecy will exist, too. He who possesses UFO technology is capable of ruling the world. Hence, the designation of secrecy may be applied to UFO information and data. Such secrecy may apply to any other information about some other incomprehensible phenomenon, and the principle used is this: let us first make it classified information, and then investigate it. If the State does possess UFO secrets, it can only learn about them in the established order, that is, through individuals who have clearance to handle secrets, and only through authorisation of competent agencies, and only because of some specific reason. No other exceptions would do. And, certainly, appeals to make such information public would not do much.

In the same article Ajaja mentioned that in 1993 the KGB, based on the request of Pavel Popovich, who was then President of the Ufological Association, gave the Ufotsentr headed by Ajaja, some 1300 documents related to UFOs. Among them reports of official agencies, commanders of military units, and information sent by private individuals. (In our chapter about KGB and UFOs we have described and used portions of the 124 pages of information given to Pavel Popovich by KGB in 1992; is Ajaja talking about the same batch of documents?). According to him, the Lyubyanka (that is, the KGB) was getting rid of an "unnecessary headache", and Russian Ufologists were expanding their database of UFO knowledge.

Ajaja did not elaborate about accusations that he stopped viewing UFO phenomenon as an extraterrestrial civilizations hypothesis. He did mention that if it would be proven that UFOs are not related in any fashion to extraterrestrial civilizations (and so far there is no proof of that), the ranks of Ufologists will thin out, and their quantity will turn into quality. In all fairness to this controversial researcher, he did not consider UFOs to be "aliens", or extraterrestrial beings even in 1990. In an interview he gave to Vechernyaya Moskva newspaper (March 24, 1990), when asked about the nature of UFOs, he gave a rather detailed answer. When UFOs are sighted, people observe their polymorphism. A variety of different shapes are associated with the unidentified flying objects. A UFO changes its shape in front of the observer's eyes. It is likely that UFOs can alter the state of matter, and human beings so far cannot understand how this is achieved. This is what Soviet Ufologists explain as energy-informational exchange. Academician V. Kaznacheyev studied this problem in 1990. Many people, continues Ajaja, visualise the UFO phenomenon rather simplistically. Extraterrestrials travelling in some craft, like we do in our spaceships, visit Earth, and then leave. This is not exactly the case. First of all, it has not been proven that they are extraterrestrials. Frequent encounters with them indicated that they live next to us, exist on the same planet with us. Lately, collection of those materials that confirm hypothesis of invisible field forms of life, the "thinking ether" mentioned even by ancient Greeks, begins to resemble an avalanche. The extraterrestrial visitation hypothesis is very stable but no one thinks about proof. And sometimes people jump to hasty conclusions. They find, say, a bolt or a piece of metal that is impossible to produce in a laboratory of some plant, or a workshop, and come to a conclusion that extraterrestrials produced it. And if, let us say, Soviet plant "Hammer and Sickle" did not produce the find, then immediately, a new "sensation" is born. The issue is much more complicated. In the last ten years there have been (according to Ajaja's) calculations, several million UFO landings. It would be impossible to study or probe a planet in this fashion. There would not be enough resources or objects to do so (UFOs). Apparently, this is co-existence, isn't it? "They" exist in the invisible part of the electromagnetic oscillation spectrum, as was confirmed through photography. We have a very narrow range of vision. It is as if we walked through the dark forest one night and our light comes from a flashlight. That is our angle of vision, our light. We do not know what is next to us, and we simply cannot see it. It seems that "flying saucers" are a defensive receptacle, temporarily created by field life forms, the "ether intellect", to ensure movement of its fragments, at great speeds in a dense environment, the atmosphere. When the need in such a "saucer" disappears, it vanishes in front of our eyes...Such safeguard for security are needed because of last years' cases of abductions of humans; humans who never came back. The Ufological Commission has researched this issue, and according to their information, among hundreds of thousands of those who disappeared without a trace, there are five and a half thousand individuals, who possibly were abducted by UFOs.

This interview presents some curious numbers, but the glaring absence of any mention of underwater UFOs and cases of sightings of strange underwater craft raise a number of questions. Ajaja knew, perhaps better than anyone else among Soviet Ufologists, the number of such sightings. He even met with Soviet counter-intelligence officers of the Navy who had encounters with underwater anomalous phenomena. Yet, he remains silent now, as he did in 1990. We believe that there may be fascinating documents in the files of the Soviet and now Russian intelligence and counterintelligence services of the Navy (certainly, not only in Russia). But we doubt that such files will ever become public. We are not criticizing Ajaja, for that is not the purpose of this book, and we wanted to make sure his opinions are given a fair representation.

In 1997 Vladimir Ajaja, former director of the Ufotsentr and President of the Ufological Association of CI, received his Ph.D. in Philosophy. He became a professor. This followed a decision by Russia's Top Attestation Commission in Moscow. The Commission judged Ajaja's achievements by the number of books he published on the subjects of anomalous phenomena and UFOs. Prior to this, only the Tomsk Polytechnic Institute allowed doctorate papers for Ufology in the framework of professions related to environmental protection and technical methods of protection of the environment. Thus, Ufology has become both a technical and philosophical discipline. This was reported in the Issue 9, 1997, of Chetvertoye Izmereniye i NLO newspaper.

In 1998 Ajaja published a book titled Inaya Zhizn or Another Life.

Then, on May 25, 1999, Department of Justice of Russian Federation approved establishment of the Academy of Informational and Applied Ufology. According to Ajaja, this step is a logical result of the development of Department of Ufology and bio-informatics of the International

Informatization Academy). The International Informatization Academy (IIA), founded in 1990, is an independent self-governing social scientific institution. It is an associated member of the United Nations Organisation (UNO). The membership of the Academy consists of well known scholars, prominent specialists, and distinguished statesmen who are devoting themselves to the solution of fundamental theoretical and applied problems in the field of information science and who are furthering the development of information processes and technologies in various scientific and cultural spheres. Its website is:

http://www.cnshb.ru/MAI/mai.htm

According to the articles of the Academy, it is a non-commercial organisation that would function under the ethics of voluntarism, equality, self-rule, and lawfulness. The Academy is a legal entity. The Academy has the following tasks: to assist in raising the level of scientific and informational levels of fundamental and applied Ufological research; and training of experts in Ufology according to international standards. The Academy has Councils of Philosophical Science (headed by the Academician of the International Informatization Academy, V. Ajaja), and Councils of technical, medical, and biological sciences).

There is a websit for those who are interested in the ACADEMY OF INFORMATIOLOGICAL AND APPLIED UFOLOGY (AIAUFO).

It is: http://ufoacademia.narod.ru/ and this is where Vladimir Ajaja may be reached.

MARINA POPOVICH

This courageous woman is a distinguished test pilot, a scientist with a doctorate degree in flight technology from the University of Leningrad, a Lt. Colonel, and a highly decorated aviator. Today Marina Lavrentyevna Popovich heads a private aviation company. She is a journalist, and a published author of six books. Because of her efforts, Russian Ufologists were able to find out many hidden facts and covered-up incidents. She had personally observed UFOs three times in her life, once during an expedition to the Pamir Mountains, to find the Yeti. There were forty people in the expedition, including her daughter, and they all observed a UFO from an altitude of 4000 metres up the mountain. A spherical object over a nearby gorge emitted a ray. Another time she and her husband observed a giant UFO over the Mitino area. It was a giant, elongated object, some 250 metres long. An airplane flying below it was barely seen. She estimated the object to be at the altitude of 20 kilometres. The UFO left behind a vortex trail. The last time Marina Popovich observed a UFO was in June of 1996, at 3: 00 a.m. The object made no sounds, but produced complex manoeuvres. It also emitted pulse-like bursts of illumination. Marina woke up her spouse and guests, and they also observed the object.

She almost graduated from the cosmonaut training school many years ago. But she was dropped from the program after Pavel Popovich, the general she was married to, convinced high officials that she was not suited for space flights. By doing so he probably saved her health. If anyone is qualified to define what a UFO is, it would be this remarkable woman: she flew all Soviet aircraft, from AN-22 transport planes to MIG-21 supersonic jets. She holds 90 flight records.

Marina Popovich is a very clear-headed person: according to her, 90 percent of sightings are not UFOs but easily explainable phenomena. She mentioned a laboratory in Tver that was assigned the task of interpreting UFO photographs sent to them. Just like her, the researchers there could not explain 10 percent of sightings. In her interview with ANOMALIYA newspaper in 1996, Marina Popovich mentioned a top scientist at National Academy of Sciences in the United States, who has carefully researched Martian photographs. The American told her that he had studied the photographs inch by inch, very thoroughly. He and another scientist revealed to Popovich that there is a Sphinx-like structure on Mars.

Marina Popovich is firm in her beliefs. She is certain that the inventions of Leonardo Da Vinci, the writings of Jules Verne, and the science fiction of Ray Bradbury were technology transmissions from outer space. The three men have been used as mediums. She considered former Soviet President Gorbachev to be an extraterrestrial "front man" because he caused profound historical changes.

When Paul Stonehill met her in 1991, she was sure that the secret files on UFOs would become public. At the time, Marina Popovich became something like a spokesperson for Soviet UFO study groups. She estimated that it would be a long while before all such secret files will be open for inspection. Marina Popovich knew of over 14 thousand UFO sightings that took place in the USSR between 1966 and 1991. When she spoke at the Whole Life Expo in Los Angeles that year, she broke the news that underground Ufologists in the USSR who went public with their beliefs were either fired or placed in psychiatric hospitals. But even Marina Popovich was not aware of many strange UFO sightings and phenomena that took place in the Soviet Union, and came to light after 1991. She was kind enough to share information and photographs with the Russian Ufology Research Centre. Marina Popovich is a concerned ecologist, because she was able to find out what horrible damage the Communist regime had caused Russia and other countries that comprised the USSR. She saw rivers drying up, dying lakes and ponds, ozone holes, and toxic spills. Russia's ecology was ravaged even before the Chernobyl incident. Economic plight of today's Russia and poverty in her native land saddens her greatly.

As for the UFOs that cannot be explained by natural phenomena: as a trained pilot she takes them for what they are: spacecraft of extraterrestrials. Marina Popovich is certain that human beings are not the only intelligent creatures in the Universe and those others are indeed paying us a visit. Marina Popovich's address is on file in the Russian Ufology Research Centre.

ANOMALOUS PHENOMENA TEXTBOOK

The Volgograd State University published the very first Russian textbook dedicated to UFO phenomenon and anomalous phenomena in 1999. The author is Gennady Belimov, a professor of the Volzshky Humanitarian Institute, who teaches a course in Ufology and bio-energy exchange in nature. The title of his textbook is Netraditsionniye I poiskoviye kontseptsii v yestestvoznanii or Non-traditional and Explorative Concepts in Natural Science. The textbook reflects development and concepts in the area of the unknown by Dr. Vladimir Ajaja (Ph.D., Philosopjy), Y. Fomin, one of Russia's prominent researchers, V. Avinsky, a noted researcher and proponent of ancient astronaut visitation hypotheses, as well as other Russian and foreign scientists.

This textbook had to be written because there is no systematic literature about anomalous phenomena. His conviction that there is justifiability behind the issue of search for extraterrestrial civilizations is based on foundation of theories of ancient philosophers: Plato, Epicure, Pythagoras, Democritus, and others. At the dawn of human history they talked of many worlds inhabited by sentient beings, about immortal souls, and other things that modern science just now begins to realise. It is time, believes Belimov, to abandon fearful rejection of new ideas, and to approach practical development of learning of unknown natural phenomena and environment.

UFO MUSEUM

In October of 2000 we learned that a new museum opened it doors in Moscow. There is little information about the museum except that it is described as Museum of Parapsychology and Ufology. Visitors can find out about ESP, telekinesis, levitation, and other subjects. Andrey Li is the Museum's director. According to Moscow Times the Museum is located at 9/8 Bolshoy Gnezdnikovsky Pereulok, Building 3, third floor. It may be worthwhile to contact Russian Ufologists to find out more about the Museum.

IN MEMORIAM

Alexander Sergeyevich Kuzovkin passed away on May 5, 2001. He was a well-known Soviet and Russian researcher of UFO phenomenon. He graduated from the Moscow Chemical Machine Building Institute in 1980, at the age of 40. From 1977 through 1988 Kuzovkin worked with Felix Zigel. In 1989-90 he, as a leading expert of UFO photography (and photography of "invisible" beings), conducted a seminar together with E. Semyonov (Ecology of the Unknown). By 1990 Kuzovkin possessed over ten thousand reports of UFO sightings. He believed that Earth was a living organism, maimed and injured by poorly thought through grandiose projects of mankind. He was afraid that our hullabaloo around anomalous phenomena and UFOs, as well as tactless interference with their world could cause unpredictable consequences. He mentioned in his interviews that Russian science still refused to consider UFO phenomenon as anything serious, while research centres in the United States knew the seriousness of the phenomenon; Ufological research was conducted in Europe, and special UFO research departments functioned in China. In 1993 Kuzovkin officially rejected any further research in the study of anomalous phenomena, and burned most of his archives and photographs of UFOs.

Alexander Kazantsev, truly one of the founding fathers of Soviet Ufology and science fiction, passed away on September 13, 2002. He was 96 years old. We have dedicated a number of pages to this great Soviet writer and thinker in our book. He was indeed a believer in the Communist future of the world, but his beliefs did not reflect the reality of Soviet life. Yet he was a very popular author in the USSR, and his books were printed in huge quantities in the 1960s and 1970s. A. Kazanstev was a strong proponent of the ancient astronaut hypothesis.

This is by no means meant to be a definitive list of UFO researchers in the former USSR, but in the opinion of the authors of this book they are probably some of the most influential figures in modern day UFO research. Western researchers cannot imagine what life has been like, and still is for many people in the former USSR. The authors would like to pay tribute here to all those above mentioned researchers and organisations as they are a credit to Ufology, not just in their own countries, but to the subject in general on an international level. Much of their work has gone unnoticed in the West, but we hope in some small way that our book will help give them the recognition they truly deserve.

CHAPTER 39

UFOLOGY IN UKRAINE

RIAP

Research Institute of Anomalous Phenomena (RIAP) was established in 1992 by VERTICAL Aerospace Company. RIAP considers itself to be an independent research entity engaged in scientific studies in the areas of UFO phenomenon and the non-classical SETI (Search for Extraterrestrial Intelligence). The Institute, according to the RIAP Bulletin, Issue 1, 1994, performs its investigations in strict conformity to requirements of the scientific method and in close cooperation with the CIS Academy of Cosmonautics, as well as Russian and Ukrainian Academies of Sciences.

The Institute is primarily involved in the following research areas: development of methods and strategies of active monitoring of UFOs by means of radar, optical, infra-red and other detection systems; instrumental studies of alleged landing sites; impact on biological systems and UFO samples; creation of an efficient system of reconstruction of an anomalous event on the basis of witness testimonies; creation of a unified UFO database and a computer expert system to identify genuine UFOs (GUFOs); development of physical models of GUFOs; psycho physiological investigations of contactees and abductees; and studies in the history of Soviet Ufology.

The SETI research of RIAP involves the Search for Alien Artifacts on the Moon (SAAM) program. This includes the search for sunlight reflections from flat (mirror-like) surfaces of hypothetical ET objects; search for other probable artificial ET phenomena on the Lunar surface; examination of the possibility of interaction between the terrestrial and extraterrestrial civilizations on the Moon; and, finally, simulation of probable ET strategies for the Moon.

There are other UFO research projects of great importance to science undertaken by the RIAP. The Scientific Council and Advisory Board of the Institute includes such Russian and Ukrainian specialists in the UFO research and SETI field as A.V.Arkhipov (radio astronomer who has discovered supposed ETI radio sources near some distant stars), A.V.Beletsky (historian who researches pre-1917 UFO waves in Russia), Yu.A.Fomin (doyen of UFO studies in Russia), Dr. L.M.Gindilis (astronomer and SETI expert), Dr.

327

Yu.V.Platov (Vice-Chairman of the Academic UFO Study Group, whose activities are described in our book), Dr. V.K. Zhuravlev (investigator of the Tunguska explosion), and others, including a group of well-known Western scientists, scholars and engineers.

Throughout the years RIAP has published interesting and informative articles in its Bulletin. Among such we would list articles written by Alexey Arkhipov (about Lunar anomalies; ancient astronauts' visitation), and Dr. Vladimir Rubtsov (history of Soviet and post-Soviet Ufology). Generally, issues of the Bulletin contain informative articles written by Ukrainian and Russian scientists and researchers. The Bulletin is also published in English, and that helps promote UFO information exchange between researchers in different countries.

To reach RIAP, write to: Research Institute on Anomalous Phenomena, P.O. Box 4684, and 310022 Kharkiv-22, Ukraine.

STRANGE METAL

On October 14, 2000, Ukrainian newspaper Zerkalo Nedeli published an article by a journalist from the town of Nikolayev about a strange piece of metal fragment that fell from the sky a year before. The piece weighed hundreds of kilograms, but the incident received no reaction from authorities. It fell down near the town of Nikolayev. Local villagers surrounded it, for such heavy pieces falling from the sky are not regular occurrences in Ukraine. Some men tried to break the piece into smaller fragments using heavy hammers, to no avail. They finally brought the strange object to a local metal recycling centre, but those in charge refused to accept it due its strangeness. Finally, one of the residents phoned astronomers. Volunteers brought the piece to the Nikolayev Observatory...where it was dumped in the backyard.

Members of the Meteorite identification commission of the observatory decided that the piece of metal in their backyard was definitely not a meteorite. Then scientists from Kharkiv Institute analysed it, and found out that the strange piece has a unique chemical composition.

Alexey Arkhipov, a radio astronomer from Kharkiv (and a member of RIAP), thinks that the unusual find is made of a strangely heavy metal, not used in aircraft or space technology. It may be an artifact from outer space, perhaps of alien technology.

UKRAINIAN UFOLOGISTS AND RUSSIAN MILITARY SECRETS

At the end of 2000, Ukrainian Ufologists from the city of Sumi sent a letter of inquiry to the Russian Federation Defence Ministry. Copies of the letter were sent to Nikolay Subbotin of RUFORS and Alexander Bogdanchikov of Neveroyatni Mir magazine.

On October 8 and 15, REN-TV showed a program titled Voyennaya Tayna

(Military Secret). Allegedly, the producers received exclusive materials from the Russian Federation Defence Ministry regarding the recently declassified UFO archives. The program showed previously classified reports of UFO sightings over military units, the questionnaires distributed among Soviet military branches regarding anomalous phenomena; and unique video films of strange objects over military bases. The program featured Aleksandr Plaksin, leading expert of the Ministry for anomalous aerial and space phenomena, and Major General of the Air Force Nikolay Antoshkin. Ukrainian Ufologists from the Sumi Centre of Ufological Research Society "Contact", referred to Russian Constitution as to why the Defence Ministry should release such information to them.

V. Romanchenko is the Chairman of the Society, and a well-known researcher (those who want to reach Contact should write to: P.O. Box 303, Sumi-7, 40007, Ukraine).

Nikolay Subbotin supported this inquiry, but had several reservations about it. His opinion is important for those interested in UFO research in modern Russia and Commonwealth of Independent States.

He explained that the documents shown in the program were never secret or classified. Vladimir Ajaja, who was contracted by the Ministry of Defence, USSR, produced the Instructions mentioned in the program. That is according to Ajaja, of course. It was not at all difficult to obtain a copy of the Instruction; any officer who served in the Soviet/Russian armed forces between the years 1982-1995 was able to obtain such an instruction. As for the declassified KGB documents, they are the same 124 pages of documents given to Pavel Popovich by deputy head of KGB, Sham. We discussed the Instructions, and the KGB released documents in other chapters.

Then there is a problem between Russia and Ukraine regarding the strategic archives of UFO sightings:

According to Russian newspapers, Russia would postpone Ukrainian payments for delivery of natural gas if Ukraine would transfer to Russia those archives of the Soviet anti-aircraft forces that were left in Ukraine after the fall of the USSR. Ukraine hosts one of the largest bases of the strategic bombers, the TU-160 and TU-95MS aircraft. It is precisely at this base that the super secret joint archives of unidentified flying objects and anomalous atmospheric phenomena sightings of the anti-aircraft defence are kept.

The value of the archives is very high for the needs of Russia's national security. According to Russian defence Ministry officials as well as representatives of the Security Council of the Russian Federation who participated in the summit between both nations, based on the data in the archives it was possible to accurately predict the time and the place of UFO sightings. This helped the Ukrainian military assure necessary safeguards, for such sightings usually take place near strategic sites (such as nuclear power stations and military bases), and also get information about the UFOs sighted. Apparently, the military tried to establish contact with UFOs, too; for example, in the Poltava region, at a military base.

This worries Russia, for if Ukraine monopolises control over the archives, it will advance its position, and leave Moscow behind. Allegedly, Ukraine finally agreed to transfer to Russia those parts of the archives that contain information about UFO sightings over the Russian Federation.

Ukrainian Ufologists received a reply on November 21, 2000. It said that the Air Force did not participate in the REN-TV program, and all inquiries should be directed to the program's producers. Nikolay Subbotin again analysed the letter, this time the one received by researchers from Sumi. He finds it quite interesting that the response was received from the Air Force press agency, and not the Defence Ministry. The response was not clear, no matter what agency sent it.

We know that UFO phenomenon had been investigated by such Soviet state agencies as Academy of Sciences and Ministry of Defence. Just recently Yuri Platov and Boris Sokolov confirmed this in their published report History of National UFO research in the USSR. Sokolov was actually coordinating (as he stated in the report) anomalous research between 1978 and 1989 in the Ministry of Defence and the Academy of Sciences.

But regardless of the scant documents available today, we do not know how the research proceeds today. Nikolay Subbotin points out that the program did continue until 1996, when it ended, according to Platov. Hence, over 18 years funds had been allocated for research, personnel, and equipment. It is highly dubious that the findings of the governmental UFO research program were what Platov and Sokolov described them to be (as we have discussed before - authors).

Results of the research demonstrated that most of the phenomena perceived by witnesses as something anomalous actually has natural explanations. For the most part such phenomena are connected with human technological activities of the last decades, and rare forms of natural phenomena. Then Platov and Sokolov negate UFO landings reports, accounts of contacts with pilots, and reports of abductions.

Nikolay Subbotin points out that he personally talked to a colonel of the Rocket Forces who investigated a UFO landing case (tall aliens were also observed then). There are other interesting and varied reports, as we have demonstrated in our book. Hence, Subbotin finds Platov and Sokolov's "official" position incomprehensible.

ODESSA UFOLOGY
This warm Ukrainian city has been in the forefront of UFO research years ago. It all began in 1968, when an article about UFOs was published in Znamya

Kommunizma newspaper. I. Lisakovsky, who wrote the article, and the editor of the newspaper were brave people, for the Soviet reality at the time was not kind to Ufologists. This article, entitled Mystery of Flying Saucers caused the black market prices for Felix Zigel's books and Ajaja's audio lectures to rise dramatically. Igor Nikolayevich Kovshun, who died a few years ago, professor and director of the Odessa Astronomical Observatory, was presenting lectures about UFOs in the Odessa Planetarium. In 1989 he and others formed a UFO research group (IGRAYA).

Its purpose was to attract attention of general public and scientists to such anomalous phenomena as UFOs. The group consisted of mathematicians, physicists, medical doctors, psychologists, students, workers, and other interested residents of sunny Odessa. They published a newspaper, too, Zagadki Sfinksa. Odessa Ufologists contacted Paul Stonehill's newly formed Russian Ufology Research Centre in 1991, and exchange of information began to flow.

There was even a TV program, UFOs OVER ODESSA. The group evolved into the UFO Centre of Odessa, and a regional organisation of Ukrainian Ufological Association. As time went by, life became more difficult in the newly independent Ukraine, and people were concerned more about their survival and jobs. Still, the research continues, sightings are reported and investigated, and Odessa Ufologists still meet monthly in the Youth Palace of Odessa.

UKRAINIAN COUNTER-INTELLIGENCE

N. Nepomnyaschy published a very interesting book, Stranniki Vselennoy or Wanderers of the Universe (Moscow, 1999). According to Sergey Paukov, who worked in the Ukrainian counter intelligence where he collected and analysed information about "flying saucers", special services of many countries are interested in the subject of UFOs.

Reports of UFO activities in Ukraine were sent to people like him.

We need to mention here a very peculiar videotape film shown on Ukrainian TV on August 1st, 2002. A disaster took place on July 27, 2002, Saturday, at 12:45 in the afternoon, at the Lviv military and civilian airfield. The program that actually showed a strange object was broadcast August 1st, by Kiev television.

That sad July day marked a disaster for Ukraine's Air Force and those people who had the misfortune to observe the flight of an SU-27 aircraft from the ground. When the aircraft crashed, it killed 85 people, wounded 199, and ended careers of some top Ukrainian Air Force brass. The TV program clearly showed, on videotape, birds near the doomed SU-27, as well as a mysterious white-coloured object shaped as a cigar or a cylinder. The object was flying parallel to the aircraft's flight, moving from side to side behind it. The experts did not believe the object to be the cause of the air disaster. On August 4, the videotape was shown in Russia. Apparently, German television station RTL received the tape from the Lviv, Ukraine, journalists, and the Germans in turn gave the tape to the NTV of Russia. The only conclusion reached by experts is that the object was not a bird and not fragments of the SU-27. It was not an insect either, for another camera videotaped the same. Actually, the trajectory of the flight of the object was like that of a missile.

Since the demise of the former USSR countries like the Ukraine have gone their own way and UFO research is no exception. No longer suffocated by the old communist regime Ukrainian Ufologists are allowed to conduct their research out in the open and they, like their counterparts in the former USSR, have played and are still playing an important part in UFO research in what was part of the Soviet Union.

CHAPTER 40

UFOs TOO, LEAVE TRACES

Russian scientist Alexei Burenin has analysed UFO accidents in Ukraine, Komi Republic, Maritime Territory, North Caucasus, and Rostov region. He graduated from the Physics-Chemical Department of the Mendeleyev Institute of Chemical Engineering in Moscow. He is a Candidate of Sciences (Tech.), as well as deputy director-general of the UFO Centre. A. Burenin was interested in an article written by A. Leshabo and published in the weekly Nedelya (Issue 4, 1993).

Leshabo observed a flat round object of a bluish colour. To its left was another of roughly the same size and the same shape, but greenish in colour. They were approaching each other slowly and silently, and when the remaining distance between them was about five kilometres, they became motionless. Suddenly a red sphere separated from the object on the right and began floating slowly towards the neighbouring object. The one on the left sent a white ray in the direction of the approaching sphere. The colour of the sphere began changing to white of increasing intensity, the sphere grew in size, then there was a sound like a clap, the sphere sizzled and, changing its trajectory, plunged toward a bee garden, The ray vanished almost instantly after the clap, and the two objects began drawing apart, each in its own direction, slowly and majestically, until they disappeared from view. A greenish slag-like mass, looking like some kind of a blob, lay near a tree stump. It still had warmth in it and was quite hot.

Experts at the Russian Federation Institute of Aircraft Materials (VIAM) and the Sevkavgeologiya geological association analysed samples of the pumice-like glassy mass that remained on the ground. The analyses revealed most unusual properties, and are published in AURA-Z Magazine (Issue 1, 1995, "STAR WARS" over Pyatigorsk, Alexei Burenin's article). An analysis of the literature suggests (according to Burenin) that the phenomenon observed by Leshabo over Pyatigorsk was one of those cases that may be tentatively classified as an "exchange of information" between UFOs.

Interesting results were also obtained by analysing samples from the site of a UFO disaster that occurred near the town of Uchkuduk, in Uzbekistan, most probably in 1990. We tried to obtain detailed information about the incident from Russia/CIS, but did not succeed. The disaster over the Kyzylkum Desert remains a mystery to Western researchers (few have even heard of it).

Burenin was able to uncover some details. Russian investigators believe that the UFO was burned by some unknown means, and the fiery mass, something like plasma, descended to the surface of the Earth and cooled gradually. It reminded Burenin of the phenomenon observed over Pyatigorsk, and there is also a correlation between chemical compositions of the samples. The enhanced contents of silicon in both cases may be related to the high temperature (1500-1600 degrees Celsius) effect of the fiery mass on the silicon-containing soil with the formation of a melt.

Such melts are known in science as being caused by meteorite impacts or lightning discharges, but being accompanied by damage to the earth's surface and a scattering of surface material. None was recorded in either of the two cases.

In 1974 a glowing sphere was observed flying over the city of Donetsk in the Ukraine. The sphere was traveling along the Gorlovka-Donetsk line at the speed of an airliner. Sometime later its movement stopped and it blew up, lighting up the night sky and the ground over an area with a radius of 100-150 kilometres. Soon thereafter people in the city at the nearby mining towns began to find pieces of a gray metal; when rubbed against metal objects it gave off a multitude of sparks. Until 1992 it was impossible to carry out a documented chemical analysis of the material, and the sample was kept at the North Caucasus branch of the Ufological association. During that period the material began to crumble into a fine powder.

The colour of the powder was variously determined with the passage of time as silvery, bluish-gray, and greenish. An analysis performed at specialised laboratories in Rostov-on-Don showed that the powder-like substance was homogeneous, practically insoluble in water or organic solvents, soluble in dilute mineral acids, non-flammable and not destroyed by flame. When subjected to calcinations at temperatures of up to 800 degrees Celsius, its mass remained practically unchanged, but its colour changed to a reddish-brown (brick red). The substance was neither radioactive (background 80-120 micro roentgens per hour) nor magnetic. The sample contained rare earth elements.

It is interesting that an analysis of a fragment found on the river Vashka (Komi Republic of the Russian Federation) in 1976 was also found to contain rare earth elements. This case is covered in another chapter of this book. The sample intensely emitted sparks when a hacksaw was applied to it. Some researchers believe it is a remnant of the Tunguska Object. The Vashka Object controversy is described in Chapter Ten of this book.

The presence of zirconium, lanthanum, yttrium, and praseodymium was also established in the remains of a glowing sphere that blew up near Dalnegorsk (Hill 611).

334

In 1992, a UFO landing was reported from the Two Sisters hill near the town of Belaya Kalitva in the Rostov region. At this site, too, a circle nine metres in diameter, and there was a black deposit in the soil.

A. Burenin believes that the records of visual observations of UFO crashes and landings, supplemented by experiments and an analysis of the scientific literature, make it possible to treat these objects as flying machines of a planetary level created by unknown rational beings who possess technical superiority to us largely because of the use of unknown technologies. Whether or not he is correct in his assumptions remains to be seen.

Vitaly N. Vorobyov is a scientist who had helped launch the Beloyarsk Nuclear Power Station and design and construction of the Bilibin Nuclear Power Station. He also participated in the Soviet Buran shuttle program. Prior to 1991, Vorobyov had spent 15 years conducting UFO research (including the study of UFO landing sites, according to him). In an interview published in a provincial newspaper Chas Pik (Issue 31, 1991), Vorobyov revealed interesting aspects of Soviet UFO research.

He learned about UFOs in 1976. He also found out that one such object had landed near a local village (Durnovka, a large Cossack village in Novoanensky area of the Volgograd Region. Vorobyov met with F. Zigel, and his semi-underground UFO research group (5 to 6 people at the time). Vorobyov met with Zigel, and they decided to organise an expedition to the area of the alleged UFO landing site. Initially only Vorobyov and Lev Chulkov, a well known personality in the Soviet UFO research, went to the site. Vladimir Serebryannikov later joined them. Vorobyov recalls that he became interested in the UFO research because he was fascinated by the idea that Earth could be visited by extraterrestrial intelligence. But also, as an expert in the field of aircraft and space technologies, having researched information and data collected by Zigel's group since 1962, Vorobyov was convinced that "flying saucers" demonstrate unusual flying traits that could not be explained by modern know-how. Any vehicle would disintegrate into fragments immediately were it to repeat the movements that UFOs have performed. It is as if the UFOs were not made of matter.

Hence, Vorobyov dedicated his life to the study of the mysterious objects, for he wanted to comprehend their power engineering, and to adopt it to aircraft and space exploration vehicles of our own planet.

He and his colleagues arrived in Durnovo too late, some two years after the alleged landing. All (but one) witnesses have left the village (graduated from a school). The remaining witness was fearful of something, and refused to accompany Vorobyov to the landing site. But they did find the site, in an area behind the village cemetery. It was a circle of burned grass, some 18 metres in diameter. Two years after the alleged landing nothing had grown in inside the circle (the surrounding area was full of lush grass). Then neither

Vorobyov nor his colleagues possessed any tools for research; but they just wanted to see the site. Years went by and his experience grew. He recalls the "angel hair" samples from New Zealand, somehow brought to the Soviet Union. Late I. Kirichenko, who also actively studied the Tunguska Phenomenon, analysed it. Vorobyov, in 1991, had possessed a sample of matter collected at the site of the Ivanovo landing. In 1989, in the town of Ivanovo, the following, according to Vorobyov, took place. On December 31 of that year a UFO hovered over the town and "fired" two fiery spheres. They burned up after falling into the snow. Vorobyov told the newspaper that he had whatever remained at the site after the combustion. The material is amazing, especially the structure of certain fragments. Although Vorobyov knows physical metallurgy very well, he had never before seen anything like it. What he had in his hands was metallic ceramics emitting foul odour (like the New Zealand samples). Certainly it was slag, but it also contained particles that did not burn. The substance was made of a spherical-like structure. Professor Smirnov, a Ph. D. of Medical Sciences, studied photographs of the substance (made with the help of powerful Japanese electronic microscope). He said that the structure reminded him of an albumen structure of certain microbes. The substance also was a good conductor of electricity. There are different resistance points within the substance. When enlarged, it shows that the structure is metallic. But for truly detailed research Vorobyov needed very precise microelectrodes, because the diameter of a sphere was less than 60 microns. Alas, we do not know what happened to Vorobyov's research after 1991.

UFO landing traces are as common in the former USSR as they have been in other parts of the world. As yet there is no definitive proof that we are dealing with technologies beyond our own, but we do have some examples of tantalising evidence that may just point in this direction.

CHAPTER 41

UFOs OVER THE CHECHEN BATTLEFIELDS

ITUM-KALE

As the First Chechen War intensified during the winter of 1994-1995, UFOs began to visit the area quite frequently. On December 14, 1994, Russian newspaper Izvestiya reported two sphere-shaped, fiery objects performing complicated manoeuvres over the battleground. They also hovered above the Dolinsky settlement. Eyewitnesses included both the journalists who reported the story, as well as the local Russian military commander.

A cigar-shaped object was reported to have hovered over a northern suburb of Grozny for over three hours. Later the same object was sighted over the Pervomayskaya settlement during a battle between Russian armoured forces and Dudayev's troops.

In 1997 a number of Western and Russian Ufologists received a strange e-mail message, written in poor English. The author signed his name as "Eddie EDISSON". His claim was that a "Flying Apparatus" was blown up and crashed in Chechnya, in November of 1995.

During the war in the Chechen Republic-Itchkeria, in November of 1995, in the mountains of Chechnya, near the settlement Itum-Kale, a flying craft of an unknown design was blown up, stated mysterious Eddie EDISSON. It was possible to collect some fragments of this craft at the crash site. Among the Chechen forces there were a number of scientists and engineers, technical experts, who were able to determine who had manufactured the unknown apparatus. Despite the raging battle and personal dangers, Chechen technical experts assembled fragments of the crashed and destroyed craft, and compiled preliminary research results and prepared hand-made drawings.

These research activities were designated as top secret and were placed under the personal control of the President of Chechen Republic-Itchkeria, Jokhar Doudaev. The results of such research activities were reported to him personally, and he was the only one to have kept all of the research materials.

Jokhar Dudayev perished in an explosion on April 21, 1996. When he died, his brief case, where he kept his personal archives about the UFO, burned with him. Several pages were recovered and kept as a record.

Three of the pages describe the UFOs design. Two of the pages contained technical sketches, made by unknown artists. After the war ended, an investigation ensued. It was fruitless, because all of the known members of the technical research group perished in the war. No other eyewitnesses of the UFO crash were found. No one knows where the fragments of the crashed UFO are buried. A surviving bodyguard of Jokhar Dudayev picked the three slightly burned pages at the site of the explosion on April 22, 1996. He turned them over to whomever Eddie EDISSON represented. In his opinion, even the remaining pages reveal, with a high degree of probability, secrets of how UFOs operate.

He also surmises that if the remaining fragments of the crashed UFO are discovered, mankind would find answers to the long-awaited questions. Basically, Eddie EDISSON was reaching out to UFO researchers to get an address of a UFO research laboratory or a university, to recreate and construct a model of the UFO that exploded in November of 1995.

Mikhail Gershtein has undertaken his own investigation, after he read Eddie EDISSON's email. No one he asked knew about the Itum-Kale incident. But he did find out about yet another UFO "crash" not far away from Chechnya. Gershtein published his article about it in NLO magazine.

The Alagir region of the Northern Ossetia had reported to the Ministry of the Russian Federation for Civil Defence, Emergencies and Elimination of Consequences of Natural Disasters (EMERCOM of Russia) on February 26, 1995 about an "airplane disaster. Local residents claimed that an airplane crashed to the ground, and the sky had become crimson from the ensued fire. A helicopter from the city of Vladikavkaz left for the crash site; the MIG-8 craft carried a group of rescuers from the EMERCOM on board. It took them four hours to thoroughly search the area, pointed out by local residents, but the rescuers were not able to recover neither bodies of the perished pilots, nor any aircraft fragments. They did find areas of the burned out grass at the site.

Gershtein believes that even Russian military do not doubt anymore that Chechnya was and is under a close surveillance by aliens from the outer space. As an example, he cites an article published in the newspaper of the Northern Caucasus military district in 1995. The article is appropriately titled "Chechen crisis under UFO observation".

In the article, Aleksandr Ursov from the city of Grozny recalls the 15th of August 1995. At 8 pm, one could observe a group of seven UFOs in the sky. Their flight altitude was approximately 15-20 kilometres. They were inside a bright greenish transparent cloud, of elliptical shape. Flying ahead of them were three huge orange spheres with very long, yellow-reddish tails. Behind them, two orange triangles with long, yellow-coloured spiral tails (two tails for every triangle). Behind them were two small spheres with identical tails. Ursov adds that if we consider the altitude, the objects must have been quite huge.

Ursov was able to see another sighting on May 16, 1995. It took place at two o'clock at night. A bright ruby-coloured light suddenly illuminated a quite common cloud at the south-western suburb of Grozny. Two thin pillars of bright red light flew out from the centre of the cloud. They flared up at the same time, disappeared, and then re-appeared some 2 or 3 seconds later over the centre of the city. The pillars hovered in a vertical position, then became enveloped by clouds, and began flaring up either by bright or dull reddish lights.

In November of 2000 strange reports of a UFO over Dagestan made global news. Basically, the story can be summarised this way:

An alleged UFO had alerted Russian border troops (the Derbent units) near Dagestan, a Republic bordering Chechnya. Dagestan is one of the republics of the former USSR. It is located between Caspian Sea on the East and Caucasus mountains on the West, the date of the incident: November 14, 2000. Details of the incident were reported to the Dagestan Ministry of the Interior. At 1:45 a.m. (Moscow time) a rapidly moving target was registered in the area of the Kazmalyar and Novaya Filya, of the Magaramkent region of Dagestan. The area is at the border of Azerbaijan. The unidentified flying object flew at an altitude of 100 metres from the direction of the mountains toward the Caspian Sea. The UFO contained three lights, each at a distance of two metres from each other. Two minutes later the object disappeared from sight of the Russian border units. At the time neither the border units, nor the Ministry of the Interior representatives could determine the nature of the object.

But Russian online newspaper Gazeta.ru announced later that the unidentified flying object, emitting three beams of light, and sighted on November 14, 2000, was actually a "Russian spaceship". This revelation was presented to Russian journalists by Colonel-General Yevgeniy Balkhovitin (head of the Northern Caucasus Directorate of the Federal Border Troops). He did not go into any details about the spaceship. But Balkhovitin did emphasise that this piece of information was related to the border troops from the central command post of the Air Defence Forces.

Igor A. Leskov provides a valuable insight into this mystery. In his brief article "On the trail of the Dagestan UFO", published in the RUFO Vestnik online newsletter (Issue 8(11), I. Leskov provides the following explanation.

He happened to have resided in the Derbent area. This is the same area where the November 14, 2000 incident took place. Leskov, a researcher himself, never knew that anything anomalous ever took place in the area. He was quite surprised when his mother recalled that she and her friend observed an unidentified flying object in that area some seven years before. She visited her son, and happened to see the Vremya broadcast about the incident in November of 2000. That prompted Leskov's mother to recall what she was a witness to, two years ago.

The sighting she had in 1993 took place just before dusk. The object was moving completely noiselessly, at the altitude of approximately 100 metres. It descended and hovered on occasions, and its size was that of a large airplane. Leskov's mother was reminded of a dirigible (cigar-shaped, with somewhat narrow ends). But the object lacked a gondola and other attributes of a blimp. In the middle section of the UFO (close to the rear end) she saw small square-shaped "windows' (illuminated by a yellowish light); she could also see moving shadows behind the windows.

Leskov believes the military explanation that the November 14, 2000, UFO was an apparatus of Earth origin. He writes that several years after the incident related to him by his mother, similar sightings took place quite frequently, but to the north from the area of Derbent, closer to the town of Buynaksk. Some reports about the sightings made it to the pages of the local media. Strangely, no reaction from the Russian military followed, although the Chechen warfare was in full swing.

I. Leskov mentions the secret testing range of the Russian Navy not far away, at the Caspian Sea. It is quite probable that there were new tests of a "UFO" in November of 2000. He also mentions that according to those who had witnessed a launch of a missile from the sea level, the object can be seen for miles around. It looks like a very beautiful pillar of light, going up from the sea toward the sky, and later dispersing by trailing concentric circles.

Mikhail Gershtein also mentioned another possibility: the UFO sighted on November 14, 2000, could have been a Russian-made drone. They were used quite frequently during the warfare in Chechnya; their size is similar to the reported size of the UFO.

We conducted our own investigation into the matter of a drone.

According to Russian journalist Vyacheslav Fyodorov (http://www.warlib.ru/), the UFO sighted over Dagestan on November 14, 2000 was actually an advanced Russian weapon, an unmanned aerial vehicle (UAV).

Combining Mr. Fyodorov's information and our independent research, the following was determined:

In March of the year 2000, the Russian Defence Ministry had approved an unmanned reconnaissance system Stroy-P (unmanned reconnaissance complex or PRC). The system was created in the Yakovlev Experimental Design Bureau, a major Russian military aircraft manufacturer, (OKB imeni Yakovleva) named for A. S. Yakovlev, a famous Soviet aircraft designer. The Yak Aircraft Corporation is now a privatised Russian aviation corporation. Pchela (a drone component of the complex) was built, as far as is known, at the Kishtim Radio Plant, with the help of the Smolensk Aviation Plant (while the Smolensk Aviation Plant joined with the Yakovlev Design Bureau in March, 1992 to form the Yak Aviation Company, the two entities seem to be operating separately); the official maker of the Pchela is Kulon Scientific Research Institute (R&D Institute of Aircraft Technology). This system, or complex, includes a launcher on caterpillar-fitted platform, two vehicles and ten (initially, five) Pchela-1T 061 aircraft. The Stroy-P complex was accepted for service with the Russian Army in 1997.

A Pchela (remotely piloted reconnaissance drone that provides television surveillance of ground targets) weighs 130 kilograms (loaded), has an operational range of 110 to 150 kilometres, can fly at altitudes ranging from 100 metres to 3 kilometres, and cruises at speeds from 11- to 150 kilometres an hour. Combat-recorded range: 55 kilometres. Its flight endurance is 2 hours (it needs 20 litres of gasoline for this). Its power plant is piston plus two solid rockets take-off boosters (power at 32hp). Onboard of the Russian drone are a video camera, a still camera, a mapping camera, and a secure radio. It uses a parachute for landing. Pchela is probably equal in capability to many Western UAV in the same class. However, it is a slower, tactical unmanned aerial vehicle than, for example, the Russian the 800-kilometre-per-hour Reis UAV.

The chronology is as follows: in 1982, the Soviet military gave instructions to the A.S. Yakovlev Design Bureau to develop a small, remotely piloted aerial vehicle (distantsionno-pilotiruemiy letatel'niy apparat, or DPLA). The person in charge of the project was a talented designer, Yuri Yankevich. Years later, a DPLA-605 Pchela was developed. This was first Soviet UAV capable of monitoring ground targets with an on-board television camera that had a real-time downlink. Later, Pchela (Russian word for a honey bee), the unmanned tactical reconnaissance drone (bespilotnyi samolet, in Russian), was modified to Pchela-1T (TV observer), Pchela-1IK (new version), and according to www.aviation.ru/Yak/, to Expert, a 5-th generation unmanned tactical reconnaissance drone to replace Pchela from the Stroy-P system.

Back in the summer of 2000 the Russians were conducting test flights of their Pchela-1T light unmanned reconnaissance aircraft, according to Mr. Fyodorov. Apparently, Russian media carried stories about the "airplane-robot" and its onboard TV camera. The Pchela drones tested in November of 2000 are also equipped to fly in the night-time and have infrared vision capability. The timing of the UFO sighting over Dagestan and the tests of the Pchela drones coincide.

Similar "UFO" flew into the Soviet Union back in 1969, and turned out to be an unmanned American espionage aircraft. The Soviets were sufficiently impressed, and their government ordered that a similar aircraft be developed per Soviet standards and equipment. However, the Soviets were designing their own unmanned spy planes back in the late 1950s and 1960s. We can be certain that some UFO sightings through the years of the Cold War were nothing but tests of such aircraft observed by innocent bystanders.

Meanwhile, the Pchela was incorporated, as a weapon, by Russian armed forces in 1997. There is a special unit dedicated to the use of unmanned aviation systems in the town of Akhtyubinsk, in the Astrakhan province of southern Russia (a Russian state aviation research centre is located there as well). Russian Bees are sold to foreign buyers, too, and have been featured at the Russian pavilions at the international aviation exhibitions. The Russians have used the Pchela in Chechnya, but Mr. Fyodorov doubts that the Russian military has utilised the weapon's potential fully. However, Russian Military Parade magazine (1999) claims something different. Their information came from a source in the Russian Defence Ministry.

This source claimed that decision to use PRCs in Chechnya to provide continuous aerial reconnaissance and target designation data for the Federal troops has been taken after analysing the results of combat operations in Dagestan. The fact is, when suppressing the fire positions of the rebels, the Russian troops were in lack of reconnaissance information, transmitted in the real time mode. Also, in 1995, the Stroy-P complex was already used in Chechnya (a Pchela weighed 138 kilograms at the time).

According to www.rg.ru/english/Archiv/2000/0114/1.htm, the unmanned air reconnaissance military unit was situated on the mountain Goiten-Kort near Khankala. The "plane-robot" proved its unique abilities having received a lot of valuable information that saved hundreds of lives. But the Russian Defence Ministry lacked funds to procure the upgraded weapons (according to the information from 1999; obviously, in the year 2000 the funds to procure upgraded Stroy-P complexes were found).

According to the same source, the Pchela-1 RPC made 10 flights in Chechnya, with the total flight time accumulated of 7 hours 25 minutes. Why would the Pchela be operated over Dagestan? To provide the round-the-clock control over 200 kilometres of the Chechnya border, and to block the attempts of rebels to penetrate the adjacent territories, according to the Military Parade's source. In 2000, the same magazine had an interesting article written by Nikolai Novichkov, Editing Director of the ITAR-TASS Department of Scientific and Technical Information. The author claimed that due to financial restraints, the Defence Ministry has not yet purchased a single new Stroy-II complex and currently has only three earlier produced sets (the article was published in early 2000), one of which was tested in Chechnya.

Russia's Defence Ministry is expected to spur adoption for service of the Pchela-1T RPV (or RPC-authors) with night vision equipment. The Pchela-1T RPVs employed in Chechnya (at the time Mr. Novichkov's article was published - authors) were equipped with only day surveillance TV cameras. The Pchela version, fitted out with infrared night-vision devices, was developed a long time ago, but its tests still had not been completed in early 2000 due to lack of funds. In November of 2000 the tests were performed, as the sightings reported confirm. Another confirmation of the tests can be found here:

http://www.vor.ru/science/madeinrus15_eng.html

The "UFO" sighted over Dagestan, it appears, was one of Russian Army's tactical reconnaissance assets.

By the way, in 1989 a Nikolai Novichkov was one of the editors of the English-Russian Dictionary of Antimissile & Anti-satellite Defence (Moscow Military Publishing House). The dictionary had unidentified flying object as an entry (page 353). We believe he is the author of the article in Military Parade. This is a footnote in the turbulent history of UFOs over the USSR.

There was another curious sighting in the area a short time later. "Residents of Chervishevo in the Tyumen region" west of Baku and the Caspian Sea "saw an unusual phenomenon Thursday," November 16, 2000. "An RIA (Russian news agency) correspondent reports that at approximately 6:30 p.m. local time Ludmilla Kovaleva and her young daughter, Yulya, went into the yard of their house" in Chervishevo "and could see 'a small dot with a long shiny tail' for several minutes." "Ms. Kovaleva said this was the second case in the seven years she and her family have lived in the village. The Kovalevas saw 'something that looked like a comet but with a long tail' back in April 2000."

"Nobody knows what it might be, an unidentified flying object, a meteorite fragment, a comet, a satellite or the aftermath of some flight test carried out at a military base nearby."

The information about this sighting was published in UFO ROUNDUP Volume 5, Number 48 November 30, 2000 Editor: Joseph Trainor.

http://ufoinfo.com/roundup

We still have no finite explanation as to the nature of the UFO sighted in Dagestan in November of 2000. Just as we do not know what has been sighted in Chechnya, a place that has experienced two wars in the last ten years.

Because of the complex conflicts that take place in the area, and international intrigues, no doubt influenced by Caspian Sea's oil reserves, on occasion UFOs are a useful subterfuge.

Here is an example:

On November 17, 1999, three Russian helicopters violated Georgian airspace and fired on a Georgian village, prompting the foreign ministry to make a formal protest against Russia's "act of aggression against a sovereign state".

(Itar -Tass, 18 Nov 1999 via Nexis)

This was not the first time. Russian planes bombed a Georgian village in August and an Azerbaijani village in October. Both times the Russian military initially denied responsibility. This prompted the Moscow daily, Izvestia to run the headline "UFOs bomb Georgia." (Izvestia 27 August 1999) The bombings might have been a result of gross inaccuracy and negligence on the part of the Russian military (other military forces throughout the world committed similar "errors"). Or, perhaps, they were calculated threats to test the resolve of Georgia and Azerbaijan; as well as a chance to test the NATO's reaction to the bombings.

Researchers have to be very careful when dealing with UFO reports emanating from such war torn areas of the world as such information can be inaccurate at best. We have seen also that the Soviet authorities are quite prepared to blame their own activities on UFOs in a form of psychological warfare. Whether or not all UFO sightings from the Chechen battlefields are the result of such psychological warfare remains to be seen, but it is highly unlikely that some of them certainly were.

CHAPTER 42

UNUSUAL DEVELOPMENTS

There have been numerous UFO reports since 1991 that deserve closer observation. Perhaps after reading the description provided, and the time of the sightings, Western researchers will be able to correlate them, and find a pattern.

Kaliningrad has had its share of secret military projects and sightings. As reported in ANOMALIYA newspaper in 1992, the strangest one occurred in May of 1991. Two witnesses observed a cube-shaped object of light-gray colour in the sky late in the afternoon. It flew at the altitude of 200 metres. The UFO's edges turned black after a while. The object descended, turned around rapidly, and vanished at great speed.

Professor K. Volkova, a medical doctor, and a keen observer reported that on July 31st, 1991, she stayed in the Leningrad area. The doctor saw a strange large and dark object across from the Sun. Some time later to the right of the Sun, a row of silvery-yellow objects was formed, at equal distance from each other. Then another, identical row (four objects in each) was formed to the left of the Sun. Then everything vanished.

In early October of 1991 residents of Arkalyk, Kazakstan, reported a UFO. The object appeared on the eve of the Soviet-Austrian space crew landing. Witnesses described it as a saucer with a semi-transparent halo, and rays that emitted in several directions. Local newspapers reported that similar UFOs have been sighted in the area previously, always flying the same route, north to south and towards the landing area for Soviet cosmonauts.

Years went by, and another report came from Kazakstan. The incident took place in July of 1996. On a highway, not far from the capital city, witnesses sighted a spherical object of blue-red colour combination. The automobiles in the area suffered from stalled engines, and the humans were paralysed with fear for several minutes. Then, just one month later, the air defence units of Kazakstan registered another UFO over Alma-At. As reported by Colonel A. Dobrinin, on July 24, a diamond shaped object of bright silvery colour periodically sent a thin green ray to the ground. The UFO too, experienced bursts of muted red and yellow lights. The military observed it for over an hour and a half, while it hovered over the area, its shape, size, and location never changing.

Several reports came from Byelorussia, and one actually made it to the pages of Vecherny Minsk newspaper (September 9, 1997). A former pilot observed an arrow-like large object in the sky, at about 300 metres over the ground. The UFO emitted different colours, and emitted rays of light. The pilot remained silent for a few days, until he read a sighting report of the same object in a newspaper.

THE BARNAUL SIGHTINGS

Barnaul, one of the oldest cities in West Siberia, emerged at the time of Russia expanse into the international arena, after reforms instituted by Czar Peter the Great propelled the huge country forward.

Akinfy Demidov, a factory owner from the Urals, sent by the great Czar to establish Russian industries in the untamed mountains and lands full of mineral wealth, selected a suitable site for a new and larger metal works near the mouth of Barnaulka River, at the foothills of the Altai Mountains. The city was founded in 1730.

Today Barnaul is an important industrial centre. There are more than 120 thousand people employed there who produce diesels, metal-cutting lathes, forge presses, steam boilers, tires, synthetic fibres, technical carbon, boring machines, cotton cloth and faceted diamonds.

The Altai Territory (its area, including Gorno-Altai Republic, is 262 thousands square kilometres) is part of south-western Siberia, which attracts many tourists. It borders on Kazakhstan, and the Novosibirsk and Kemerovo Regions, and the Republic of Altai. We have discussed UFO phenomenon related to Kazakhstan, Siberia, and areas in the Altai throughout the book. As for Novosibirsk, it too is visited by unidentified flying objects. On October 20 of last year, Vecherniy Novosibirsk newspaper reported that Monday the 23rd of October, in the evening, a very bright star appeared over the area. It emitted triangular rays. The sighting lasted several minutes. Then the "star" disappeared instantaneously, (just as quickly as it initially appeared in the sky). The trail left behind was similar to the trail of a jet.

The Altai Territory is not that far away from the Baikonur Cosmodrome and the Semipalatinsk nuclear testing range. There is a lot of electromagnetic radiation released at both sites, and some proponents of ET hypothesis believe that UFOs need such energy to recharge their power supplies. Others believe that "UFOS" over the Altai Territory are Russian-made craft, tested over the Cosmodrome. Still others point to Tibet for possible explanations. There is a strong belief among some Russian researchers that the Himalayan, Pamir, and Tien Shen mountains are huge reservoirs of cosmic energy (or that the areas contain underground cities where advanced civilizations found their refuge).

According to Sobesednik magazine (Issue 6, 2001), there were just six recorded UFO sightings over the Altai Territory from 1930 to 1949. But in the last fifty years, over 112 sightings have been recorded.

Vostochny Express newspaper reported a number of interesting sightings in its issue dated 14, 1991. A report from the Shekhonainsky region described a UFO that looked like a "second moon". This "moon" actually emitted rays that explored the settlement below, and was soon joined by a similar object that also emitted rays. The objects moved about noiselessly. Eyewitnesses reported UFOs over Leninogorsk (eastern Kazakhstan) to be shaped as dumbbells.

In the flood-lands of Gromotukha River one of the local dwellers actually reported meeting face to face with an anthropoid creature, three metres tall, wearing a spacesuit. The denizens of Bolshe-Narimskoye town and nearby auls (villages) reported numerous UFOs that explored nearby fields and industrial plants. Passing cars below the hovering UFOs would experience stalled engines. In the Zaysansky area Soviet border guards were alerted after a UFO spent several hours over the land. In Ust-Kamenogorsk, at the same time as in the Shekhonainsky area, three UFOs were reported; they, too, emitted rays. To summarise: the UFOs of 1991 in the Altai area were reported over a territory the size of France. The Altai has become, once again, an attraction to the unidentified flying observers of life below. Did the ever-increasing (and sudden) local pollution levels attract them? Let us recall that in September of 1990 a powerful explosion took place at the Ul'binsky Metallurgical Plant. This is where fuel for nuclear power stations was produced. As a result of the explosion, a huge amount of poisonous beryllium was released into the atmosphere. Is it that the UFOs, just as in Chernobyl, arrived to check on human-generated destruction of nature and environment? Another explanation of the 1991 flap could be due to the fact that the Soviet Union was disintegrating rapidly, a historical process equal to the fall of the Roman Empire. Why would "they" miss watching it?

Another, more recent, disturbing report came from the Altai Mountains. There was a confirmation of it, published in NLO magazine (Issue 8, 1997). The area itself, not far from Mongolia and China, has been used by Soviets for secret facilities. The Gomzyakov family travelled through the reservoir, on a boat, June 6 (Friday night) of 1997. They sighted a luminescent flying object, moving at the speed of some 500 kilometres an hour. It turned around over the Ob River, and flew towards Novosibirsk. One hour later the group came to their destination, and as they disembarked, all were able to observe a UFO over the Krutikha Village. The object was engulfed in a gas cloud of a brownish hue, and it emitted powerful floodlights downwards. The witnesses were fascinated by another object (to the right), reflected by powerful light: it was attached to the UFO, its size was about eight times larger than the UFO, and its shape was that of a sickle. Another UFO, identical to the emitting gas substance, flew in front. It, too, emitted brownish gas, but in a different, systematic manner. The incident lasted for over fifteen minute, and then the UFOs flew towards Novosiborsk. The smell left behind reminded eyewitnesses of the smells coming from furnaces of metallurgical works.

UFOs, as we can see, are attracted to Barnaul. Recently there have been numerous sightings of strange objects in the sky.

On October 31, 2000, in the evening, people sighted a luminescent object, slowly moving to the north-east. There have been sightings throughout November of last year; UFOs were reported to be multi-coloured, sometimes they would "flare up".

In May of 2001, the night of 21st of the month, an object hovered over the old part of town. This report comes from a local newspaper Svobodny Kurs. The object changed its shape during the forty minutes of its presence in the area. The shapes included a sphere, a cylinder, a triangle, and a glowing dot. No sounds were recorded. According to the newspaper, there was a sighting back on Janury 21st, in the landing area of the Barnaul Airport. When pilots of a private company jet sighted the UFO, they refused to fly their Il-76, and turned back. The UFO was a sphere, it was initially orange, and then turned violet-green, and finally red. When observed through binoculars, the object looked to be of an elliptic shape. It was not large, about the size of a soccer ball. It initially hovered over the airport, and then started a slow movement, its speed some 10 to 20 kilometres, from left to right, and vice versa. After an hour and a half the UFO departed toward Pavlovsk. The last thing observed by air traffic controllers at the Barnaul Airport, was a red glow that flared up in the rear section of the object (now, a semi-sphere). Then the UFO disappeared. The local anti-aircraft military units were immediately notified, but did not register anything on their radars. By the way, according to Sobesednik, the crew acted according to the instructions in place. Such instructions were issued in late 1980s, after a UFO chased a passenger jet in the area of Kaliningrad... The UFO would follow the jet through its flight, occasionally assuming a shape of an airplane. After the incident, Soviet Ministry of Civil Aviation issued special instructions to all Soviet airports: UFOs are not to be approached closely; if provoked by UFOs, disregard such provocations; in turn, do not provoke UFOs; observe everything, write everything down in great detail, and send reports to the commission of flight safety. The Barnaul Airport officials did precisely as instructed, and also sent inquiries to Semiplatinsk and Baykonur. There was nothing sighted at both locations. One week later the same UFO was sighted over a nearby settlement of Gon'ba. Another strange incident took place in the Malakhovo Village, later same month.

According to Sobesednik, there were at least two other incidents with UFOs at Soviet airports. In 1962 (the same year that Menzel's book debunking UFOs was published in the USSR), the Moscow Vnukovo Airport experienced a strange incident. A UFO was able to evade all Soviet air defence-tracking systems, and hovered over the airport for two hours.

In 1985, the city of Gor'ky (now Nizhni Novgorod) airport reported UFOs flying at speeds of 6000 to 7000 kilometres per hour.

In March of 2001, residents of Barnaul observed a UFO over the city's eastern suburbs. It reappeared on the 6th, 7th, and 9th of the month. Its s hape was that of a sphere. Nothing happened to its shape on the first day, but later it started changing its shape, "danced around" in the sky, increased and decreased its size, "exploded" like fireworks, split apart into pieces, and rejoined again, changed its colours and moved around erratically.

Eduard Gozhin, a UFO researcher from Siberia, has stated in a letter to the RUFORS Round Table that a book published in Tomsk (Russia), provides an adequate explanation.

The title of that book is "Monitoring Atmosferi Sibirskogo Regiona", and it contains a chapter regarding the January sighting.

While Mr. Gozhin does not possess the book, he was able to summarise the author's explanation. The UFO is but an electromagnetic "clot" in the atmosphere. There is a laboratory, dedicated to the research of similar phenomena. Such phenomena (systems, per Mr. Gozhin) are caused by human activities - an interference with ecological equilibrium in nature. Basically, Mr. Gozhin wanted to indicate that Russian scientists study such "UFOs", and have achieved some tangible results in their work.

Hence, he is of the opinion that the Barnaul Object is no UFO, but a phenomenon created on Earth. Gozhin is not fluent in English, but those who want to reach him, should do so by writing to the authors of this book.

Whether Western researchers have similar sighting within their files is of course a great interest to us. One of the reasons for writing this book is to open up areas of further research and exchanges of information between UFO researchers in the East and those in the West. For far too long Soviet UFO sightings have not been available to Western researchers and while our book will not solve all such problems it will no doubt help a great deal.

CONCLUSION

No long ago, Yuri Smirnov described in his newspaper the state of contemporary Russian Ufology. He said that gone are the days of Soviet UFO research, as other aspects of Soviet life, was largely sheltered from Western influences. There was some, quite scant, one-way information exchange with foreign UFO research groups limited basically to receiving occasional Western publications.

Thus, Soviet Ufology remained "pure", and free from influences of yellow and tabloid press. Scientific and military research conducted in the USSR was a forbidden subject, and only after the Gorbachev's perestroika Soviet UFO researchers and those in the West interested in their research did find out some details. The KGB, too, had its own programs and data collection, partially revealed in the early 1990s. Occasionally we see and hear sensational bits of information about other KGB UFO research aspects, and while such information may be true, we simply do not have the evidence in our hands to support it. In our book we make every attempt to describe as fully as possible Soviet and Russian UFO cases, research areas, prominent personalities involved in such research (military, intelligence agencies, and civilian), opinions and viewpoints of those who were and are serious in their approach to the study of anomalous phenomena. Obviously, we will not give forum to dubious contactees; spinners of tall tales; sociopaths who deny Westerners the right to write about Russian Ufology and who denigrate esteemed Russian and Ukrainian researchers that happen to have different views; UFO cultists, and other similar types. We thank those who have helped us in our endeavour: Nikolay Subbotin, Mikhail Gershtein, Vadim Chernobrov, Anatoly Kutovoy, Yuri Orlov, Genrikh Silanov and many other Russian UFO researchers, kind, intelligent, open-hearted people dedicated to the pursuit of knowledge.

CO-OPERATION ACROSS THE OCEAN

A serious effort to study the UFO phenomenon jointly and to share information was initiated in 1991. The Joint American-Soviet Aerial Anomaly Federation (JASAAF) was formed, thanks to the efforts of Dr. Richard Haines. Paul Stone hill helped him translate some announcements and the invitation to Soviet Ufological organisations to join the Federation. It looked so promising back then. The co-signers to the document establishing the federation included the Mutual UFO network, J. Allen Hynek Centre for UFO Studies, and the Fund for UFO research in America. In the USSR the co-signers were the All Union Inter-branch Scientific and Coordinative UFO Centre (SOYUZUFOTSENTR), and the Scientific Research Institute for the Study of Anomalous Phenomena. The co-directors were Vladimir Ajaja in Moscow, and Dr. Vladimir Rubtsov in Kharkov (or Kharkiv, as it is known today) in Ukraine. Haines, a retired NASA scientist, has travelled several times to the former Soviet Union. The Federation was to be a bridge for serious investigators of both nations. Actually, the federation translated and published some of Felix Zigel's works, and created an awesome file of UFO phenomena-related news clippings and articles from the USSR (some were translated, too). Chaotic changes and troubles that beset the former Soviet Union precluded any serious joint research projects. There has not been any significant joint activity during the last eight years: times have not been easy for former Soviet Ufologists. However, Dr. Haines remains optimistic, and we share his hopes for a better tomorrow.

Our book is not meant be definitive, as that would be impossible, but it is meant to show that UFO research has been and still is very active in the former USSR. We hope that by publishing this research and investigation we will enable greater co-operation between East and West in what some have called 'The Greatest Mystery Known To Mankind'. Only time will tell if we have been successful or not.

Paul Stonehill and Philip Mantle.

HEALINGS OF ATLANTIS

Quality Products for your Mind, Body, Spirit & Soul

Please visit our online store:
www.HealingsOfAtlantis.com

Holistic Workshops ◎ Monthly Horoscopes ◎ Moon Phases
Crystals ◎ Tarot & Oracle Cards ◎ Flower Remedies ◎ Organic
Aromatherapy ◎ Organic Soaps & Shampoos ◎ Jewellery ◎ Runes
Greetings Cards ◎ Crystal Balls ◎ Incense & Incense Holders
Candles & Candle Holders ◎ Feng Shui ◎ Angels ◎ Books ◎ CDs,
DVDs
and much much more….

www.HealingsOfAtlantis.com

Also available from Healings of Atlantis:

UFO Case Files of Scotland
(Amazing Real Life Alien Encounters)
By Malcolm Robinson

The subject of UFOs has been hotly debated. Are UFOs space vehicles from another world? Are they top-secret military aircraft of some kind? Or are they simply a figment of our imagination? If we are totally honest none of us really know for sure, but one thing we can say with complete accuracy is that whatever UFOs are, they do not respect any international boundary or border.

Malcolm Robinson is a UFO & Paranormal Researcher with over 30 year's expertise and has had 'hands on' experience with each of the cases contained in this book. Malcolm has lectured extensively on UFOs and the Paranormal all over the UK and Ireland and was the first Scot to lecture on American soil in Laughlin Nevada in 2009.

In the publication of Malcolm Robinson's first book, he looks to enlighten you with the most fascinating UFO cases that Scotland has to offer. This is an epic book, a book that clearly shows that Scotland as a country has been touched by the UFO presence. This book will leave you with little doubt that mankind is dealing with a very real and bona fide phenomenon, as the witnesses in this book can clearly testify to.

www.HealingsOfAtlantis.com

Also available from Healings of Atlantis:

Time & Time Again
(My Family and Reincarnation)
By Kenneth N Gould

This is a completely true story, a chronicle of a chain the most incredible and fascinating events which have taken place in the author's life. These are not ordinary events but encounters with the next world which can only be deemed as proof of the after-life.

Kenneth N Gould recounts how his 'Grannie Alice' from beyond the grave, request him to act as her saviour and her pen; her chronicler and agent on this earth; and how she informed him of the tasks required to fulfill her wishes, which have now been accomplished.

Additionally to his grandmother's own story, unexpectedly and astoundingly he has been led to the conclusion that reincarnation has occurred with respect to another member of his remarkable family.

This book must surely become a classic in the field of the paranormal. For anyone with even just a fleeting interest in this subject and family history, to read it is a must.

If you doubt reincarnation and life after death, then it is time for you to think again.

www.HealingsOfAtlantis.com

Also available from Healings of Atlantis:

The Ghost Hunting Files
(Ordinary Peoples Encounters With The Supernatural)
By Natalie Osborne-Thomason

Can a doll become possessed by the spirit of a child? Can an evil ghost drive a family from their dream home by his actions in the night? Can a child relay from the beyond, that a deadly vaccine supposed to promote health caused her death and could potentially kill other innocents? All these questions are answered here, and many more besides. The truth is out there and it's far stranger than fiction...

Natalie Osborne-Thomason is an experienced member and investigator of 'The Ghost Club' based in London. She became interested in the paranormal after experiencing it first hand. Living in a haunted mill cottage for seven years, she felt a desire to find out more. She joined 'The Ghost Club' in this quest and through careful study learned how to set up an investigation and the techniques of interviewing witnesses. She has also studied some of the scientific breakthroughs and reasons for some of the phenomena.

The life of a paranormal investigator is an exciting adventure. You will read about dolls possessed by the dead, voodoo curses and black magic. You will discover mysterious orbs and ghosts caught on film. The fleeting glimpses of another world that appears far stranger than we could imagine. Many of the cases are recent and fresh, most of them will surprise and some have a twist in the tale worthy of the best fiction.

www.HealingsOfAtlantis.com

Lightning Source UK Ltd.
Milton Keynes UK
21 May 2010

154477UK00004B/2/P